D1712941

ALL IN THE
FAMILY

A Cultural History of Family Life

SUANNE
KELMAN

VIKING

VIKING
Published by the Penguin Group
Penguin Books Canada Ltd, 10 Alcorn Avenue, Toronto, Ontario, Canada M4V 3B2
Penguin Books Ltd, 27 Wrights Lane, London W8 5TZ, England
Viking Penguin, a division of Penguin Books USA Inc., 375 Hudson Street, New York,
New York 10014, U.S.A.
Penguin Books Australia Ltd, Ringwood, Victoria, Australia
Penguin Books (NZ) Ltd, cnr Rosedale and Airborne Roads, Albany, Auckland 1310,
New Zealand

Penguin Books Ltd, Registered Offices: Harmondsworth, Middlesex, England

First published 1998
10 9 8 7 6 5 4 3 2 1

Copyright © Suanne Kelman, 1998

All rights reserved. Without limiting the rights under copyright reserved above, no part
of this publication may be reproduced, stored in or introduced into a retrieval system,
or transmitted in any form or by any means (electronic, mechanical, photocopying,
recording or otherwise), without the prior written permission of both the copyright
owner and the above publisher of this book.

Printed and bound in Canada on acid free paper ∞

CANADIAN CATALOGUING IN PUBLICATION DATA

Kelman, Suanne, 1949–
All in the family: A cultural history of family life

ISBN 0-670-86656-3
1. Family — History. I. Title

HQ503.K44 1998   306.85'09   C97-932760-1

Quotation on p. 67 excerpted from *W.H. Auden: Collected Poems*, edited by
Edward Mendelson. Copyright © 1940 by W.H. Auden. Reprinted by permission
of Random House Inc.

Visit Penguin Canada's website at www.penguin.ca

*To Georgia, Jackie, Vicki,
Leslie and Allan*

and in memory of David M. Berger

CONTENTS

Preface / ix

CHAPTER ONE   The Birds & the Bees / 3

CHAPTER TWO   Two by Two / 25

CHAPTER THREE   Love & Loss / 53

CHAPTER FOUR   Bringing Up Baby / 79

CHAPTER FIVE   Make Room for Daddy / 115

CHAPTER SIX   One Big, Happy Family / 149

CHAPTER SEVEN   The Hidden Enemies:
Church & State, Part I / 185

CHAPTER EIGHT   The Christian Family:
Church & State, Part II / 231

CHAPTER NINE   From Patriarchy to Romance / 261

Notes / 301

Bibliography / 337

Index / 345

I'VE ALWAYS BEEN interested in families, because my own plays such a large role in my life. I was deeply startled to learn in university that the extended family was dead, because I had grown up in one. For part of my childhood, we lived across the street from my mother's sister. I spent almost as much time with my cousins as with my sisters. My maternal grandmother lived with us for a while after her second husband died. Sundays were devoted to visits to other assorted relatives.

There were difficult times, of course, but I often find family life *fun*. I like the sense of being part of a shared tradition. I love hearing stories about my own people and their parents and grandparents. At the same time, I also sometimes find it stifling: the obligations, the tensions, the criticisms, the lack of privacy. I was and remain fascinated by the ways people negotiate the delicate balance between their families' demands and their own desires.

I occasionally found ways to sneak my own interests into my work. As a high-school student, I ran into serious trouble with physics. My grade hovered near the failing point, and my parents hired a tutor. He advised me to make up stories to fix the scientific principles in my mind. I did. I created a universe of mommy neutrons surrounded by rebellious but dependent baby electrons. I found a pattern of pursuit, capture and instant rejection in the play of positive and negative charges. My solution nauseated my physics teacher, Major Markham, but it raised my grades from the low 50s to the mid-70s.

For much of my working life, I had to recognize my own interests as an aberration. The question of families failed to interest my high-school teachers, university professors or colleagues in broadcast journalism. The academics saw personal life as a feminine concern, lacking intellectual interest. The journalists vastly preferred stories that included weapons, government corruption or constitutional wrangling. I sometimes found myself tiring of this impersonal, rather masculine diet. I secretly shared the attitude towards history summed up by one of Jane Austen's heroines: "the men all so good for nothing, and hardly any women at all—it is very tiresome."[1] But I never admitted publicly to such an unfashionable vision.

In the wake of the rebellious 1960s, I also became aware that some of my fellow-students and colleagues were mystified by my closeness to my own family. It gradually dawned on me that my friends from elsewhere in the world understood perfectly why I headed up to my mother's place on weekends; it was the Canadian WASPs who were slightly shocked. The difference crystallized for me a few years later. A few of us were chatting about our parents at the radio show where I worked. The executive producer, a Pole, turned to a silent WASP and said, "You white people don't have families, do you?"

But of course, they do. By the mid-1980s, it was even possible to produce the occasional story on some issue of personal life as a rare treat. Date rape and the trials of the working mother were acceptable, for instance—as long as you dealt with them in a politically correct way. The academic world, especially in Europe, began to write about the history of personal life, but with an intellectual subtlety utterly unsuited to current affairs broadcasting. History was acceptable when it concerned the reunification of Germany or South Africa's Rivonia trials, not when it dealt with the daily lives of medieval peasants.

Over the years, my frustration grew. I was tired of bloodshed in Lebanon and Quebec politics. I left my job to work freelance, and discovered a wealth of new markets that welcomed writing on family issues. Over the past ten years, I have produced radio series on intimacy, marriage and weddings; written about both male and female violence within the family; and discussed endlessly on radio and television the joys and miseries of romantic love.

I find that the family, unlike politics, never becomes boring. I was particularly lucky in gaining approval for three series on love and marriage for the CBC radio show *Ideas,* because of the amount and depth of the research they required. I learned a tremendous amount. Moreover, once the shows aired, I learned that all this research on the family, much of it very recent, came as news to my audiences, too. I was delighted and even unnerved by the passion with which listeners responded—by the emotions the programs sparked.

At the same time, I was amazed at how little even well-read North Americans knew about the history of family life. Writers on the family tend to fall into three major schools of error: Most people think that until this century everyone lived in large, happy, caring families, with at least three generations crammed into every farmhouse. In recent times, the more familiar nuclear family has been branded by some on the left as a capitalist perversion unique to the industrialized nations. Meanwhile, many intellectuals have absorbed the French theory that the family was a purely economic unit for most of history, until the West invented romantic love during the Middle Ages.

In working on both the *Ideas* shows and this book, I have become convinced that every one of these ideas is wrong. I am particularly grateful to the anthropologist William Jankowiak, who confirmed what I suspected all along: romantic love is a universal human emotion.

My aim in this book is not to moralize or prescribe: I have no answers. I am all too conscious of how much I have omitted here. I have paid virtually no attention to psychology, for instance, preferring to dwell on the structure of families through the ages. No one book on the family can hope even to glance at the millions of questions we now know enough to ask. All I aimed for was filling in some of the gaps; I wanted to provide some historical context to let us think a bit more rationally about the way our families function now.

Many experts would object to my selection of material and the interpretations of it that I come to. That's fine with me. I would be ecstatic if people put down this book and started arguing. I want to provide a basis for discussion.

My personal interest in these and all other questions concerning family life has sharpened dramatically since 1994. In January of that year, three friends gave me a truly unique birthday present: the responses to a Companions Wanted ad they'd placed in a Canadian newspaper. I wanted to give up after three abysmal dates, but the donors insisted I try again. In May, I am going to marry the fourth man I agreed to date. At the age of forty-nine, I have suddenly acquired a husband, a stepson and in-laws. Like me, my husband-to-be comes from a large extended family.

It has not been an easy decision. I very much enjoy the freedom of modern life to live alone and selfishly. But I also recognize the value of what a friend once called "the discipline of domesticity"—the moral qualities we can only develop by living with other people.

Many, many people have generously given me invaluable help with this book. Above all, I owe thanks to my patient editor at Penguin, Meg Masters, and my copy editor, Mary Adachi. Stuart McLean often took time from his own hectic schedule to read my work and offer wonderful suggestions. I learned a great deal from the conversations I have enjoyed for the past twenty years with Bronwyn Drainie. Marjorie Nichol provided uncritical enthusiasm at the times I needed that most.

I am grateful to Sara Wolch at *Ideas*, Ivor Shapiro and Caroline Connell at *Chatelaine*, and Nancy Gottesman at *Shape* for assignments that helped me to formulate my ideas on family life. The work of the following former students at Ryerson Polytechnic University provided some of the thoughts in this book: Don White, Finbar O'Reilly, Barbara Karadimos and Lisa Joyce.

A number of academics and journalists were both generous and honest in the interviews they provided for the research that shaped this book. I want to thank Janice Boddy, Natalie Zemon Davis, Barbara Ehrenreich, Helen Fisher, Beatrice Gottlieb, Gunnar Heinsohn, William Jankowiak, Norma Joseph, Bonnie Kreps, the late Christopher Lasch, Maggie Scarfe, Lawrence Stone, Dr. Federico Allodi, Deborah Tannen and Susan Treggiari for the time they devoted to our interviews. I only wish that the reader could hear their wonderful, thoughtful voices on the page.

I owe thanks to William Johnston, Meg Fox, Ana Ferraro, Daniel Cooper and Hargurchet Bhabra both for our many discussions of the issues in this book and for finding me a husband.

Finally, I would like to thank and embrace the people who taught me the most important things I know about family life: Georgia, Jackie, Vicki and Leslie Kelman, and the dozens of relatives to whom we are linked, and Allan Fox, who is my own new family.

ALL IN THE
FAMILY

The Birds & the Bees

HERE IN THE WESTERN world, most people have a fairly rigid idea of what constitutes a family: one man, one woman and their children. For us, the constellation of father, mother and child seems the shape of nature itself. We tell the story of Papa Bear, Mama Bear and Baby Bear breakfasting together, even though real Mama Bears and their cubs generally steer clear of Papa. Outside of fairy tales, Papa Bear seeks Mama's company only for mating, and is apt to see Baby himself as breakfast.

We do recognize additional family members, but we don't tend to see them as part of the household. It's no fluke that Red Riding Hood has to walk through the forest to get to Grandmother's house. The widespread belief that the nuclear family is a recent development is false, at least when it comes to much of Europe and North America. Household size has been relatively small there for many centuries. Homes crammed with several generations of an extended family were and remain the exception.[1]

Other societies have very different family structures, which they, too, see as perfectly natural. In much of Asia and Africa, for instance, Red Riding Hood wouldn't have to venture through the forest to visit at least one of her grandmothers.[2] In many cultures, her paternal grandmother would certainly be somewhere about the shared house, keeping a sharp and far from friendly eye on Mother's cooking and housework.

In a very few traditional pockets of Nepal, India and Tibet, the family displays a more striking difference from our own norms. For them, the "natural" family consists of a couple, their sons, the sons' communal wife and the children she has borne. This arrangement, polyandry, disturbs all our ideas of what is natural, since it rests on the belief that men can share a woman without jealousy. On the other hand, it's a useful system for areas with meagre resources, since it conveniently limits population growth. Four or five brothers can impregnate an awful lot of women, but a single woman—especially one who breast-feeds her children on demand for several years—can only produce a limited number of babies.

The few tribes who still practise it probably don't see their preferred family type as a concession to economic necessity. For them, it is both natural and moral. It enjoys scriptural justification, after all: polyandry's supporters can argue that if one wife to five brothers was good enough for the heroes of the epic poem the *Mahabharata,* it's good enough for ordinary mortals.

Obviously, both of these kinds of families have some claim to being natural, since people manage to live in them. But they are far from being wholly natural, or they would not vary so profoundly from culture to culture. When it comes to humans, it no longer makes much sense to talk about a "natural" pattern. Instinct does not guide our behaviour in the way that it controls the reproductive lives of other animals.

It's important not to overemphasize our own uniqueness in this respect. Animals aren't as mechanically predictable as we used to believe. Ethologists have discovered far greater variations—and deviance—in animal behaviour than we realized even a decade ago. Many birds, once seen as models of monogamy, have turned out to be stealthily adulterous.[3] Other avian species, such as the jacana, have turned out to be polyandrous: Successful females keep male harems of up to four intimidated males.[4] Our closest relatives, the chimpanzees, vary their usual riotous promiscuity with spells of monogamous seclusion that can last for weeks, even months.[5]

Nonetheless, versatility in the rest of the animal kingdom has sharp limits. Other species simply don't have the choices available to humans. Consider a problem that plagues Western nations, the absconding father. Human males can decide that the economic and emotional burdens of family life are simply too great—so they disappear. That fecklessness is not an option for one of nature's model parents, the emperor penguin. Each year, he finds a mate, cavorts briefly with her, then waits around until she lays a single egg. She promptly heads out to sea in search of fish; she's been fasting for about forty days, as has he.[6] Dad is left in charge of incubation.[7]

For the next few weeks, he's stuck tending his egg out on an Antarctic glacier. He gets no rest: He and the other males form a phalanx that moves ceaselessly forward, with the front row constantly dispersing and trudging to the back. That way, each penguin is surrounded by the relative warmth of his fellows almost all of the time. It's the only way to avoid death by freezing.

If Mama hasn't returned by the time the egg hatches, Dad secretes an esophageal fluid to keep Junior going. Even when Mom waddles back, Dad continues to brood his chick for up to ten days after its exit from the egg. Only then—more than a hundred days since his last meal—can Dad start the journey to open water and a well-deserved breakfast.

It's not much of a life, but the male emperor penguin has no options. No government will ever have to hunt down a defaulting penguin father. No emperor penguin couple decides to put off child-rearing until they've perfected their fish-catching skills. Every year of its adult life, the male emperor penguin will feel irresistibly driven to mate and go through the whole gruelling ordeal again.

The system is not perfect, but it has what the French call *les défauts de ses qualités,* the flaws of its virtues. One built-in problem emerges if a male dies before his egg hatches or his mate returns. Since not everyone gets to mate, and not every egg hatches, the obvious answer here would be adoption. And penguins are all too eager to adopt—that's the trouble. If an egg is left unattended, childless penguins rush towards it and fight for it with such reckless intensity that it's invariably trampled to bits. That's wasteful, but it's an inevitable by-product of the craving that keeps the whole system going, the penguin passion for eggs and chicks.

That's where human beings seem to differ sharply from the rest of creation. Biologists tend to see all of life as an unending struggle to reproduce and ensure the survival of one's own genes. Even when some newly discovered quirk of animal behaviour doesn't appear to fit the pattern, further study usually finds a link to the battle to multiply and replenish the earth with one's own stock. The adult blue jay, jackal or wolf who postpones his own sexual life to help out his parents is raising siblings, whose genetic material is close to his own.[8] The adulterous female chickadee is hedging her bets, gambling that the next-door neighbour might provide better genes than her mate's.[9] The philandering male snow goose, having seen his legitimate issue safely hatched, ups the ante by trying to rape his neighbours' wives.[10] The possessive male chimp who coaxes or coerces a fertile female into a spell of monogamous seclusion is attempting to ensure that her children will be his, something he could never achieve if the rest of the troop were around. There are exceptions, but when an animal adds some kind of fillip to his or her sex life, it usually makes genetic sense.

But there are human drives and desires that make no sense at all in this Darwinian vision of existence. They amount to genetic suicide.

In other animals, some of our behaviour could be explained as part of the struggle to procreate. Thus, the red-sided garter snake sometimes dabbles in transsexual behaviour, mimicking female pheromones during mating. But it's a ploy that tricks other males into courting him while he hunts for a receptive female.[11] Bonobo chimps toy with gay sex, but it's a mere sideline, an aspect of their willingness to couple with just about anything.[12]

In contrast, a substantial percentage of human beings (though research now suggests it's nothing like the 10 per cent that had become the accepted figure[13]) is exclusively homosexual, a guarantee that they will leave no genetic legacy. Pedophilia, celibacy and deliberate childlessness all have the same result.

At first glance, the same thing seems to hold true for contraception, abortion and infanticide. But that may be an over-simplification. Animals may not take the pill, but they do frequently dispose of unwanted offspring, before and after birth. Under conditions of stress, females of many species spontaneously abort or reabsorb their unborn young. They may also trample or even eat their infants.[14]

Paradoxically, their behaviour makes genetic sense. If an animal is so threatened that this particular brood will not survive in any case, why waste valuable energy that could be redirected at another try for genetic immortality? If her brood is going to die anyway, why should a mother waste the valuable protein she can reclaim by eating her young?

In the wild, then, genetic self-destruction is often a logical, if brutal, reaction to an emergency. But for some species, as any farmer can tell you, captivity sends reproduction anxiety spinning out of control. A surprisingly large number of domesticated ewes try to trample their newborn lambs to death. I once spent a hellish spring afternoon on a farm acting as a human buffer between lamb and rejecting mother. Farmed female minks are notorious for infanticide and cannibalism; mink farmers must separate mother and babies at once.

Zoos frequently face an even more daunting obstacle, because animals raised in cages may have trouble figuring out the mechanics of mating. Many animals don't instinctively know *how* to have sex, especially if they fail to get adequate maternal care. Raised in unnatural conditions like a zoo, they are apt to direct their sexual urges towards the wrong objects. As the zoologist Desmond Morris notes, in a sentence I treasure: "In captivity, for example, certain carnivores have been known to copulate with their food containers."[15]

Even species that don't confuse lunch with love may lose their enthusiasm for reproduction behind bars. Captivity's dire anaphrodisiac effects can be measured in the size of crowds eager to see baby pandas, tigers and gorillas. Each one born represents man's triumph over his feral hostages' reservations about the whole business of carrying on.

And that's where we come in. To my mind, all human beings everywhere grow up in captivity. It has been millennia since the first hominids descended from the trees, learning for unknown reasons to walk on two feet. It has been a long, long journey from bashing nuts and shells with stones to our own world of airplanes, skyscrapers, computers and microwave ovens. So it's really not surprising that our conduct, at least in animal terms, often seems hopelessly screwed up.

If we assume that we lost our natural pattern somewhere along the way, the obvious question is: Where did we start?

It's a hot issue, because we tend to assume (without a shred of evidence) that what is natural must be best. Dan Quayle, the Pope and other Western conservatives, for example, believe that Adam and Eve set the pattern for what is natural: one man and one woman, united for life, with any children they may conceive. In Islamic culture, a growing number of even more conservative theologians would argue that what is both natural and ordained is one man and one or more wives, for as long as the man chooses. There are feminist theoreticians who believe that a natural life would involve one woman, any children she chooses to bear and raise, and whoever else she feels like sharing with at the moment.

When I was a child, the popular image of humanity's natural state was summed up by cartoons of cavemen pulling their women around by the hair. We imagined a world in which dominant, jealous men spent their days hunting mammoths and sabre-toothed tigers. Their wives waited meekly home at the cave, tending the kids and doing a little basic cooking in return for all the meat they could eat and a large collection of fur wraps.

From the nineteenth century on, there has been a growing suspicion that things weren't actually like that. It's no accident that new theories about the lives of early humans suddenly proliferated in the last century, because they depend heavily on Darwin's theory of evolution. Iconoclasts, abandoning the story of Adam and Eve, began to consider the implications of man's descent from the apes.

But which ape? Because human behaviour varies so widely from culture to culture, we fall into a number of patterns. If you looked at life today in Saudi Arabia, you would assume that we behave a lot like gorillas, whose alpha males jealously guard their harems from any encroaching males. If you turned to Roman Catholics and examined their beliefs—although not invariably their practice—you would conclude that humans mate monogamously for life, just like gibbons.

Today, almost all experts on the issue of early human life accept that we probably behaved a lot like today's chimpanzees. In some ways, this makes sense. We know, for instance, that they are our closest relatives, identical to us except for a meagre 4 per cent of DNA. But there are also some difficulties with the idea that today's chimpanzees represent our original pattern. For if that is true, here's what would come naturally for us:

Most women would mate with most men, though the top male (the president, let us call him) would make sure he had *droit du seigneur* over the most fertile women. Sex would be an intermittent affair, indulged in to spectacular excess during the woman's estrus but totally forgotten by her for years at a time when pregnant or rearing a young child. This estrus would be announced to everybody in sight by her pink and swollen rear end, which would prove irresistibly fascinating to every male who saw it. They would try to monopolize such females for weeks at a time, forcing them to go away on a "consortship" with them; they would not always succeed and would quickly lose interest when the swelling went down.[16]

Obviously, this doesn't have much in common with life for us now. The human female exhibits no obvious signals to indicate when she is fertile, nor do most of us alternate marathon gang-bangs with years of celibacy. While women are physically capable of having sex with many men in rapid succession, it's not generally the kind of thing they enjoy. In our world, that level of turnstile promiscuity is usually associated with coercion, as in gang-rape, or the profit motive, as in prostitution. While some pornography might suggest that human females are sexually insatiable, most women do not in fact want to take on entire football teams at a time.

Similarly, many human males today pay attention to and spend time with women outside their fertile *years,* never mind outside their fertile days. It's true that "top males" sometimes still attempt to monopolize desirable women, but fertility isn't usually the issue. In general, the last thing a CEO or political leader wants from his mistress is a pregnancy.

On the other hand, the chimpanzee's pattern is not monolithic, and it does show an embryonic version of a very common human pattern. Female chimpanzees may find themselves laying everyone in sight (with the exception, generally, of their closest relatives),[17] but enterprising males may also hustle them off into romantic seclusion in the forest for as much as three months at a time. Sometimes the females head for the trees with the eagerness of a lovestruck adolescent girl setting out on a date. But they can also behave more like a traditional Chinese or Hindu bride, weeping all the way. Jane Goodall and her staff note that female chimps frequently seem unwilling to leave the troop, and have to be intimidated into co-operating by threats and violence. They often manage to slip away, or to call to other troop members they can hear in the distance.

On two occasions, the human observers watched the female's rescuers—males—attack the abductor. That's unusual. When a male gorilla or baboon catches one of his females in a compromising situation with another male, he will invariably take out his rage on *her*. But chimpanzee females aren't owned by individual males; they're more like rentals, available for exclusive use only for set periods. Thus, a high-ranking male may frighten other males off a really attractive female during her estrus, although it's difficult to exercise the level of ceaseless vigilance necessary to keep a female in heat faithful.[18] The chimpanzee's sex life exhibits a spotty combination of promiscuity and possessiveness.

What seems the likeliest scenario for humans is a gradual shift in balance. Among chimpanzees, the seasonal estrus-sparked orgy is much more common than the extended *tête-à-tête* in the woods. Most research and writing on this subject today are based on the assumption that we, too, began with a sexual free-for-all, but moved on to more discriminating mating as we evolved. If this was our original system, though, you can see why some men feel a lurking resentment about both marriage and any female coyness or prudery. If there is such a thing as race memory, deep in the male subconscious lies the recollection of that golden time when women took on all comers and begged for more.

Moreover, there were no strings in the golden age. The male chimpanzee plays no role in child-rearing. All he has to do is to participate in the occasional orgy, coax or threaten some female into a long dirty weekend, or—if he's reached a high enough rank—keep a sharp eye on some particularly attractive siren to keep her away from the rest of the guys during estrus. That's it. He will never face child support, junior hockey car pools or school fees. He doesn't worry about being a good father; he doesn't know he *is* a father.

Clearly, something changed, because this isn't the life we lead. There are several schools of thought as to exactly what happened, and why. Let's start with the most obvious: If you compare the anatomy of female humans and chimpanzees, you can see why the party had to end. The original hominids walked on four feet and gave birth to scrawny, lithe infants capable of clinging tenaciously to the fur on Mother's back. Because Mom used all four feet, that back was usually a horizontal surface, ideal for perching. It was comparatively easy, as it is for other primates today, to tote around a baby on a daily forage for food.[19]

It's no longer so easy for us. About fifteen million years ago, drastic environmental changes sharply reduced the forests where the first hominids hung out, leading a timid, fructarian existence.[20] These early humans landed on the plains, and took to walking on two feet.

Unfortunately for the female contingent, our back muscles continued to hang from the spine, not the shoulders, which made pregnancy a singularly uncomfortable struggle against gravity.[21] Our babies changed, too. Humans give birth to plump little butterballs, whose chubby fingers can't gain a decent grip on our smooth, almost hairless flesh.

The reader might well wonder why we developed such inconvenient idiosyncrasies. A truthful answer would be that we have no idea, but in the pages to come I'll look at some of the possible explanations for our strange shapes and comparative baldness. We do know that human babies are born at an extremely early stage of development in comparison to other mammals. We're almost certain that's because otherwise the heads containing their large brains couldn't make it through the birth canal.[22] Precisely because their mental capacities will eventually leave their primate cousins trailing in the dust, they have to leave the womb prematurely.

Whatever caused their peculiarities, our babies clearly can't perch on Mommy's back. They lack the strength, dexterity and proper shape for perching on anything. Nor can Mommy cradle the child easily under her belly—both her back and her front now present vertical surfaces.

So Mom is stuck with a baby she has to carry—in her arms, at least until she figures out how to fashion a sling from a hide. Moreover, that burden will rapidly grow from a passive bundle of seven-odd pounds to a squirming toddler of twenty, thirty, then forty pounds. As anthropologist Helen Fisher says, early women found themselves faced with the problem of surviving while carrying—at all times—the equivalent of a forty-pound bowling ball.[23]

To make things worse, we're talking the long haul. Human babies not only emerge from the womb with a distinctly meagre collection of survival skills, but they take longer than other animals to acquire more. A mare nudges a colt to its feet within minutes of its birth. A baby antelope can manage a reasonable gallop in a couple of hours. But the human mother will wait months before the kid is self-propelling, and years for him to pick up a decent speed. If she and her child are to survive, she's going to need help. Her need will be particularly fierce at the beginning of her reproductive career, when she'll have no older children to lend a hand at food-gathering, baby-minding and mutual protection.

Up till now, males have been interested in her only during her estrus, and their attitude to her offspring has ranged unpredictably from benevolent tolerance to sudden irritable hostility. Aside from driving off the occasional intruder or predator, or a bit of companionable grooming, they have never been of the slightest use to her. At this point, however, the time has come to rope in Dad.

The question is: How to do it? In a very general sense, we know the answer: individual males and females started to forge deeper, longer-lasting bonds. But different researchers and theorists are deeply divided about the nature of that bond. This is important: Your vision of these original human pairings has a profound influence on the way you will see the human family today. If you hold on to the image of a Neanderthal clutching his club and dragging a submissive female into their shared cave, you're assuming that marriage in all its forms has an underpinning of coercion and violence. You'll believe—with a respectably large contingent of researchers and writers—that abduction was the basis of all early marriages.

If, on the other hand, you believe that the original humans came together out of mutual desire, then all the institutions that remove choice from mating—arranged marriage, purdah, penalties for adultery, forbidding divorce—are essentially perversions of our nature. I also see no problem with accepting elements of both theories, since the truth probably lies somewhere between the two.

In the 1960s and 1970s, the mystery of early human life fascinated the reading public. There was a spate of popular books on the subject by men like Robert Ardrey, Desmond Morris, Lionel Tiger and Robin Fox. Together, those four represented what we might call the man-as-hunter school of human evolution, because they explained the changes that made us human largely as products of the male switch from foraging fructarian to predatory carnivore.[24] One of their critics, Elaine Morgan, lumped them together as "the Tarzanists." It's not an entirely unjust barb. Desmond Morris may have called his first book on the subject *The Naked Ape*, but it was the hunting ape who truly engaged his imagination.

Thus, humans learned to walk upright so that man-the-hunter could use weapons to bring down his prey. We lost our fur lest man-the-hunter overheat while on the chase. We developed speech so that man could plan strategy with his hunting buddies. Meanwhile, woman engineered some spectacular physical changes of her own so that she could entrap one of the hunters as her personal butcher shop *cum* furrier.

She stopped signalling her estrus so that man-the-hunter wouldn't know when she was fertile—she could keep him guessing. Since this deprived her of the dramatic sexual swelling that accompanied estrus, she put on a seductive layer of subcutaneous fat that made her buttocks look swollen all the time. Then she shrewdly developed rounded breasts that mimicked her new buttocks and pouting lips that looked somewhat like her vagina. Bingo! Now she could transmit sexual signals from the front as well as the back.[25] Humans' characteristically protruding noses, fleshy earlobes, subcutaneous fat and sensitive hands all developed to add to the erotic delights that kept man-the-hunter firmly attached to woman-the-sexpot.

Morris's language seems almost to imply that woman did all this *on purpose,* but he doesn't mean that. Almost everyone writing about evolution falls into a convenient shorthand that misleadingly suggests intention. Pamphlets about the rain forests of Costa Rica make it sound as if cunning non-toxic opaque butterflies deliberately cultivated transparency to mimic poisonous clear-wing butterflies. The pamphlet's authors are presumably aware that no butterfly has the intellectual capacity to keep a comparative body count and then act on that data. No matter how amazingly intricate and deliberate nature's processes seem, all we know is that evolution apparently rewards butterflies that develop clear wings, poisonous or not. We are evolution's slaves, not its masters.

In the same way, when Desmond Morris and the other male-oriented evolutionists write about women's anatomy changing to entrap males, they don't mean that a wily female hominid sat down and decided to grow big breasts and buttocks to increase her popularity. Nonetheless, they're already suggesting far more than we can really know. I suspect that some men find big breasts and behinds sexy simply because they associate them with women, and thus with sex. *Why* women have them remains an open question.

I do not personally care for the idea that evolution was designed primarily to boost sexual enjoyment and the male ability to hunt. It seems to me to slight the role and importance of women. I should confess that my own bias here is one despised in scientific circles. Like Elaine Morgan (to whom I owe a tremendous debt), I favour the idea that mankind evolved on the seashore. For Morgan, man is not the naked or hunting or sexy ape; he and *she* are the aquatic ape, the title of one of her books.[26]

In Morgan's theory, the aquatic ape learned to walk upright because she spent a lot of time in the water avoiding the sultry heat that had destroyed her forest home. In the course of keeping her head above the waves, she got used to standing erect, on two feet. She and her brothers learned how to use tools and weapons by bashing harmless shellfish and aquatic mammals with rocks until they got the hang of it. It may be fanciful, but the aquatic theory makes more sense to me than the idea that man perfected his hunting skills on the run, bringing down his first mammoth just after he first learned to balance on his hind legs.

Scientists detest the aquatic theory of evolution for an excellent reason. It is pure theory, without an atom of physical evidence to support it. It's also messy, because it requires faith in an unexplained U-turn. Few of us now spend our days paddling around tropic seas and idly whacking open a few crabs for dinner. The aquatic theory rests on the assumption that when the weather improved, for unknown reasons, mankind moved back inland.

But, valid or not, the aquatic theory certainly offers some sensible suggestions for the modifications that make us human. If it were true, for instance, we would have developed our layer of subcutaneous fat—unique among primates—for the same reason as whales and dolphins: to keep warm in the water. Water is cooler than human blood, and a far more efficient conductor of heat than air. That layer of fat would be the natural equivalent of a scuba diver's wet suit.

Similarly, our buttocks and breasts wouldn't become rounded as a sexual come-on. There is, after all, nothing intrinsically sexy about plumpness, nor is the breast a universal turn-on. A West African university lecturer once treated me to a cheerful, condescending lecture on comparative sexuality. He found the European interest in breasts childish—grown men slavering over something that was only good for feeding babies.

To a large extent, Morgan agrees. The female breast, in her argument, started to soften and stick out even more because we'd lost our fur. Our babies could no longer cling to the breast itself. That meant a nursing mother would be stuck holding the kid upright, flush against her chest, through each feeding. It's hard work—a rounder bust would let her hold the child at a more comfortable angle. And why not? It seems reasonable that not *every* physical evolutionary change related to the sexual act itself. Sex, after all, is only the opening round in the reproduction game. Surely, some of the modifications that transformed us from apes to people must have benefited stages further along the cycle.

These ideas are far less popular than those of the Tarzan school. There's still a general acceptance of Morris's explanation for the human female's anatomical burgeoning. To keep males and females together to raise their young—and to fill the "relationship void" created when the young adult naked ape separated from his doting parents—we had to develop an ability to fall and stay in love. For this, Morris noted quite correctly, a "prolonged and exciting courtship phase" helps.[27] And how to achieve this lingering, thrilling courtship? "The simplest and more direct method of doing this was to make the shared activities of the pair more complicated and more rewarding. In other words, to make sex sexier."[28]

That would explain why human beings indulge in much more and varied foreplay than other primates, spend much longer on the sexual act itself and generally make such a commotion during it. (On the other hand, Elaine Morgan points out that other animals make far less fuss than we do about a lot of other natural functions, like vomiting and childbirth. For all we know, other primates may find orgasm an ecstatic experience, without feeling any need to bond because of it.[29]) For humans, unlike most other species, sex is also a year-round activity. The other primates, as has been noted, enjoy sex only when the females are in their most fertile phase, their estrus. Yet it's on tap for humans at virtually all seasons. These continuous, rich sexual pleasures are supposed to enhance the bond between the couple and keep them from tiring of one another.

In *The Naked Ape,* Morris argued that the increased sexual intensity of human relationships created what he called a "pair bond," keeping the couple together to provide the optimum care for their young. That isn't exactly true. A pair-bonded animal generally remains tied to his or her mate until one of them dies, or at least until the end of a breeding season. Only 3 per cent of mammals of any kind create pair bonds. Among primates, only the gibbon qualifies.[30] It seems most common in vilely antisocial species—the gibbon is a nasty piece of work unable to tolerate even his own adolescent offspring.[31]

But when it comes to their mates, the pair-bonded are programmed for fidelity. If humans were indeed a pair-bonding species, you would have married the first guy or girl you dated in high school. You would be constitutionally incapable of seeking a divorce *at least* until your children were old enough to fend for themselves. You might have to wait until death carried one of you off. There would be no desertion. However else you can describe human love, it is not a pair bond.

The difficulty with making human sex so much more interesting is that the interest isn't exclusive. Sex, now thoroughly enhanced by evolution, can prove even more interesting with someone other than your lover or spouse. The U.S. divorce rate—still about 50 per cent[32]—provides evidence of the sexual bond's inefficiency in keeping couples together. The physical and emotional changes that transformed the original promiscuous little ape make being human a lot more fun, but they don't make our love lives stable.

In fact, more recent research on our patterns suggests strongly that human love has a built-in expiry date. Helen Fisher summarized the new data in *The Anatomy of Love* and concluded that people suffer from a four-year itch.[33] That is, the decision to separate or divorce occurs most commonly in or around the fourth year in societies all over the world.[34] From that conclusion, Fisher theorized that the initial rush of sexual attraction and bonding sustained early human couples through the conception, birth and most dependent years of a single child.[35]

Once the child progressed from infant to toddler, the couple might either stay together or split. It's the same arrangement we find in most species of birds, who mate with a different partner each year to raise a new clutch of eggs. As a reproductive strategy, it's a pattern with an obvious pay-off; it increases genetic diversity.

Other evidence lends some support to Fisher's theory. Children under the age of four are at far greater risk of being murdered than older children,[36] and the killer is often a stepfather. (At least one African tribe permitted a woman's new lover to kill any of her children under that age.[37]) It makes a kind of sense. After the first four years, children make fewer demands on the mother. As we'll see, they spend much of their time in play groups, leaving her free to attend to her work or her new mate. They are less of a threat to a new relationship, less wearing on the nerves all round.

Research into the nature and duration of human love also backs Fisher. Psychologists know that the passionate, thrilling attraction we call infatuation does not last a lifetime. It has a maximum shelf life of three years.[38] By the end of that time, the all-embracing, I'll-die-if-I-can't-have-her, please-let-him-phone kind of love is either gone or transformed into a gentler, less exhausting attachment. People can continue to love one another for a lifetime, but a crush has a limited run.

A pattern of four-year relationships would not add comfort or stability to human life. Fisher acknowledged in an interview with me that these original partings may well have been just as traumatic as a contemporary divorce. After all, a four-year limit doesn't run on schedule like a train, so the partners would not usually tire of one another at the same time. It hurts to be abandoned; if you have even the first stirrings of a conscience, it hurts to do the abandoning. As Freud wrote, "Why don't we fall in love over again every month? Because with every parting something of our heart is torn away."[39] The early humans, just like us, must have suffered.

The pain must often have been more than purely emotional for the absconding female. When the sexually possessive apes—baboons and gorillas, for instance—catch their paramours *in flagrante delicto*, it is not the intruding male who pays the price. The cuckold invariably chooses to drub or bite the female, to remind her that adultery is a bad idea. If our human ancestors were familiar with the eternal triangle, then the *crime passionnel* probably wasn't a stranger either.

On the other hand, there is no reason to assume that early human couples faced nothing but ecstasy followed by misery. People are capable of two different kinds of sexual love, and only one of them turns life into an emotional rollercoaster. First, we can feel passion, the pounding-in-the-heart desire that's inspired thousands of love songs and romance novels. As humans, we are *programmed* to be capable of mad infatuation, which is physically rooted in a powerful neurochemical cocktail. Our bodies, for instance, produce phenylethylamine, or PEA.[40] It induces, in Helen Fisher's words, "elation, exhilaration, and euphoria," a perfect description of the first stages of love. PEA packs such a wallop that it can be physically addictive; the man or woman who flits from one fling to the next is a PEA junkie. The sensation of being in love—or deprived of love—is determined by our phenylethylamine levels.

The second type of love, the feeling of attachment, often gets overlooked because it packs less of a kick. But it, too, has a physical basis. Attachment—the comfort we find in the company of a familiar and trusted partner—is accompanied by a soothing tide of endorphins. Unlike the adrenaline rush of fresh passion, attachment doesn't impel us to break into a song or a tango. Nonetheless, it feels good. *West Side Story*'s "Maria" is about passion. *Showboat*'s "My Bill," with its combination of realism and emotion, is about a time-tested attachment: "I love him, because he's, I don't know, because he's just my Bill."

The man-the-hunter school doesn't completely ignore the existence of attachment. The new love bond, after all, is meant in part to fill the gap created by adult independence from parents. Nonetheless, the emphasis is very much on courtship and sex, the high-voltage phase of our relationships. But that's not all there is. Most of us don't spend our lives drifting from one wild affair to the next. Our relations with each other aren't based exclusively on fabulous sex; our world couldn't function if they did. We are bound together by more complicated bonds than an enhanced sexual relationship; for us, sex is very rarely simply sex.

That's probably true of most other complex species. Even bonobo chimpanzees, who start humping as a response to just about any stimulus, seem to use sex as a kind of universal social lubricant.[41] Humans didn't invent foreplay; other species court and caress and fondle before they get down to business. Birds dance and sing in courtship with more verve than Ginger Rogers and Fred Astaire.[42] Many courting animals offer gifts, sometimes of a value well beyond candy, flowers or even a fur coat. The orb weaver spider, for instance, proffers the ultimate love token, since the female devours him as they couple.[43]

But humans add more to sex than any other species. To a far greater extent than other animals, for instance, we imitate infantile behaviour in courtship to re-create the original parental tie. We use baby names and baby talk to inspire parental protectiveness in our lovers. Conversely, we also mother our lovers, fussing over their health and misfortunes, offering food in restaurants and our own kitchens. Human beings can have totally unadorned sex, in the style of "Wham, bam, thank you, ma'am." But in our romantic relationships, sex isn't like that. We stroke and kiss and nibble, using many of the gestures we learned as infants. Like other primates, we groom each other, patting a lover's tie into place, or offering a soothing back rub.

Drawing on our one uniquely human characteristic, we talk in courtship for hours on the phone in adolescence, endlessly in restaurants and beds later on. Women in particular crave shared talk, that aimless but richly satisfying flow of conversation.[44] We also like to share activities that may have nothing to do with sex, making dates to watch movies, hike, bowl, skate. For men, doing things together is often the essence of bonding, which is why so many women find themselves watching football, camping or fishing in the early years of the relationship. (I write as a woman who has backpacked in the Grand Teton mountains, exhausted but game, to indulge a nature-loving partner.)

Given all this, it seems to me that sex for humans became not so much sexier, but less purely sexual. We added a wealth of emotions and behaviour from other relationships to an original, less complicated primate sexuality. So it also became more infantile, more nurturing, more altruistic and more intimate.

There is a final, important point here. Later writers challenge the idea that human evolution was shaped so exclusively by male needs and interests. There is, to take one crucial example, a different way of looking at the question of gaining food by sexual bonding. It's true that a woman with a gentleman friend would stand a better chance of getting some meat for herself and her kids. But it's also true that the gentleman friend might welcome, after an unsuccessful hunt, some of the sustaining snacks that she and her family had foraged.

The hunter school of evolution essentially portrays women and children as parasites, conveniently ignoring the fact that women and children perform their own work. Hunter societies are more accurately termed hunter-gatherer. While the men are out bringing down big game, the women and children are busy scooping up nuts and berries, herbs and insects, seeds and small prey. In surviving hunter-gatherer societies, the female-headed gatherers routinely supply two-thirds or more of the calories the whole population consumes.[45] Foraging is simply more reliable than the hunt. Elaine Morgan argues that early males developed deeper relationships with individual women not only to ensure a source of regular sex, but to guarantee access to a steady supply of gathered food.

It's unclear what role these hungry or lustful hunting males played in their children's lives. It's unlikely that they recognized that the children *were* theirs for the first few millennia. It requires a certain amount of intellectual sophistication to work out the link between a session of slap-and-tickle and the birth of an infant, and then to deduce the male role in the process. The anthropologist Bronislaw Malinowski reported that the Trobriand Islanders still hadn't figured it out by the time he arrived on the scene in the 1920s. Moreover, they firmly rejected his scientific explanation of conception, on a variety of grounds. I particularly admire their argument that the pregnancies of some of their more spectacularly ugly women constituted evidence that conception did not require sex. Much later in this century, the journalist Alex Shoumatoff wrote of an encounter with the Cayapo, a tribe in South America that still hadn't quite figured out the whole business. They told Shoumatoff that pregnancy was the result of eating a particular phallus-shaped fungus— although they also seemed to recognize that they descend from their mother's husbands.[46]

Nonetheless, the males would have figured in the lives of children because they had started to spend time with individual females. These early humans had developed a new subdivision within the troop: the couple. Although force may sometimes have been involved, it seems to me that many of these long-term romances must have been based largely on preference. For what it's worth, the patterns of courtship and romance persist wherever people are allowed some degree of personal freedom. Moreover, the overwhelming majority of societies do recognize the existence of romantic love, even if they frown on it.[47]

That would be news to many otherwise well-educated people, because it's the well-educated who are most likely to get the history of the human family wrong. When I was in university, I learned that romantic love had been invented in France in the Middle Ages. Until very recently, anthropologists were taught that romantic love was a purely Western phenomenon, not to be sought in any other societies they were studying.[48] Many still believe it.

This belief is founded on the shapes that the family took as civilizations developed. When a society becomes more complex, it also tends to become increasingly intolerant of the unstable, anarchic nature of human love. Precisely because the bond between two lovers is so strong, all cultures try to bring it under some kind of control. To some extent, all succeed. The history of civilization is one of continuing war between private passion and public order, and neither side can ever claim complete victory. But it is astonishing that people are so often willing to suppress the expression of their own desires and natures so completely, to live in harmony with profoundly uncongenial social rules. It is a phenomenon that has profound effects on the romantic and sexual bond.

Two by Two

THERE IS A YIDDISH saying: "Every pot has a lid." In Barbados, they say, "Every piece bread got its cheese." Both sayings are meant to comfort the single; each suggests that everyone has a fated partner, a match arranged by Providence. The underlying message, of course, is that our world is like Noah's ark: people belong in twos. The unpaired human makes many cultures uneasy. Women, in particular, seem to take a tireless interest in covering the pot with the lid, the bread with the cheese.

That interest can be highly intrusive. A friend of mine in Toronto once kindly gave a lift home to one of her mother's friends. She was in her late twenties at the time. The older woman started up as she turned the key in the ignition. "So why's a lovely girl like you still single? You're doing it to spite your mother, aren't you?"

As a teenager, I thought that this nagging insistence on marriage was a peculiarity of my own Jewish group. Then I attended my first wedding in Africa. I watched an imposing matron plant herself in front of a sheepish young man. "So when are you going to get married? We're all waiting, you know." I'm sure she would have loved a phrase I remember from a comic novel of the 1970s: "Even Frankenstein found a bride, so what's wrong with you?"

Now, something clearly happened to human beings after we left the trees, because other primates take no interest whatsoever in promoting the matches of others. For unknown reasons, juvenile chimpanzees do work hard to pry apart mating couples. But no chimpanzee has ever been observed in the process of matchmaking. The human urge to promote togetherness is a later development.

There are really two issues here separating us from our chimpanzee cousins: we pair up, and our societies interfere in the process. Marriage is about as close as humans come to a universal cultural value. There is no solid evidence for a single society that has or had *no* form of it. Moreover, most cultures take a keen interest in it. In Thailand, in Italy, in India, in Zimbabwe, the first question the solitary female tourist encounters is: "Where is your husband?"

But while marriage may be universal, its forms are myriad. That's obvious from even a cursory look at the first step in marriage, the way that couples get together. Different cultures have chosen thousands of systems to match the pot with the lid, the bread with the cheese. I wish I could explain how all these systems evolved, but we have no solid answers for that. At later periods of history, we *can* trace what happened, through the codes governing marriage developed by formal governments and churches. But here let's look at those patterns we can't explain. These are the systems and values so deeply imbedded in individual societies that their origins have been lost, and they are assumed to be "natural."

Let's start with one fact we ought to know, but often forget. Most societies celebrate marriage as a joyous occasion. In Judaism, it is a religious duty to "rejoice with bride and groom," right up there with visiting the sick and comforting the bereaved and attending the house of study. The crucial word here is "rejoice." Individual weddings may be fraught with tension, but there are very few societies in which they are not *supposed* to be happy events.

Yet you would never know this from much of the literature on the history of marriage. The historian Will Durant, for instance, wrote of its origins: "Individual marriage came through the desire of the male to have cheap slaves, and to avoid bequeathing his property to other men's children."[1] Anthropologists and sociologists are equally likely to treat marriage as an institution that concerns only the distribution of property and the legitimizing of children. I've heard it argued that *all* marriages were originally abductions. Feminist scholars have suggested that slavery is an outgrowth of early forms of marriage, and that men derived both institutions from their experience in domesticating animals.[2]

Now, it must be admitted that the history of the family contains a hefty share of coercion, possessiveness and brutality. But a vision that restricts marriage to those elements is culturally blinkered. It requires both ignorance and arrogance to believe that marriage is always about property rather than emotion. If that were true, the idea of an affectionate and largely equal union would be a recent and almost exclusively Western innovation. And a full examination of forms of marriage around the world makes it clear that's not true.

Nonetheless, marriage in most societies is *not* linked to romantic love: you have to discuss the two separately. In the West, we expect people to find their own mates and to marry for love. Because our society is so dominant, we tend to mistake our place in the world. As countless historical dramas have shown, sometimes we project our own system on to all other cultures. We imagine medieval knights and aristocratic Roman maidens and Indian princesses making love matches. That's simply not the way it was. But we also sometimes assume—especially within the academic world—that we are the first society ever to permit choice or to value love in marriage. And that's not true either.

It is true that our system horrifies less permissive cultures. In her memoir of life in China in the 1930s, Nora Waln records the reaction of a middle-aged woman to the news that Chiang Kai-Shek's Republican party disapproved of arranged marriages. "Ah! Yah! Then when this Republic gets itself established girls will have to go out and hunt for their mates? If their families cannot help them get married, then they will have to become bold and deceitful, preying on any man they can get yet pretending that they are not wanting one. Only the most artful will mate! Shy, plain, good maids will wither into a fruitless old age!"[3] Despite her disapproval, the intervening sixty years have firmly established the love match in urban China at least.[4]

But pre-revolutionary China was far from unique in its banning of love matches. Helen Fisher cites the Tiwi, a tribe whose marriages are arranged before *conception*. The Tiwi live on Melville Island, just off the northern coast of Australia. Their society is a gerontocracy, ruled by the old.[5] (Once again, we have no idea how they developed such as system.) When a girl begins to menstruate, she joins her father and one of his friends in the bush for a brief betrothal ceremony. She is not going to marry this man who is old enough to be her father. Her daughters are. The girl pretends to be asleep while her father places a spear between her legs. Then he hands the weapon to his friend, who ceremonially calls it wife. From that point, the friend is entitled to marry any female children the girl bears.[6] This system seems based on a vision of marriage as a loveless exchange of property, namely women.

To Western eyes, Tiwi women seem powerless, traded by men like cattle.[7] But that's not the case. Fisher writes, "Every son-in-law must cater to the needs of the woman who will bear his brides, and a mother-in-law can break this contract if his gifts and work are paltry."[8] There is no such thing as a simple and straightforward marriage system; human beings are too complex to make that possible. There is always a gulf, indeed a conflict, between a society's idea of marriage and its actual behaviour. Look at our world: a love match is no guarantee that a woman—or a man—will encounter respect and consideration in marriage.

Some cultures find a middle ground between our own romantic and individualistic system and the monolithic severity of, say, premodern China or Saudi Arabia today. One rather lovely example is the Igarot, a small tribe in the Philippines. I learned of their traditions from the anthropologist Renato Rosaldo, who teaches at Stanford University.

Like us, the Igarot marry for love, even though their hunting and farming society offers no opportunity for what we would call dating. The young couple starts with flirtation, that universal dance of talking, teasing and lingering looks. If the attraction deepens, they move on to exchanging gifts. The girl may embroider clothing for the boy; he may fashion some jewellery for her. These gifts don't constitute a commitment; things aren't serious yet.

Rosaldo's informants told him they knew they were in love when the other person visited their dreams. They meant that literally. The Igarot believe that the soul travels during sleep. They have encountered the Western insistence that dreams are a product of the subconscious mind, but they dismiss it. They argue that in dreams they often travel along strange, unknown rivers. If dreams took place only inside their own heads, they conclude triumphantly, then they would dream only of the rivers they already knew. So the soul must visit new places during sleep. Given that, if someone's soul joins you in sleep, it must be the real thing.

This is a beautiful, romantic vision of love. Unfortunately, the next stage tends to dissipate its gentle glow. At this point, the two families find out what's going on, and they take over. In our society, discreet or open bickering sometimes accompanies the planning of a wedding. The Igarot take that to an extreme. The two families enter protracted and openly hostile negotiations, largely about property. It's not a time for banter or courtesy; each group's status is on the line. The quarrelling and insults can become so nasty that the bride may try to retreat. She rarely is allowed to do so.

Once the arrangements and the exchange of goods are finally settled, the couple marries. The man moves in with the woman's family. They will spend little time together. He will spend his days hunting with her male relatives. Once the hunt is done, he'll join them in taking care of the children—theirs and eventually his. Farming, the women's work, is much more time-consuming than the hunt, so among the Igarot day-care is largely a male concern.

The couple may remain fond of each other, but they won't have much opportunity to indulge their attachment. The Igarot live communally. Sex is not a problem; all longhouse societies politely pretend that the act is invisible and, if necessary, silent. But privacy is at a premium. If a couple needs time alone for confidences or a quarrel, their only option is to head for the open fields. Under these conditions, it's inevitable that romance will eventually lose its bloom.

Note that the Igarot pattern of courtship and love is not particularly unusual. The love match is not an exclusive Western preserve. But many societies *do* make a sharp distinction between love and marriage. They see love or sexual attraction as too flimsy a basis for a lifelong partnership. They intuitively accept Helen Fisher's findings that romance has a built-in time limit.

Every society finds its own balance between its members' desires and its own craving for order. Contrary to a widespread Western misconception, the vast majority of cultures recognize and experience romantic love.[9] But they also recognize that romantic love is an inherently unstable, antisocial and anarchic force. For that reason, all societies attempt to channel it, and some try to suppress it altogether. For, while love and sex can be purely private matters, marriage is inevitably a public one.

It's important to recognize that all cultures interfere in *some* way in the pairing-up process. There is nowhere on earth where you can marry anyone you choose, and in many places, even today, you have absolutely no choice in the matter at all.

Many cultures, including our own in recent decades, try to solve the problem of love or at least sexual curiosity by letting individual lives mimic the evolution of human mating behaviour. They permit a kind of sexual playtime between childhood and child-bearing. This lets young people indulge their hunger for romance or simply promiscuous sexual experience before they settle down to the serious business of family life.

Thus, premarital experimentation is tolerated and even encouraged in some cultures in the Pacific islands, sub-Saharan Africa and parts of Asia.[10] In the West, moral conservatives see our new sexual permissiveness as a fatal decadence. But in comparison to some societies, our sexual lives in adolescence and early adulthood are relatively tame. In a global context, the striking feature of our behaviour is not our promiscuity, but the length of time we spend playing the field. We marry late and, increasingly, we fail to marry at all. Hugh Hefner would be an unthinkable character in many societies, which expect people to outgrow an obsessive interest in sex by the middle years.

Surveys of our actual sexual behaviour, however, make it clear that we are no champions.[11] We compare poorly, for instance, to the population of Mangaia, an island in central Polynesia.[12] There, boys and girls began to have intercourse with a wide variety of partners as soon as they hit puberty. There wasn't a scintilla of romance in these relations. The Mangaians neither demanded nor expected even affection as a condition for sexual pleasure.[13]

Instead, they placed great emphasis on sexual technique. Young men took pride in the number of their partners and the orgasms they were able to induce. Both boys and girls were supposed to enjoy a wide variety of sexual experience before marriage.

Marriage was an entirely different matter. Matches were arranged by parents, without consulting the prospective bride or groom. The couple would have shared an economic and reproductive life, not necessarily an emotional one. In the early years, the man might have continued to dally with other women, but his wife was expected to behave herself. Affection, understandably, didn't play a major role in Mangaian marriages, although sexual jealousy did.[14]

That pattern of riotous youth followed by sober adulthood is not restricted to small and obscure cultures. Readers may remember an account of rural Japanese courtship customs late in the last century in James Michener's novel *Hawaii*. A man was free to visit a willing single woman. If he returned to her three nights in a row, their society automatically recognized the couple as married. If he changed his mind on nights one or two, the man could withdraw without causing any loss of face.

Now, Michener was writing about an old-fashioned and isolated community where traditional ways still survived. But the custom he describes was a normal one even for aristocrats in Heian Japan. (It's safe to assume that upper-class families monitored their daughters' visitors closely, so the apparent intrigue may well have disguised an arranged match.) It is precisely the way in which the fictional Prince Genji marries Lady Murasaki.[15] Yet the traditional Japanese image of marriage is a singularly unromantic one, based on stern ideals of duty and self-control.

Why does the second stage have to be so much less fun than the first? Why don't societies simply let the party last forever? Why do they inevitably take control, trying to regulate individuals' sexual lives and dictating who may or may not get together?

There are many answers to that, often related to the common human obsessions with property and blood lines. But the first answer is a single word: incest. Each culture draws a line separating relatives who are permitted partners from those it considers too close for comfort. (Many cultures eventually come to draw other lines, of course, to prevent marriage between different castes, social classes, religions, etc. But incest is always the first line.) Members of your immediate family are usually the first names to be crossed off the list. Both Sigmund Freud and Claude Lévi-Strauss saw the suppression of incest as the essence of civilization, one of the uniquely human traits that distinguishes our lives from the animals'.

As it turns out, Freud and Lévi-Strauss were wrong about that. Many animals avoid sexual intercourse with their closest kin, and even the most promiscuous primates rarely attempt sex with their own mothers.[16] For biologists, the reasons for this selectivity are obvious. In the simplest possible terms, we all carry some genes that are duds. The battle for survival ensures that such genes will be recessive—codes that usually lie dormant, checkmated by a dominant healthy gene. Otherwise, your whole genetic program would be in jeopardy, since a serious defect or illness limits your chances of living long enough in good enough shape to reproduce.

In other words, you do your chromosones a favour if you choose a mate whose genetic baggage is substantially different from your own. If you get together with someone whose genetic map isn't all that different from yours, the chances of cancelling out a defective chromosome plummet. The more closely related two parents are, the higher the risk of disease and early death for their offspring. Biologists call this destructive phenomenon "inbreeding depression."

This is not just a theory. A Czech study examined the medical histories of 160 children born of incest with a father, a brother or a son. (It speaks volumes about the weakness of the human incest taboo that such a study was possible.) Almost half of them failed to survive long enough to have children. The problem did not lie in the mothers' genes themselves—the study included a control set of ninety-five children born to the same women by non-related fathers. Ninety per cent of this non-incestuous group survived long enough in adequate health to have children of their own.[17]

Many higher animals seem to know this instinctively, and can recognize their close relatives, probably by smell. Human beings, less nasally gifted, generally share the aversion to sex with close relatives, but they develop it in a different way. We know now, largely through studies of Israeli *kibbutzim*, that people raised together as children rarely develop a sexual interest in one another. One study of the marriage patterns of 2,769 second-generation *kibbutzniks* found not a single marriage between people raised together as children.[18]

Now, the *kibbutz* example works particularly well because that system raised unrelated children of the same age *exactly* like siblings. Children of both sexes shared a dormitory and washroom, showered together, studied together, worked together. The taboo is less likely to be absolute in other systems—an English upper-class home, for instance, where siblings may spend much of their childhoods in separate boarding schools.

Nonetheless, I've witnessed this sibling effect in action myself at a coed British university residence in the early 1970s. Ironically, parents and university administrators had fought mixed residences tooth and nail, no doubt imagining full-scale, term-long orgies. Their fears were largely groundless. A few couples got together in the initial weeks, and shared beds contentedly thereafter. But by the Christmas break, the rest of us had pretty well lost sexual interest in one another, and were seeking excitement in groups who lived somewhere else, *anywhere* else. Sharing housing during the precarious early years of maturity had transformed us into a group of surrogate siblings.

Most human beings also come to feel what we could almost call an instinctive aversion to sex with their mothers, once (assuming Freud was right) they have passed beyond the infantile stage of uninhibited incestuous desire. It's not a mechanism you can always count on, but sexual relations between mothers and sons are relatively rare.[19] While researching a series of articles on abuse in the family, I encountered many stories of father–daughter incest, but only *one* alleged case of sex between mother and son. Nonetheless, it does happen. The Roman Emperor Nero, to take a famous example, reportedly had an affair with his mother, Agrippina. While historians undoubtedly exaggerate some of the excesses of the imperial family, the details of this particular scandal sound plausible.

Meanwhile, historians and social workers can offer countless examples of sex between daughter and father. It's a relationship where our own incest taboos seem dangerously weak. Biologists have a ready explanation for its relatively higher prevalence: men invest less of their time and energy in child-rearing than women. A woman has a limited number of chances to raise a healthy child. Each attempt uses up nine months of pregnancy. If the child survives, birth heralds several years of intense maternal activity. Since a child conceived with her own father, brother or son has a high chance of being drastically flawed, it makes little sense for a mother to risk incest under anything but extraordinary circumstances.

The Bible offers one example of this loss of the incest taboo in such extreme conditions. Lot's daughters decide to throw the genetic dice while hiding from God's wrath in a cave with their father: "The eldest daughter said to the younger, 'Our father is old and there is not a man in the country to come to us in the usual way. Come now, let us make our father drink wine and then lie with him and in this way keep the family alive through our father.' . . . In this way both Lot's daughters came to be with child by their father."[20]

Lot's daughters obviously reasoned that bearing a child with genetic problems—not to mention a severe social stigma—was better than bearing no child at all. In the Bible, the whole thing is their fault; their father is a guiltless victim. That's not the way it usually happens; it's the woman who is more likely to resist incest. A male has much less to lose. His investment is automatically lower, because he will not become pregnant. He may not even have to help raise the child. His risk declines dramatically if his society allows him to commit infanticide. Then he can dispose of an obviously flawed child. He has less evolutionary need for feelings against sex with his female relatives.

There are a few groups that have weighed the risk and decided to tolerate incest between father and daughter, or sister and brother. What advantage could outweigh the risk of passing on serious genetic deficits? The answer is usually power and property. Incest was permitted and even encouraged, for example, in some royal families where the crown passed through the female line. If you're the king by virtue of your marriage to a hereditary queen, the death of your wife is not only a personal tragedy but the end of your career. So it makes sense to marry the heir to the throne—your daughter. That is precisely what kings traditionally did in the royal houses of Iran, Peru, Hawaii and possibly Samoa.[21] Similarly, ancient Egyptian royalty permitted the marriage of brothers and sisters. The practice of incestuous marriage may once have been more widespread among the ruling classes. Certainly the myths of many cultures, including Greek and Japanese, start with gods who mate with their own parents or siblings.

But cultures that allow sex and marriage with close relatives are extremely rare. Most societies draw the line at least a few steps outside the nuclear family. Some go much further. In traditional China, people with the same last name couldn't marry, on the grounds that they must have shared a common ancestor at the dawn of time.[22] (Confucianism considers male descendants part of a single family, no matter how many generations removed.) South Korea maintained a similar ban for 689 years, finally rescinding it in July 1997. The rule imposed considerable hardship in a country where 20 per cent of the population is named Kim; some 60,000 couples were already living together without being able to marry.

Each society finds its own particular balance between the incest taboo, and the desire to keep power and assets in the family. Most societies, for instance, see sex with uncles and aunts as too close for comfort, but there are tribes that strongly encourage marriage between uncle and niece.[23] Many cultures have grave reservations about marriage between cousins, and a substantial number forbid it.

Yet there are Arab cultures, particularly among the Bedouin, that *insist* on cousins marrying, perhaps because it keeps the dowry in the family.

(Such societies generally differentiate between what anthropologists call "parallel" and "cross"-cousins. Your father's sister's daughter is a cross-cousin. His brother's daughter is a parallel cousin. Most of these cultures encourage cross-cousin marriage, but in some of them parallel cousins are seen as the ideal mates.)

In these cases, as with the royal houses, the decision comes down to a weighing of costs. The genetic risk is outweighed by the prospect of material or political advantage.[24] Once the custom is established, of course, its pragmatic origins may well be lost. Human beings have an unfortunate tendency to invest their social systems with sacrosanct values over time. In his book *Villages*, Richard Critchfield told the story of an Egyptian girl who decided to resist marriage to her cousin.[25] Everyone in her village knew that the boy's father was a drunkard, and that he was no prize himself. But public opinion hardened against her. Her refusal to submit to a life of misery was seen as blasphemous and obscene—even though there is no religious basis for the custom of cousin-marriage.

So far, all of this is tidy in terms of logic, if not in its impact on actual human lives. But incest among humans is not confined to a few privileged sub-groups of selected societies. If you read the newspapers, you know that incest—in the form of the sexual abuse of children—shows up regularly in our courts. I would not place complete faith in any statistics on its incidence, but it is clearly no rarity. If you talk with sex-abuse counsellors or read the literature on the subject, you may be tempted to reverse the question that so intrigued Freud, Lévi-Strauss and many, many others. Perhaps we should ask, not why people tend to avoid incest, but why our inhibitions against it seem weaker than those of many other animals.

The answer, to my mind, probably rests in our estrangement from instinct. For humans, all things are possible. We cannot be trusted to avoid those relationships that jeopardize our genetic futures. We need a set of rules—which leads, eventually, to other rules, governing other inconvenient human tendencies like infatuation, self-will and fickleness.

It is conceivable that incest only becomes common in decadent societies: ancient Rome, ancient Egypt, the modern West. The alternative is almost too horrible to contemplate. Consider the possibility that many other cultures hide rates similar to our own of forced incest between father and daughter, uncle and niece, brother and sister. Then remember that many societies demand virginity of their unmarried women. Their own male kin must kill them if they are found to be unchaste. And their virginity will inevitably be tested on their wedding nights; numberless cultures require some variation of a public display of the blood-stained bridal sheet.

If incest were universally common, many girls would fail the test. That would mean that untold numbers of them throughout history have been murdered for harlotry by their own violators.

In spite of all this, incest remains an exception, even a rarity in the history of family behaviour. No matter how many people deviate from the norm, the great mass of humans have always operated on the principle that you can't mate with your own closest kin. (As a friend of mine explained to his four-year-old son, who had just announced plans to marry his mother: "When I went looking for a wife, I didn't stay home and marry Grandma. You get out there and find your own wife, too.") Given that, humans need systems for meeting and mating with partners outside their families.

You might ask, of course, why they need partners. As we've seen, the answer for women seems to lie in the extreme helplessness of their young. They also needed men for protection, for meat from the hunt, and quite possibly for companionship. Similarly, men wanted their own women for dependable sex, for the tremendously useful work of females and children and—at least in the view of many anthropologists—because they desired their own offspring. I'll be returning to this extremely common belief, because it shapes the way we see history and because I'm suspicious of it. I've never understood what men need legitimate children *for*. But even without that assumption, one or more female partners are a highly desirable acquisition for a male in any hunting-gathering society.

Now, you might think that finding a helpmate would be fairly simple—that partnerless men and women could just head out to the woods or the savannah to check out likely prospects. But in a great many societies, that's not how it worked. Instead, the men gained control of the whole process. Somehow they learned to trade their daughters and sisters, first for other women, and eventually for other goods and favours.

This trading in wives is a particularly puzzling piece of human behaviour. Chimpanzees bully females, but they don't trade their sisters for food or mates. So, how did human societies get to this point? The answer, unfortunately, is that we don't know. We can safely assume that the incest taboo precedes this human barter; such cultures must already have developed a strong sense of the need to marry out of their own group. But the trades couldn't have worked unless girls were indoctrinated almost from birth to accept their duty to obey the men who controlled them.[26]

Lévi-Strauss believed that such exchanges were among the earliest forms of human communication: Here, you take my sister, and I'll take yours. (I can't help picturing the parallel communication of the women themselves during these sociable little exchanges—clinging to a brother's leg and whimpering, perhaps.) Whatever the drawbacks, this kind of arrangement guards against inbreeding without dooming most people to celibacy.

A surprising number of societies still operate on this basis. The Tiwi are one obvious example. There are (or were) tribes in Dahomey that operate on a kind of floating deficit basis. A husband is in debt to the friend who has provided his bride until he can return the favour, usually in the person of his own daughter. That means that debts can pile up for decades. Moreover, it may become necessary to transfer the obligation, since women do not materialize on command. To quote the anthropologist Laura Bohannan: "If there are only sons, or if the daughter dies before she is of marriageable age, the heir of the husband, as soon as possible, gives a girl from his compound to the heir of the best friend. The obligation is then cancelled."[27]

It's possible, even under a system like this one, that the woman may have some rights, that she may not be treated badly. But it's inarguable that many societies do regard women and children simply as slaves, to be used, mistreated, even sold. Even now, in many areas of the world, young women routinely leave their homes weeping, to share the bed and fortunes of a stranger, surrounded by the often hostile members of his family. In practice, he and his relations may hold the power of life and death over her, as witness the problem of bride burnings in India.

I still remember with horror a news story from the early 1980s. A Nigerian girl, married before her teens to a much older man, had persisted in running away. He beat her the first two times. The third time, to prevent any further escapes, he cut off both her legs. She died. She was fourteen years old.

Even when marriage is wholly controlled by men, it is not inevitably a miserable and enslaving condition for women. But it's important to recognize that some cultures manage to function while pretty much leaving women to their own devices. A prime example can be found in particular communities of the Nayar caste along India's Malabar coast. They fascinate anthropologists, because their marital arrangements break all the rules.[28] They succeeded in providing children, avoiding incest and guaranteeing the purity of their blood lines, all the while letting their women lead happily independent and exceptionally varied sexual lives.

At first glance, their system seems common enough. Their women must be married off very young. It's a grave disgrace for a girl to be single by the time she starts menstruating. Her family generally gives her to a rather older man. She meets him for the first time at a group marriage ceremony. The Nayar like to marry off several girls at once.

Up to the last century, the couple then spent a few days in seclusion. If the girl was approaching puberty, they might well have sex. And that was that. The couple needed never see one another again. By the time anthropologists had arrived to study them, the Nayars had abandoned even the pretence of secluding the newlyweds. After the ceremony, the "husband" has no further obligations to his "wife." She and her children owe him one thing: They must observe ritual mourning for him when he dies.

You may well wonder where the children come from, under these peculiar marital conditions. The answer is that the Nayar wife spends her nights entertaining a collection of visiting "husbands." Observers have estimated the number of rotating guests at from three to twelve. If a man arrives to find his "wife" already occupied, he is free to sleep on her verandah. Nights aren't cold on the Malabar coast.

Unlike the woman's ritual husband, visiting husbands do have economic responsibilities to their part-time wife—or wives. By any standard, however, these are fairly limited. He owes his wife gifts of clothing, special foods and grooming luxuries. If he fails to deliver these at the appropriate times, he is signalling the end of the affair.

In our world, these gifts of non-essential items seem the domain of the lover, rather than of a husband. But the Nayar male has one further obligation that elevates his role in the woman's life. If she becomes pregnant, one or more of her husbands is supposed to acknowledge paternity and pay her midwife.

It's a practical system. The woman and her children remain with her family, sharing their property. There are some restrictions. Her male relatives would not tolerate a liaison with a man of a lower caste, for instance, and sex with her own kin is absolutely out. But as long as she avoids incest or the contamination of a misalliance, she can do as she pleases. The only risk she runs is the silence of her lovers. A woman who fails to find a "father" for her child is in serious trouble. In the past she would have faced death.

The Nayar system intrigues anthropologists precisely because it is atypical. In most societies, marriage involves a complex web of obligations and responsibilities. The real anomaly of the Nayars is the man's freedom from the burden of maintaining a wife and children. Instead, he is responsible for the maintenance of his own female relatives.

That system of obligation to siblings, rather than mates, is not entirely unique. A number of West African tribes use a kind of knight's move for bequeathing property: one step to the side and one step down. That is, a man must leave his property to his *sister*'s children, not his own. Echoes of that system may have helped to form what anthropologists sometimes call the Jamaican model of marriage, in which a woman may have several children by different men, marrying late if at all. While the legacy of slavery is a major factor in this easygoing family system, it also relies on strong bonds and sharing among the woman's own relatives. Her brothers, too, may be relatively negligent fathers but exemplary uncles.

And that raises an interesting question about the issue of the legitimacy of children. As I've already noted, one of the most popular explanations for the development of marriage is men's "need" for their own offspring. What is never explained is why men need them.

If it is a question of survival of the species, the woman's own family can be at least equally effective in supplying resources and guidance. Societies like the Nayar prove that. Nor do we have proof that men have a *genetic* need to produce their own, recognized offspring. What they have is a genetically programmed desire for sex. The need for their very own children has to be a later development. As the last chapter noted, it requires a broad intellectual leap to link a round of slap-and-tickle and the birth of a child, and there are societies that got by for millennia without clearing that particular gap.

There are also societies—admittedly, a small minority—that simply don't care much. Asia's few remaining polyandrous societies, for instance, work on the assumption that it's enough for the kids to be your own blood. Since they descend from one of your brothers if they're not technically yours, there is no point in being picky. This may not have been an unusual attitude in earlier stages of human development. Some of the nineteenth-century theoreticians about the family speculated that our original pattern was a form of group marriage. Even now, the Nayars seem able to tolerate a degree of uncertainty about paternity without undue anxiety. In our own society, hundreds of thousands of men are helping to raise other men's children, acquired either through marriage or adoption. Many of them do rather well at it.

There have been cultures where fatherhood didn't count for much. As late as this century, the Zuñi of New Mexico had an exceptionally relaxed system of courtship and cohabiting. The woman owned her own house. She would invite a man to share it—for as long as she wanted. If she tired of him, she could simply leave his pipe and other personal possessions on the roof of the hut. When he came home, he had no choice but to gather them up and head home to Mother. It was socially acceptable for him to weep and carry on, but not to resort to violence. Any children of their union belonged to her and her people.[29]

Under this system, there were marriages that lasted a lifetime. In those homes, the constant presence of the father would ensure that he influenced his children's lives. But he was not a *necessary* figure; the woman's relatives could look after the child's material and spiritual well-being.

Now, the Zuñi cherished self-control and amiable social relations above all other values. That ethos made for exceptionally gentle child-rearing practices, and peaceful, pleasant relations between the sexes. Their culture is historically unusual. But it should be noted here that women generally seem to fare best in marriage in societies where they control property. Among the Nayar and the Zuñi, women had their own houses. Women also do comparatively well in hunting-and-gathering societies, where they control the bulk of the food. Among the pygmies of the Congo, the women built and owned their own huts. If they quarrelled with their husbands, they simply started dismantling the marital home leaf by leaf. There is a wonderful account of a husband who figured out how to back down without losing face just as his wife had finished tearing off the leaves and was starting on the supporting sticks. No, no, he told her; only the leaves were dirty, the sticks were fine. After a few seconds of startled thought, the woman headed down to the river to "wash" the dirty leaves. Peace had returned to the home front.[30]

An interesting line of feminist thought has developed from the news that relationships between the sexes in societies like the pygmies'—pre-agriculture and pre-herding—tend to be more egalitarian. It's also based on the prevalence of goddess worship in the early stages of society—a form that a later patriarchy almost always replaces with a male pantheon of divinities. This is the belief that the original human pattern was matriarchal, until evil males brought the golden days to an end.

The difficulty with this is that no one has ever found evidence for a genuinely matriarchal society. The only exception that I know is based on extreme and recent social change. In the Khasi tribe of northeastern India, men today complain bitterly that the women run everything. The Khasis are a matrilineal society, in which the family name and property pass from mother to daughter. Families tend to invest in their daughters' education, rather than their sons', since the daughters are the guardians of the family's property and posterity. In marriage, the wife holds the cards. Her husband lives with *her* family, under the authority of *her* mother. She and her sisters will inherit the family's wealth.

But it's not as simple as it seems. First, the mother's brother is an important member of the household, often its real head. Second, social change has thrown off the balance of Khasi life. At one time, the men were warriors, away from home for months at a time. The women became accustomed to running everything on the home front. (The Western world experienced a milder version of the same upheaval in the two world wars.) When Khasi men were warriors, however, they would have been far more powerful than the unemployed and despised figures they've become. Aside from any other consideration, pillage would have been a source of income. Today, without warfare, the men have no source of self-esteem, or of leverage at home. No wonder an educated female Khasi says bitterly, "Our men are little more than breeding bulls."[31]

A society like the Khasis' is rare to the point of freakishness. In the vast majority of cultures, the lives of women are distinguished by fewer rights, lower status and far less power than men enjoy.

That's why it's necessary to stress those relatively rare societies that offer models of partnership in marriage—precisely because the picture of family life in the chapters that follow will so often be distressingly grim. It is hard not to be horrified by the unnecessary cruelty of many of the systems that human beings have endured and even supported. It is important to recognize that brutality and subjugation are not inevitable ingredients of family life. And it's also important to acknowledge that a harsh order often victimizes men as well as women and children.

As evidence for that last point, let me offer the admittedly untypical example of the Dobu, an unfortunate group living near the Trobriand Islands.[32] The Dobu are untypical because their social order is so vicious. There are reasons for that: unlike the Trobriand Islanders, the Dobu inhabit a most unwelcoming environment, featuring poor fishing and grudging volcanic soil. They have, in response, developed a social system based largely on competition, treachery and malign magic.

Their social unit is the *susu,* a village composed of a small band of maternal kin and—some of the time—their spouses and children. Each *susu* is a closed unit, profoundly hostile to all outsiders. A road always skirts it, so that strangers won't enter it. Nor are its internal relations distinguished by warmth or confidence. Husbands and wives share neither work nor the magic spells upon which all growth and prosperity depend.

How, in such a society, do people manage to marry mates from other *susus,* as the incest prohibition demands? The arrangement relies on a combination of coercion and lust. The adolescent male may not sleep in his own home. He therefore sneaks into neighbouring *susus,* to share the huts of a variety of available girls. He is wise not to sleep too soundly; if he values his freedom, he must be on his way well before dawn.

In the course of time, lust or exhaustion will make him careless. He will sleep in. He awakens to find the young woman's mother— now his mother-in-law—glaring at him. His paramour's relatives assemble and stare at him silently for an unnerving half-hour or so. Then his mother-in-law hands him a hoe and says, "Go dig."

For the next year, he will work on his in-laws' patches of yams and on his own family's, too. In his wife's *susu,* he may not eat in front of other people, nor use their names. They will take every possible opportunity to humiliate and harass him. The only thing that makes the system endurable is that he will return with his wife to his own *susu* for the following year. For the rest of their lives, they will alternate the limited comfort of living with their own kin and the unadulterated misery of living among hostile strangers.

It's a bad system for men, women and children. (The children, raised by warring parents, are regarded as intruders by their father's family. They lose all rights even to enter his *susu* upon his death.)

Note that Dobu men used to be prized workers on the worst ships of Asia. Understandably, they would endure almost any hardship to get away from home.

The Dobu are a cultural rarity. Scarcity has shaped a society that drains all pleasure and trust from human relations. But they serve as an important reminder that a rigid social order is hard on everyone. Coercive systems may exact the highest price from the least powerful members of a society, but they create more than enough misery to go around for everyone.

Nonetheless, in less hopelessly antisocial cultures, a system may not always be as harsh and unfeeling as it seems. Take a feature of marriage in other cultures that often appalls Westerners: the dowry or the bride-price. To us, it's difficult to determine which alternative is the more degrading: cultures that demand a hefty bride-price in return for women's labour and reproductive services, or cultures where the insistence on a dowry suggests that you can't even give women away.

Nor are we alone in our distaste. The Paharis of northern India do not generally pay a bride-price; the dowry is a more familiar pattern in all of Hindu India. But a financially strapped family may offer a bride without a dowry and accept money from the groom's people for the wedding expenses. This system horrifies more conservative (and affluent) Paharis, who ask, "How can you sell a daughter you love?" Their opponents defend the system on grounds of principle, not expedience. They say that the groom's family should not accept charity, should not take the girl without paying for her.[33]

What we may fail to realize is that the exchange of property can act as a guarantee of the woman's status and treatment. As in psychoanalysis, the payment creates a sense of value. If a girl brings a substantial dowry into a marriage, her in-laws will not want to lose it by returning her. If they have paid an equally substantial amount to acquire her, they may appraise her worth on that basis.

The reality may be less humane, of course. The elderly Nigerian groom presumably paid a bride-price for the child-bride he killed through amputation. A daughter who will need a dowry may be regarded by her own family as an unwelcome burden. We know that families in such societies are apt to stint on their daughters' food and education: Why waste resources on an asset that's ultimately only going to benefit someone else? But the possibilities are not as limited as we sometimes assume.

While we can never be sure of practices before recorded human history begins, it seems a safe bet that the bride-price arrangement preceded the dowry system. In the beginning, a man or his kin paid for the woman they were acquiring. At some later and more complex stage, the woman's family began to send her off with her own worldly goods, signalling her value to her new relations. In most societies where marriage involves an exchange of property, both sides contribute. Nora Waln describes the days leading up to an upper-class Chinese wedding in the 1930s, with the bride's family sending gifts of meat and sweetmeats—and the groom's family reciprocating with almost identical offerings.[34] What began as a straightforward sale has become an intricate web of obligations and social gestures.[35]

That softening process can apply even to the most apparently brutal practices. As I mentioned earlier, I have heard the argument that the institution of marriage derived from the forced abduction of women. If you look at marriage in a global context, that is clearly untrue. There is not a vestige of it in the early Japanese pattern, in the Hindu system, among the Zuñi or the pygmies. But it's not an unreasonable argument if you look at parts of Asia and Europe, particularly around the Mediterranean and in the Balkans.

Gunnar Heinsohn, a professor at the University of Bremen in Germany, kindly instructed me on the current wisdom concerning marriage in ancient Rome. He and other authorities on the family now believe that the rape of the Sabine women was no myth. He sees the first Romans as slaves who had revolted—a militaristic tribe desperately short of women.

In his vision of events, the Romans abducted their wives from tribes whose women had enjoyed substantial sexual freedom. He bases his argument on early Roman law, which emphasized the control of women. It was, for instance, a capital offence for a woman to drink wine, to leave her husband's home without permission or to kill her child on her own initiative. Professor Heinsohn reasons that the Sabine women had previously controlled their own sexual and reproductive lives. Significantly, the only capital offence possible for a male was to appear naked before a woman other than his wife. The laws were designed to make sure that a powerful but possibly unattractive husband need have no worries about his wife's fidelity or his children's paternity.

Moreover, with the power of life and death over his children, he could make sure that his family was composed of healthy sons and perhaps one daughter. The girl could be bartered for a bride for his own first-born son. His younger offspring would have a strong incentive to head out to war, so that they could capture wives of their own. To Professor Heinsohn, it seems clear that the Romans deliberately imposed the demands of a patriarchal and militaristic society on women who were not accustomed to obedience.

And equally clearly, it worked, at least for a while. The Sabine women eventually made peace between their male relatives and the men who had become the fathers of their children.

As we'll see, there is nothing unique about this pattern of subjugating women. From the ancient Middle East to contemporary Bosnia, rape and impregnation have been a favourite method of bringing enemy women under control. Moreover, there are a few societies that still practise marriage by capture. In 1996, in Zenica, Bosnia, an Islamic holy warrior arranged the abduction of Eldina Mesinovic, fifteen, a schoolgirl on her way home.[36] A local imam tipped off the girl's family when the "matchmaker" came to arrange a quick ceremony. They managed to rescue her, with no help from the police. The report continued: "Enraged at the girl's escape, four mujahideen came to her home where they beat her father and uncle."

But abduction doesn't tend to be a durable marital system in the long run. Rome's women, for instance, never truly settled down happily under their husbands' thumbs. By the time the Republic fell, a startling number of them were not the sober, chaste, industrious wives of their men's ideals. Similarly, the practice of abduction itself has a tendency to lose its force over time. It becomes ritualized— perhaps because a prisoner doesn't make an entirely satisfactory companion and bed-mate.

An enchanting example of ritualized abduction can be found among the Wodaabe of Niger. (Most readers will have encountered the Wodaabe on their television screens, in commercials for Coca-Cola or British Airways, or in Michael Jackson videos.) They are a nomadic people, about seven million strong, living off their camels and herds of cattle and goats.

The Wodaabe prize beauty above all else. Their men adorn themselves spectacularly for regular celebrations in which they dance to display their grace, their looks and their charm. As might be expected, this emphasis on beauty and appeal is not divorced from sex. But the Wodaabe have found ways to limit its potential for social damage. In *Millennium: Tribal Wisdom and the Modern World*, David Maybury-Lewis writes:

> Wodaabe philandering takes place within an elaborate set of rules
> that allows for romantic sexual passion while preserving the stabil-
> ity of the family. Within one's lineage—and there are fifteen sepa-
> rate lineages among the Wodaabe—a man may only marry one
> woman, and this marriage is arranged at childhood. It is called the
> *kobgal* marriage. Affairs are not outlawed within one's own lineage,
> but they can never lead to marriage. It is considered dangerous and
> disruptive to the entire lineage to carry on one of these affairs for

too long, and while it is going on, it must be very discreet. Wodaabe etiquette says, "What the eyes do not see did not happen," which means that rumours and suspicions have to be ignored . . .[37]

The illicit affair, however, is not the only recourse for enlivening life. Maybury-Lewis continues: "A far more common source of romantic adventures is the practice of wife-stealing between different lineages."[38]

The word "stealing" is not entirely accurate here. The most common arena for initiating an abduction is the Geerewol celebration, an annual festival whose highlight is a week-long dance competition among the men. Up to a thousand of them at a time vie to be chosen the most beautiful and charming. (The judges are three unmarried girls, selected for *their* beauty.)

In addition to the throng of dancers, there are thousands of onlookers. Yet somehow, in the midst of this crush, couples manage to signal their desire to meet silently, using only the eyes. That tryst may lead to the decision to elope. Maybury-Lewis writes:

What is extraordinary from the Western point of view is that the decision to run away together, made "from the heart" as they say, is often reached very quickly. A Wodaabe couple may arrange a meeting, sleep together once, and decide to marry. If they are already married to others . . . and her husband is anywhere near, he will give them chase. But this is a ritual, strictly for show. He usually accepts that if his wife wants to leave, there is no point in trying to stop her . . .[39]

There are two factors that make this recklessness all the more extraordinary. First, the absconding woman will never enjoy the status of a *kobgal* wife in her new home. Her arrival at her new home is not a pleasant one. Her husband leaves her at a distance from his camp, where she huddles under a blanket, waiting for his established wives to accept her existence. They are certain to resent her, not only out of sexual jealousy, but because she will place further strain on resources that are already pretty limited. Even once their anger has softened, the new wife can never own as much as the socially endorsed *kobgal* wife, who will always take precedence over her. Yet this "abduction" of respectably married women is a regular occurrence. The Wodaabe apparently consider the world well lost for love.

Maybury-Lewis points out that the bolting wife's loss of property may not seem disastrous to her, since the Wodaabe don't own much to begin with. Moreover, an unhappy wife can always return to the camp of her own birth family if life becomes intolerable.

It is the second drawback of absconding that would give many other cultures pause. The departing wife leaves her children behind. They will grow up, without her, in her husband's lineage. It's a system that provides stability in their lives. But for most of the world, the idea of a woman leaving her children for love—possibly repeatedly—seems abhorrent, and unnatural.

Nonetheless, individual women in many societies have made the same choice. Early in this century, the wife of a Nottingham professor left her husband and children to share the tempestuous life of D.H. Lawrence. In this decade, an American woman named Susan Smith deliberately drowned her two children in terror of losing her lover.

Coming and going, love can be a most destructive force. All cultures try to restrain the problems it causes, and none ever completely succeeds. As we'll see in the next chapter, love is no easy force to control.

Love & Loss

What men call gallantry, and gods adultery,
Is much more common where the climate's sultry.
                    —Lord Byron, *Don Juan*

"Well, I think adultery is a filthy habit," said Rose, *"like using*
someone else's toothbrush."
                    —Alice Thomas Ellis, *The Sin Eater*[1]

"He that is without sin among you, let him first cast a stone at her."
                    —John 8:7

EVEN UNDER THE MOST rigid social systems, human mating
patterns are singularly untidy. Our literature and love songs bear
witness to the frequent misery of our romantic lives: think of Tris-
tan and Isolde, Lancelot and Guinevere, Romeo and Juliet, Frankie
and Johnny, Charles and Camilla, and Diana and Dodi. Almost all
of our great love stories end in the tragedies of death or betrayal.
They have to, because passionate love is ephemeral. Indeed, it's hard
to find models for an attachment that isn't doomed to fail. Two San
Francisco psychologists, Erica Chopich and Margaret Paul,[2] told me
in the early 1990s that they would give a thousand dollars to anyone who could name a love song that was *not* about what they called
a dysfunctional relationship. (I suggested "Lulu's Back in Town,"
but they weren't familiar with it.)

Our messy problems would be incomprehensible to, say, the
common loon, who mates contentedly for life. Perhaps the secret is
separate vacations: loons enjoy a same-time-next-year relationship,

wintering apart. Each spring, two Canadian naturalists note, couples get reacquainted through "an elegant, quiet, diving courtship waltz when they return to their original honeymoon lake..."[3] Only death can prevent the annual rendezvous; for loons, the magic is never gone.

This is not necessarily true for humans. We have half the loon pattern; we tend to pair up. The overwhelming majority of us spend most of our adult lives in some form of marriage. But our pair bonds can be dangerously fragile. They do not protect us from falling out of love; they often fail to keep us from falling in love with someone else.

This is not a recent observation. It has not escaped the attention of the social anthropologists and other theoreticians who examine the evolutionary basis of our behaviour. Today, writing on the subject has veered sharply away from Desmond Morris's comfortable vision of contented monogamy. For humans, one partner is often not enough. That's one reason why 84 per cent of recorded cultures have permitted polygyny.[4]

Our fickleness makes sense, at least in genetic terms. As we've seen, monogamy is not necessarily an advantage to a male. The man who keeps a harem, like the compulsive philanderer, is playing the odds: sheer numbers increase his chances of genetic survival. This is not, of course, his conscious aim. Like the prehominid female sprouting breasts, he is evolution's tool, not its master. But their genes seem to impel a lot of men into playing the field. A lot of researchers have gained new respect for the old rhyme, "Hogamous, higamous, men are polygamous; higamous, hogamous, women monogamous."[5]

That belief predates the field of evolutionary psychology by millennia. Will Durant, in *The Story of Civilization*, wrote from the assumption that primitive cultures (what he called "nature peoples") often find monogamy immoral and unnatural.[6] He saw traces of an ancient communal right to a tribe's women in a few surviving folk patterns. These included some societies' periods of sanctioned licence, such as Saturnalia and Mardi Gras. He also drew on the hospitable wife-lending of the Inuit and a few other tribes, and "the *jus primae noctis*, or right of the first night, by which, in early feudal Europe, the lord of the manor, perhaps representing the ancient rights of the tribe, occasionally deflowered the bride before the bridegroom was allowed to consummate the marriage."[7] (Durant did not seem to consider the possibility that the practice reflected instead the traditional right of the lord of the manor to enjoy the best of everything at all times.)

Durant contended that polygamy was "well-adapted to the marital needs of a primitive society in which women outnumbered men." He continued with a thought very much in vogue when he wrote this book, the 1930s: a suggestion that we return to a system in which "the most able men" could have several wives, and thus a large number of offspring.[8] It distressed Durant that successful men in the West were marrying late and having few children.

Now, Durant's belief that the world is loaded with extra women is common. The prophet Mohammed advocated polygamy in part to provide for war widows. But there is no reason to assume that women did greatly outnumber men in most early societies. While hunting and combat no doubt carried off many men, childbirth in unhygienic surroundings must have finished off a balancing number of women. Durant's eugenic arguments have been unpopular since the Allied victory in the Second World War—they're too reminiscent of the Nazi master-race theories.

In any case, Durant's theory is based on the supposition that earlier civilizations were meritocracies. Maybe—but I suspect that status would become hardened into hereditary privilege fairly early. Any dolt could presumably inherit the wealth and rank that made him a desirable match.

But Durant was right about the reality of polygyny. He concluded that even in polygamous cultures, most men had only one wife.

Today, we know that when a culture permits polygyny, only 5 to 10 per cent of the male population is likely to practise it.[9] (There are exceptions. In some West African cultures, 25 per cent of older men have two or more wives.) In Durant's own words, "The mass of the people practised a monogamy tempered with adultery, while another minority, of willing or regretful celibates, balanced the polygamy of the rich."[10] He concluded that monogamy is artificial, a distortion created by civilization.

I remember the first time I encountered this argument. It was in Sierra Leone, where I taught university for a year. My remedial English class was discussing their essays on their families. One of the braver men took it on himself to explain to me that men *have* to be unfaithful. Their physical nature requires more than one woman, while women are perfectly satisfied with a single man. He braced himself for a flood of missionary-style horror. Instead, I asked him to come up with some numbers. He conferred with his cronies, then suggested that a healthy man needs sexual access to four or five women at any time.

I led him through the logic of his argument: Most men are visiting more than one woman. Each woman, being naturally monogamous, is faithful to a single man. But it takes two to tango. Where the hell are all those extra women coming from?

It's a question I continued to ask for many years. In most cultures at most times, women do *not* significantly outnumber men, except as the result of catastrophic war.[11] So there are only two possibilities. Either a few women keep very, very busy, or a lot of women aren't wholly monogamous after all.

There's clear evidence today that the second proposition is correct. We have learned that what's sauce for the gander is sauce for the goose. The adulterous male cannot count on the little woman's unwavering loyalty. As an old Motown song asks, "Who's making love with your old lady, while you are out making love?"

I'll admit that this came as a shock to me. When I started the research that eventually led to this book, I had assumed that male concern about female infidelity was largely paranoia. But men have good reason to worry. A 1993 survey of Americans, *The Janus Report of Sexual Behavior,* found that 26 per cent of married women had had extramarital affairs. Surveys by *Cosmopolitan* and *Penthouse* magazines have reported higher numbers. Now, those numbers are suspect for the general population, which may be more sexually conservative than people who read *Penthouse* or choose to fill out surveys on the most intimate aspects of their lives. But even the National Opinion Research Center at the University of Chicago, after questioning a random demographic sample, placed the infidelity rate at 12.2 per cent for men and 11 per cent for women over the previous two years.[12] Another recent American study found that around 10 per cent of children had been sired by someone other than their legal father, who believed them to be his own.[13]

It's possible, of course, that North American behaviour is aberrant. Even there, some communities behave better. Adultery is more prevalent in large cities, where it's easier to hide a liaison. Obviously the rates are apt to be lower in countries where there's little opportunity for dalliance, because men and women do not work together or because women are restricted to the home. The surrounding culture also has to have some impact; I wouldn't want to risk an affair in contemporary Iran.

But there are cultures where the adultery rate is a lot higher than 11 or 12 per cent. There are obvious examples: the decadence of Rome's later period, or the biblical Sodom and Gomorrah. Much of Renaissance Europe was licentious to a degree that would shock the modern world. William Manchester wrote, "To the ladies in the Nérac court of Marguerite of Angoulême,... extramarital sex was considered almost obligatory. Those wives in the *noblesse d'épée* who remained faithful to their husbands were mocked by the others. To abstain from the pleasures of adultery was almost a breach of etiquette..."[14]

The same ideal of aristocratic promiscuity has reigned in many other courts. The ladies of the imperial palaces of Heian Japan lived in purdah, hidden from men behind screens. Nonetheless, their fiction, diaries and pillow books make it clear that the illicit liaison was one of their major pastimes, governed by its own arcane code of etiquette.

But adultery is not a private preserve of royalty. It can permeate a whole culture. One fascinating example is the Mehinaku tribe of Brazil, studied by the anthropologist Thomas Gregor. It would be a gross understatement to say that Mehinaku men are enthusiastic about sex. They told Gregor, "Good fish gets dull, but sex is always fun."[15] They describe their sexual relations as "delicious" and "succulent." (Note that their standards of beauty are rather different from ours. Mehinaku men favour women with heavy but firm thighs and calves, large breasts and nipples, "small close-set eyes, sparse body hair and tweezed eyelashes."[16])

Mehinaku women are generally both more pragmatic and more emotional in their approach to affairs. They want human contact with their lovers, but they also willingly exchange sex for gifts of fish, beads or soap. Some of the least attractive men in the village had racked up impressive totals of lovers. The men generally ignored older women as sexual prospects, but, as they aged, could continue to make conquests themselves by offering gifts.

The women also showed much greater variation in sexual behaviour than the men. The average Mehinaku man, Gregor computed, is carrying on 4.4 extramarital affairs. The women, in contrast, have "either a very large or very small number of boyfriends. The three most sexually active women in the village account for almost 40 percent of the total number of liaisons..."[17]

As you might expect, the Mehinaku are not prudes. But, like us, they feel strongly that the act itself must be private.[18] Moreover, spouses are highly jealous. A chief explained, "Women's vaginas are very dear to men... No one lets his wife have sex with others. You must not let a husband see his wife while you are propositioning her."[19] Affairs must be concealed. Couples sneak into the woods, often using a child as a go-between.[20] Bolder lovers will hide behind the woman's house, waiting for her to come out to work or urinate. Her husband may be only yards away.[21]

This is the kind of behaviour that drives missionaries wild, but humans may come by it naturally. It is perfectly possible to argue that adultery is part of our genetic heritage—an intrinsic feature of our animal nature. Certainly we are not the only species that can't be trusted. Recent research has established that many animals are not the paragons of virtue we once believed. Take birds. A guide to the Ontario wilderness makes the female chickadee seem positively sordid: "Lower-ranking female chickadees sometimes fly to the territory of a dominant male for an illicit liaison, then return to their nests on the wrong side of the tracks to have their cuckolded husbands help raise their blue-blooded brood."[22]

Red-winged blackbirds are equally naughty. The males are polygamous, maintaining harems of up to four wives. But the harem sometimes cheats with interlopers while the males are off feeding. A researcher discovered that almost 30 per cent of the hatchlings are the products of extramarital affairs.[23]

There are animals that manage to cheat even without "marriage." Chimpanzees, as we've seen, are a highly promiscuous species. Yet, even with built-in variety, females seem to crave the exotic. They have a weakness for males from outside their own troop, and will sneak off to meet them. Other primates also seem to prefer strangers. I remember a television documentary in which a young female monkey squatted near an interloping male, devouring him with her eyes. As she inched ever nearer, he kept *his* eyes on the males of her troop in terror. Lust eventually overcame prudence, but the male was clearly tense and distracted throughout their brief coupling.

He was right to worry. His species does not have a *laissez-faire* approach to a female's sexual straying. There are animals who seem more philosophical. The male puffin carries on even after he's caught his wife *in flagrante delicto*—perhaps hoping to keep her in a good mood for his next try at genetic immortality.[24] Primates tend to be less tolerant. An erring female gorilla or baboon can expect to be soundly drubbed and possibly bitten.[25]

Changing partners can be a nasty business even among mammals in a group marriage. A group of male lions taking over a pride kills the infants. The massacre wipes out the DNA of their predecessors, and brings the females back into estrus.[26] Male langurs do the same thing when they fancy a nursing mother.[27] It may be brutal, but it's genetically practical. Helen Fisher found at least one African tribe that permitted a woman's new partner to kill any of her children under the age of four.[28]

Nonetheless, I don't think it's wise to discuss human beings purely in terms of genetic strategies. Evolutionary self-interest is not the only factor in human behaviour. All but the most rabid animal-rights activist would agree that our relationships are emotionally more complex than those of other animals, and possibly more profound, so academic aloofness can take us only so far. I remember being on a television panel about love several years ago. A distinguished scholar from the University of Chicago provided a detailed and detached description of Victorian attitudes. But by the end of the panel, he opened up enough to say, "Let's face it—we all suffer like dogs in love."

We suffer because our love is not always requited, and because it does not always last. In 1991, I prepared a radio series on intimacy for the Canadian Broadcasting Corporation. For it, I interviewed a friend whose girlfriend had just left him. Lying in bed, too depressed to get up, he remembered the "glow" and the "magic" of the past. In contrast, he described the misery of the present: "Bereft. You feel bereft. . . . A big treasure, a huge treasure, the most important treasure, . . . your most precious jewel is no longer yours. It's gone. It's horrible." (The treasure eventually returned home, and they've been together happily ever since.)

Two experts interviewed for the same series summed up the problem of love succinctly. Gunnar Heinsohn believes love is a lose-lose proposition: "Either people hurt you by leaving you, or people hate you for leaving them." Bonnie Kreps, a Canadian film-maker and author,[29] was more graphic.

Borrowing from Shakespeare, she calls the infatuation form of love "sparkledust." In our interview, she said, "It starts out of nowhere, it stops out of nowhere. Boing! You're dumped . . . Or you dump somebody. You know, it's like click-click, a cut in a film— a person is gone. Very painful. Profound, excruciating pain."

Bonnie Kreps doesn't believe it has to be this way. She advocates learning to love "without losing yourself"—fighting off the sparkledust of passion.[30] In other words, just say no to infatuation. I got a similar message from a rather different source a couple of years later, when I was working on yet another radio series—this time on marriage. Dr. Suzanne Scorsone, director of the office of family life for the Archdiocese of Toronto, expressed some impatience with the idea that we are genetically programmed to commit adultery. "You could say we have a genetically programmed urge to steal because we covet," she argued. "We have animal desires to do what we want, and we just make a decision not to do it. . . . In all of these areas, we're going to be tempted, but with the grace of God . . . we decide we will do what is right."

This is sensible advice, but rather hard to follow. We do not always seem to have a choice about the kind of love we feel, when we feel it, or whom we feel it for. Our genes propel us into frenzied desire, and they may also dictate our exit from it. As we now know, that old black magic springs at least in part from changing levels of dopamine, norepinephrine and phenylethylamine.[31] Our experience of love relies in part on this powerful cocktail of natural amphetamines, which boost energy and spark euphoria. This fizzy, heady brew makes us want to skip, to run, to dance.

If these chemical goodies are suddenly withdrawn, you get the feelings that land a healthy young man in bed, moaning about his lost treasure. Energy dies, the world loses its sparkle, the sky turns grey. This loss of love is our favourite musical theme, the subject of countless arias and torch songs.

And, even if love lasts, it changes. It hits a new stage, one that is woefully underrepresented in our literature, movies and music. Eventually, after the amphetamines have peaked, a new chemical mix of oxytocin, vasopressin and endorphins kicks in. You start to feel a more temperate and stable sense of attachment to your partner. It's the kind of love that united the mythical Philemon and Baucis, whose only request to the gods was to let them die at the same instant. Nick and Norah Charles of *The Thin Man* series, with their camaraderie and wisecracks, are clearly another couple who have survived the sparkledust stage.

That's an achievement, for a lot of affairs never make it to the serenity of quiet attachment. Passion, the force that brings a couple together, is wildly volatile. Shakespeare captures it perfectly when Romeo transfers his affections instantly from Rosalind to Juliet, or when the two couples in *A Midsummer Night's Dream* change love objects with the rapidity of ping-pong balls. A sprinkling of sparkledust, and women long for girls disguised as boys, or a queen dotes on an ass. Love messes up our lives.

Unfortunately, humans crave sparkledust. Federico Allodi, a Toronto psychiatrist, discussed the problem for my radio series on marriage: "You know, each one inside of us has a dragon that always wants more and more flesh. The dragon is called love." Dr. Allodi says some people realize that the dragon is insatiable, and try to ignore him. Others keep feeding him, at the cost of recurring pain and guilt. For if you're addicted to passionate love, you have to keep changing partners. You cannot stay at the infatuation stage permanently.

In sociobiological terms, the amphetamine cocktail grows weak and your partner suddenly fills you with irritation or ennui. If Helen

Fisher's four-year-itch theory is right, your genes are set up to start fault-finding about the time that your first child is ready for nursery school. (You can't short-circuit the process by staying childless, either. The break-up rate is much higher for childless couples.)

And so—click-click—you desert or you're deserted. If may work out well genetically for the race as a whole, but it's hell for individual people.

Now, contrary to conventional academic wisdom, that pain is well-nigh universal. Thanks to William Jankowiak of the University of Nevada and Edward Fischer of Tulane University, we know that romantic passion is recognized in 147 of 166 cultures studied by anthropologists.[32] We came to that knowledge late. Because social scientists had been indoctrinated to believe that romantic love was an isolated phenomenon, they did not look for it, and often did not recognize it when they saw it.

Jankowiak did not start out as a specialist on romance. During his student years, his instructors firmly squelched his interest in the subject. But it resurfaced when he was doing field work in China in the early 1980s. He had arrived assuming that socialism would have stamped out private passion; he expected a nation of puritans. Instead, he found a culture obsessed with love and marriage. Everyone wanted to know if he was married, if he had a girlfriend. People welcomed questions about their own romantic lives—or fantasies. And because their society is so rigid and repressive, their stories were often tragic.

Jankowiak was intrigued. Classical China relied on arranged marriage, supplemented (for men) by secondary wives, concubines, prostitutes and a wealth of pornography. But its folklore and street stories were tales of passion, very much like our own. The story of Chang Po, who eloped with his lover in the seventh century, is startlingly like *Manon Lescaut*. The overt morality of these stories manages to stay within the bounds of orthodoxy, because their illicit affairs always end tragically. But, as with us, they offer the audience the vicarious pleasure of forbidden desires.

In an interview, Jankowiak told me about the day he started this line of research, when a man revealed an attachment to a dancer who had left him. "I might even have contemplated suicide," he told the anthropologist. Jankowiak found even more painful love stories in rural China. One woman told him she had begged her family to let her marry the man she loved, but "all things weren't equal." Married against her will to a wealthier man, she fought him for four months before sharing his bed. It is a tale straight out of *Fiddler on the Roof,* but with no happy ending. "My heart belongs to someone else," she said, after years of marriage.

I found the same fascination with love during an interview with a young immigrant from China. Because of the sensitive nature of the discussion, she asked to be called simply "Ooming"—no name. Ooming is a divorcee. When I asked her what she looked for in a man, she reeled off a list of essentially practical virtues: reliable, affectionate, willing to share housework, intelligent, educated. I asked about love, and she was shocked that she hadn't started with it: "Oh, did I miss that? . . . I think that is the most important thing. I would put love as my top priority."

Ooming resented the idea that China has no tradition of romantic love, citing both the same folk stories as Jankowiak and the classic *Dream of the Red Chamber.* She admitted that these stories end unhappily, "but that shows people have this desire for love. Unhappy endings only show that other powers prevent this happening. But people's desire is still there." She did acknowledge, like a number of Japanese women I've met, that one Western novel has played a major role in popularizing the hunger for love in marriage. With its long-suffering heroine and its muted but happy ending, *Jane Eyre* has a female cult following in much of the Orient.

All this could still suggest that the ideal of romantic marriage is a recent phenomenon, buoyed by a few fictions with no basis in reality. But even in China, there have always been people who count the world well lost for love. One of their stories forms the basis of Jonathan Spence's magnificent history *The Death of Woman Wang*. It is the story of an unhappy wife who ran off with a lover in 1671. Her husband took her back—then killed her as she slept beside him.[33]

Another turns up surprisingly in Nora Waln's memoir of the final years of an extremely traditional Chinese family, in *The House of Exile*. Waln went to live with the Lins as a young woman in 1920. The family was so strict that its women travelled in closed chairs, so that no one could stare at them. All marriages were arranged. Yet the House of Exile owed its existence to a most undutiful romance. The founder, Lin Fu-yi, fell in love with the daughter of his supervisor while working to extend the grand canal for Kubla Khan. He was eighteen; his lover, Sun Li-la, was fourteen. Lin was a married man. Sun Li-la's father was unwilling to let his daughter accept the lower status of a concubine. So the girl climbed over the wall, and joined Lin at the quarters he had already arranged for her. Lin rudely rebuffed his grandfather's pleas to return home after the death of his legitimate son. But Sun Li-la, filled with pity for the old man, gave him her eldest son to carry on the family line.[34]

The Lins retained a repressed love of romance. Waln's closest companion, Mai-da, obediently renounced the Manchu prince she wanted and married the man her family chose. He died, murdered during the Nationalist uprising, leaving a letter and package to be delivered when Mai-da had finished her period of mourning. He had diverted money from his own family to allow her the independence to marry the man she really loved. The letter urged her to do so.[35]

Romantic love is so sturdy that it can spring up even in arranged marriages. In 1990, in Toronto, Homaira and Humayan Kabir married.[36] Their parents had arranged the match. Homaira later told a reporter that her community's approach to marriage was pragmatic: "Are the boy and the girl from a similar social setup so that there is compatibility in their thinking? Is the boy educated and gainfully employed and is the girl of a sweet and compromising tempera- ment so as to get along with her new family? Do they have sound moral values and a clean past record? If these basic questions are satisfactorily answered, then there is no reason why the marriage should not work." Before their marriage, their only time alone was the occasional phone call. At her home, everyone else monopolized his attention. Nonetheless, Homaira fell deeply in love. She said, "I would watch him from afar and long for the day when he would eventually be mine."

My male African students would never have admitted to such feel- ings. They, too, came from societies that frowned on romantic love. Before I entered the country, I eavesdropped on a conversation at the Sierra Leone embassy in London. A group of young men were deploring the coming nuptials of a friend. "Only two reasons for marry," one of them said to his friends. "Na money, na family influ- ence." Later, when one class was studying *Romeo and Juliet,* a baffled male student asked me why a man would kill himself for a woman, when there were so *many* women.

Yet most of the women and quite a few of the men had a pas- sion for romance comic books. The Mills and Boon romance nov- els sold better than thrillers. The anthropologist Helen Regis found the same half-repressed fascination with love among the Fulbe, another West African tribe. They regard love as a shameful weak- ness—yet lovesick young men find themselves hanging around the desired one's hut, risking ridicule for a glimpse of the beloved.[37] In the words of William Jankowiak, "The Fulbe have a tremendous incentive not to fall in love, yet time and time again, they fail."

The Fulbe cannot resist the pleasures of the earliest stages of love—the sight of the loved one, the shared glance, the secret smile. Of course, that sets them up for future pain, since their unromantic society will never let them possess the object of their desires. They are doomed to suffer the loss of love, and we humans really hate that. We aren't even keen on sharing it. W.H. Auden said it best:

For the error bred in the bone
Of each woman and each man
Craves what it cannot have,
Not universal love
But to be loved alone.

If the experience of love is universal, so is the agony of jealousy.

There is, however, a widespread belief that the sexes are jealous in different ways. Dr. David Buss, a psychologist at the University of Michigan, has explored the sexual predilections of some ten thousand people, representing thirty-seven cultures around the world.[38] He found many differences between the sexes. According to his research, women are usually more tolerant of sexual infidelity than of any loss of attention or resources. Conversely, at least in his findings, men are indifferent if their wives prefer the company of others, but go wild over sexual straying.[39] According to this vision of human jealousy, the reactions of a spurned man and spurned woman are qualitatively different.

I have some reservations about this distinction. I know men who are deeply jealous of their wives' families and friends. Conversely, some of my female friends would be unable to forgive even the most casual sexual indiscretion in their husbands or lovers. I've also encountered people of both sexes who seem able to tolerate open sexual infidelity in their mates—couples who have what used to be called "an understanding." Most of these marriages seem to me to have a short shelf life, but I know one such couple who are coming up to their fiftieth anniversary.

Nonetheless, you can compile plenty of evidence that the sexes are generally jealous in different ways. The *crime passionnel* is overwhelmingly a male prerogative. Similarly, although there are women who stalk former partners (and even men they simply *want* as partners), stalkers are much more likely to be male. Both sexes may resent a partner's roving eyes and thoughts, but men are more apt to do something about it. The Canadian writer M.T. Kelly once told me of a visit to Iran. He had encountered a trio—a man walking ahead of two women, presumably his wives—and one of the women looked up and met his eyes. The man turned and knocked her down.

I have never seen that kind of behaviour in a woman outside a comic strip or old movie, although I know it happens. Women *are* capable of violent jealousy. Jean Harris is a classic example, and a good illustration of David Buss's theory. She had tolerated frequent sexual infidelity in her lover, Dr. Herman Tarnower of Scarsdale Diet fame. She shot him only after he'd actually dumped her—click-click—for his secretary, Lynne Tryforos. Harris claimed that she had intended only to kill herself in front of Tarnower, but the jury didn't buy it.[40] (Neither do I.)

Jean Harris became a feminist *cause célèbre*, rather to my horror. The idea that lovers are property strikes me as wrong in itself, and inevitably more dangerous to women. But I do accept the idea that Harris's jealousy was peculiarly female. She always denied that she was jealous of the secretary who had supplanted her in Tarnower's affections. Her baffled rage was directed entirely at him. Her testimony at the trial suggested that she felt she was saving him from himself. She had identified with him so completely that she felt she held the key to his true nature, which his affair with a mere secretary was subverting.[41]

For women like Jean Harris, the loss of a loved man can feel like the loss of themselves. The end of a romance robs them of too much, because they have invested so heavily in the relationship, and derive so much of their self-image from it. Simone de Beauvoir captures it perfectly in her novella *The Woman Destroyed*.[42] The narrator of that story is in hell because her husband has left her for another woman (whom she despises), taking with him her image of herself as loved, valuable, worthy of respect as a person. She repels advice and assistance designed to help her rebuild her life—she doesn't *want* to rebuild it. Having identified with her husband so completely for a couple of decades, she subconsciously believes that her depression is punishing him. And to some extent she is right, although he soon begins to distance himself from her pain. I have seen women writhe in precisely the same anguish, deprived of an identity by the loss of the love that defined them.

There are, of course, less pure emotions in female jealousy. As we've seen with the Wodaabe, a reluctance to share material resources also figures in the mix. Resentment is inevitable in societies where women take their status from men. Britain's notorious Old Bags Club, composed of discarded first wives, urges the abandoned spouse to seek revenge. Its founder set an example by inflicting irreparable damage on her ex-husband's clothes and car.

In spite of all this, many societies expect women to stifle any anger or hurt they might feel when their men move on, emotionally or physically. Major civilizations from Sumeria to the Mayans to China tended to assume that women ought to be able to cope with their husbands' infidelities, without expecting any reciprocal toleration from men. Even officially monogamous cultures didn't really expect men to stick to one woman. Other men's wives were generally taboo, but slaves, servants and courtesans were fair game. The little woman could presumably console herself with the reminder that such women had no official rights or status—they weren't really *wives*.

A number of cultures, as we've already seen, have found a way to make legitimate what we would see as adultery. They expect women to live harmoniously in polygamous households, to share a man without friction. It sometimes works. Norma Joseph, a professor of religion at Concordia University in Montreal, discussed the history of polygyny in Judaism with me for the marriage radio series. She stressed that the laws governing it were onerous—each wife was entitled to equal property and sexual access. Relatively few Jews ever practised it, and it became taboo for European Jews in about 1000 A.D. But it remains permissible for Jews from the Arab world, and Joseph has a friend, an Iraqi Jew, who grew up in a home with two wives.

Strange as it may seem to us, it was the first wife who nagged her husband to add to the household. She was childless, and extremely lonely. She chose a cousin she liked. Her husband resisted at first, but she eventually got her way. Joseph's friend grew up regarding both women as his mother. He has only happy memories of the love shared by his three parents. His stepmother evidently felt no sense of loss in splitting her husband's affections with another, younger woman.

There is even an organization in New York today that wants to bring back the option of multiple marriage—or at least concubinage—in Judaism. It is called *Shalom Bayis,* literally "household peace." The group argues that the system would let a man marry a woman of outstanding character, well-suited to raising his children. Then he could satisfy his personal desires with a better-looking concubine. (He could also have sex more often, since orthodox Judaism bans intercourse during a substantial chunk of a woman's monthly cycle.) Concubinage would also provide a role for unmarried women. But note that *Shalom Bayis* is very much a fringe group. A leading rabbi said of them, "They're crazy, fanatic idiots. They have nobody of heavy rabbinic stature behind them. Not even anybody mediocre."[43]

Nonetheless, I don't think most women relish sharing their homes and husbands, even where polygamy is socially accepted. The Bible itself provides examples: Sarah forcing Abraham to banish Hagar and Ishmael to the desert, Peninnah and her children taunting the childless Hannah. The harem is not necessarily a happy place. The Chinese book and film *Raise the Red Lantern* present a hellish vision of the seething jealousies it can contain.[44] Rivalry and bitterness seem almost inevitable when women have to compete for attention and resources, not only for themselves but for their children.

The aristocrats of Heian Japan clung to a double standard that seems to me particularly unjust. Aristocratic women were largely confined to their own rooms, communicating with men by notes in exquisite calligraphy. It's clear, especially from the memoirs of one Lady Nijo, that they were expected to take lovers. Refusing illicit love was seen as selfish and priggish. Accepting it, however, involved terrible risks, especially if the woman became pregnant or her husband found out. But the man who stayed faithful to one woman was an object of ridicule. Women were expected to suffer torments of jealousy. But they also knew that their lovers would flee if they complained about neglect. There was no escape from almost constant unhappiness.

Very few cultures expect men to suffer jealousy in silence. Although they often come up with religious and social justifications for the double standard, the underlying argument is genetic. Samuel Johnson expanded on this theme to his ever-receptive biographer, James Boswell:

"Between a man and his wife," said Dr. Johnson, "a husband's infidelity is nothing. They are connected by children, by fortune, by serious considerations of community. Wise married women don't trouble themselves about infidelity in their husbands." Boswell remarked, "To be sure there is a great difference between the offence of infidelity in a man and that of his wife." Johnson said, "The difference is boundless. The man imposes no bastards upon his wife."[45]

For most of history, the larger civilizations have shared the conviction that men have both a need and a right to be sure that their children are genetically their own. I began to realize the intensity of this doctrine during an interview with Natalie Zemon Davis, an expert on European history and the author of *The Return of Martin Guerre*.[46] She told me that medieval Europeans genuinely believed that bastards were morally inferior—as passionate and untrustworthy as the bastard Edmund in *King Lear*. They were seen *literally* as bad seed, liable to infect and destroy the line they invaded. Professor Davis believes that the medieval obsession with legitimacy may have had its roots in the intense competition for property, but it clearly became almost wholly irrational. Nothing else can explain the transcendent silliness of medieval beliefs about virginity. Scholarly treatises discussed the clarity of a virgin's urine, in comparison with the cloudy liquid excreted by the experienced female.[47]

The Middle Ages were not unique in this obsession with female sexual purity. The ancient Romans, at least in their earlier years, were partial to the legend of Lucretia, who killed herself after losing her honour. Her husband's cousin Sextus showed up late one night when her husband was away, and asked for a bed. He then entered her room and told her that if she refused his advances, he would kill both her and a slave, throw the naked corpses into her bed and claim he had punished her for harlotry. She submitted. When her husband returned, she summoned him and her own male relatives, told her story, then stabbed herself to death.[48]

She chose her audience properly. Under early Roman law, the wife's male kin were supposed to punish her if her husband returned her with evidence of adultery. Presumably, the practice reflected an earlier matrilineal society, where a woman remained the property of her own clan. In Rome's later years, the harshness eased somewhat. An adulterous couple might merely be exiled to different, desolate islands.[49]

The Mayans took a slightly different approach. Husbands had the right to kill the men who had cuckolded them by dropping large stones on their heads. Interestingly, the husband did not get to kill his wife, whose shame was considered sufficient punishment. Since she would henceforward live as a pariah, this apparent clemency might have been realistic rather than merciful.[50] The ancient Hebrews, however, did stone the adulterous woman as well as her partner, and let the whole community join in the stoning. (Christ obviously considered the penalty excessive.) Stoning is also the punishment dictated for adultery by the Koran, and is still practised in countries that observe Islamic religious law.

As we'll see, this abhorrence of adultery can ripple out, creating a male obsession with female chastity. The obsession with female honour may grow until men are fixated on the purity of their women. A man may consider himself responsible for guarding the behaviour not only of his wife and daughters, but of every female in his family. Thus, when Odysseus finally returns from his long journey, it is his right and duty to execute the maids who have dallied with his wife's suitors. His son, showing a precocity gruesome to modern readers, begs for the opportunity to carry out the killings himself.

This concept of honour is still very strong in the Arab world. Saddam Hussein of Iraq, in a 1987 speech, declared that men had the right to kill with impunity *any* female relative caught or even suspected of "misbehaving," and he promptly passed a law to that effect.[51]

This is not evidence of any unique barbarity on the part of Iraq or its leader. Many Arab cultures would thoroughly approve of such moral orthodoxy. In 1996, in the West Bank, two Bedouin brothers, Ali and Suleiman Mileyhat, confessed to killing their cousin Taghreeb Mileyhat. She had been engaged to Ali, but he had broken it off when rumours started to circulate about her and her sisters. Taghreeb had remained on good terms with Suleiman. He invited her for a walk in the hills, then helped his brother to murder her.[52]

Their own community unconditionally approved of their conduct. Even the girl's mother did not blame the killers, and begged that they be released. The Palestinian police seemed almost equally sympathetic. Colonel Mohammed Salah, director of the Palestinian criminal investigations bureau in Ramallah, explained to the press: "For the Arabs, it was a heroic thing to do." He added, "Unfortunately, the girl was a virgin"—the rumours that led to Taghreeb's death were unfounded. The Palestinian attorney-general acknowledged that there had been twenty-five such murders in the two years before Taghreeb's death.[53]

That implacable enforcement of female purity is by no means exclusive to Islam. Even today, it would seem perfectly normal in parts of Asia, Africa and Europe. It is firmly embedded in the Western tradition. Roman moralists referred admiringly to the austere example set by Verginius in 449 B.C., when he stabbed his fifteen-year-old daughter to death to save her from dishonour.[54]

In spite of all this, there are societies that expect *men* to keep their jealousy in check at least some of the time. Among the Nayar and other polyandrous cultures, for example, men are clearly willing to opt for a kind of corporate sexual ownership—controlling any jealousy of their brothers or other members of their clan or caste. The Inuit, as is well known, have practised wife-swapping (or lending) under certain circumstances, judging that the creation of loyalty between hunters outweighs the need for sexual exclusivity.[55] Among the Zuñi, as we've seen, males have no right to resent female philandering, although a woman may throw out a man if *his* outside affairs become notorious.

The male concern with fidelity also seems to ebb considerably in decadent cultures. Lady Caroline Lamb, the lover of Lord Byron, eventually lost her place in society—but not because of her affair. It was her indiscretion and outrageousness that so infuriated her mother-in-law, Lady Melbourne, who—like Lady Caroline's own mother and aunt—had herself enjoyed a rich extramarital sex life. Nor is this some peculiarity of the English aristocracy. Henry IV of France was equally blasé, at least in legend:

There is a characteristic incident told of a call he made without warning on his mistress, Gabrielle d'Estrées, at her Paris house at 12, rue Gît le Coeur. Gabrielle was not alone when Henry entered the building. Her companion barely had time to scramble under the bed when the King entered. Henry seated himself affably, ordered an enormous meal sent up, and when it came handed a partridge to the quaking Gabrielle, helped himself to another, and then tossed a third under the bed. "Can't let the poor devil starve," he said.[56]

In my own youth, there was a brief wave of approval for this indifference to sharing a partner's affections and body. When I was a university student, the works of Abraham Maslow were very much in vogue. Maslow, a Harvard psychologist, was concerned with self-actualization and transcendent experience, but the theory that caught the spirit of my age involved jealousy. Maslow saw it as a neurotic and unnecessary emotion. The fully self-actualized person would not feel it.

I have to say I knew even then that this was nonsense. It was a theory that ignored the realities of time and human energy: there are only twenty-four hours in a day, so a man with several lovers would have to spread himself pretty thin. Nonetheless, I know men and women who bought Maslow's philosophy, and paid dearly for it. A friend of mine, a psychologist, remembers struggling in therapy with her "jealousy problem" during her years at university in California. She was convinced it was wrong to resent her partner's philandering.[57]

Today, as a therapist, she says she'd tell any patient that such resentment is perfectly natural and justified. The poet W.H. Auden was right: we do crave to be loved alone. Children want it, and compete with their siblings for it. I know a young child who headed up the stairs towards his wailing infant brother, clutching a hammer and muttering the ominous words, "I'm going to fix the baby." A little later, girls in particular want *best* friends, friends who like them more than anyone else.

There is no perfect solution to the dilemma of romantic love. We want it to last forever, and it rarely does. In the past, at least in the West, the answer was to force people to stay together, no matter how unhappy they were. Today, Westerners are free to kiss and part, and they do. In the words of Professor Gunnar Heinsohn, "Essentially, we have replaced one form of misery with another." More harshly, the distinguished British historian Theodore Zeldin writes with contempt, "The consumer society not only allows women to buy new gadgets and clothes all the time, it can also mean enjoying men and discarding them like an unfinished meal . . ."[58]

That sentence makes my hackles rise in an instant feminist reflex. Why shouldn't women be allowed to chop and choose if they wish? And yet, I know I can't trust that response. Like many of us, I remain deeply ambivalent about the issue of fidelity. In my first year of university, I found myself deeply annoyed by Chaucer's poem *Troilus and Criseyde*,[59] a standard tale of love and betrayal. I detested Troilus's self-pity, his sense of having been wronged. It was 1966: I felt that Criseyde had every right to change her mind and move on to another man.

Yet in my personal life, I resented male fickleness. When her boyfriend dumped my best friend, I was filled with sympathetic indignation over her misery. I remember discussing the boyfriend's perfidy with a fellow student, a male West Indian. He was outraged at my anger; he saw it as a sense of entitlement, an arrogant assumption that women (especially white women) somehow *owned* men.

Perhaps one day a better answer will emerge from the current flood of research on love itself. Maybe we'll all learn Bonnie Kreps's trick of loving more coolly, with more self-possession. But not everyone is optimistic. The late Christopher Lasch's posthumous work, *Women and the Common Life*, is devoted to the principle that intense academic and official scrutiny has caused a "drastic shrinkage of our imaginative and emotional horizon,"[60] with no compensating benefits. He saw a modern world in which people behave in the same rotten old ways, while finding new ways to justify their misconduct.

No wonder, then, that so many societies frown on love, especially as a basis for marriage. Love is a most anarchic force in human life.

It threatens all social institutions, because it creates a competing bond. A love-sick woman may forget her obligations to her own people, and most cultures are proprietary about women. (Even today, a Muslim man may marry a Christian or a Jew, but a Muslim woman may marry only another Muslim.) The man who is madly in love may neglect the really important things—the hunt, the herd, the army, his ancestors, his parents.

To complicate our relationships even further, the enamoured couple usually comes to face further claims on their time and affections. For most of history, all over the world, passion has eventually transformed lovers into parents.

Bringing Up Baby

THE COMEDIAN ELLEN DEGENERES used to have a routine that started, "I don't have any kids." She'd pause, then add with a boyish swagger: "That I know of." The sheer absurdity of it always brought down the house. For while men can and do worry about whether their children are really theirs, few women ever have occasion to doubt the maternity of their children. Childbirth is not something you can fail to notice. It's true the popular press carries an astounding number of stories about women who make it to the final stages of pregnancy in total ignorance. Their missing periods, tender breasts, morning sickness and weight gain somehow fail to register.[1] Even for these human ostriches, however, reality eventually intrudes. The first contractions can sometimes masquerade as indigestion, but the birth itself is unmistakable.

The tricky part of motherhood is what comes after labour. For a fish or a turtle, that's not a problem. Once the eggs are out of the body, Mom's role is usually over. She swims away, leaving her young to fend for themselves. Most of them won't make it, of course, but she's hedged her bets. Cold-blooded animals lay lots of eggs—dozens, hundreds, even thousands. Mammals play the numbers game differently, bearing few children but lavishing energy on them. For us, birth is only the beginning. Our very name comes from the way we feed our infants—through our breasts, the mammaries. From agoutis to zebras, all mammals suckle, clean and to varying degrees educate their children.

For cats or pigs, that behaviour is largely instinctive. In general, they bond passionately with their newborn offspring, and lose interest gradually as the litter learns to cope on its own. Once upon a time, we believed that human mothers also functioned largely on instinct. That's no longer true today. Throughout this century, various schools of thought have argued that there is no such thing as a human maternal instinct. According to their theories, maternal behaviour is learned, a cultural product. Moreover, they've sometimes argued that it's an *unnecessary* cultural product. They've maintained that children do not need sustained and exclusive attention from any one adult, including their own mothers. This conflict has influenced the way hundreds of thousands of children have been raised, and it continues today. The question is: Do women *instinctively* want and love their children?

Now, if we think of human beings primarily as animals, the idea that there is no maternal instinct seems insane. If there is one thing that female mammals adore, it's babies. In *The Descent of Women*, writer Elaine Morgan describes a set of psychological experiments using rats. The rats had already learned to press a lever to receive food and, later, sex. (The female rats' appetite for sex was far more voracious than the males'.) Then someone tried a new reward: When a female rat pressed the lever, she got a newborn baby rat. She went on pressing until she was too tired to push, and her cage was knee-deep in infant rodents.[2]

In most places, for much of human history, there's a general assumption that women share that passion for infants. Look at the Bible. Rachel, Jacob's favourite wife, tells him bluntly: "Give me children, or else I die."[3] She is so desperate that she asks him to make use of history's first known surrogate mother: "And she said, Behold my maid Bilhah, go in unto her; and she shall bear upon my knees that I may also have children by her."[4] In a later book, we find the same misery in Hannah, another barren wife. At the Temple Hannah prays for a child with such fervour that the priest Eli assumes she is drunk.[5]

The love of babies is not restricted to societies—like the world of the biblical matriarchs—that place great value on fertility. Whether by nurture or nature, we are programmed to adore infants. Morgan explores this theme in a passage that has stayed with me through the twenty-odd years since I first read it:

> In several species—including the untender baboon—the response to a newborn infant is universal. Not only does the mother's status shoot up; other females cluster around, making submissive gestures, hoping she will allow them to take the infant from her for a while. Even alpha males, though without the submissive gestures, approach her with the same intention. But she retains the right, and the determination, to take it back from anyone if it cries ... I remember in my own childhood in a Welsh valley when a mother took a new baby around to friends and relatives and neighbours to show it off ... There would be an involuntary chorus of "Aw!" at the first sight of the baby's face emerging from the shawl. Someone would always say "Can I hold him for a bit?" The mother would graciously grant the boon, but would take him back if he cried.[6]

This is a familiar scene. I've seen the same begging rivalry to hold a new baby at family parties and on ferries in Africa and at television studios. All over the world, it would seem, women melt over a newborn. Shown pictures of babies in pupil-dilation experiments, they involuntarily send out the equivalent of a wolf-whistle.[7] Their eyes dilate and their temperature rises in an excitement as strong as anything pornography can generate. Advertisers know that; it's no accident that commercials use babies to pitch everything from tires to cameras. Nothing else is so successful at riveting a viewer's attention.[8]

Our fascination with infancy is so intense that it extends to other baby animals. Many of us feel a surge of protective affection for kittens or puppies, or even those mature animals, like pandas and koala bears, that look like babies. Apparently we're not alone in this. In 1996, a female gorilla in a St. Louis zoo tenderly rescued a child who had fallen into her compound. Even our ideal of female beauty mimics the appearance of infants: big, well-spaced eyes; broad forehead; clear skin.

We've learned only recently that this fascination with infants might actually be encoded in our chromosomes. There really *is* a motherhood gene in at least one species. In 1996, Dr. Michael E. Greenberg announced the discovery of a gene, fosB, that controlled nurturing behaviour in female mice.[9] In the journal *Cell*, Dr. Greenberg wrote, "Ordinarily, a female mouse put in a cage with her babies will crouch over them and keep them warm within a minute." In contrast, he noted, "When this gene is missing, mice show no interest in their babies. Instead, they curl up in a corner and let the young ones die." The gene is also present, although less pronounced, in male mice. Humans have it, too, although its role in our behaviour has not been established. Dr. Greenberg's research is suggestive. It might help to explain the extraordinary range of maternal feelings we find in people. Maybe the indifferent or murderous mother simply lacks the gene that bonds most mothers to their children.

It would certainly make sense for us to be genetically coded to love babies, because they need us so badly. They're born in a state of extreme immaturity. For the first few months, someone has to take care of all their needs, because they're shaped all wrong for self-sufficiency. They take longer than any other primate to grow up. Anyone who's ever raised a child knows it's a tremendous amount of work. Babies have to be kept fed, warm, dry and often amused. They're subject to sudden terrifying illnesses and endless colicky screaming. They are absolutely unable to comprehend the priorities of the adult world. Unlike colts or piglets or a tiny clinging monkey, they have to be carried for several frustrating months.

So all over the world, new mothers work in a haze of sleep deprivation, punctuated by the baby's piercing wail. It would make sense for mothers to find powerful emotional compensations to temper the frustration and fatigue. To put it simply, it helps a lot if you love your kid. And many women do. You might not realize that from reading current scholarly works on the history of maternity, which tend to see strong maternal love as a very recent historical development. But most mothers do feel a passionate attachment to their children, at least part of the time. Most people—not just mothers—also *enjoy* infants. Babies provide a lot of pleasure.

V.S. Naipaul, in his novel *A House for Mr. Biswas*, describes a scene shortly after his hero's birth that perfectly captures the delight and almost awe that many cultures feel for infants. Naipaul describes a twice-daily ritual of massage and exercise for the new child. Adults touch the baby's toes to his shoulder and his nose. The ritual is half treatment and half game. It ends with a clap and a laugh, stimulating the baby's emotions as well as his body.[10]

That playful, physical pleasure is a biological necessity. You can't just shove food into babies and hope for the best. They have to be touched. Human children, like all primates, need at least a semblance of love to ensure physical and mental health. Scientists have experimented raising infant monkeys without any contact with their own kind, or any affection or handling from humans. They grow up deeply disturbed and apparently incapable of sex. This is not a recipe for genetic survival. In fact, we now have evidence that a caring mother produces calmer, more adventurous offspring, at least among rats. A Quebec team discovered in 1996 that rats whose mothers nursed, groomed and licked them had lower levels of stress hormone, even after an anxiety-producing experiment.[11]

We know that emotional neglect can have drastic effects on human children. In 1996, British researchers finally ascertained why neglected children sometimes stop growing, even though they continue to eat adequately. A study of twenty-nine unusually short children revealed low levels of growth hormone, even after some kids binged on food. The levels shot up quickly when the children were hospitalized, away from their abusive families.[12]

Stunted growth is by no means the worst thing that can happen to neglected children. Without at least some warmth and tenderness, they can die. They did so and continue to do so in orphanages that cannot or will not provide them with some attention and affection. I have a friend who was adopted at the age of fourteen months, in his case just in time. He is black, and the orphanage staff apparently resented him on that basis. They were horrified that his adoptive family preferred him to a white child. He has been told that it took several months before he resumed eating normally, and started to gain some badly needed weight.

He was lucky. In 1994, a boy named John Ryan Turner died at his home in Miramichi, New Brunswick. He was three years and eight months old, and he weighed just twenty-one pounds, the normal weight for an eleven-month-old baby. Mere hours after his funeral, his parents were charged with manslaughter for failing to provide the necessities of life to him. A neighbour testified that John's body shook as he struggled futilely to drag himself up the back steps of his home. In response, his mother, Lorelei Turner, reportedly yelled, "If you can't get up the steps, you'll stay out!"[13]

The defence argued that John's parents were innocent, because his starvation was self-inflicted. Both denied that they'd deprived him of food, and I believe them. I think that he starved himself to death. Expert witnesses agreed, but in ways that didn't help the Turners' case. A pediatric neurologist told the court that emotional,

rather than physical abuse caused John's death. The doctor explained
John's self-starvation as a subconscious choice: "If his world was
impossible to live with or live in, then nature took over and said,
'We cannot survive; we'll stop eating and waste away.' "[14]

It should be noted that the boy initially enjoyed a good relationship with his father, although his mother apparently rejected him at
birth. The father, Steven Turner, told the court he deliberately withdrew from his son in the hope that the mother would finally bond
with the boy. (Both parents were reported to dote on John's younger
sister, Amanda.) It was his mother who truly seemed to hate John.
Other witnesses testified that John spent his final days bound to his
bed in a dark bedroom, gagged with a sock. His body was covered
with self-inflicted bruises, cuts and bites. In the end, the Turners
were found guilty, not because they had starved the boy, but because
they neglected to get medical help for him as he wasted away before
their eyes.[15]

Not all unloved children die. Barbra Streisand claims that her stepfather hated her so much that he wouldn't buy an ice-cream cone
for her when he was treating the rest of the family—he said she
was too ugly.[16] That rejection seemed only to add fuel to her desperate need for success, which she achieved. Similarly, Tina Turner
went to live with her grandparents when she was three years old,
because her parents abandoned her. The grandparents didn't want
her either. She has said: "I wasn't cuddled as a child. I wasn't
caressed. I was just unwanted. . . ."[17] Obviously she survived, and
did very well. But her personal life, especially her long submission
to an abusive husband, suggests real damage. Adults who survive
an unloved childhood may remain stunted in more than one sense.

I know people who have weathered precisely this kind of emotional neglect. In the 1980s, friends of mine in Africa adopted a
Zimbabwean child who had been abandoned at birth. She spent
the first few months of her life in an orphanage. When I first
encountered her in 1986, she was two years old. She seemed almost

catatonic. After four years of life in a loving, attentive family, she had become another child, lively, intelligent and affectionate. She was particularly captivated by the photographs I had taken of her younger self.

I wonder, however, what her life will be as an adult. I referred earlier to the friend who had started to starve himself just before he was adopted. Today he looks like a success story. He is a brilliant scholar and teacher, an adventurous traveller, a delightful companion. But he actively dislikes being touched. His discomfort with physical intimacy is so acute that he can barely stand to let someone else light his cigarettes.

It's important not to exaggerate the dangers of emotional neglect or harshness, because most women already feel so insecure about the way they raise their children. We know only that children need some attention and love; we have no idea how much. The psychologist Jerome Kagan wrote in *The Nature of the Child* that our own society is uniquely obsessed with the quality of parental love: "The psychological power ascribed to parental love, or its absence, has a parallel to the potency attributed in other societies at other times to spirits, loss of soul, sorcery, sin, gossip, God, and witchcraft.... A mother's love for the child is treated as a mysterious force which, if sprinkled plentifully over young children, guarantees salvation."[18]

Kagan is making a solid point. We posit a kind of mystical force in the quality of a mother's love—and we're not alone in doing it. This irrational belief has caused a great deal of damage; women are blamed for every mishap, every illness, every failure. For decades, Freudian psychiatrists assured the mothers of autistic children that they were at fault; the inadequacy of their love had damaged their children. All societies that I know have a tendency to confuse cause and effect when it comes to mothers. In *The Naked Ape*, Desmond Morris wrote of constantly crying babies: "A comparison of the parental behaviour of mothers with cry-babies and those with quieter infants gives the answer. The former are tentative, nervous and anxious in their dealings with their offspring. The latter are deliberate, calm and serene."[19] It apparently never occurred to him that a couple of months of a constantly screaming baby might make anyone—even a British expert on animal behaviour—"tentative, nervous and anxious."

Mothers are not good at dismissing these unending accusations of inadequacy. Because we can think, we are vulnerable to guilt about the way we raise our children. But the fact that children need love does not mean that they will wither and perish from the occasional harsh word. You don't have to walk on egg shells for the first five or ten or eighteen years of a child's life. We know that cats feel an instinctive love for their kittens, but an irritated feline mother doesn't hesitate to discipline her offspring with a smart cuff or a sharp shake by the scruff of the neck.

These bursts of irritation are perhaps even more inevitable for us than for other mammals. It takes so much work to raise a human being. If our children are going to survive, they have a huge amount to learn. Admittedly, we're not the only mammals in the education business. A chimpanzee teaches her young a wide variety of skills, including the use of tools. We have pictures from the Gombe reserve of a chimp showing her young how to "fish" for termites with a straw.

But human lessons go well beyond Elementary Fruit Gathering or Nest Building 101. In any society, children have to acquire a huge body of knowledge. To begin with, there's speech—not a small assortment of multi-purpose grunts and hoots, but a working vocabulary to cover all occasions. Then, even in the most primitive cultures, kids need to know what's safe to eat and where to find it and how to prepare it. It takes ages to teach children all the skills and information they need to survive, whether they grow up in Manhattan or the Kalahari. Anywhere in the world, they also must learn how to negotiate the intricate social patterns of their own group. And for the first years of life, it is almost always the mother who does the teaching.

In genetic terms, it would make sense for humans to feel a deep and durable bond between mother and child, preferably an even stronger one than other primates. And there is considerable evidence that we do. Women truly do lay down their lives for their children.

In the summer of 1996, a mother in British Columbia died saving her six-year-old son from a cougar. Cindy Parolin, the thirty-four-year-old mother, had just started a horseback camping trip when the cougar frightened her son Steven's horse and he fell. Parolin leapt from her horse and went after the cougar with a stick. It turned on her, allowing two of her other children to carry Steven away and get help. It came too late for her.[20]

You don't have to die for your children to feel deeply about them. Most women do willingly put their children's needs and often desires before their own. And they receive compensating pleasures, because they also enjoy their children. In her novel *Don't Tell Alfred,* Nancy Mitford (childless, but a devoted aunt) puts these words into the mind of her heroine, Fanny: "I am always pleased when my children turn up. The sight of them rejoices me, I rush forward, I smile and I embrace."[21] Most of the women I know feel the same way— as long as their children aren't in the rocky years of adolescence.

For all that, the vision of maternal love is clouded in our Western culture, in part because our vision of motherhood is deeply ambivalent. We are leery of maternal love, because we don't want it to remain too strong. In North America and most of Western Europe, the idea is that your children—especially your male children—are supposed to outgrow you. If they still need you after adolescence, you have failed. This does not make things easy for mothers. They are supposed to fulfil their children's every need in the early years, and then to fade quietly into the background. No wonder Fanny, that doting mother, is uncomfortable with her role in her sons' adult lives: "In moments of introspection I often thought that a woman's need for children is almost entirely physical. When they are babies one cuddles and kisses and slaps them and has a highly satisfying animal relationship with them. But when they grow up and leave the nest, they hardly seem to belong any more. Was I much use to the boys now?"[22]

Fanny turns out to be rather more use to her sons than she anticipates, and all of them ultimately admit to a restrained, quintessentially British fondness for her. Other cultures are less reticent. In many societies, people remain passionately and enthusiastically attached to their mothers long after they've grown up.

I saw that when I taught in Sierra Leone. As a novice lecturer, I got stuck with a remedial English class for science students, all male. Early in the term, inspired by my own curiosity, I asked them to write an essay on their families. To a man, they adored their mothers. (To a man, they also detested their fathers, but that's a story for a later chapter.)

Their mothers clearly provided their most intimate relationship; they were far more detached about their girlfriends. They were not embarrassed about enjoying their mothers' company and attention. Several noted that their mothers had paid for all their schooling, and they were grateful for it. Most of the people I know today would cringe at Freud's belief that the relationship between mother and son was the deepest and most satisfying of all loves. My students had no trouble with it at all.

This bond is not unique to Africa. In at least one European country, the strength of the bond between mother and child has become a social problem. Italy suffers from a generation of what it calls *mammoni*—mamma's boys.[23] A newspaper article in 1996 told the story of Giovanni Istroni, a sound technician who was still living with his mother and two brothers at the age of thirty-eight. The brothers were forty and thirty-five. Istroni told an interviewer he didn't understand why the women he dated wanted to live with him in a new household: "It's not like my mother. She needs me. She doesn't ask for any guarantees. It's a more freely given love." More than 50 per cent of twenty-nine-year-old Italian men still live at home with their parents.

In 1996, a court in Ferrara ruled that a twenty-four-year-old man had the *right* to live with his mother, even though he was earning a living (as a gas station attendant) and his disenchanted mother swore *she* would leave home if he didn't. "There is something profoundly sick in a society of eternal *bambini* [children] who love only their mothers," a commentator wrote in *La Repubblica*. Perhaps understandably, Italy's marriage and birth rates are among the lowest in Europe.[24]

Given all this, you might ask how anyone could question the existence of a maternal instinct. There is, however, plenty of evidence against it. There are all sorts of possible proofs that many women do not want children, and do not care for the ones they have.

The birth rates of all developed countries provide a stunning indication that women are very different from the rats in the experiment Elaine Morgan cites. We do not have an infinite hunger for babies. Women in affluent societies tend to produce fewer than two children apiece—not enough to replenish their own populations.[25] Given access to contraception and a decent standard of living, most women don't seem to want very many children, while some of us don't want any at all. It's a trend some political leaders find most unsettling. The government of Singapore initiated its own dating service for university graduates, hoping to nudge its educated élite into reproducing. The premier of Quebec, Lucien Bouchard, ran into some trouble in 1995 when he remarked: "We're one of the white races that has fewest children. . . . That suggests we haven't solved our family problems."[26]

Quebec's low birth rate is by no means a unique phenomenon. Jérôme Carcopino, writing at the start of the Second World War, censured the decadence of upper-class women two millennia earlier in his book, *Daily Life in Ancient Rome:* "Some evaded the duties of maternity for fear of losing their good looks; some took a pride in being behind their husbands in no sphere of activity . . . ; some were not content to live their lives by their husbands' side, but carried on another life without him at the price of betrayals and surrenders for which they did not even trouble to blush. Whether because of voluntary birth control, or because of the impoverishment of the stock, many Roman marriages at the end of the first and the beginning of the second century were childless."[27]

Today in Japan, the government is projecting that the population will fall by more than half over the next century. In 1996 in the farming village of Kyokushi, the municipal government began to offer more than $6,000 to women who had four or more children. It also dangles other incentives to fertility. They're not working.[28] (There has been no attempt to implement a suggestion by the country's current prime minister, Ryutaro Hashimoto. As finance minister in 1990, he told cabinet that in order to raise the birth rate the government should discourage women from going to college.[29]) As we'll see in later chapters, many societies (especially, but not exclusively, militaristic ones) have tried to entice or coerce their women to bear more children.

Our current minuscule fertility rates are not entirely a question of choice. Scientists estimate that about 15 per cent of the female population is infertile. Sexual diseases, environmental pollution and the Western tendency to delay child-bearing all play a role here. There is clear evidence that many involuntarily childless women desperately want babies. Otherwise, there would be no fertility clinics—with their expensive, demanding and very chancy medical procedures. Nor would Western couples be raiding the orphanages of Central and South America, China and parts of the former Soviet bloc.

Nonetheless, except for certain orthodox religious groups, even the most fertile women in our world rarely give their reproductive abilities free play. A family of the size of, say, Ethel and Robert Kennedy's is a rarity in the West today.

We know that women often tried to limit their families in the past. The success rate must have been quite low in some cultures. The ancient Egyptians, for instance, put their faith in plugs made of crocodile dung, or tampons of ground acacia leaves, dates and honey on cotton.[30] The Romans knew a variety of methods: some possible, some dubious and some potentially lethal. Women in the Greek city state of Cyrene between 400 and 600 B.C. relied on silphium, a plant so successful in preventing pregnancy that it became a major export. Unfortunately, they harvested it to extinction.[31]

Today in the developed world, with several reasonably safe and highly successful methods available, contraception is obviously a major factor in reducing birth rates. But it's not the only one. It is impossible to ignore the contemporary tendency to use abortion as a form of birth control. We terminate pregnancies at a staggering rate. In 1993, 1.3 million abortions were performed in the United States.[32] In Canada, the rate now stands at 26.9 abortions for every 100 live births.[33] Data culled from a Statistics Canada study found that about one in three Canadian women had had an abortion.[34]

Nor is this a purely North American phenomenon. Women in the poorest countries continue to bear child after child, but social chaos or even dramatic change seems to inhibit the desire for children. In the turmoil of post-Communist Russia, abortions outnumber births two to one.[35] In 1995, a private U.S. study predicted that those rates would lead to a "population catastrophe" in the former Soviet Union. The study's author, Carl Haub, found that the decision to abort was based largely on economic fears. He said, "People ask themselves: 'Can I afford to bring another child into the world?' The answer is definitely no." He added that when Russian women were asked what they would do if they were pregnant, only about one in seven said she would carry the baby to term.[36]

The popularity of abortion today is unprecedented in human

history, for reasons that will emerge in later chapters. But women in other places and times often attempted to end an unwanted pregnancy. Unfortunately, their methods were neither reliable nor safe. Ancient Roman women used herbs and douches, even though the risks were terrible. We know that didn't dissuade them, because the government eventually made abortion a crime.[37] In Britain, right into this century, working-class women could try the legendary hot bath and bottle of gin. Upper-class women could go horseback riding, hoping to jolt the fetus loose. Lacking horses, the reluctant mother could always try a knitting needle—quite possibly perforating the uterus and dying of infection as a result.

Abortion is not universally safe today. A peasant in contemporary Rajasthan can book a legal abortion in a clinic, at a cost of between ten and thirty dollars. But a study by the Indian Council of Medical Research found that one woman in three still prefers to hire a midwife, magician or witch.[38] Herbs, magic and massage seem safer to them than surgery. The official government estimate for illegal abortions is six hundred thousand a year, but other studies place the rate in the millions. The toll is terrible; an estimated twenty thousand women a year die from illegal abortions, and hundreds of thousands more are disabled from hemorrhaging and infections. Dr. S.G. Kabra, a physician in Jaipur, says, "Septic abortions are killing more women than pregnancy itself." But the government clinics are too expensive for many women, nor is their own reputation good. The death rate from legal abortions in the Indian state of Rajasthan is forty in every one hundred thousand—four times the U.S. rate.[39]

There are societies where abortion is not possible, either because it is not available or because the legal risks are too great. The unwilling mother still has options. Anywhere in the Western world, she can put up the child for adoption. She pays a price, of course; there is still a significant social stigma attached to giving away a child in our world. We don't even approve of women who voluntarily give their husbands custody after a divorce.[40] (Obviously that attitude is not universal; there's no evidence that the Wodaabe condemn the woman who leaves her children in order to take a new husband.)

A related and more acceptable option is to hand your children over to other relatives. It's an arrangement that predates organized social services. In the past, a woman without the desire or ability to raise her own children could ship them off to relatives. (In the higher reaches of the social scale, kindly and fertile relatives occasionally bestowed one of their children on barren kin.) In many cultures today, it's still a common practice. In the so-called Caribbean model of the family, a mother (usually unmarried) frequently leaves her children with her mother while she goes elsewhere to earn a living. In Europe and North America, any number of middle-class families are dependent on a Caribbean or Filipina nanny whose own children live with a grandmother or aunt.

Women also can and do simply abandon babies, often in the full knowledge that the child will die. In 1996, Los Angeles County failed to solve the deaths of ten infants found in dumpsters, trash cans or at the sides of roads. Social workers estimate that there is at least one undiscovered abandoned baby for each one found. *The Los Angeles Times* called it "the perfect crime."[41]

It isn't always. In early 1997, police in Camrose, Alberta, charged a young woman with infanticide, interfering with human remains and improperly disposing of a human body. The mother, Melanie Murphy, was an unmarried twenty-year-old student at a Christian college. A custodian found the corpse in a garbage bag while he was cleaning the hallway of the first-year students' dormitory.[42] A more notorious case caught America's attention the year before. In Newark, Delaware, a teenaged couple named Amy Grossberg and Brian Peterson—high-school sweethearts and both honours students at college—were arrested and charged with first-degree murder after a motel employee found a dead, newborn infant in a trash bin.[43]

These children are often dead before their bodies are dumped—

smothered, strangled or shaken to death. But not all absconding parents are murderers. Newspapers regularly carry stories of living infants found by the garbage man, the motel clerk, the passing pedestrian.

In our society, abandoning a child is a serious crime. We arrest people even for leaving their children home alone unattended for any length of time. But abandonment is not an uncommon strategy if you look at the whole of human history. It has always proved tempting for unmarried women in puritanical cultures. It has sometimes been the only option for people who could not hope to feed another child. Even before the first Foundling Hospitals were established in the seventeenth century, a hard-pressed European mother might leave her newborn on the steps of a monastery or convent.[44] In Rome, Greece and other ancient societies, there were recognized drop-off points, where the child would either find rescuers or die.

Our own era has seen waves of mothers voluntarily giving up their children. In the last days of its Communist regime, Romania banned contraceptives and abortions, in an effort to boost its population. The result was orphanages crammed with unwanted children.[45]

The mass abandoning of babies throughout the former Soviet bloc has proved a blessing to childless couples—and singles— in the West. I personally know three families that have acquired children from former Communist countries. In one case, Russian authorities shipped a baby boy, sight unseen, to a single mother in Canada. He cost her $10,000.

There are societies where none of these options are available to the unwilling mother. There is a final choice: You can kill the child outright. Not all cultures find that a horrifying idea. Remember that child sacrifice has been a religious duty in untold numbers of civilizations, including parts of the ancient Middle East, southern Asia, South and Central America. Elsewhere, children were often seen as expendable. Even affluent Roman families might keep and raise only the firstborn female child, exposing any later ones to die. Female infanticide remains a problem in some areas of the world, including China.

To be fair, men have generally controlled infanticide. We do not know how the mothers felt or feel about losing their newborn children. The Roman matron or ancient Mayan mother may have been sick with grief. But infanticide is not an exclusively male prerogative. Women kill their children, too.

They sometimes do it in moments of madness. Take the notorious case of Elisa Izquierdo, murdered in New York at the age of six by her cocaine-addicted mother, Awilda Lopez. At the time of her death, Elisa had cuts and bruises on virtually every inch of her body. She had been sexually violated with a toothbrush and a hairbrush. Awilda finally killed her daughter by throwing the child against a concrete wall.[46] Her mind unhinged by drugs, she thought Elisa had been placed under a spell.

It would feel wonderful to write that this was an isolated incident. Sadly, it is not. My own local papers carry similar stories. In 1993, a crack addict named Patricia Johnson killed her daughter Shanay, whom she had whipped with belts and coat hangers, punched and kicked—knocking out three teeth—and scalded in a bathtub. Like Elisa, Shanay had been returned to her mother by the authorities, *after* an investigation of reported abuse.[47]

These mothers, and hundreds like them, may not be entirely responsible for their actions. But there are cases of infanticide that are not sparked by madness or drug abuse. There are women who kill their children deliberately, for practical reasons. In February 1996, for instance, in Dayton, Ohio, Terressa Jolynn Ritchie was convicted of killing her four-year-old daughter after the child caught her having sex with a neighbour.[48] Her lover testified at the trial that Ritchie attacked Samantha with the cast on her broken wrist and a wrench after the child caught them in the act. In September of that year, a mother in Ceres, California, was charged with failing to feed her severely disabled five-year-old twin daughters. Brittany and

Breanne Kinn had cerebral palsy and muscular dystrophy. When police removed them from their home, the hospital found the girls weighed twelve and sixteen pounds, about right for a three-month-old baby. The mother, Tonya Kaye Walker, told police she could no longer afford the supplemental baby formula the twins needed— so she let them starve.[49] Finally, there is the notorious example of Susan Smith, who drove her car into a river and let her children drown rather than lose her lover.

But that kind of calculating infanticide hasn't always been a rarity, at least for infants. I've already mentioned the prevalence of child abandonment in human history, generally in the full knowledge that the child will die.

There are subtler methods of disposing of an unwanted infant. Until the modern period in Western history, for instance, "overlaying" was a common cause of death. Women supposedly rolled over their children as they slept, smothering them.[50] Judges and juries usually ruled that the deaths were accidents and the mothers, while careless, were innocent of murder.

Some of them probably were. A number of deaths attributed to overlaying must have been cases of Sudden Infant Death Syndrome. Others among the mothers charged may have been drunk enough to accidentally crush a baby. But human beings aren't totally unconscious during sleep. Adults usually manage to control their bladders and bowels. It's impossible to avoid the conclusion that separate beds aren't the only reason that overlaying has disappeared from the courts. Many, if not most cases were unquestionably deliberate murder.[51] As proof, overlaying faded from the eighteenth century on, with the rise of Foundling Hospitals where unwilling mothers could safely abandon their offspring.

How can women do such things to their children? Shari Thurer, in her invaluable book *The Myths of Motherhood*, tried to find a comfortable answer by arguing that abuse is most prevalent in misogynistic societies.[52] (She acknowledges that there are other factors, from life-threatening danger to mental impairment, but she gives misogyny top billing.) It's a tidy solution, but I think an incomplete one. All kinds of stresses seem to trigger women's rage against their children: starvation, social upheaval, marital neglect, drugs and alcohol. I can't quite swallow the idea that a Detroit crack addict sold her fifteen-year-old son to her drug dealers because she lived in a misogynistic society.[53] I believe that misogyny is just one factor. Perhaps, like sheep, we turn on our children when we feel stressed and trapped.

Whatever the reasons, the ugly truth is that not all women love their children. I learned as an adult that one of my great-aunts was appalled that my mother chose to breast-feed. Raising her own two children in the 1930s, she turned to bottle-feeding with profound relief. Babies, she once told my mother, reminded her of peeled rats. She could barely stand to touch them.

It is a short leap from the truth that some women don't want children to the theory that *no* woman really wants children. In this century, several schools of thought have concluded precisely that; society alone creates the cult of self-sacrificing motherhood. They proceed from the premise that intense maternal love is a product of our minds, not our instincts.

The early Bolsheviks, to take a major example, argued against individual maternal love, planning a state in which all children would be raised in collective nurseries.[54] That way they could get rid of the "bourgeois" notion of the family, and free women to work in the factories and fields. Inspired by this liberating vision, parents in the original *kibbutzim* of Israel spent one hour a day with their children, who then returned to their group homes.

The Bolshevik experiment soured quickly. Soviet leaders were soon extolling maternity as somehow uniquely Russian.[55] In today's *kibbutzim*, children live with their parents. Some of the 1960s feminists shared the revolutionary distaste for the nuclear family and biological ties. I can remember radical speakers urging a collective approach to child-rearing, if not a straightforward rejection of the very act of reproduction. The most extreme position was held by Valerie Solanas, the woman who shot Andy Warhol. She saw maternity as a male conspiracy, and happily pictured a future, all-female world populated by test-tube babies.[56]

Solanas had no lasting influence on feminist thought, perhaps because she was barking mad. But her beliefs are not that far from the vision of Shulamith Firestone, a theoretician whose influence has been enormous. In *The Dialectic of Sex,* Firestone called for "the freeing of women from the tyranny of reproduction by every means possible."[57] She envisioned a society in which the blood tie to the mother would eventually be severed. To help things along, Firestone wanted scientists to hurry up and develop an easier way of producing children, "so that pregnancy, now freely acknowledged as clumsy, inefficient and painful, would be indulged in, if at all, only as a tongue-in cheek archaism, just as women today wear virginal white to their weddings."[58]

Not everyone was willing to go that far; others were more realistic about the limitations of science. But many feminists argued that there was no need for women to raise the children they bore. In *The Female Eunuch,* Germaine Greer wrote that if she had a child, she would hand it over to be raised by Italian peasants.[59] (She and her friends would visit often from England, of course, for a kind of working holiday.) Nor was Greer alone in advocating twenty-four-hour day-care centres, where a mother could happily dump her child at any time. But Greer recanted in her later book *Sex and Destiny,* and expressed bitter regret that she was childless. Today, the feminist movement tends to embrace the idea of women as mothers (only by choice, of course), and to link the interests of women and children as one.

It is our society's intellectuals who lead the assault on maternal instinct today. Scholars like Philippe Ariès and his disciples have attempted to prove that medieval Europeans were essentially indifferent to their offspring. In his work *Centuries of Childhood*, Ariès examined medieval art and documents, and discovered an inattention to childhood, especially infancy, that he interpreted in part as a lack of feeling. He concluded that high infant mortality rates and other, more abstract factors limited parents' love and individual interest in their offspring, especially in the children's dangerous early years.[60]

The anti-maternal-love school has a considerable body of evidence to draw on. If earlier Europeans loved their children, why did the richer ones ship their babies off to wet nurses in the country almost the instant they snipped the umbilical cord?[61] If mothers cared about their babies, why did they leave them to squirm, swaddled, in their own filth, often for an entire day?[62] Why did they shake and rock them so forcefully as to stun the poor infant into a stupefied silence?[63]

Some of the historians who ask these questions have concluded that strong maternal feelings are a recent innovation, impossible in earlier ages when relatively few babies survived to adulthood. They see profound parental affection and concern as a cultural product. They assume that women were fairly casual about their kids until society imposed an exacting and artificial idea of devoted maternity

Now, the arguments of the Bolshevik and feminist schools are easy to refute; they have failed to survive the passage of time. The Russians discovered that the family bond is not so easy to break, and that institutions (at least the ones they developed) do not do a terrific job of turning out well-adjusted and healthy children. The early feminist zealots discovered that a lot of women don't want to be liberated from having and raising children. Ariès and his crew, on the other hand, will never face the test of time. They are writing about the past, and about precisely that personal, intimate layer of history that can never be fully accessible. Still, I find some of their arguments less than convincing.

There is, first of all, the question of interpretation. I was particularly struck by an anomaly in *Centuries of Childhood* that at least one other writer has noticed. It's a quotation from Mme de Sévigné, describing the reaction of a fellow aristocrat to the death of her little daughter. Ariès uses it as evidence of pre-modern maternal indifference. Mme de Sévigné wrote: "She is greatly distressed and says she will never again have one so pretty."[64] But the mother, Mme de Coetquen, only made this decidedly ambiguous remark after she regained consciousness. Her first response to the news of her loss was to pass out. As Ferdinand Mount asks in *The Subversive Family,* if she was so indifferent, why did she faint?[65]

Ariès also relies heavily on iconography. He reasons, for instance, that if medieval artists generally portrayed children as miniature adults, then their society had little sense of childhood as a separate state. It's an interesting theory, but not entirely persuasive. To begin with, it ignores the role of convention in art; it assumes some degree of realism in all forms, plus substantial creative competence. Its reasoning sometimes strikes me as tortured. Ariès makes much, for instance, of the fact that adults and children wore clothes of the same fashion and cut, suggesting to him once again that the medieval mind was impervious to the differences between the two states. But medieval robes and tunics, unlike three-piece suits or a Merry Widow corset, were pretty comfortable garments. Like today's jeans and running clothes, they were sensible and practical garments for children and adults.

Then there is the issue of gender. Ariès acknowledges that most of the artists whose work he examined were male. Meanwhile, the women were raising the children.[66] The sculptor's wife or the monk's mother may have had a far more accurate sense of the nature of infancy and childhood.

The deepest weakness of the intellectual attacks on maternity seems to me to lie in the question of intent. It's true that pre-modern

Europeans often did a rotten job of raising their kids. They never seemed to learn from experience. So vast numbers of children continued to die at the supposedly healthy homes of rural wet nurses. Toddlers left on their own all day were killed by accidents, by fires, by wild or domestic animals.

But that doesn't mean their parents didn't care about them. In many cases, the adults simply had no choice. Which is the greater risk: leaving a baby by the fireside or taking it along as you work in the cold and, quite likely, rain? How do you child-proof a hovel? Many peasant practices were dictated by economic necessity. Others were the product of tradition. Swaddling may have been a bad idea, but it didn't express hostility. On the contrary, the medieval mother or nurse swaddled a baby with the best of intentions. Very young babies often find swaddling reassuring; it re-creates some of the security of the womb. As the weeks went on, the child would of course start to struggle against it, but the surrounding adults had good reason to ignore his unhappiness. They were firmly convinced that early swaddling would foster strong, straight limbs.

In fact, stupidity explains a great deal of behaviour that might suggest indifference or hostility to children. One of the most dispiriting features of the history of the family is the idiocy of many child-rearing practices around the globe. People cling ferociously to lethal traditions, or seize with instant enthusiasm on some equally destructive innovation.

Consider one of the Ariès school's pet pieces of evidence: the medieval European peasants' reliance on dangerously violent rocking and shaking to soothe their babies into slumber.[67] The parents never seemed to notice that these practices didn't work terribly well, or that the occasional baby was killed or maimed for life by severe jolting. Ariès and his followers take this as proof of negligent, apathetic parenting. But maybe the parents meant well. Maybe, given that they were undernourished, uneducated and overworked, they simply weren't very bright.

I have certainly seen a similar imperviousness to experience in other mothers. To take just one example from my personal knowledge, Sierra Leone has one of the highest infant mortality rates in the world. Moreover, the rate for male babies is much greater than for females. Poor hygiene, malaria and bad water all play a role. But they're not the chief culprit. A rural doctor explained to me, in intense frustration, that the primary cause of this exceptional death is food.

To be specific, it is highly spiced food chewed by the mother and forced into the infant's digestive tract. Many women believe that they should start their babies on solid food very early. They feed their infants precisely what they eat themselves: oily, spicy stews. Babies, being much more sensitive than adults, at first reject these chili-laced concoctions. So the mother holds the child's nose shut and shoves the food into its mouth. The child generally chokes, sending fragments of meat and hot pepper into the lungs. He or she dies from a respiratory infection. The gender ratio is out of whack because mothers value their sons more than their daughters. They literally kill their sons with kindness.

Stupid child-rearing practices, however, aren't the exclusive preserve of Third World peasants. Nor does the error always lie in clinging to a destructive tradition. New ideas can be every bit as wrong-headed. The educated middle class of the United States provided a wonderful example of the flight from common sense during the 1930s. Swayed by the behaviourist theories of Dr. John Watson, thousands of American mothers raised their babies on rigid schedules, with the absolute minimum amount of touching.[68]

They genuinely believed that responding to a baby's crying would somehow "spoil" the child. Their children were kept warm, fed and clean—and that was that. Unless a diaper needed changing, you picked up the kid only to feed him, usually at four-hour intervals.

There is a portrait of this form of child-rearing in Mary McCarthy's *The Group*, a picture obviously drawn from personal encounters.[69] The poor, harried mother spends wretched hours listening to the baby wail. The kid is savagely hungry because the mother's breasts don't provide enough milk. Her doctor husband insists that she try to breast-feed to give his son the benefit of her antibodies. Even after that crisis ends (they switch the boy to a bottle), the child is raised as if he were a machine. The parents make no concessions to his fears, desires or helplessness.

By the time the boy has hit the usually terrible twos, he's become a well-behaved, if rather listless child, who takes his revenge by resisting toilet-training. He causes his mother agonies of embarrassment by suffering the occasional "accident." We don't know how he'll turn out later in life. But I don't think anything good can come from raising a baby without fondling or games or personal attention. It seems to me a recipe for creating an adult filled with hunger and rage.

Modern child-rearing "breakthroughs" can also be physically damaging and dangerous, just like the violent rocking of the Middle Ages. In the 1970s and 1980s, many North American parents happily put their infants into "walkers," secure in the knowledge that the child would be both entertained and motivated to use his own limbs. Then we discovered that it was bad for kids to rest their weight on still-undeveloped legs. By that time, of course, a number of children had already plunged down staircases.

The triumph of ideology over common sense is by no means restricted to the West. In Maxine Hong Kingston's *The Woman Warrior*, Kingston's mother brings her sister over from Hong Kong late in life. The sister has been abandoned by her husband, now a successful—and bigamous—doctor in California. Kingston's mother, a hardline traditionalist, instructs her sister to march into the husband's house and claim her rightful place. The children of her husband's second marriage will of course recognize his first wife as their true mother: "The children will go to their true mother—you. . . . That's the way it is with mothers and children."[70] The mother's world view is so thoroughly Confucian that she apparently expects a genetic recognition and acceptance of hierarchy.

At the opposite extreme, I have seen children spoiled rotten by parents fixated on a different, Western philosophy. In the 1950s, I knew a boy whose life struck me as idyllic. His parents, great fans of psychiatric theory, were determined to spare him all possible frustration, in order to protect him from developing inhibitions. I suppose they succeeded; he *was* wholly uninhibited. I did my best to avoid him. I can still remember my own parents' horror, almost awe, when they learned that the boy got a present *every day* that he didn't play some vicious practical joke on his schoolteachers.

I've seen the same kind of indulgence shown for different ideological reasons. In 1986, I visited friends in South Africa, during the last years of the apartheid regime. I watched, rigid with disapproval, as a young white mother let her four-year-old son slap, kick and punch her—and anyone else foolish enough to wander into his orbit. When I asked my friends what the hell she was doing, they explained that she wanted her boy to grow up without any fear of authority, to make him a better freedom fighter. She, too, had achieved at least a partial success. He certainly was a fighter.

All of these people truly loved their children. Their mistakes and ineptitude did not spring from indifference. (Even Maxine Hong Kingston's steely mother reveals a fitful tenderness in later life.) Moreover, women aren't invariably willing to sacrifice their own instincts and notions to someone else's theories. There is a moving example of resistance in Emmanuel Le Roy Ladurie's *Montaillou: Cathars and Catholics in a French Village*. A couple had joined the fanatically religious Cathars sect, who instructed the woman to stop feeding her infant daughter. The father agreed to impose on the child "the ultimate fast" of the sect until she died. But as soon as he left the house, the woman put the child to her breast. She later told a court, "I could not bear it any longer. I couldn't let my daughter die before my very eyes."[71]

There must have been many such moments throughout history. The tragedy is that our parenting skills and sense are so unreliable. Still, humans aren't the only species to display varying levels of parental skill and involvement. Domestic cats, to take one example, are not all equally capable mothers. A treasured pet may, like some spoiled aristocratic beauty, prove to be a most negligent parent. The rats in the stress experiment cited earlier showed extreme variations as mothers. Some paid very little attention to their young.

To take an example closer to our own natures, there are both great and mediocre mothers among Jane Goodall's chimpanzees at Gombe. Flo, the troop's sexpot and matriarch, was a terrific mother in her vigorous middle years, raising one confident, curious female and a pair of male future leaders. In old age, however, she seemed to lack the energy to control her last baby. Spoiled rotten and excessively dependent, he died of grief shortly after her death. Other females seemed less competent even in their prime. Goodall's notes reveal at least one nervous and overly protective mother, who infected her offspring with her own anxieties.[72] While Flo was relatively patient and generous with her daughter Fifi, one of the other mothers was often ill-tempered with her child, and invariably reluctant to share her food.[73]

Of course, even in chimpanzees, parenting behaviour is a product of both nature and nurture. Flo's daughters will almost certainly become able mothers themselves, having absorbed the skills of an experienced and intelligent model. The children of the more nervous and less competent mothers may not manage so well.

As I've already noted, primates raised in laboratory conditions, deprived of nurturing from and contact with their own kind, are unlikely to need parenting skills, since they have no interest in sex. A human female, however, may end up having sex and children no matter how deprived her childhood was. Women in many societies have no choice about marrying. Without access to contraception, they also have no choice about bearing children. Their societies shove them into marriage and maternity with at least as much zeal as a zookeeper pushing two reluctant pandas into mating.

That's not a frivolous comparison. If human mothering patterns seem a trifle erratic, it may have to do with our uneasy mix of nature and nurture. We all raise our children in a zoo; we live in societies that watch us and shape our behaviour. No one can question the existence of a maternal instinct in other mammals, because you can see it in action. But when human mothers behave in the same way, we don't know if nature is at work. No human female ever raises a baby on instinct alone.

It's hard even to set any kind of standard for good, appropriate human mothering. Which values do you choose? In her study of a southern Indian village, *Family Web*, Sarah Hobson records the women's explanation of their harshness with their children: "'How can we treat them softly?' said the women. 'They wouldn't survive their lives.'"[74] Similarly, the Spartan mother was dedicated—at least in theory—to raising fearless warriors, an aim that promoted the harshest discipline. Many cultures feel that indulging children, instead of pushing them towards adulthood, is not real love.

That attitude would shock an Inuit or Balinese mother; she would not dream of striking a child, that visiting gift from the gods. Once, European missionaries were horrified by this gentle approach to child-rearing. Today, Asians and Africans are frequently appalled by the insolence and self-indulgence of the permissively raised Western youngster. Meanwhile, in the jungles of South America, the Yanomamo mother is thrilled when her son shows budding aggression by beating her with a switch (provided, please note, by his delighted father).[75] She is elated by precisely the kind of juvenile violence that sends a contemporary North American mother racing to her child-care manuals.

Our ideas of appropriate maternal behaviour are at least as various as our ideas of romantic love. I realized that truth during my year of teaching in Sierra Leone. The bond between mother and baby there seemed to me much stronger than it is in Canada. A young baby is carried all the time, usually by its mother. Mothers traded in the market, did laundry, cooked and farmed with a baby attached to back or hip in a sling fashioned from a piece of cloth. This was not possible, obviously, for women who worked in offices. But they were able to spend most of their leisure time with their children. Their society doesn't segregate children from adult social life to the extent that we do. Most mothers were with their infant children every minute, because they also share their beds with their youngest child.

On the other hand, except among the educated élite, women didn't seem to pay much attention to teaching their children skills. There was far less of that urgent Western concern about getting the baby to walk and talk. Perhaps because of that, perhaps because of the all-consuming bond with the mother, young babies seemed to me much less sociable than the ones I'd known in the West.

But that changed fairly quickly. By the age of three or four, the baby would join a play group of other children. The shy baby soon changed into a mischievous, curious, almost flirtatious child. From that point, a new dimension entered the relationship of mother and child. The love between them remained strong. But the mother also became a disciplinarian—often a very harsh one by our standards. Almost everyone accepted that hateful adage, "Spare the rod and spoil the child." The result often looked like cruelty to me. Yet it did not damage the bond between mother and child. As I've noted, adult men adored their mothers. Their mothers had pushed them, and they were grateful for it.

There are many other places where the good mother is not the forbearing, all-accepting creature that we applaud. There are plenty of societies that define the mother as a stern disciplinarian, a woman who shows no misconceived softness towards her children. Here is a portrait of a mother from Sholom Aleichem's "Hanukkah Money":

Between sips of chicory she cuddles the baby at her breast and digs her elbow into the child on her knee. "Look at you eat, you pig! May the worms eat you!... Mendel, don't make so much noise! I'll give you such a crack that you'll turn over three times! Oh, my heart, my soul, my comfort. What, murderers, you want more food? All you do all day is eat, eat, eat! Why don't you choke!"[76]

This particular portrait is an unflattering one, but that's largely because the cursing fails. The children are uncontrolled brats. The invective itself isn't the mark of a bad mother. It's not all that far from Tevye's admiring descriptions of the maternal skills of his wife, Golde, another great curser and slapper. As in Africa, the Jewish *shtetls* of Europe valued the mother who kept her children on the straight and narrow. It was a world that saw children largely as adults in the making, to be rushed into proper behaviour. It was not a culture that encouraged hugging or touching children after infancy. The aim was not to produce a happy and well-adjusted child. It was to produce a pious, respectable and self-supporting adult.

At the opposite extreme lies the contemporary mother in Japan. Even the most conscientious Western mother seems like a monster of selfishness next to her Japanese counterpart. Japanese mothers do not thwart their toddlers in any way. The Asia expert Ian Buruma notes that "appeasement appears to be the Japanese mother's favorite tactic."[77]

The patience of the Japanese mother is unequalled. She is an endless font of concern and love. Buruma notes: "Being a Japanese child, especially a boy, and most of all an eldest son, is as close as one can get to being God."[78] I've stayed with a family in Kyoto where the mother routinely cooked three different meals each night for her husband, her daughter and her son. She felt that all the members of her family were entitled to the food they wanted. It's no wonder that in popular Japanese culture, the figure of the motherless child is always good for some tears. Mother is the only source of dependable, uncritical love most Japanese will ever know. There is little danger, nonetheless, that Japanese children will become spoiled, since their teachers and peers soon browbeat and bully them into shape.

But if the children *do* turn out badly, it's their mother's fault. If her husband drinks too much, if her children do badly at school, if any scandal touches their house, somehow she's to blame. I've noticed in both Japanese life and literature a kind of mystical belief in the mother's power. It's as if she could control her family's behaviour through some kind of subconscious force, if she would just concentrate hard enough.

That subconscious belief in the mother's omnipotence isn't restricted to Japan. It is one of the burdens we add to the mix of nature and nurture we bring to parenting. I suspect it's a holdover from earliest infancy, when our dependency on the mother is complete. It's an attitude captured perfectly by the writer Tobias Wolff in his story "Firelight":

> I was shivering like crazy. It seemed to me I'd never been so cold, and I blamed my mother for it, for taking me outside again, away from the fire. I knew it wasn't her fault but I blamed her anyway— for this and the wind in my face and for every nameless thing that was not as it should be.[79]

That mystical dimension in our vision of motherhood can be completely literal. In many societies, the mother's magical abilities are right out there in the open, fighting the evil spirits that threaten her children. In a lot of the world (including parts of our own), people believe that survival depends in part on our relations with the supernatural. The good mother is the woman who knows how to placate the forces of evil, and can teach her children the same arcane lore.

In all sorts of places, women must race to familiarize their children with elaborate sets of taboos. Terrible dangers can lurk in a single banana (if eaten by a female), a bit of pork, a bowl of rice prepared by someone of the wrong caste. Children have to learn how to propitiate their gods or God, how to live without offending the unseen world. Ignorance of the necessary rules is as life-threatening as starvation. And until children are old enough to know the rules, it's usually the mother who's responsible for keeping them safe from harm.

There's a simple and familiar example of this approach to child-rearing in the movie *Hester Street*. The film is set early in this century among the Jewish settlements of New York's East Side. The heroine, newly arrived from Europe, conscientiously protects her son from the evil eye as he's about to leave the safety of their flat. She throws a pinch of the salt and spits three times. My own grandmother used the same formula. But this fear of supernatural harm is not restricted to Jews, or to an earlier era. A Uruguayan grandmother I know begged her daughter to pin something red on her child's coat as a prophylactic against the evil eye—she was terrified of leaving such a pretty little girl unprotected.

These spells and charms satisfy a deep emotional hunger. They reflect our obsession with protecting children from the pitfalls of this world and the next, our yearning to keep them safe from all harm. In all cultures, no matter how different their other standards are, the first test of the good mother is that her children survive and prosper. She must therefore be ever-vigilant.

The second test is that her offspring grow up to fulfil whatever standards of good behaviour their particular society holds. But those standards are so wildly different that one culture's good mother may seem like a monster or a lunatic in other places.

Our own culture's vision of maternity, shaped by widespread mis-understandings of Freudian theory, is particularly exacting. Shari Thurer writes in her book *The Myths of Motherhood:* "Popular

mother culture implies that our children are exquisitely delicate creatures, hugely vulnerable to our idiosyncrasies and deficits, who
require relentless psychological attunement and approval. A senti-
mentalized image of the perfect mother casts a long, guilt-inducing
shadow over real mothers' lives."[80] She puts it more bluntly when
describing contemporary mothers' terrors: "One false move and
their precious bundle of joy will turn into an ax-murderer."[81]

This is a sensible point. Bruno Bettelheim issued the same message (rather late for him and the rest of the Freudian clan) in the
book *A Good Enough Parent*.[82] It's a liberating concept: You don't
have to be perfect to raise physically and emotionally healthy children. Nor do their characters depend entirely on their mothers. But
Thurer is wrong about the uniqueness of our perfectionism. In many,
many other cultures, mothers worry that one wrong move might
doom their children. It's less obvious because they're concerned
about a different set of moves. But mothers worry all over the world
if they're doing the right things, if they are *good* mothers.

There is no perfect answer to balancing our instincts and our
culture, no perfect way to raise a child. I believe there is a maternal instinct, but one that is neither universal nor totally dependable.
It can dissolve under the influence of various external and internal
pressures. Statistics pretty well establish that it has difficulty with-
standing desperate poverty and a surrounding atmosphere of violence. Addiction can destroy it. I suspect that overcrowding causes
it to plummet.

Moreover, human life is far too complex to let us raise children
on instinct alone, even if such a thing were possible. You need a
working brain to be a decent mother. It seems to me that a sensible, well-intentioned woman could do a good job of raising a child
without genetic assistance. I want to stress that idea because at this
moment in Western development we're fixated on the importance
of bonding between mother and child. Experts are telling women
that they must bond with their kids at birth, or the game is over.

What does that mean for the adopted? Lobbying agencies for them tell their clients that they will never find wholeness until they've bonded with their biological mothers.

This emphasis on the biological link strikes me as bizarre, given the number of people who feel like misfits in their own biological families. If bonding with your natural family is the answer, why do so many children, living with their own parents, secretly fear, believe and sometimes wish that they were adopted? Why do so many mothers reject and abuse the children they've borne?

Certainly their cultures and own upbringing play a role; perhaps there is a genetic component here as well. For all we know, some kind of anti-maternal hormone may stream through some human systems. Finally, although it is a most unfashionable judgment to make, I think character plays a major role. Good motherhood requires many of the major virtues: patience, selflessness, self-control, compassion. There are times when you need all of the big three: faith, hope *and* charity.

In any case, few women in the course of history have had the chance to raise their children exactly as they wish, in accordance with nothing but their own feelings and values. We have travelled light years from our earliest female ancestors, whose babies were wholly their own. Even today, with the nuclear family in disarray in so much of the world, Mom and the kids aren't usually on their own. Unlike their prehominid forebears, they have learned to make room for Daddy.

Make Room for Daddy

My mother always deferred to my father, and in his absence spoke of him to me as if he were all-wise. I confused him in some sense with God; at all events I believed that my father knew everything and saw everything.
—Edmund Gosse[1]

My father was frightened of his father, I was frightened of my father, and I am damned well going to see to it that my children are frightened of me.
—King George v[2]

I would have liked to have a father.
—Barbra Streisand[3]

FISH GOTTA SWIM, AND birds gotta fly—and their males often gotta take care of the kids at the same time. The emperor penguin is unique only in the rigours of his environment, not in his self-sacrificing devotion to his chicks. In fact, he fares rather better than the male African hornbill, who seals his mate into a hollow tree with mud when it's time for her to lay her eggs. The male leaves a tiny hole for her beak through which he then must feed her and their four chicks non-stop. By the time the rest of the family is ready to break out of the safety of its sealed home, Dad is usually dead from exhaustion.[4]

In many other species, the males play a major part in protecting, feeding and tending their young. It's the male demoiselle fish who tirelessly guards the eggs he's fertilized long after Mom has made watery tracks.[5] It's the male jacana (along with the other guys in the harem) who gets stuck with brooding the eggs.[6] Nature has made them competent, self-sacrificing parents.

Things can go wrong, of course. Not all males get a chance to *be* fathers. In an overwhelming majority of species, the female exercises some form of choice when it comes to mating. Her standards are as rigid as they are arbitrary: the peacock with a substandard tail or the yellow-thighed manakin without some really fancy dance steps is out of luck. Parental ability and commitment vary, which is why the female albatross tests her suitors' loyalty and reliability for as much as five years before settling down.[7] Finally, just like females, dads can turn on their young at times of crisis. If the male demoiselle fish can no longer cope with the surrounding predators, he'll join them in polishing off his brood. But these are exceptions. In much of the animal world, Dad is programmed to be a caregiver.

Paternity is by no means, however, a universal value, particularly once you leave the finned and feathered for the furred. Among many mammals, fathers contribute nothing but sperm. Their energies are channelled into the competition to mate. After that, Mom is on her own. Indeed, as with male bears, fathers can represent a serious threat to their offspring, and Mother may have to keep an eye on Dad as a potential predator. From elephants down to dogs and cats, parenting among mammals is often strictly a female concern.

That's certainly true of our closest relatives, the chimpanzees. To be fair, many of their males show a general benevolence towards the troop's young, and they share the female fascination with newborns. But paternity has no place in their female-headed family order. Jane Goodall did observe cases of males trying to raise orphaned children, but those were their siblings, not their offspring.[8] Among chimpanzees, the feeding, protection, grooming and education of the young are almost exclusively maternal chores.

Where do humans fit into this sweeping range of paternal patterns? It's a puzzling question. As we've seen, the general assumption in most scientific writing today is that our original pattern was very close to the chimpanzees'. Yet if you look at the sum of human history, you might well assume that fathers are the pivot of our social

order, the family's *raison d'être*. Many societies work on the principle that nature and divine law conspire to place men at the head of
the household, legitimately demanding obedience and unswerving
loyalty from their wives and children. Among the Lele of West
Africa, children are taught, "Your father is God."9 Until fairly
recently, many Western families operated on the same principle. In
a tract on domestic duties, the Puritan William Gouge wrote,
"Though an husband in regard of evil qualities may carry the image
of the devil, yet in regard to his place and office, he beareth the
image of God."10

The vision of the dominant and possessive father and submissive mother and children is so pervasive in so many societies that
we often project it onto the rest of nature. We still grow up with
images of an animal world organized into cosy nuclear families—
with Daddy in charge. Perhaps the glut of nature documentaries on
TV today will help a younger generation to grasp that neither Papa
Bear nor male elephants have the slightest desire for visitation rights,
and that Mommy Beaver and the female jacana, more aggressive
than their mates, are the boss.

That news would prove a shock to men in a wide range of cultures. Paternal supremacy is a central tenet of—to choose just a
few examples—both books of the Bible, the Koran, Hindu theology, Confucian philosophy and the laws of ancient Greece, Rome,
Sumeria, Babylonia and Assyria. The anthropologist Ruth Benedict,
writing about Japanese society in 1946, observed: "Even today a
father of grown sons, if his own father has not retired, puts through
no transaction without having it approved by the old grandfather.
Parents make and break their children's marriages even when the
children are thirty and forty years old. The father as male head of
the household is served first at meals, goes first to the family bath,
and receives with a nod the deep bows of his family."11

This is not some uniquely Japanese quirk. Many cultures allow
a man the right to control both his children and his wife, or wives.

The journalist Jan Goodwin learned that lesson in Pakistan, when she befriended the twelve-year-old daughter of an Afghan refugee. The girl's father traded her for another young girl, swapping a daughter for a wife. Goodwin's friend, Maria, tried to resist. She was a child who loved school and longed for more education. But she could not hold out against a steady diet of physical abuse. As her grandmother told Goodwin: "A man has the right to beat the women in his family. There is nothing you can do."[12]

To be fair, there are cultures that value paternal gentleness and altruism. Among the Trobriand Islanders, for instance, the pioneering anthropologist Bronislaw Malinowski noted in the 1920s that

> the husband fully shares in the care of the children. He will fondle and carry a baby, clean and wash it, and give it the mashed vegetable food which it receives in addition to the mother's milk almost from birth. In fact, nursing the baby in the arms or holding on the knees, which is described by the native word *kopo'i*, is the special role and duty of the father... The father performs his duties with genuine natural fondness: he will carry an infant about for hours, looking at it with eyes full of such love and pride as are seldom seen in those of a European father. Any praise of the baby goes directly to his heart, and he will never tire of talking about and exhibiting the virtues and achievements of his wife's offspring.[13]

But the harsh system Goodwin encountered is very common. In Chapter 2, I pointed out that men succeeded in gaining complete control of marriage in some cultures. The corollary of that, of course, is complete control of the offspring of those marriages. In much of the world, a child is literally the father's property. A father in ancient Sumeria, Babylonia or Assyria had the right to offer his wife or kids to pay off a debt.[14] In pre-revolutionary China, a poor father often sold a child—usually a daughter—into slavery or prostitution. It still happens today. In 1996, a beleaguered Palestinian refugee in Lebanon tried to sell one of his sons. His motive was filial devotion; Nabil Rifai put his seven-year-old son Bilal on the market to pay for his father's kidney treatments.[15]

Fathers wield enormous power even in societies that don't permit selling children outright. As mentioned, Lele children—especially boys—were taught to revere their fathers. The ethnographer Mary Douglas wrote: "Boys were taught, 'Your father is like God. But for his begetting, where would you be? Therefore honour your father.' They were taught that the debt which they owed him for his care of them in infancy was unrepayable, immeasurable. It was very shameful for a man to show disrespect to his father. Fathers were expected to avoid their grown sons, so that the latter should not feel bowed down with the burden of respect."[16] That may seem like an extreme example, but beliefs weren't all that different in China or Japan until after the Second World War, while similar attitudes persist to this day in other Asian and African cultures.

In our world, it's easy to lose sight of the exalted status of fathers elsewhere. For instance, our own Western societies have come to believe that children—especially young children—are generally better off with their mothers. You might think that the one unalterable certainty of family life would be the mother–child bond, especially given the inescapable necessity of breast-feeding without some fairly recent technology. But it is precisely this bond that many "advanced" civilizations try to weaken in favour of the father. It seems a likely factor in the popularity of wet-nursing for so much of European history; farming out a child severely weakens the bond between mother and child, and leaves the mother free to devote herself to her husband. Respect for the mother's rights is a recent development in our culture. Until the last century, we, too, saw children as the father's property.[17]

Many cultures still do. As we've seen, the Wodaabe of Niger regard the child as the property of the father and his clan, so the mother must leave her offspring behind if she wants a new romance.

The Koran awards all parental rights to the father, so throughout the Islamic world he automatically enjoys custody rights.[18] That leads to a sadly common problem after divorce: men from the Islamic world abduct their children when Western courts award mothers custody. Back home, there is little danger that authorities will heed a court order favouring a woman, particularly a foreign woman or a Muslim woman who has developed a Western streak of insubordination.[19]

Meanwhile, the West attaches importance to the rights of the father in other ways. In 1995, an American doctor, John Kessel, sued Anne Conaty and her parents for defrauding him of his parental rights. He and Anne Conaty had been engaged, but she had broken it off when she discovered he was seeing another woman. By that time, she was pregnant, and Kessel knew it. She did not want to raise the child herself, but she also had no intention of granting him the paternal rights he was seeking. Rather spitefully, she gave birth in hiding from him and promptly gave the child up for adoption. The Conatys' lawyer claimed that Kessel had originally urged Anne to get an abortion. Nonetheless, a jury in Huntington, West Virginia, awarded him *$7.835 million*,[20] placing a surprisingly high value on the joys of fatherhood.

The amount might well strike most of us as excessive, but much of the world would join the jury in backing the father's rights. There is a tendency, both in societies and in individuals, to see children as male property. One horrifying manifestation of that is the high number of cases in which rejected men kill their children and themselves. Although the result is the same, these cases are different in motive from the murders recorded in the last chapter, where violent child abuse results in death. These men often love their children, and kill them deliberately and sadly. The murder may be rooted in suicidal despair; it's as if killing their children is an extension of killing themselves. All over the world, there are dozens of cases each year of men slaughtering children when their marriages break up, or when they decide for other reasons that their own lives are unbearable.

I can choose cases at random from a file I've kept for only a couple of years: In September 1995, a Montreal man leapt from a bridge clutching his four-year-old son. His marriage had broken up two years earlier; he was driving the boy home after a weekend in the country together.[21] A month later, a man in Hamilton, Ontario, killed himself, his nine-year-old daughter and his seven-year-old son, apparently because he had lost his job and his marriage had collapsed.[22] In the same month, a Toronto man burnt himself to death with his eight-year-old son and his four-year-old daughter, evidently because his wife was planning to leave him.[23] In January 1997, a man in Tacoma, Washington, *threw* his two young children out of a third-floor window during a fight with his wife.[24] I could fill an entire book with similar stories.

We don't know how many children die under circumstances of this type; police statistics don't usually focus on motive. We do know that men are more likely to kill or injure their children than women. In 1993, a statistical analysis of figures gathered by the Children's Aid Society in Ontario revealed that fathers were cited in 54 per cent of the cases of physical abuse.[25] Since many children under CAS supervision are being raised by single mothers, that small majority actually reflects a fairly substantial split between the sexes.

The level of violence we're discussing here goes far beyond the occasional exasperated slap. The head of a child-protection unit in Halifax told me he sees a disturbing number of babies injured by severe shaking—severe enough to kill a third of the victims, and inflict permanent damage on another third, damage on the order of blindness, cerebral palsy or retardation. He added that the vast majority of perpetrators were men acting as parents—fathers, stepfathers or the mother's boyfriend.

But, as we've seen, women are capable of this level of violence, too. The statistics on child abuse of all kinds do not provide evidence that women are usually good parents, and men bad ones. They do, however, suggest that the two sexes often fail as parents in different ways. The CAS study found that mothers were cited in 82 per cent of the cases of neglect. (To be fair, many of these women do not have partners, which somewhat skews the statistics.) Men, unsurprisingly, were the perpetrators in 90 per cent of the sexual abuse cases. Despite the occasional well-publicized case, few women are interested in forcing their children to have sex, even where that is a physical possibility. But an alarming number of men seem to have no internal inhibition against forcing their attentions on their daughters, and sometimes their sons.

I've heard social workers speculate that male violence and sexual abuse of children may be rising because men now spend more time with children. But historical fact contradicts that argument. The medieval father might not have been with his younger children during the day, but he was crammed into a tiny shack with them all night. Moreover, he slept with them. In pre-industrial societies, men spent a *lot* of time with their kids, because they all worked together. The modern father—or stepfather—spends rather less time with his children than some of the world's gentlest male parents in hunter-gatherer tribes.

If we allow folklore as evidence—an admittedly dubious procedure—it's clear that fathers often figure as very bad news in legends. It's true that the stepmother is the all-purpose villain in European fairy tales, but the nightmare of the dangerous, devouring father runs through many myths and religions. For the ancient Greeks, for instance, the original god was a spectacularly poor parent, imprisoning all his offspring until the Titan Cronus rebelled against him. Cronus in turn swallowed *his* newborn children by his wife and sister, Rhea, until he was overthrown (through her trickery) by his son, Zeus.[26]

But cruelty and dominance are far from the whole story of fatherhood. There is such a thing as a good father. You might not guess it from a lot of the current literature on the family, but there are men who are patient, nurturing, self-sacrificing and loving with their children. The Trobriand Islanders aren't the only men who dote on their children. Take the Aka pygmies, a hunter-gatherer-trader tribe in the south of the Central African Republic and the north of the People's Republic of the Congo.[27] In an extended observation of fifteen Aka fathers, a researcher found that they held their infant children 20 per cent of the time spent in camp. They played with their children, hugged, kissed and cleaned them.

Individual fathers can be equally nurturing elsewhere. A student once gave me a tape of an interview with a Canadian who ran an orphanage in Cambodia until the fall of Phnom Penh. In it, she described a man who for six months would bring his little daughter to her every day: "She was like a little princess, he fed her no matter how little food he had." Necessity finally drove him to leave the child with the other orphans, but he returned every day until he was sent to the front to fight. He never returned.[28]

This is not a unique or even unusual story. The Bible offers examples of men consumed by the love of at least one of their children. In Genesis, the patriarch Jacob originally refuses to let his youngest boy, Benjamin, accompany his brothers to Egypt. Jacob has already lost his other favourite, Joseph, and he tells his sons, ". . . my son shall not go down with you; for his brother is dead, and he is left alone: if mischief befall him by the way in which ye go, then shall ye bring down my gray hairs with sorrow to the grave."[29] And when King David wins his battle against his rebel son Absalom, he is heartbroken: "O my son Absalom, my son, my son Absalom! would God I had died for thee, O Absalom, my son, my son!"[30]

Most of us can find similar examples from our own lives. While trekking in Kashmir in 1983, I was accosted on the side of a Himalayan mountain by a man carrying a small, flushed child. He had transported her over God knows how many miles at the sight or news of our party, seeking whatever medical help a group of visiting Westerners could provide. Our guides told us the girl was his daughter. Her hectic flush, hacking cough and emaciation suggested tuberculosis, and we offered to help him get her to a hospital, in the city, more than a hundred miles away. We might as well have advised him to take her to the moon; he couldn't abandon his flock and family for so long. He left with a fistful of Tylenol, a vision of despair.

Nor does it take tragedy to create paternal feelings. I know men who are far more involved with their children than their wives are. They typify the "New Father"—a figure I'll be returning to. The New Father does more than change diapers, mix formula and remember hockey practice. He is intensely involved with his children, as sensitive to their emotional needs as any woman. I've spent time with a father who agonized about leaving his four-year-old son with friends for a single evening. Another father told me half-jokingly that he regards La Leche's proselytizing for breast-feeding as a sinister plot to exclude fathers from babies' lives. *He* preaches the egalitarian benefits of bottle feeding. No wonder: among his fondest memories are the seven a.m. feedings that were his designated private time with a son who is now twenty-one years old.

Nor is the loving father some recent development in human evolution, a measure of the progress we've achieved. The historian Joyce Tyldesley stresses that children were far more than status symbols for the ancient Egyptians:

> Both husband and wife appear to have loved their offspring dearly, and Egyptian men had no misplaced macho feelings that made them embarrassed or ashamed of showing affection towards their progeny. To produce a large and healthy brood of children was every Egyptian's dream, and babies were regarded as one of life's richest blessings and a cause for legitimate, if occasionally exaggerated, boasting: we must either assume that the 11th Dynasty army captain claiming to have fathered "seventy children, the issue of one wife" was over-counting to emphasize his virility, or else feel deeply sorry for his wife.[31]

Even the harshest father may love his children. The father of the Victorian poet Elizabeth Barrett Browning has been immortalized as a model of the dictatorial patriarch, thanks to the play and movie *The Barretts of Wimpole Street*. His control of his adult children included an absolute ban on marriage, which is why his daughter Elizabeth had to elope. (There is now a theory that Mr. Barrett feared his West Indian family might have black ancestors. Nineteenth-century genetic theory included a belief that even a trace of African blood in one parent could result in a coal-black child.) Yet Elizabeth Barrett wrote these words to Robert Browning in August 1845, "But what you do not see, what you cannot see, is the deep tender affection behind and below all those patriarchal ideas of governing grown-up children . . ."[32]

There are entire societies where men value nothing more than children. In Sierra Leone, I once endured a furious lecture from a plumber who had just fixed my toilet. Pausing at the door (he was a very large man, and practically filled the entrance), he asked me censoriously where my husband was. When I answered that I didn't have one, he thundered at me, "The Bible says, 'Be fruitful and multiply and replenish the earth.'" In the ensuing theological debate, it was obvious that my childlessness disturbed him more than my single state. Like many of the people around me, male and female, he was perplexed and troubled by my failure to have borne even a single child at the advanced age of twenty-five.

He couldn't understand why I wasn't interested in the most desirable of all life's blessings: children. Most of the men around me in Africa shared this passion for offspring. They valued even babies born to them outside marriage. A startling number of men, including senior academics, freely acknowledged their "outside" children. (One venerable scholar was widely rumoured to have adopted and raised his illegitimate daughter; certainly the girl looked just like him, and her adoptive mother clearly detested her.)

And if children were welcome even outside the bounds of marriage, you can imagine the craving for them inside it. The man who cleaned my flat once a week once asked me about "birth pills." He was not, as I initially assumed, seeking contraceptives; he wanted fertility treatments for his wife, who was fifteen years old. (He wouldn't tell me his own age, but I suspect he was in his late teens.) They had been married for a year, and he was seriously alarmed by her failure to conceive. He worried she would leave him; he feared the ridicule of other men; and, above all, he wanted a child.

I have to admit that his desire was actually more specific. He wanted a son. Almost everywhere in the world, men tend to value boys more than girls, and to be more involved fathers if their offspring are male.[33] There are cultures that view female children as a calamity. In most of India, for example, a daughter will be transferred to her husband's family at great cost. No wonder one researcher found a sharp difference in attitudes to male and female children: "The birth of a boy is a gift from God to parents whereas the birth of a girl is a debt incurred with God."[34] Nor is this attitude restricted to men. A southern Indian wife in Sarah Hobson's *Family Web* expressed no desire for daughters. She said, "The minute we have a son, I'll have the operation. The sons work and feed us. The girls go away to another house. A son is nice for anything."[35]

Yet personal feelings often override belief. Despite the burden imposed by the need to marry off daughters, some Indians nonetheless love them. The brilliant television series *Lovelaw* quoted a surprising Tamil proverb about the ideal family: "A son to light your funeral pyre, a daughter for joy." No doubt my steward in Sierra Leone would have accepted and loved a daughter, even if he would have preferred a son.

In the West today, we are not thrilled at the idea of two very young teenagers starting a family. But that hunger for offspring in such a young couple would have made perfect sense to the ancient Egyptians. One piece of scribal advice runs: "Take to yourselves a wife while you are young, so that she may give you a son. You should beget him for yourself when you are still young, and should live to see him become a man."[36]

From a genetic point of view, this lust for fatherhood makes only partial sense. The man who wants to ensure genetic immortality should certainly be trying to have children—but not to raise them. His priority should be impregnating the maximum number of women, a quest that can only be hampered by raising a family. Sociobiologists work from the assumption that women are looking for a small number of high-quality males, while savvy men are looking to get laid by anything young enough to conceive.

In Chapter 3, I mentioned the book *The Evolution of Desire*, by University of Michigan psychologist Dr. David Buss. Buss surveyed some ten thousand people, representing thirty-seven cultures.[37] In an interview about his findings, he told a reporter that "men's sexual strategies tend to be short-term and promiscuous." He added that men "will consider sharing their genes with any woman who meets their mating standard: young, healthy, physically attractive. They tolerate situations where their partners form a deep, non-sexual relationship with someone else, but are subject to mad fits of jealousy at the prospect of sexual infidelity." In other words, as the reporter noted, "Men may be slime, but they come by it naturally."

Women, in contrast, tend to take the long view. Dr. Buss found they wanted an average of five partners during their lives—versus a male ideal of eighteen. Moreover, women all over the world place less emphasis on beauty than on economic success, reliability and commitment.[38] That makes sense, too; a helpful, productive, powerful partner will increase female chances of raising a brood of healthy, prosperous children. It's the standard genetic vision of the sexes' conflicting roles. Yul Brynner summed up this conventional view of gender for all time in *The King and I*, explaining loftily to Deborah Kerr that the bee flies from flower to flower to flower, but the flower does *not* fly from bee to bee to bee.

But some bees do settle down with a single flower. The Trobriand Islander is one example of a man who invests energy, time and emotion in children—even though he has no claim on them, and they may well not be his. That's an extreme version of male altruism, but in much of the world men stick with one woman at a time (even in societies that permit polygyny), and help—more or less—to raise their kids. On the other hand, there have always been men who specialize in raiding flower after flower, leaving their conquests to raise the children, and others who bolt after a taste of domestic responsibility.

That kind of fecklessness is on the rise in both the industrialized and the developing worlds. A lot of men, for whatever reasons, have decided that family life is not for them.[39] Unfortunately, most of them don't choose to renounce sex at the same time. So the number of single-parent, female-headed families is rising exponentially. In Canada, single mothers now head one in five families; their numbers have tripled over the past thirty years. Moreover, half of all divorced fathers do not pay any of their court-ordered child support, and another quarter pays only a part of it.[40] In the United States, nearly two out of every five children live without a father: 38 per cent in 1995, up from 17.5 per cent in 1970.

Nor is this phenomenon unique to the wealthier nations of North America. Two cultures—the Black Caribs of Belize and Samoans in American Samoa—have absentee father rates of between 30 and 50 per cent.[41] The proportion of single-parent, mother-headed families is soaring in much of Latin America, Europe and Africa.[42]

Even if they stick around, not all men are thrilled with the financial and emotional responsibilities of fatherhood. Genetic imperative to reproduce or no, a lot of men do not respond with enthusiasm to the news of impending fatherhood. A decade ago, a colleague asked me to speak to his wife, pregnant for the first time. He'd just seen a film about birth at their Lamaze class, and he'd almost fainted. He wanted at all costs to avoid the delivery room. He argued that his wife barely knew him; they'd only been together for two years. He was hoping she'd opt for the assistance of some female friend she'd known longer.

Let me hasten to add that in the end he attended the birth of both his children, and became a devoted parent. But not all men develop strong paternal feelings. I've watched marriages and relationships crumble because the man didn't want children, or didn't want to add a second set to his offspring from an earlier marriage. A lot of men also seem to take longer than women to adjust to the fact of parenthood. I may be particularly sensitive to that possibility because of an incident in my own life: When I was three months old, my mother left me briefly in my father's care. She returned to find him walking down the street with a friend, deep in conversation. "Where's the baby?" she asked in horror. His answer was, "What baby?"

I survived my father's spell of paternal forgetfulness. But that absent-mindedness can have grisly and tragic results. In June 1997, a California man drove to work, forgetting that he was supposed to drop off the baby at day-care. In the course of eight hours in a stifling car, the child died. I found that my own friends talked about this incident a number of times over the following few days. One man, an extremely conscientious and loving father, told me that it haunted him because *it was the kind of thing that could happen to anyone.* It reminded me inevitably of a conversation many years before with another colleague. He'd taken his young daughters to the beach, and had returned briefly to his car. When he came back, one of his daughters had disappeared. She surfaced a few moments later, sputtering and choking, and he raced to the water to scoop her out. He told me soberly the next morning that he hadn't slept that night. He lay awake, tortured by the recognition that he was never going to be able to relax his vigilance. His daughters were his hostages to fortune.

These men adore their children. Yet even in strongly patriarchal societies, something about affluence and industrialization often seems to dull the male desire to reproduce. An article on Japan's dangerously low birth rate quoted a childless Tokyo housewife: "My husband doesn't want kids at all, and I don't particularly want them either. My husband just doesn't like them. He doesn't like annoying things. And since he wouldn't help out raising them, I don't want kids either."[43]

That idea of children as a nuisance and a burden seems to be on the rise. Even in Africa, one of my colleagues seemed positively buoyant over losing one of a pair of newborn twins. He told me cheerfully that he couldn't have afforded to raise two children anyway. That attitude would have shocked my plumber or my cleaner—neither of whom had nearly as much money as the pragmatic university lecturer. Most of the men I know in North America might shrink from admitting to such cynical materialism, but they might well share the sentiment. If men do have a genetic desire to sire children, some cultures manage to do a good job of repressing it. The ancient Romans often approached the responsibilities of family life with extreme reluctance. In our own contemporary Western world, plummeting birth rates tell their own story. In men as well as women, individualism and the possibility of other forms of self-fulfilment seem to erode the desire for parenthood.

Moralists naturally see this as evidence of our own degeneracy. American politicians—from vice-presidents Dan Quayle and Al Gore down—are concerned about the divorce rate, paternal fecklessness and other forms of family breakdown. The answers proposed range from outlawing no-fault divorce to restricting welfare payments for single mothers to Newt Gingrich's nostalgic fondness for the orphanages of Boys Town. (Gingrich may suffer from an inability to separate fiction from reality: *Boys Town* was a highly sentimental movie, based on the orphanages established by the legendary Father Flanagan—Spencer Tracy in the movie. Newfoundland's Mount Cashel, a real orphanage where boys were systematically raped and beaten, apparently escaped Gingrich's notice.)

But the return of tradition may not provide much of a solution for our current problems. It is quite possible that we are simply returning to the earliest traditions of all. Here is Will Durant's summary of primitive family life:

> So slight is the relation between father and children in primitive society that in a great number of tribes the sexes live apart. In Australia and British New Guinea, in Africa and Micronesia, in Assam and Burma, among the Aleuts, Eskimos and Samoyeds, and here and there over the earth, tribes may still be found in which there is no visible family life; the men live apart from the women, and visit them only now and then; even the meals are taken separately.[44]

Durant is wrong about some of the details. For instance, most Inuit (his word, Eskimo, is now considered a derogatory term) actually live in small, fluid households that generally do contain at least a woman, her children and a man. But he's right about the essence. A lot of societies do not stress paternity. Young children live with their mothers (and in some cultures, I regret to say, the pigs) in the women's longhouse until the boys are considered old enough to join the men. Fathers may have rather more symbolic value in such cultures than Durant realized, but they play no real part in raising their children.

And there are societies which go even further in dispensing with fathers. The Nayar, as you've read, make do with purely ceremonial husbands and fathers. A woman's children address her lovers indiscriminately as "lord."[45] Similarly, there are very few cultures where a woman's strongest tie is to her brothers, with whom she and her children live. Married couples rarely co-habit, and husbands remain outsiders, marginal in their children's lives.[46]

In addition, there are a number of cultures and sub-cultures in which fatherhood is more of an idea than a reality. In large parts of the Caribbean, for instance, many fathers play no role in their children's lives, and provide no support for them. A ground-breaking report on this pattern found that men somehow managed to be both dominant and marginal to their families. One woman told the study's authors, "Women do run the households. West Indian men don't like to do any work at all either. . . . Those that do work to support their families usually do not make enough to support their drinking habits *and* their families. So women have to go to work too . . . Women are used to supporting themselves, so they do it when the men are here and when the men are gone as well. They tell their daughters not to depend on men, but on themselves. They should tell the sons to have responsibilities, but they don't. It is the women who become responsible."[47]

More detached observers have drawn the same conclusion. An earlier study of Jamaican family structure noted that it was quite common for children never to have seen their fathers, or to have "only the most casual acquaintance with them."[48] The author described the families as "matricental" and "maleless."[49]

To be fair, later research suggests that Jamaican men in low-income, intact, common-law families may actually be as involved in child-care as fathers in most other cultures.[50] That is not, however, a particularly impressive level of involvement. The time these Jamaican fathers reported spending on child-care was one-half to one hour a day. And that's normal. Around the world, men in most cultures spend about a third as much time on their children as mothers do.[51]

Finally, even in societies where two parents are the norm, death ensures that many children will grow up without fathers. That's particularly true of death in warfare. The massive conflicts of this century, for instance, left many women widowed and with little chance of remarrying. (The odds against North American women fell further because a staggering number of North American men brought home wives from overseas.) A British writer who grew up in this kind of fatherless home noted tartly that her childhood underlines the truth that "not all happy families are nuclear families."[51]

Given all this, you have to ask if fathers are necessary. If individual families and entire cultures can manage without them, are they perhaps an unnecessary frill? After all, most male birds and a few fish have little choice about good parenting. Their genes apparently spur them into action as soon as the eggs appear. If male humans can exhibit such disparate patterns with their children, it seems unlikely that they have any kind of similar mechanism.

Yet all societies have some kind of idea of fatherhood—even those, like the Trobriand Islanders, that didn't recognize men's biological contribution to making babies. If human males are not imprinted with paternal feelings, how on earth did that happen?

It's of limited use to turn to other primates for the answer. Our patterns of fatherhood vary so wildly that we resemble virtually *all* of our relatives, even the distant ones. Moreover, primates themselves are capable of varying their mating behaviour. Savanna and hamadryas baboons are so closely related that they can interbreed. Yet their social systems are completely different. The dominant hamadryas baboon has a harem of up to ten females—females he's scooped up as youngsters. He "mothers" them in their presexual years—grooming them, but also keeping a sharp eye on them at all times. Hamadryas females become passive, unlike their savanna cousins. Among savanna baboons, the females are (in Alex Shoumatoff's words) "more assertive and political . . . Groups of females form to defend access to certain trees whose nutritious fruit enhances their reproductive success. New males are not admitted to the band without their consent."[53]

Both of these patterns are not entirely unknown among humans. Jan Goodwin's friend Maria, for instance, would recognize the defeated obedience of the hamadryas female. Even a premarital parenting stage, while uncommon, isn't completely unknown in human marriages. In the novel *The Tale of Genji*, Lady Murasaki is originally Genji's ward, and he treats her like the child she is. She is initially deeply disturbed and angry when he begins to have sex with her, although she soon comes to love him. That daddy-turned-lover scenario remains a common female fantasy: think of *Emma*, or *Daddy Longlegs*, or even *Gone with the Wind*. (There is an academic theory that Rhett Butler represents the good mother, rather than a father. Think of his crooning competence with his daughter, Bonny.). As for the matriarchal savanna baboons—I have seen women exercising exactly the same kind of control in Third World villages and government ministries and university faculties.

The pattern I find most interesting belongs to yet another species of baboon, the olive. Helen Fisher notes that these baboons form "special friendships," in which a courting male hangs out with a female: "Often this companion becomes the social father of a female's young. He carries, grooms, cuddles, and protects them. But he uses these infants too. If another male threatens him, a male grabs the infant and holds it to his chest. This instantly stops the attack."[54]

Obviously, baboon fathering is very much a hit-and-miss affair. Not all males form bonds, but the possibility is there. It's closer to the human condition than, say, the unwavering paternal commitment of the penguin, the gibbon or the jacana. It adds a new dimension to the chimpanzee's family life, which is pretty well restricted to Mom and the kids. For the baboon, it's a genetic advantage to be good with children; his assistance and loyalty earn him the female's sexual services, giving him a shot at progeny of his own.[55]

Olive baboon females aren't stupid. They bestow their affections shrewdly. A male courting a high-ranking female takes a test—she makes him babysit while she forages for food or otherwise entertains herself. The lone male, dolefully tending a baby, is a magnet for other females, becoming "the local heart-throb," in the words of one nature documentary. But he patiently repels the interlopers, holding out for the affections of a female who can share her own high status.[56]

Fisher believes that humans developed a more consistent model of these special friendships once environmental and physical changes made single motherhood too difficult. Females, like their baboon cousins, became more attracted to males who were good with children. That wouldn't be the only factor in the equation, of course. Presumably some females would be willing to hook up with a male whose rotten parenting skills were balanced by a spectacular talent for finding food. More aggressive males may have been able from the beginning to force women into accepting them, just as female chimpanzees can be coerced into temporary consortships.

The behaviour of the doting Trobriand father mirrors several features of this pattern of primate behaviour. The offspring of both olive baboons and chimpanzees belong to their mother's troop. Similarly, Trobriand society is matrilineal. The children belong to the mother's family. Moreover, the olive baboon male is a father by virtue of his relationship to a mother—and so is the Trobriand Islander. He is the woman's "husband," and therefore, in a limited sense, her children are "his."

The issue of legitimate paternity doesn't enter into the equation at all. Indeed, as I've already noted, the Trobriand Islanders didn't recognize the male role in conception as late as the 1920s. I suspect that many, many other cultures came late to this particular scrap of knowledge; I don't think there's anything instinctive about it. We may yet find out that *women* actually have some sort of biological tie to their own children. There are, after all, female animals who can recognize their own children by smell and cry. (Accurate identification is of some importance among animals that live in large herds.) I know women who claim the same skill. But I am not aware of any male animal with the ability to distinguish his own offspring by scent or sound. (The rhesus monkey may be one exception; they seem to recognize all of their kin, presumably by smell.)

So it is indeed a wise child who knows his own father—and vice versa. American studies on babies born in the 1930s revealed that a startling number of them were not their legal fathers' offspring.[57] Furthermore, a study in 1996 claimed that physical appearance isn't much help in sorting out who's whose.[58] Its authors found that children don't really resemble either parent much, except for a passing likeness to the biological father at the age of about one. The researchers speculated that such a resemblance might be a survival tool.

I have to say that I'm deeply suspicious of those results. I've seen lots of children who look a great deal like one or another of their parents. Think of acting dynasties: both Jane and Peter Fonda are obviously their father's children, while Natasha Richardson and Isabella Rossellini clearly resemble their mothers, Vanessa Redgrave and Ingrid Bergman. Such resemblances, however, seem to me to be decidedly weak during a baby's first chubby, button-nosed year. In any case, for a number of children any resemblance to the biological father could be counterproductive, if not downright suicidal.

Still, children do sometimes resemble their fathers. Presumably that similarity provided one clue about the nature of human reproduction. After all, the first humans cannot possibly have worked out the complicated and unlikely progression that leads to birth. I feel confident that the original prehominid male took on children because they came in a package with a woman. And women were desirable because they provided sex—not to mention a relatively reliable source of food. As you'll remember, gatherers bring home a lot of goodies. In that context, the children must often have been an asset, with their sharp eyes and nimble little fingers.

I would like to believe that this productive exchange of goods and services was a universal model for the earliest human families. But I suspect that there have always been variations. From the beginning, we probably had at least the three arrangements used by chimpanzees: the virtual ownership of a desirable female by a high-ranking male; the free-for-all; and the temporary romance. Of course, evolutionary changes would have altered the place of children in all these forms of relationships. Female chimpanzees don't have much to do with males when their babies are small, because they don't go into estrus. Human children remain dependent for a much longer period of time, while their mothers are never out of season. The sexual marathon might well become less appealing to females, while it would make sense for human males to develop a stronger interest in the young than most other primates.

I favour this idea of the development of the family in part because it explains some of the behaviour I see around me. Certainly I have seen families based only on power, with brutal, dominant fathers. That was true even in the *Leave It to Beaver*–style suburbs where I grew up. I used to visit a schoolmate whose mother was not allowed to join us for tea in the evening until her husband came home. I've seen him roar with anger because he thought she'd disobeyed him; everyone (including me) was terrified of him. I've interviewed women who've lived with psychopaths whose energies were devoted to the physical and psychological torture of their families. (I will never forget a phone interview with a man who had shot and stabbed his ex-wife, leaving her blind in one eye and in permanent pain. I detected no trace of remorse. "We are all victims," he opined piously.) But I also know men who delight in fatherhood and family life—who see their wives and children as the centre of their lives.

As we've already learned, most anthropologists believe that male devotion is a human idiosyncrasy that evolved because the rigours of raising children were too oppressive for women to manage on their own. Desmond Morris, a major player in popularizing that idea, concluded that humans started to behave like other hunting animals once they progressed from being mere foragers to true predators. "Like the paternal wolves . . . the hunting ape males also had to carry food supplies home for the nursing females and their slowly growing young. Paternal behaviour of this kind had to be a new development, for the general primate rule is that virtually all parental care comes from the mother."[59] So human couples developed a strong sexual and romantic bond to ensure that Dad brought home the meat instead of camping out with the guys and scoffing all the protein himself.

The new system had some major advantages: ". . . the development of a one-male-one-female breeding unit meant that the offspring also benefited. The heavy task of rearing and training the slowly developing young demanded a cohesive family unit."[60] As we've just seen, of course, that cohesive family unit doesn't *have* to be a nuclear family. A strong tie to siblings or other maternal kin could serve the same purpose, and sometimes does. But Morris also presupposes that men need to feel sure of female loyalty—essentially, that men need to own women. If humans didn't pair up, the men would squabble over the females. And that could have an unthinkable result: it could interfere with the hunt.

Morris does note, with endearing understatement, that our family systems were "never really perfected."[61] That could, of course, be the result of grafting a fundamentally unnatural behaviour pattern onto the free-wheeling, loose-loving apes that we descend from. But there is a later theoretical embellishment that makes more sense of our difficulties with family life.

Morris himself hints at it, then veers away. In his discussion of the development of the nuclear family, he explains that throughout the animal kingdom, when the burdens of child-rearing are too great for a single parent to manage, "we see the development of a powerful pair-bond, tying the male and female parents together throughout the breeding season."[62] That takes us to the concept popularized by Helen Fisher—the idea that we're actually programmed to stay together for about four years, at which point both bee *and* flower start giving their neighbours the glad eye. But the four-year-itch theory takes us only so far. It does nothing to explain how the control of children passed from mother to father in so many societies. A tendency to serial monogamy also doesn't account for that male ownership of women we see in such a wide range of cultures. We return to the great conundrum: how did the last person to join the family get to run the whole show?

It doesn't help to explain the primitive societies whose men swap daughters and sisters for wives, but Helen Fisher blames the plough. Her theory, bolstered by the work of many other scholars, is that women have a comparatively comfortable degree of freedom and autonomy in hunter-gatherer societies.[63] Although males provide the most desirable and protein-rich form of food, meat, women and children can be relatively self-sufficient. It is difficult to keep any-one under permanent control under such conditions of constant mobility, and there seems to be less desire to do so. Familial pos-sessiveness is not one of the characteristics of the !Kung people of South Africa, for instance. Among the pygmy tribe described by Colin M. Turnbull in *The Forest People,* even parenthood is com-munal. Children call all adults Father or Mother. They know who their own parents are, but they get traded around as the necessity arises.[64] That makes sense, because children are a communal resource for hunter-gatherers; everyone routinely shares whatever he gathers or kills. In *The Harmless People,* Elizabeth Marshall Thomas watched a group of Bushmen carving up a gemsbok, and noted that "any animal is divided at once by a rigid system of rules, some meat given to each person rather than kept as a communal supply or portioned to families."[65]

Some analysts have concluded that subsistence by foraging and hunting encourages egalitarianism and the sharing of child-care. Among the Aka of central Africa, for instance, husband and wife have to work together to trap small animals in a net; if they don't co-operate, they'll go hungry.[66] Similarly, men and women among the Batek tribe of Malaysia work together both in hunting and gath-ering, and their fathers are highly involved in child-care.[67]

This system could persist even when humans began to develop more sophisticated methods for procuring food.[68] The Igarot are a perfect example; their women farm small, unploughed tracts while the men hunt. As we've seen, the men take over the care of the children when they return to camp.[69]

The plough, according to Fisher, changed all that. Men could farm much larger tracts of land, but at the cost of far more labour. It has become a cliché in anthropological writing to call hunter-gatherers the first affluent societies. They may not have much, but they meet their needs with only a few hours of work a day. A man farming even a couple of acres, on the other hand, needs all the help he can get. Children become an extremely valuable resource, so women's reproductive role becomes paramount. Will Durant makes the same point in *The Story of Civilization:* "Children were economic assets, and men invested in wives in order to draw children from them like interest. In the patriarchal system wives and children were in effect the slaves of the man; the more a man had of them, the richer he was."[70]

Given such values, the general status of women inevitably declined. In this vision of prehistory, men suddenly cared more about legitimate offspring, being unwilling to leave their land to other men's children. Nor could they be casual about the break-up of a marriage; a farm is not a convenient thing to divide. The woman, smaller and less aggressive, had no choice but to remain with the land-owning man.[71]

In an interview with Helen Fisher in 1994, I raised two problems that continue to puzzle me about her theory.

First, patriarchy is also extremely common among herding people, who are on the move all the time and have no use for ploughs. Their property—the herd—is easily divisible. Yet herding societies are generally far from egalitarian. It's true that the Wodaabe allow women to up and leave, but the male keeps the children. Other herders force their females into far more restricted lives. Among the tribes of Afghanistan and the Bedouin, the patriarch has formidable powers.

That's true of most other nomadic, herding cultures. Take Jacob Bronowski's description of the Bakhtiari in *The Ascent of Man:* "The role of women in nomad tribes is narrowly defined. Above all, the function of women is to produce men-children; too many she-children are an immediate misfortune, because in the long run they threaten disaster. Apart from that, their duties lie in preparing food and clothes. . . . But the girls and the women wait to eat until the men have eaten."[72] The Bakhtiari don't qualify as particularly harsh, either. Modern Saudis are the descendants of nomadic herders, and their women are among the most restricted in the world.

As I mentioned in an earlier chapter, Gerda Lerner and other feminist scholars have their own explanation for that: men got the idea of domesticating women and children from taming animals. It's an unpleasant idea, but a highly plausible one. Nonetheless, it does not answer my second problem with Fisher's theory: why would property, whether land or animals, aggravate men's desire to control their women and ensure the legitimacy of their children?

In all of my research, I have yet to come across a satisfactory solution to that mystery. Nonetheless, the theory seems, at least in part, to work. While there are many exceptions, it is possible to trace a pattern in the rise of human civilizations. They become less equal. It's true that the ancient Egyptians and Minoans were relatively egalitarian in the sexual roles of their upper classes, but they do not represent the norm. If you look at Rome, or at the successive empires of Sumeria, Babylonia and Assyria, what you find is an erosion of the rights of women, and the consolidation of male power.

At some point in the evolution of a complex culture, that process seems to start to reverse. Thus, in North America and much of Europe, the male desire to dominate a wife and many children appears to have waned sharply. The same thing is happening in Japan.

It's not just that a lot of men no longer want children. Those who do seem to want a new role within the family. For instance, many Japanese fathers are becoming understandably unhappy about their working hours and their consequent absence from their homes. (Japan failed to reach the government's official target of 1,800 annual work hours per worker by April 1992. The average number of hours in 1991 was 2,016.) In the 1980s, Japanese television commercials targeted the go-ahead worker, chained to his desk. Now the focus is shifting to what the journalist Jennifer Veale calls "soft and cuddly images of family life." One ad even showed a man cooking for his *wife*, a radical innovation. Between commercials, the comic father has become a staple in programs with names like *My Home Papa* and *Trendy Papa*.[73] In the context of Japanese society, the bumbling father represents an extraordinary break with tradition, one that may stem from male fatigue with the onerous roles of wage-earner and moral centre of the family.[74]

We don't really understand why any of these changes occur. We don't understand why fathers can be deeply involved or indifferent, brutal or affectionate, not just in different cultures, but within the same one. After an exhaustive review of research on fathers' involvement with their children, Patrice Engle and Cynthia Breaux concluded that men are more likely to participate fully in raising their children if their cultures encourage a high level of involvement, if they live with their wives and children, if their relationship with the wife is harmonious, if they are able to support their families financially and if they work with their wives in a co-operative way to provide that support.[75] It's a beginning, but those criteria exclude an awful lot of families and societies. Nor do they explain why fathers play such a feeble or negative role in so many cultures.

I can't find any genetic justification for some of the family systems humans have developed. Many of them create a great deal of misery for little benefit. It is true that the father's power to sell or kill a child can make sense in some contexts. Sacrificing one child may help the family as a whole to survive. A recent book on China's great famine of 1958 to 1962 claims that there were cases of infanticide and cannibalism among desperate families during those hungry years.[76] There were similar reports out of North Korea as it headed towards starvation in 1997.

But the case of the Palestinian refugee mentioned earlier in this chapter cannot be explained in those terms. In genetic terms, a son is of far more use to a family than an ailing grandfather. Some of our patterns of fatherhood seem to defy rational justification. The Victorian father who forbade his children to marry—as did Elizabeth Barrett's father—was committing genetic suicide. The man who marries off his daughter to some antiquated patriarch is doing no favours either to her or the human race.

Or consider the Mossi, a polygynous and patriarchal tribe in Burkina Faso. Among them, fathers and eldest sons live in permanent, simmering hatred. Fathers detest the offspring who will succeed them, those living reminders of their own mortality. Because of this, they try to avoid them. As one chief explained to an anthropologist, "Since he is going to inherit everything I own when I die, why should he come close to me now?"[77]

This is a far, far leap from the doting Aka and Trobriand father. To a far greater extent than motherhood, paternal behaviour is shaped by external forces and by the *ideas* that a man holds about the father's role. Its malleability is attracting more than academic interest these days, when the numbers of fatherless households are rising so sharply over almost all of the globe. (China is one large and notable exception.) The Western world is obsessed with the problem of paternity today. Politicians and writers deplore the absent father, Robert Bly mourns the damage he does his sons, and social analysts try to figure out where on earth he's gone.[78] Bill Moyers ran into considerable flak a few years ago for suggesting that irresponsible and missing fathers were the cause of much of the poverty in America's underclass, but that has become a respectable point of view now.

For some purposes we have even come to operate as if Dad were gone for good. In North America and Western Europe, social and health services increasingly devote their attention exclusively to mothers and children, as if the father did not exist.[79] One researcher has suggested that American social services of all kinds classify fathers as good or bad guys solely on the basis of their financial support of their families. There is no sympathy for the man who cannot find work, and no recognition of any other benefits to be derived from his presence in the family.[80]

At first glance, this may seem particularly strange because we're in the middle of a love affair with the idea of fatherhood. From *Kramer vs. Kramer* to 1997's *Fathers' Day,* Hollywood's favourite romance is the one between a man and his kids. Newspapers can routinely run lists of the dozen or so recommended new books on fatherhood to celebrate Dad's day each year. (For 1997, *The Globe and Mail*'s round-up included *The Prodigal Father: Reuniting Fathers and Their Children; Pregnant Fathers: Becoming the Father You Want to Be; The New Father's Panic Book: Everything a Dad Needs to Know to Welcome His Bundle of Joy; A Father's Book of the Spirit: Daily Meditations; The Sixty Minute Father: How Time Well Spent Can Change Your Child's Life;* and *Be a Man: Letters to My Grandson*— that last by actor and National Rifle Association aficionado Charlton Heston.[81]) And, as I've noted, this obsession with good fathering isn't simply a fantasy; there are men out there who are trying to live up to that rigorous ideal.

It's even possible that the two phenomena—the perfect father and the invisible one—are actually linked. In the early 1990s, I produced a radio series on intimacy and romance. In it, the psychologist Herb Goldberg (author of *The Inner Male, What Men Really Want* and a large number of similar self-help books) offered a novel and disturbing perspective on our contemporary fascination with relationships. He felt that the sixties were obsessed with community because it was dying, the eighties were obsessed with materialism because

the good life was ending, and the nineties had fixated on relationships because the ability to connect with other people was about to
disappear.[82] He conceded that pockets of genuine relationships might
survive, along with pockets of upward mobility and a few scattered
genuine communities. But his theory would suggest that the good
father is an endangered species.

There are schools of thought that wouldn't see him as much of
a loss. They define the nuclear family as an institution based on
power, rather than on affection or even the welfare of most of its
members. And there's no question that it is at least partly true. Many
past and contemporary societies seem to be organized largely to protect and hallow the rights of males.

But it's dangerous to dismiss fathers lightly, simply because we
may have managed without them until we came down from the trees.
Many of us are fortunate enough to have gentle and loving fathers,
who have enriched our lives enormously. Not just in the contemporary West but almost everywhere in the world, you can find families who feel real affection for one another. To see the nuclear family
strictly as a patriarchal invention is to deny the joy and fulfilment
many of us find in a family life that embraces *all* its members.

You don't have to turn to Freud to recognize that fathers have
become major players in the human psyche. Children in most cultures both want and need fathers. Half a century ago, Anna Freud
recorded the reactions of a four-year-old whose father died in
World War Two: "My daddy is killed, yes, my sister said so. He
cannot come. I want him to come. . . . My daddy is taking me to
the zoo today. He told me last night; he comes every night and sits
on my bed and talks to me."[83] Studies from the 1930s on have established that male children raised exclusively by women tend to be
angrier at females and more violent in general than boys from two-
parent homes.[84]

We are just starting to learn that the presence of a concerned
and loving father in a child's life brings a number of unexpected

benefits. A U.S. study has established that children with highly involved fathers score significantly higher on intelligence tests.[85] Statistics Canada has determined that children raised by single mothers have more behavioural problems and school failures than children raised in two-parent homes.[86] Children in Saudi Arabia even seem to suffer less from diarrhoea when their fathers are home.[87]

Finally, before we write off Dad, we should note a crucial difference between many of today's female-headed homes and fatherless families in some traditional cultures. In tribes where fathers do not figure much in their children's lives, substitutes tend to fill the gap. Other male relatives, elders or the hunting group help to raise the children. In such societies, the mother's brothers may take on many of the responsibilities we see as paternal. Economically, emotionally and spiritually, they act as the fathers of their nieces and nephews.

It would make sense for all cultures to encourage a strong relationship between fathers and children—but not all do. There are a number of societies that believe men are incapable of handling infants, for instance. But they can change. I grew up in a world where fathers were characterized by their incompetence with babies and toddlers. Yet most of the fathers I know today are whizzes with diapers, formula and play group. The Chinese traditionally believe that men and babies don't mix,[88] but the one-child policy has altered fathers' behaviour in the family dramatically. (Immigration seems to have the same effect. Many of the Asian fathers I see toting around babies in Toronto's Chinatown are obviously loving and able parents.)

We don't understand much yet about the extreme diversity of paternal behaviour. Fathers are influenced by the economies and cultures in which they live, the structure and nature of their families, their own natures and upbringing, and the characteristics of their children.[89]

That last factor is an important one. As we've seen, men generally prefer boys to girls. The child's own personality also plays a role: anyone copes better with a happy-go-lucky child than a chronically fretful one. Finally, most men want to be sure their children are truly their own. In almost all cultures, they greatly prefer their own children to other men's. We know that they generally care far less for stepchildren than for their biological ones. In many cultures, the legitimacy of their children is a male obsession.

That concern can ripple out from the actual couple involved to a much larger circle of relatives. Just like women, men in many cultures do not control their own relations with their spouses and children. They do not live in nuclear families, and their own wives and offspring may not be their closest ties. It is time to take our exploration of the family to its next level: to the large and complex tangles of kin who constitute a family in so many places.

One Big, Happy Family

A man is a bundle of relations, whose flower and fruitage is the world.
—Ralph Waldo Emerson, *Essays*, First Series, *History*

THE TORONTO TRANSIT COMMISSION traditionally offers a "family fare" late each summer, to encourage visitors to the Canadian National Exhibition to leave their cars at home. For a set price, you can take as many subways and buses as you want all day—as long as your family includes no more than six people, only two of them adults.

For much of the world, this would seem a pathetically inadequate number. In cultures that do not restrict fertility—by birth control, abortion or infanticide—the number of children alone can run into double digits. My own father was the youngest of seven children, not counting a stepsister by his father's previous marriage. Another friend was one of nine siblings, thanks in part to a set of twins.

Among Catholics, orthodox Jews and Moslems, and many other groups, those numbers would not set records. The average Saudi Arabian family has six to ten children.[1] Alex Shoumatoff interviewed a descendant of a former king of the Akan, a Ghanaian tribe. His informant told him that the king, Nana Sir Ofori-Atta, had about a hundred children by some twenty to twenty-five wives, plus a few mistresses.[2] The king would have needed an awful lot of family passes to get the kids to the midway.

As you can see from the last example, the allowance for *adults* would be a problem in many societies. Even in monogamous cultures, a household can contain far more than two adults. In much of Asia, Africa, southern Europe and Latin America, the nuclear family is not the standard household unit. You can see it as a tourist in India. The vacationing Hindu families at the Red Fort or Taj Mahal—people with enough money to go sightseeing for pleasure— often feature several adults of both sexes and a horde of children. As sociology texts tell us, Indians often live in what's called a "joint family," a variation of the extended family. In it, brothers and their wives and children share a home, even after their father has died.[3]

Now, there is a widespread assumption in our world that those big, complex extended families are the norm, and that our own nuclear family is an aberration. We've come to believe that people only started recently to live in what's known as the "conjugal unit" or the "family of procreation." (The family you grow up in is your family of orientation. You and your spouse and children form the family of procreation.) We've come to believe that until now, everyone everywhere lived in large, extended families—that people married and had children without ever leaving home. We picture an entire globe consisting of farmhouses crammed with grandparents and aunts and uncles and a horde of happy cousins.

This is simply not true. The anthropologist George Murdock, who compiled the seminal *World Ethnographic Sample*,[4] wrote that the nuclear family exists—alone or within or beside other models— in all cultures.[5]

In an analysis of our information about 192 societies, he found that 47 formed only nuclear families, 53 had polygamous but not extended families and 92 lived in some form of the extended family.[6] Later studies have established that nuclear families predominate in hunter-gatherer societies and in the most industrialized modern nations, with the extended family prevailing in cultures that depend on farming, especially farming combined with animal husbandry.[7]

The nuclear family is certainly embedded deeply in our own Western roots. The historian Beatrice Gottlieb has established that household size has been fairly small in much of Western Europe for a longer time than we had imagined.[8] In the northern countries, people married late—the average age for lower-class women was twenty-five—and only when they had the resources to let them live and work on their own, independent of their families.[9] The whole point of marriage was the establishment of a separate household. If you couldn't manage that, you postponed the wedding, quite possibly until the death of a parent brought you a little property of your own.

Alternatively, you might never get to marry at all. Gottlieb notes, "Historic demographers have suggested that single adults made up at the very least 5 percent of the population and in many places 20 or 25 percent."[10]

Nearer the Mediterranean, several generations and nuclear families might well share one overcrowded home, or palace, or farm, but many northern families could have moved comfortably into a contemporary bungalow. Gottlieb has looked at records going back to the thirteenth and fourteenth centuries, and found a consistent pattern. Large, complex households were the preserve of the top level of society—royalty and aristocrats. Our vision of the past has been skewed because we've focused on the more accessible and glamorous lives of the blue-blooded rich.

We make the same mistake when we look at the ancient Romans. Some of the imperial family lived together at times, quite possibly because the emperor had every reason to keep a sharp eye on his potentially treacherous relatives. But further down the social scale, the household unit was much smaller. Even in the later years of the Empire, when many Romans had amassed considerable wealth, the average domestic circle wasn't huge. The largest estate might house a *paterfamilias*, his wife, a few sons or unmarried daughters and, of course, some slaves.

Once the *paterfamilias* died, his sons became heads of families in their own right. As one historian notes, under these circumstances the Roman "felt no attachment to his brothers and uncles but that dictated by private feelings or family strategy. Whether or not a group of brothers would live together in the family mansion was simply a question of convenience and money."[11] Not everyone waited until the father's death to establish a separate residence. We know that sons of Cicero and his friend Celius rented an apartment precisely so that they wouldn't have to live with their parents.[12]

The average well-to-do Roman household looks crowded to us because of the addition of slaves and servants. That's normal: in the past, extended families often embraced not only blood kin, but menials who were seen as an integral, if inferior, part of the household. As late as the fifteenth century, a Florentine patrician named Leon Battista Alberti wrote *Della famiglia*, an inquiry into the quality that "exalts and ennobles families." His definition of the family included "Children, wife, other relatives, retainers, and servants."[13] I'll be returning to the issue of slaves as family later in this chapter.

There are many examples of Murdock's thesis that the nuclear family exists even when it is not a culture's dominant unit. Take the Hopi Indians. In the past, they seemed to live exclusively in extended kin groups. Like the Zuñi, they were traditionally matrilocal; a bridegroom moved in with his wife's mother and sisters.[14] (The extended family—the sib—can take many forms. In some cultures, notably among the Chinese, paternal kin absorb the women who marry in. Among others, like the Hopi, Zuñi and the Ashanti of Ghana, a husband joins his wife's family, and becomes a member of it.) Even today among the Hopi, the wife's mother may live with a couple if she's a widow. But the nuclear family was a force in their lives even before European values intruded. The bond between husband, wife and children had its own acknowledged importance. It was not a wrenching change for the Hopi to shift to the Western nuclear pattern. Today they generally live in conjugal units: man, wife, children.[15]

You can even find a kind of nuclear unit among the Marquesans, inhabitants of a clutch of islands near the northern limits of French Polynesia. They used to live in one of the world's rare polyandrous arrangements: a home could consist of a man and a woman, a woman and two or more men, and even two men and two women—the result of a married man setting up house with a married woman.[16] From our point of view, the relationships seem extended—perhaps rather too far—but the household is organized around the nucleus of the chief couple.

Of course, many of the world's major cultures do (or did) favour extended families. It was the ideal in pre-revolutionary China, where the model household consisted of "three or preferably more generations living under the same roof, constituting a household of some twenty, thirty, or more members, presided over by a head, or patriarch."[17] That would still seem a model arrangement in much of the Arab world and in parts of the sub-continent.

Similarly, the ancient Hebrew household included a patriarch, his wives and concubines, their young children, their grown sons and their wives and children, slaves, bond servants, and sometimes strangers, men who'd attached themselves to the group.[18] A group of related households constituted a clan, or *mishpochah*, the word still used by Jews to signify the extended family. The links between these kinsmen were strong; the biblical patriarchs were forever visiting relatives, or sending their sons off to work or marry among them.

The ancient Hebrews had what anthropologists call a "deep" kinship system, one going back many generations. Think of those long lists of "begats" in the Old Testament. In many cultures, death does not end membership in the extended family. Indeed, the anticipation of death, in a society that stresses family continuity, has a profound effect on life. Thus Orthodox Jews and Hindus have a religious duty to sire sons—for Jews, to say *Kaddish*, the prayer for the dead; for Hindus, to light the funeral pyre.

In some cultures, dead ancestors are not simply remembered, but worshipped. In ancient Greece, the father's power derived not only from his control of his estates, but from his role in the family's ancestor worship.[19] Some Inuit tribes believe that the souls of dead ancestors enter their children, which is why they never spank or mistreat them.[20] Ancestor worship is a cornerstone of traditional Chinese and Japanese societies; Japan's emperor still makes ceremonial reports to his forbears. The Victorian explorer Richard Burton noted that whenever a king in Dahomey (now Benin) wanted to share important information with his ancestors, he executed a couple of messengers to pass on the news in the next world.[21]

Many societies endorsed stronger ties between extended kin than between husband and wife, or even parent and child. (Some still do.) The warriors in the *Iliad* seem much more emotionally involved with their comrades than with their wives. The ancient Anglo-Saxons rarely mention the nuclear or conjugal family in their surviving literature. They focused on the group of kin we call a sib—the whole body of blood relatives, in their case both paternal and maternal.[22]

An individual had serious responsibilities to his sib, as did it to him. As in much of the Balkan world even now, loyalty to the sib entailed automatic involvement in any number of feuds. If a member of some other clan killed one of your people, you were required to exact revenge, or at least payment. Conversely, if one of your kin harmed someone else, his relatives were entitled to wreak vengeance on you.[23] If that responsibility became too onerous, it was possible to disown your sib. If you let them down, they could also disown you. And the consequences could be dire. A disowned person was by definition an outlaw, everyone's legitimate prey.

It is extremely difficult for most contemporary Westerners to imagine life in a culture where people feel closely connected to a network of dozens or even hundreds of relatives, where duty to a family or clan overrides the demands of marital love or any kind of personal fulfilment. To begin with, that kind of family organization often demands a more complexly shaded sense of kinship than we possess. The Baganda, a Ugandan tribe, possesses sixty-eight different words for various kinds of relatives.[24] Many other groups use different words to distinguish older and younger siblings. Where we are restricted to nieces or nephews, other cultures may have different terms to distinguish the children of a mother's brother from the children of a father's sister.

That makes perfect sense in cultures with more elaborate incest taboos than our own. If you're going to have to marry your father's sister's daughter, while his brother's girls are absolutely forbidden, you'd better have words that distinguish the two kinds of relationship. The distinction is equally important in societies that give you free sexual access to one type of cousin—but not the other—before marriage. (George Murdock found eleven groups that allowed premarital sex with a father's sister's daughter, and fourteen that offered the same privilege with a mother's brother's daughter.[25]) Under those circumstances, you need different words to underline who's illicit and who's fair game.

The values of these expansive, intricate families may contrast with ours in more radical ways. In some societies, it is perfectly normal to hand over your own child to be raised by relatives. Trobriand Islanders believe it benefits the child by creating strong ties with greater numbers of kin.[26] They do not see adoption as weakening the tie between child and biological parents. Among the Inuit, it was common for married couples to let relatives or the wife's mother adopt an infant—and obligatory for the unwed mother.[27] The Baganda routinely handed over their male children to a relative chosen by the son of the father's eldest brother. Girls lived in the home of an older married brother or with a paternal uncle.[28] The Baganda believe the practice saves children from being spoiled by the over-indulgence of their parents[29]—just as medieval and Renaissance parents packed their children off as apprentices or servants.

The practice clearly endured very late in our own culture. Jane Austen, writing about two centuries ago, has two characters whose parents give them up—Frank Churchill in *Emma*, and Fanny Price in *Mansfield Park*. But her treatment of them suggests that doubts were creeping in about the wisdom of the arrangement. With Fanny at least, Austen is at pains to stress the suffering of a child swept off to an alien home, never to be treated as a full member of her adoptive family. Moreover, both adoptions essentially sever the bond with the child's own family. Fanny and Frank spend years away from their true parents and siblings, creating an inevitable breach. Fanny's new family at Mansfield waits more than a decade before suggesting that she revisit her original home.

We live in a society that has trouble with the idea of parents giving up their children in this way. We do not really understand the emotional basis of life in cultures where blood ties extend so far and so strongly. The Baganda, for instance, live in a highly hierarchical culture, burdened with heavy obligations to their superiors. The Anglo-Saxons clung to a warrior's code that placed little emphasis on family affection or individual desires. Such societies routinely demand sacrifices from their members. Perhaps our closest equivalent would be the life of a dedicated Communist in the early years of the Russian or Chinese Revolutions, or even of a Nazi during the Third Reich.[30] But even these are only imitations of total, unself-conscious membership in a homogenous tribe or clan.

It has been fashionable for several decades to argue that there is something wrong with us and our preference for the nuclear family.

There is a pervasive nostalgia for big, cohesive families that embrace more than a man, a woman and their children. The anthropologist Robin Fox has called the nuclear family "an aberrant product of capitalism and affluence, a consequence of the mobility of labour."[31] Indeed, he believes the human capacity to recognize kinship—to form and maintain extended families—was a key factor in human evolution. Similarly, his colleague Lionel Tiger has suggested that marriage was originally just an instrument for creating an extended family network by uniting two sets of kin.[32]

Fox isn't the only scholar to deplore our loosening family ties. In the early 1980s, I discussed the issue with the historian Edward Shorter, while he waited to record a script for the radio show I worked for at the time. He told me that the nuclear family and the social isolation of North America might be fine for "media bunnies" like me, but the extended family worked much better for the bulk of mankind.

This preference for the extended family is not restricted to the academic world. In 1982, I spent a month in Malaysia, teaching a course on environmental broadcasting to radio personnel from a dozen Asian and Pacific countries. One of the other instructors, far more qualified than I, was a former head of All India Radio, P.V. Krishnamoorthy. He had grown up in Burma, fleeing at the time of the Japanese invasion, and he had fond memories of his early life. In particular, he loved the long visits of throngs of relatives. He liked the adventure of all of the children bedding down on cots on the verandah, to accommodate the masses of adults. He missed the reassuring, lively warmth of that community of relations.

But nostalgia for the extended family is not universal. In some communities, for instance, there's no need for nostalgia: the extended family isn't dead. During the same course, a Tamil university professor told me she dreaded the descent of her far-flung relations. For days or even weeks, she would find herself acting as cook, confidante and sightseeing guide, without the slightest concession to her full-time job. She would no longer have any time alone with a husband she adored. The hectic round of family obligations was incompatible with her chosen professional and personal life.

That desire for privacy can creep into the most traditionally gregarious groups. In 1942, the journalist Joseph Mitchell interviewed Johnny Nikanov, a gypsy patriarch in New York. Mitchell noted that it was normal practice for gypsy couples to share their homes with their adult offspring, at least the male ones. But Johnny and his wife lived separately from their kids. Their four sons shared a tenement a couple of blocks away with their wives and children—twenty-two people in all. Mitchell quoted Johnny, "I may be peculiar . . . but I like to have room enough to turn around in."[33] As materialism and individualism rise, people supposedly lose the capacity to enjoy life in the herd.

This development does not necessarily undercut the argument that extended families are more nurturing than nuclear ones. Advocates of large, multi-generational households acknowledge that people today often shrink from living in groups, but they see that as proof that something's gone wrong.

That idea percolates through the popular imagination. When people in the West picture the past, I think they tend to see an arrangement much like the early years of the Corleone family in the book and film versions of *The Godfather*. In that fictional world, the second generation spends a lot of its free time around Mamma's dinner table, with its respective boyfriends, girlfriends and eventually spouses. The sons work for the family business (evidently import-export and extortion), deferring to their father's judgment. The daughter marries someone in the same line of work, who can join the family's assorted enterprises. The story has as much to do with nostalgia for the intact family as it does with crime.

The proof lies in the crucial scene where Michael, the new godfather, tells his mother he worries he's losing the family. She simply cannot understand the concept. For her, it's impossible to lose the "famiglia." But Michael's fears are justified. His wife turns on him, aborting his third child. Both a brother-in-law and a brother play Judas, betraying him for money. In North America, you *can* lose your family, and many people do.

There is no question that this is in some ways a real loss. A strong, supportive extended family offers advantages—practical and emotional—that no mere conjugal unit can ever provide. It's hardly surprising, for instance, that the populations of the world's great rice-growing areas tend to live in extended families. Growing paddy rice in particular requires vast amounts of boring, back-breaking labour. You need lots of people to manage it successfully. But the yield is high. Under normal circumstances (i.e., barring floods or drought), you can feed a lot of people, too. Slash-and-burn agriculture in a tropical rain forest can support a maximum of fifty people per square kilometre, but rice plantations in Bali can support more than one thousand.[34] An industrious family can feed itself and sell the surplus.

This doesn't mean that the extended family always makes economic sense. The story is different where land is less fertile and crops less productive. For Natalie Zemon Davis, for instance, there is no mystery about the small size of the average household in pre-modern northern Europe. Married couples generally set up their own homes rather than moving in with their parents because farms could not produce enough food to feed a large, multi-generational family. In an interview, she pronounced firmly that "the land would not support it."

In general, however, the extended family is most popular in agricultural economies, especially ones where technology is fairly primitive. The need for lots of labour is only one factor here. The extended family also offers the advantage of keeping the family property intact. Canadians are familiar with the thin ribbons of land along the St. Lawrence River, the result of estates being divided and redivided as each generation inherited the family property. An extended family can avoid all that; its members (the male ones, anyway) can continue to own the whole thing communally. In some cultures, as we've seen, the concern for property is so strong that blood kin have to marry to preserve it.

Extended ties can prove useful under other conditions. A nuclear family is not the ideal unit, for instance, for hunting buffalo. Elsewhere, nomadic herders may well do better by pooling a large flock and caring for it together. Apart from any other consideration, a large group will have a better chance against raids by rival nomadic herders. It's no wonder that the nuclear family is so rare in primitive societies. In the middle of a rain forest, you are apt to want the company of lots of others—plus a variety of people gathering or hunting every possible source of food.

The extended family is also more resilient than the nuclear family, a powerful benefit in societies that treasure order and tradition. A nuclear family's survival depends on two adults at most, and inevitably dies with each generation. (As proof of that, when I ask my journalism classes how much they know about their grandparents, a sizable minority cannot even name all four.) So nuclear families are of no use for preserving family traditions. An extended family does not rely on individuals for survival. It stretches back to the ancestors, and forward to all its posterity.[35]

This has practical advantages, as well as spiritual ones. Before our era of telephones, faxes and e-mail, for instance, bankers could certainly use strong family connections. The most conspicuous example would be the Rothschilds. In the eighteenth and nineteenth centuries, brothers in London, Paris, Vienna, Frankfurt and Naples all were running branches of the family firm, "all shrewdly managed and working in close collaboration with one another."[36] Technology has not destroyed all the advantages of keeping a multinational business in the hands of close kin. The Rothschild family remains a formidable force in the financial world today. The Hunt brothers, the Reichmanns and the Bronfmans all provide contemporary examples of dynastic business empires.

To survive, however, any form of family has to be able to adapt to changing circumstances. The Lins, Nora Waln's hosts in *The House of Exile,* managed that trick at least until the Chinese Revolution. By the time Waln arrived in the 1920s, the family had added a number of business ventures to its original agricultural base. It had found new markets for its crops—sending strawberries, for instance, to the European enclave in Beijing. Everyone had a role in the endless round of work this entailed; everyone shared in the prosperity it created.

The Lins' domestic relations were distinguished by harmony and consideration. They cared deeply about the happiness of all family members, including those who married in. They invoked the memory of an earlier bride at each marriage, telling the nervous young wife, "May you be as happy as the maid from Canton."[37] At times they managed to accommodate individual desires that would have splintered a less resilient group. Thus, instead of disowning the rebel son who abandoned his official wife, they designated his northern home a branch of the family, retaining both personal and economic ties with it. The words "Better establish a branch than cut off a line" were chiselled over the front gate of the House of Exile.[38]

But there is a darker side to life in an extended family. In less happy and generous families than the Lins, a bride's feelings may not count for much. Indeed, she may be seen only as a commodity, or India would not have the continuing problem of bride-burnings. These horrific murders—largely, let it be noted, a middle-class phenomenon—occur when the girl's family can't come up with the dowry her in-laws believe they're owed. The usual method is to douse the victim with kerosene as the women cook, then set her on fire. Given that so many of these deaths happen in the kitchen, the killers are often the victim's mother- or sisters-in-law.

This murderous hostility can extend even to grandchildren, despite the blood they share with the paternal family. In 1996, a British Columbia court sentenced Rashida Khan to life in prison on a charge of second-degree murder. Her husband, Abdur Khan, had already been convicted in an earlier trial of murdering Naazish Khan, his daughter-in-law, and her baby daughter, his grandchild. Naazish, a Hindu, had married the Khans' son Faisal over the objections of his Muslim family. In 1993, her beaten and strangled body was found in the trunk of the family car in Coquitlam, BC.[39]

There were no murders in the extended family Sarah Hobson studied in southern India.[40] Their community, the Gowdas of Karnataka, maintains practices rather different from those of most Hindus: they permit widows to remarry, for instance. They also encourage the marriage of uncles to nieces. Murder is presumably less of a risk for blood relatives. Yet, despite the blood relationship, some of the wives got along very badly with their marital families. (Anthropologists routinely assume that close relatives—sisters, for example—will get along better than strangers. Anyone with sisters knows better.) One son's wife, Susheelamma, constantly infuriated her father-in-law by sullenly ignoring his orders.[41]

Her resentment makes sense in the context of her in-laws' attitudes towards the wives. Susheelamma's husband told Hobson proudly, "I wouldn't beat her, not while she's pregnant"[42]—making it clear that it's open season the rest of the time. Nor would his parents or brothers intervene to defend her. As Hobson notes, "After all, they were only the women who had been brought to the house as daughters-in-law; the house was not theirs, the land was not theirs, even their sons belonged to the house and not to them."[43] Understandably, none of the daughters-in-law was happy. All of them seethed with anger against the family, essentially their owners.

This is not at all unusual. Extended families like to exercise control, in ways that can be galling. The mother of a friend of mine, a Sikh, told me in an interview that she and her husband did not have sex for several days after their arranged marriage. Her mother-in-law decided when they could go to bed together. Among the villagers of Deh Koh, in rural Iran, resentment between in-laws frequently runs so high that women leave their husbands to return to their original families.[44] (They usually end up creeping back. Their own extended families aren't terribly supportive, either.)

That is the issue that fans of the extended family tend to ignore: the struggle for power. Extended families, like any other kind, are not simply about providing everyone with financial and emotional support. They are also about trying to control other people, especially the newcomers to the group. In a quarrelsome, unhappy family—and there are lots of them—life isn't much fun at the bottom of the pecking order.

For the extended family is not necessarily a haven of warmth and affection. Underscoring that truth is the brutal reality that it often embraces not just relatives by blood and marriage, but servants and slaves. And these attendants often function as parts of the family. Forget the formality and separation that characterized the relations of master and servant in the British TV series *Upstairs, Downstairs.* In pre-modern societies, before privacy became a concern, the help lived very much with their masters, sharing their lives, their activities and often their beds.[45]

The owning class often romanticized that relationship. Both Tolstoy and Gogol show Russian masters enjoying affectionate bantering with their serfs. In *Gone with the Wind,* Margaret Mitchell (writing long after the end of American slavery) makes the figure of Mammy the moral centre of Scarlett O'Hara's postwar home. Some real-life slaves clearly came to feel genuine identification and loyalty. In Rome, for instance, if the family were a prosperous one, the home often accommodated freed slaves who'd chosen not to leave after their emancipation.[46]

Nor were slaves ever mere automatons. Human beings cannot experience themselves as property, even if they wish to do so. The cheeky servants of comic opera and the grumbling serfs in Chekhov's plays testify to the difficulty of fully controlling menials.

Precisely because of that difficulty, there's a general assumption that the first slaves were not loyal family retainers. On the contrary, they would have been captives, conquered in war. Precisely because people are so hard to control, the victors almost certainly killed or maimed their male prisoners.[47] This brutal practice did not die out with antiquity. In the early Middle Ages, it was standard wartime practice after the capture of a city to kill anyone "who could piss against the wall"—all males over the age of about three.[48] Females, however, would be easier to manage. Indeed, you had a fair chance of subduing them completely in time, by raping them and then using their offspring as hostages for their good behaviour.

Under these conditions, it seems certain that slaves would not originally be regarded as an extension of the family. They would be closer in status and image to the animals man had domesticated. Denying them fully human status would be easier in the many societies that enslaved only outsiders. Around the Mediterranean, for instance, the Greeks, Romans and Jews were not allowed to own slaves who belonged to their own people. Romans did not have Roman slaves, and so on.[49]

For some slaves—indeed, for some entire cultures—relations never became any warmer or kinder than that. Spartan society, to choose one striking example, involved capturing slaves through war and keeping these communally owned workers—the Helots—in their miserable place.[50] In ancient Greece, slaves in the mines were routinely worked to death;[51] in Rome, galley slaves lived brief lives of unspeakable suffering.

But domestic slaves are another story. If you live closely with someone over a period of time, some sort of relationship inevitably develops. How did these attendants fit into the pattern of family life? We can never truly know. Contemporary stories of servitude would not suggest a happy association. But then, we only hear the horror stories—the servant from the Philippines facing charges for murdering her abusive Saudi employer, the Western nanny caring for someone else's indulged children at the price of raising her own. Moreover, attitudes towards servants and slaves are so different in our own period that we cannot recapture the flavour of earlier eras.

The pictures we get of earlier ages are in any case contradictory. Historians sympathetic to the cultures they record take pains to stress the kindness shown to slaves. Thus Jérôme Carcopino, in *Daily Life in Ancient Rome,* notes of the Romans: "They had always treated their slaves with consideration, as Cato had treated his plough oxen . . ."[52] He does not mean this ironically. The sentence which precedes this extraordinary judgment reads: "The practical good sense of the Romans, no less than the fundamental humanity instinctive in their peasant hearts, had always kept them from showing cruelty to the *servi.*"

If that is so, it's a little difficult to make sense of the slave rebellion under Spartacus. But Carcopino does have some justification for his praise of Roman restraint. Unlike, for example, some slave-owners in the pre–Civil War American South, the Romans recognized that slaves were fully human—that they had souls.[53] Nonetheless, the slave was considered an inferior human being, because he was owned. Roman kindness, as might be expected, was not invariable. The poet Ovid had to remind his readers that scratching or stabbing a slave with a needle was unattractive and unlady-like behaviour.[54] Similarly, Juvenal satirized the miserly master who "pinches the bellies of his slaves."[55]

Because our own images of slavery derive so largely from the American South, we tend to overlook the varied meanings and status that different cultures assigned to the word "slave." Many slave-holding cultures restricted the master's rights. From the beginning of the Empire, a Roman master could not deliver his slave to the beasts of the amphitheatre without obtaining authorization.[56] Roman law was in some ways merciful: it did not treat a slave as a runaway if he had fled his master's home to beg one of the master's friends to intercede for him.[57] Towards the middle of the first century, the Emperor Claudius ruled that if a master abandoned a sick or infirm slave, that slave was to be granted his freedom—a dubious benefit under the circumstances, but no doubt kindly meant. Nero ensured that slaves had a forum to complain about their owners' injustice. By A.D. 83, the Roman had lost the right to castrate his slaves. It was clearly a privilege that Romans cherished, since in the next century Hadrian doubled the penalty for breaking the law.[58] He also made it illegal for masters to sell slaves to either a procurer or a trainer of gladiators.[59]

It is true that in the early years of the Republic, Romans had the right to kill their slaves—but they held the same power over every family member. By the time of Hadrian, they could no longer kill off the humans they owned without judicial sanction. There was clearly a progression in the Roman attitude towards slaves. By about A.D. 200, for instance, slaves were allowed to marry. The historian Paul Veyne notes that "it had previously been unthinkable that these childlike creatures should have families."[60]

Within the home, some slaves were unquestionably treated with affection. But the nature of that kindness might well be ambiguous. Among the later Romans, a fad developed for keeping a juvenile slave as a pet—much like a film star fussing over her poodle. A pretty child might be treated as a toy, quite possibly a sexual plaything.[61] These pampered favourites faced a cruel disillusionment when they reached adolescence, when they returned to a life of drudgery.

Sexual relations with slaves were normally less open and less precious. Obviously, if you own a human being, you own his or her sexuality. In Greece, in Rome, in China, the slave was a licensed sexual outlet for the patriarch and the sons of the house. The efficient owner took care to regulate the reproduction of his slaves. In Greece, where it was desirable to limit the population, a man might force a pregnant slave or concubine to abort.[62] In Rome, a more prosperous society, a master would take steps to ensure reproduction. Thus, the sale of a sterile female slave was the occasion of legal controversy. It was decided on the basis of a legal precedent involving livestock: the sale of a spayed sow was invalid if the buyer had not been warned of the operation before the purchase.[63]

The presence of slaves—sleeping with the master, bearing his children—has to have affected family life very strongly. Aside from any other consideration, a household would contain half-siblings of completely different status—some free and legitimate, some captive and unacknowledged. (The Roman could free his enslaved offspring, but never adopt or legitimize them.[64]) It creates the eerie sensation you can get in small towns in the American South or parts of South Africa, the recognition that the populace is openly divided by race but secretly united by shared blood.

It would be an error, obviously, to assume that the reactions of other cultures would be identical to our own. The slave-holding household would not always have seethed with the jealous tensions familiar from *Roots*, or the historical fiction of Frank Yerby. Some women presumably repressed any jealousy of the slaves their husbands favoured; perhaps they welcomed a respite from sex and its consequences. We know that some Roman matrons thoughtfully provided their husbands with suitable concubines and slaves. Livia, wife of the Emperor Augustus, went so far as to hunt out virgins for her husband.[65]

You can see why it is so difficult to reconstruct the emotions of vanished cultures. Try to imagine the modern equivalent of the considerate Roman wife: a contemporary woman selecting a nanny or cleaning woman as a suitable mistress for her partner, or scrutinizing her friends' daughters to identify a likely virgin. And even that is not the greatest gulf that yawns between us and Romans. For in that society and several others, the patriarch is free to enjoy sex not only with his slaves, but with those slaves' children.

I do not think it is excessively judgmental to suggest that such a system would have, at the very least, a detrimental effect on family life. The knowledge that your father is diddling your little playmates (and possibly half-siblings) strikes me as unwholesome, and unlikely to promote family trust and security.

I think it's also important to dispute the idea that people inevitably treat slaves well and wisely because that is in their self-interest. I first encountered that argument in junior high school, when a history teacher suggested that Afro-Americans might have been better off *before* Emancipation. She reasoned that slave owners would at least have taken care of their property. Perhaps she was playing devil's advocate; perhaps she genuinely held this offensive view. In either case, she was wrong. People are not always rational, especially about other people. We know that many owners treated their slaves very badly indeed, either out of emotional compulsion or because they were simply very stupid.

As a final point on this subject, it's interesting that child-care is one of the first tasks to fall to voluntary or involuntary servants. In Rome and Greece in particular, slaves were often the primary child-minders. Boys from respectable Roman homes never went out without an attending servant or slave, the *custos*, "for there was as much concern for their virtue as for that of the fair sex."[66] (This concern gives us an idea of the prevailing moral climate in the classical civilizations.) Young girls, of course, rarely went out at all, which probably meant that they passed a great deal of their time in the company of servants.

This tendency to slough the children off onto the help did not end with antiquity. Until the modern period, a French child of the aristocracy was raised—to use the term loosely—among the servants as a matter of course. Well into this century, the British nanny was certainly the closest thing to a mother that her upper-class charges were likely to know.

Even today, there are close equivalents. I remember a television documentary that I saw a number of years ago, in which young adults from the American South were filmed with their families' (inevitably black) servants. Understandably, many of them had stronger feelings for the women who'd raised them than for their biological parents. Nonetheless, almost none of them had trouble with their beloved pseudo-parents' rock-bottom wages and deplorable living conditions. One snippy young woman explained complacently that a servant wouldn't appreciate really nice things anyway so there was no point in making it possible for her to own any.

You don't have to be a political liberal to see this as unhealthy. It's a system that means that children forge their closest ties with someone they are eventually taught to despise. Yet it has been a way of life for millennia among the upper classes. Nor do I think it's disappeared today—or I wouldn't know so many Canadian pre-schoolers who talk with the marked Tagalog accent they've picked up from their Filipina nannies.

Nonetheless, there is a striking difference between our attitudes and those of past cultures. We're not comfortable about all this. We don't have maids or valets; a lot of us can barely deal with the guilt of employing a cleaning woman. (Like every other woman I know, I try to clean up *before* mine arrives.) Above all, most of the mothers I know don't feel good about leaving their offspring in a nanny's care. They're careful to stress the special qualities of this particular nanny—her intelligence, her love of children, her exalted status in the family. But that doesn't really soothe the guilt women in our society feel if they don't want to be with their children all day, every day. It might be a consolation to recognize that other societies cheerfully assumed that raising children was exactly the kind of job that you'd most want to leave to someone else.

I have dwelt at such length on slaves and servants to underline the issue of power in the extended family. Obviously, not all societies that favour extended households practise slavery. Many don't even have servants. But a strong sense of kinship can co-exist comfortably with the ownership of outsiders, and I think that will inevitably flavour the relations of the family itself. The line between slave and kin can be a thin one. There are still places where families can and do sell daughters to procurers. The callousness that allows people to trade other humans does not end with slavery. Extended families can and do sometimes treat some of their members as property. Status and self-interest may loom larger than more humane values.

Moreover, it is more difficult to work your way up the ladder in the traditional societies that favour extended families. They tend to assign value arbitrarily, rather than on any rational basis. For instance, when I first read Sarah Hobson's *Family Web*, I was struck by the family's consistent undervaluation of the women's work. The patriarch of the family complained constantly that the women did nothing, although they spent more hours a day labouring than anyone else. I've learned since that this is a consistent pattern around the world: work performed by women is rarely seen as valuable.

This delusion has profound effects. Since women are seen as less valuable, they often receive less to eat. In many cultures, they have to wait until the men have finished their meal—women eat what's left over. Yet women in many of these cultures do most of the hardest work—hauling water and wood, carrying the bulk of a nomadic family's possessions, farming. They are also often pregnant or nursing. If a culture wants healthy children, it's chosen a disastrous formula for allocating food.

No matter how low their status, however, women are rarely completely powerless. Even where they control no property, they can fall back on emotional weapons. These do nothing for the quality of domestic life, since they include sulking, scheming, open battle and even violence. Perhaps the most formidable instrument is the tongue. Fans of the extended family tend to ignore its capacity for creating drama and myth, for colouring or simply inventing conflict and scandal.

To take a wonderful example from Deh Koh: one young bride,

Golgol, lived initially with her husband in a rather desolate spot, at a distance from her own family. His family took turns spending time with the young couple. Shortly after a miscarriage Golgol returned home.

In the mouths of a variety of relatives, these events took on an amorphous life of their own. Her mother argued that if she hadn't been left alone in the wilderness all day, Golgol wouldn't have been startled by the local lunatic—which caused the miscarriage. The mother-in-law countered that Golgol failed to take sensible precautions—namely, amulets, fumigations and special beads—which caused the miscarriage. But Golgol's aunt said a bead *caused* the miscarriage—a "child-bead" to promote fertility, deadly to the unborn, and worn, of course, by one of Golgol's in-laws, Huri. Meanwhile, in Huri's version of the story, it was just bad luck that Golgol was alone when the earthquake—no one else had mentioned an earthquake—sent a wall toppling, startling Golgol and causing the miscarriage.[67] Unsurprisingly, Erika Friedl notes that the people of Deh Koh have words for "truth" and "right" and "correct"—but not for "fact."[68]

This storytelling is a major feature of life in the closed extended family. It lets off steam and enlivens an often monotonous existence. I myself have always enjoyed the assorted scandals of my own families, told and retold and embroidered over the decades. This kind of intra-family gossip and fiction can be extremely spiteful. The writer Clark Blaise was shocked by the scandal-mongering of his in-laws when he visited his wife's family in Bengal. At a family wedding, he noted: "Women who would blush in shame at a rendition of the commonest Western novels and movies will tell scandalous stories about people they hate within the family, of their infidelities, witchcraft, dishonesty, embezzlement, hoarding, favoritism, selfishness, impurity. Nothing is left out; husbands' impotence, the rape in childhood, promiscuousness of nieces, ingratitude of nephews."[69]

Blaise came to understand that these tales weren't meant to be taken literally; they were a symbolic expression of resentment and frustration. I've seen the same malicious spirit of invention at Indian weddings I've attended. At one, a complete stranger insisted on telling me—in the women's washroom—all about the bride's sister's shameful affair with a married man. She persisted even after I pointed out that I was not only a guest of the bride, but a friend of her allegedly disgraceful sister.

There are compensations for this frequent atmosphere of intrigue, of course. Advocates of the extended family often argue that it provides options. If a boy is getting along badly with his father, he can pay an extended visit to an uncle. If a mother doesn't have much time for her daughters, their grandmother can provide a balancing affection. And, to be fair, it often does work that way. At the height of a battle between bride and in-laws in Deh Koh, one of the sisters of the house takes herself off to an aunt for a breather.

But the extended family can also narrow a person's options. In the matriarchal pattern of family life sometimes called the Jamaican model, ties between blood relatives on the mother's side are very strong. As one anthropologist notes: "Some people are so kin-oriented as to believe that close friendships should be maintained only between close relatives, never between unrelated persons."[70] That's great if you like your relatives, and they like and respect you. It's not so terrific if they bore you to tears. It's even worse if they don't think much of you.

The danger is that extended families, just like nuclear ones, have a tendency to assign roles and even characters to their members arbitrarily. I write as the third generation of a three-daughter constellation on my mother's side. I am the eldest daughter, like my mother and grandmother. I was raised to be sensible and responsible, a caregiver—a role somewhat thwarted by my extreme selfishness. The second daughters were expected to be the rebels; all of them have lived up to that expectation. The third, the baby, is the family charmer.

That's relatively innocuous. But such roles can be extremely confining, even untenable. In *Sanity, Madness and the Family,*[71] by R.D. Laing and A. Esterson, the authors discuss the assigning of roles in the families of schizophrenics. The patients' parents tended to ascribe character traits and ideas to them with no reference to the patients' actual words or natures. Thus, one religious family continued to assert stoutly that their daughter never hankered after forbidden activities, a comprehensive list that embraced going to movies or dances, wearing make-up and dating men from outside their church. Yet the unfortunate patient not only wanted to do all those things; she had actually done them.[72] The identity assigned to her was impossibly limited and contradictory. Even though she'd suffered repeated breakdowns, her family (and especially her husband) continued to see her as very strong.

I remember feeling uneasily, when I first read the book, that the families of non-schizophrenics tend to do the same sort of thing in a milder way. That's fine if it covers trivial traits—like Joseph Heller's anti-hero in *Good as Gold,* who has to keep oversalting his food because his sisters are convinced that's what he likes. It's less comfortable if the family image is that you're incompetent—like V.S. Naipaul's Mr. Biswas. The extended family *can* offer respect and emotional closeness to all its members—as witness the Lins—but it is also capable of reducing its relations to a formula. More people do not always equal more closeness; they can add up to no closeness, no intimacy at all.

Fans of the extended family sometimes claim that this lack of personal fulfilment is relatively unimportant—that we value our emotional lives more than people in traditional cultures did. Extended families are most common, after all, among groups who haven't developed the individualism and materialism that characterize our society. To some extent, I agree. But I think it's possible to exaggerate our differences. It is popular now, as we've seen, to argue that our kind of romantic love is a recent innovation. Yet clearly, it is not. In the same way, I suspect that people everywhere want and need love and respect in their relationships—plus intimate connections to at least a few people. I believe that people who were isolated and unvalued within their families suffered just as we would. I even suspect that married couples, constricted within sharply defined roles, may have longed for precisely the kind of intimacy that we value.

That's not a fashionable view at the moment. The San Francisco psychotherapist John Welwood (the author of *Love and Awakening*[73]) preaches that family and marital intimacy are innovations unknown to our ancestors. He argues that personal intimacy is a new idea, irrelevant in marriages before this century. For instance, he believes that most married couples throughout history never discussed the quality of their relationship, or developed any conscious awareness of it.

Perhaps, but I see considerable evidence to the contrary. If earlier people had no emotional closeness, no need to share their feelings, why does the biblical Elkanah ask his wife, "Hannah, why weepest thou? and why eatest thou not? and why is thy heart grieved? am not I better to thee than ten sons?"[74] Natalie Zemon Davis, making the same point, said in an interview that Bertrande, the wife of Martin Guerre, told the court she believed an impostor was her husband because he knew the special words of love she liked to hear in bed. Bertrande must have been lying—but her defence makes it clear that sex was not merely an animal act for her and for the people around her.

Glückel of Hameln, a Jewish merchant's wife of the seventeenth century, provides a more telling example.[75] She left us a book written for her children, meant to encourage them to remember their beloved father and to lead moral lives. Glückel was betrothed at twelve to a man she had never met. She married him two years later. It took some time before they could set up house on their own.

The young couple lived for a year with his parents in Hameln before moving to Hamburg—where they lived with *her* parents.

If we can trust Glückel, the ties to their extended families did not weaken their own bond. She wrote that her husband "loved his wife and children beyond all measure."[76] They did not have an egalitarian relationship; he addressed her, for instance, as "child." But when she lost him, she sat down in 1690 to write her memoirs "[i]n my great grief and for my heart's ease . . ."[77] Describing his death, she wrote: "All his life my beloved companion hearkened to my troubles, and they were many, and comforted me so that somehow they would quickly vanish."[78] That sounds like intimacy to me.

I think there may be a confusion here between feeling and vocabulary. Samuel Pepys's poor wife, Elizabeth, lived too early to talk of co-dependency and the loss of intimacy on the occasions when she caught him philandering. She couldn't sit down to discuss healing their relationship. But I believe she felt more than wounded pride and sexual jealousy. She was hurt precisely because he was destroying her own trust in him, their intimacy as a married couple.

So I believe it's dangerous to assume that our emotional needs are radically different from those of earlier generations. They, too, may have longed at times for more privacy, more power, more intimacy than an extended family can generally offer. Because few of us now know how it feels to live tied to a cluster of kin, I think we tend to romanticize that kind of family.

When a sophisticated intellectual starts arguing for the benefits of the extended-family system, I'm irresistibly reminded of a lecture on China I attended years ago. The speaker's only criticisms of the entire country were levelled at her guide. "All he wanted to do was eat," she noted scornfully. A decidedly plump woman herself, she continued her tirade after the lecture, punctuating her rant by popping cookies into her mouth.

The intellectual fans of the extended family seem to me to suffer from a similarly blind self-righteousness. They want the rest of the world to live in large, tight clans, while many of them could not endure a three-day visit from their in-laws. They want a way of life for the general public that they could not tolerate themselves.

Nor do I buy the idea that extended families are somehow more natural than nuclear ones. Our animal relatives offer a range of options. Thus, while chimpanzees generally live in troops, individuals often wander off on their own. Young males and females may change troops, just like a graduate heading out to a new city today. A male, as we've seen, may lead a female into seclusion for days, or even weeks. Chimpanzees have a choice of extreme sociability or relative solitude—and so do we.

It's possible that scholars value the extended family so highly because its survival is endangered. In my travels in Asia, I've noticed the tendency to see the nuclear family as modern and up-to-date—a good in itself. I have to admit that the result of this attitude can be disastrous. One classic case is the Asmat tribe of New Guinea's Casuarina coast, now under the control of Indonesia.

The Asmat traditionally lived in extended families of up to two hundred people. But from the 1970s, Indonesia has been forcing them to live in nuclear families. The change has destroyed the co-operative day-care system that used to give mothers time to fish. The couples, together all day, grow bored with one another. The change was both abrupt and counterproductive; it is destroying the Asmat way of life.[79]

The Asmat situation is highly unusual; social change is rarely so dramatic. But it's easy to trace the same pattern among Third World immigrants to the West. It takes more time—usually at least one generation—but they almost inevitably abandon their traditional family structures.

It's easy to trace the transformation. A favourite slanderous complaint about recent immigrants to the West is that they live sixteen to a room. Germans say it about Turks, Canadians about Somalis,

Britons about Pakistanis. Two generations ago, you heard the same thing about Italians, Portuguese, Jews.

It's an exaggeration that reflects two realities. Recent immigrants often can't afford spacious housing, and many of them come from places where people are accustomed to limited personal space. In the last century, for instance, the first census in India found that the Todas, a polyandrous group, lived in huts of eight feet by ten feet—about the size of a modern breakfast nook—shared by an average of six persons.[80] Moreover, even that tiny space wasn't available to all members of the family. Women were supposed to keep to the rear, leaving the front free for the men to do their work. If you're used to similar conditions, you can probably cope with ten or a dozen people in one Western apartment.

But your children won't. They will develop the Western desire for a great deal of space. The offspring of the Jews and Italians who packed two large families into one small house live very differently today. They want big bedrooms, separate washrooms and large, imposing public rooms. Childless professional couples today routinely occupy older homes meant to accommodate two families. Men and women who grew up living three to a bedroom have kids who would regard having to share a bedroom as an intolerable violation of their God-given rights.

Note that recent immigrants often share their homes with extended family: sisters, brothers, aunts, uncles, plus their spouses and children. In their early years in Canada, my father's parents lived with my grandfather's brother—and shared a business with him, too, until some quarrel lost in the mists of time severed the relationship. When my mother's father died, she and her mother and her sisters moved in with an aunt. Necessity kept the extended family strong.

The ties are still fairly strong in both my extended families, but no one even considers living with a relative. We all have separate careers, too—there are no family partnerships. The reason is simple. In an industrialized society, you usually don't need them. There's normally no advantage to that kind of family cohesiveness once a group has established itself. It may be cheaper to share housing with relatives, but people clearly find it less pleasant when they have the choice. A family business may be useful while a set of new-comers is adapting to a new country, but after that most of us like to strike out on our own.

As the new values start to intrude, moreover, family ties frequently sour. My paternal grandfather's break with his brother is typical. In one Indian family I know, the marriages of two daughters have fallen apart. Both marriages were arranged; both bride-grooms immigrated to Canada to marry. It's possible that my friends simply chose badly, but the closeness of the wives' families was also clearly a factor. The men simply couldn't take the constant inter-ference of their in-laws. On the sub-continent, the wives' kin would have played a decidedly minor role in the couples' lives; the hus-bands' families would have dominated and absorbed the brides. Divorce is still such a scandal there that the couples might have found ways to compromise. In Canada, without the traditional social con-trols and rules, the marriages simply disintegrated.

Another, nastier case in the Chinese community illustrates the same problem. In 1996, in Toronto, a woman named Penny Cheng sued her in-laws for support.[81] She was born and raised in Canada. She had sponsored her husband, Peter Cheng, his parents and his aunt as immigrants to Canada. Her in-laws, she said, agreed to support her if she fulfilled her traditional responsibilities as a wife. By 1996, she had three children. The whole family lived together. Penny says she worked for them, running an apartment complex; her husband acted as chauffeur and translator for his parents.

In 1992, the Cheng parents said they had bought their own con-dominium; Peter would go with them for a few days to help with the move. He never came back. Three months later, his family read Penny a prepared statement, saying their financial circumstances had changed and they could no longer support her and her children.

They had already closed her joint accounts with her husband and cut off her credit cards. She then sued them for support.

She believes today that her marriage was simply a trick to get her husband's family to Canada. Their behaviour would be very difficult in traditional China. Divorce in that society is only possible under very specific conditions. There are only seven grounds for returning a woman to her birth family: "barrenness, wanton conduct, discourtesy, gossip, theft, discontented envy of others, or an infirmity misrepresented in the betrothal contract."[82] Penny Cheng was guilty of none of them.

Even today in China, it would be virtually impossible to deny support to a wife who had worked hard and had children—especially male children. Moreover, a marriage in China was and to some extent still is an alliance of two families. There, it might prove dangerous to offend Penny's family so deeply. The new environment of this country sharply alters the pattern of family relationships.

The problem is not limited to the Chinese community. Indians will be more familiar with a case that's achieved a certain fame, because one member of the extended family was a minor celebrity. In 1996, a court in Bangalore, India, permitted a family to return to the United States after their arrest over a dowry dispute. One of the accused was Balamurali Ambati, a prodigy who became a doctor at the age of seventeen. The Ambatis had been arrested in late 1995 on charges of harassing Balamurali's sister-in-law, the wife of his brother Jayakrishna. The wife, Archana, claimed the family had forced her to agree to a divorce in New York after her family failed to deliver the full amount of the dowry they owed: $16,370. The family denied the charges, and left the mother, Gomati, behind in India as a guarantee they would return for the trial.[83]

These are not isolated abuses. An article in *The Toronto Star* in 1995 found many cases of mistreatment.[84] Some women complained that their husbands had confiscated their passports and abandoned them in their home countries. Toronto lawyer Nola Crew supported their claims, saying the husbands frequently take their wives home for a "visit," dump them, then confiscate their passports and other identification. When they return to Canada—or the United States—the men tell the immigration authorities that they've separated from their wives.

Women who remain in the new country may face a different set of problems. Crew told the *Star* that many immigrant wives live under the constant threat of divorce and subsequent deportation; their husbands use it to keep them under total control. The women can end up as little more than unpaid servants for their in-laws. In one case, the new wife's husband stopped sleeping or talking with her after the first month. She continued to put in twelve-hour shifts at a factory, handing over her entire pay-cheque to her rapacious in-laws.

In spite of all this, a Toronto psychiatrist who works with recent immigrants believes the advantages of an extended-family system greatly outweigh its drawbacks, even in the New World. I interviewed Dr. Federico Allodi for my series on marriage. He feels there's a lot to be said for a culture where all of a family's adult males are responsible for the children. He draws on personal memories. "When I was a child in Spain," he told me, "any adult could tell me to behave, could assume the authority of the father." It kept him in line ... up to a point.

Dr. Allodi points out that many immigrants from Africa and the Caribbean have very loose conjugal arrangements. But, in compensation, the maternal grandparents play a very active and supportive role. The man may well disappear, but there are other relatives to take up the slack. Where individual male responsibility disappears, it's a good idea to have the balance of an extended and involved family.

Many North Americans may have trouble understanding just how deep and wide those family connections can grow. It might be helpful to scan this obituary, which ran in the *London Free Press* on June 10, 1996, for a man who had died on June 7:

Mr. Clifford "Cliff" Farquharson of London: in his 60th year. Beloved husband of Myrtle (Reynolds) Farquharson. Dear father of Collington Farquharson of Jamaica, Dennis Farquharson, Joseph Farquharson, Jennifer Morrison, Fawana Farquharson, all of London, and Beryl Matthews-Mitchell and her husband Bill of New York. Dear brother of George Farquharson and his wife Minerva, Rupert Farquharson and his wife Verna all of Toronto, Enoch Farquharson of England, Rupert Dixon, Purcell Dixon, Ronald Farquharson, Roy Farquharson, Delsford Gordon and his wife Gloria all of Jamaica, Hopeton Farquharson and his wife Elaine, Cislyn Farquharson of Florida, Donald Gordon and his wife Evan, Crysel Farquharson, Dorothy Rowe and her husband Gerald, Lucille McLeish and Merton Wisdon, all of New York. Also loved by his 5 grandchildren: Donovan, Sasha, Maranda, Gavin and Brittany and his great-grandson Christopher. Survived by several nieces, nephews, and other relatives.

That is a truly extended family.

The late Mr. Farquharson was clearly an involved husband and parent. But in the various communities of transplanted Africans—in Canada and the United States, the Caribbean, parts of Central and Latin America—the important tie is often the one to the biological family, not the marital one. The roots of this pattern go very deep. It is fashionable to argue that the weakness of the conjugal bond among Afro-Americans and West Indians is a legacy of slavery. But you find the same kind of family system in some African tribes, especially in West Africa.

One might ask, of course, which came first, the chicken or the egg. Might not men be more involved with their children if the woman's family were less strong? Certainly I know at least one man who felt that his partner's family—West Indians—pushed him out of their daughter's life. Perhaps it's not a question that can be answered. But it has profound implications for the lives of millions of children, here in a culture where the extended family tends to disintegrate.

Even where they're intact, extended families tend to create some difficulties. Dr. Allodi tells a story that illustrates one of the problems with them. While visiting a psychiatric clinic in Central America, he noticed that most of the staff—from doctors down to the receptionists—had the same surname. He asked if this was a coincidence. The director of the clinic explained that they were all related. He preferred to hire family. "But that's nepotism!" Allodi exclaimed. The director slapped his knee in appreciation. "You North Americans!" he said admiringly. "You have a name for *everything*!" What we call nepotism is a virtue, not a sin, in most traditional societies.

Even on its home turf, this kind of family loyalty causes trouble. It was the source of a lot of grief for my students in Sierra Leone. Almost all of them were on government loans, which they could pay back only by working in rural schools for several years after they graduated. (If their families had any money, they would have attended university in Britain or the United States.) They would earn a pittance. After that, they were free to find jobs—in a corrupt and devastated economy, which has deteriorated severely since my years there. At the same time, their families—large extended ones—would expect them to support and assist their relations. This is a common problem in many African societies today. One young man pointed out sombrely that people like me could afford integrity. With a couple of dozen cousins to help through school and the job market, he figured he'd have to take bribes to survive.

That unhappy admission accents one of the difficulties with any kind of family system. They don't always change with circumstances. Sierra Leone can no longer afford a corrupt government and bureaucracy; it's one of the poorest countries on earth. But the pattern of helping only blood relatives continues, at the expense of public morality. And that's not the worst case of the catastrophic effects of a system that stays frozen. The ugliest instance on earth, by far, is the case of the Ik, a tribe in central Africa.

The Ik are famous. The anthropologist Colin Turnbull has chronicled their terrible story in his book *The Mountain People*.[85] They were originally a group of nomadic hunters, until the creation of a game reserve drove them from their lands. They were reduced to a life of desperate foraging and farming in a most unpromising mountain terrain. Competition for food became the focus of life, the only activity. Their system, such as it is, is now one of mutual, endless exploitation. Turnbull noted that everything we associate with family life—affection, sacrifice, co-operation—had vanished. The Ik mother cares for her children only until they reach the age of three. After that, they're on their own.

Cruelty became one of the Iks' few pleasures. Turnbull saw adults laugh uproariously when a small child burned himself at the campfire.[86] The children, in turn, grew up without a trace of altruism; they sometimes snatched food out of the mouths of the helpless old.

The drought ended. When Turnbull returned a year later, he discovered that the Iks' social patterns had not changed, even though food was so abundant that crops were rotting in the fields. They could not travel back to anything like normal behaviour. They were trapped, paralyzed in a system so vicious that it will doubtless ultimately prove suicidal.

The Ik are unique among the tribes of this world. But I can't help wondering if other social systems don't become static in less obviously destructive ways. The arrangements cultures choose often transcend rational self-interest. But once they've settled into place, it's difficult to change them at will.

That means that we in the West don't have much choice about our nuclear arrangements. We have come to crave privacy. We don't want servants underfoot all day and night; we don't want even close relatives in our homes every day. Economic change could thwart that desire; young people, for instance, are less able to leave their parents' homes if they can't find well-paid jobs. But a return to extended households in our world would be a matter of necessity, not choice. I detect a similar tendency almost everywhere. Where people have the option of living in smaller units, they prefer it.

That doesn't mean that the nuclear family is always the right choice. The prosperous Asian countries that are moving away from extended households also prefer hideous shopping plazas to their own street markets; the worst elements of Western pop culture to their own music and theatre; garish and indestructible plastic to their natural and graceful traditional materials. (Plastic, a Thai professor of ecology once told me, is the curse of Asia.) We don't always choose what's best for us in the long run.

I want only to suggest that the nuclear family—despite the contempt heaped on it in recent years—has a powerful appeal. It has a deep hold on the human imagination. It is not a contemporary perversion bred by capitalism; it is not inevitably inferior to the extended family as a place for raising children or finding emotional satisfaction. The groups that have tried to reject it for some better model—the *kibbutzim*, the early Bolsheviks, the 1960s' communes—failed to come up with anything that works.

As we're about to see, however, those experiments do not mark an unprecedented attempt to tamper with the family. Whether extended or nuclear, families do not exist in isolation. In every society on earth, they are shaped by intentional and accidental pressures from the outside world.

The Hidden Enemies: Church & State, Part I

ALL FAMILIES HAVE A tendency to generate their own rules and codes. In university, I heard that a fellow student had been rather anxious about his fiancée's first meeting with his decidedly proper family. The prospective in-laws were also uneasy, until the young woman declined milk or sugar for her tea—Earl Grey, of course. They were reassured, then, that at least she was not irredeemably vulgar. I myself was present at a wedding where the groom's brother outlined a few rules of her new family to the bride. The one that sticks in my mind must have been a survival from an earlier period: "Drink your Coke slowly, 'cause you can only order one."

There are no societies, however, where a family gets to compose *all* its own rules. It's not possible, because no family today lives in total isolation. Perhaps there were such clans in the remote past, but they have died out. Without exogamy, inbreeding would have eventually finished them off. As we've seen, all cultures develop rules to ban or at least limit incest, to protect families from precisely that danger.

In time, all cultures impose new layers of rules on the family. These do not necessarily serve the interests of individual families: religions and governments generally have a keen sense of self-interest. So some of the rules they formulate may be designed to limit the influence of the family, leaving control in their own hands. Other laws simply impose order, by regulating the issues of property and succession, and limiting the anarchic effects of our fickle sexual passions.

Where the environment is harsh, the ruling class may want to limit the population, by restricting sexual relations or by killing off some infants at birth. (The sickly, malformed and female are usually the prime candidates.) Under different conditions, religious or secular leaders may find a large population desirable, requiring laws to reward and promote fertility.

In pre-literate societies, the rationale for such rules may eventually be lost. It is often impossible even to trace their origins. Written legal codes are a late development in human history; even the idea of "government" or "ruler" can be elastic. In the West today, we tend to divide the institutions that rule our lives into neat compartments: there is the government and, for some of us, there is religion. But it's not always that easy to draw the line that separates the family from the external forces that shape it. Divisions blur between kin and tribe, state and creed. Cultural codes become so thoroughly absorbed that they feel like part of the natural order— inevitable and immutable.

The origins of many of these commandments and prohibitions are a mystery. Two perfect examples can be found in some areas of the Muslim world, in female circumcision and the forced marriage of cousins.

The peoples who practise female circumcision often believe that it is prescribed by the Koran. This is untrue. Islam, like Judaism, has a horror of most forms of mutilation, with the notable exception of male circumcision, which both religions require. But male circumcision is a relatively straightforward operation, involving only the removal of the foreskin. (There are cultures that are much harder on men, favouring the insertion of metal objects into the penis to promote female sexual pleasure.) The female equivalent is a more serious matter; the very term "female circumcision" is a misnomer. The operation ranges from excising part or all of the clitoris to removing a large portion of the inner labia. It is often accompanied by infibulation, the sewing together of the remaining tissue to ensure chastity.[1]

Now, this is a terrible idea. At best, it inevitably reduces sexual enjoyment. (A young Muslim woman in Australia told the journalist Geraldine Brooks that she was glad that part of her clitoris had been removed: "It reminds me that my marriage is about more important things than pleasure."[2]) It also often leads to infection and even death. Scar tissue can cause pain during intercourse and complications during childbirth.

It is hard to imagine the mind—or minds—that came up with this particular way to safeguard female purity. Yet loyalty to the practice is tenacious. Both men and women in the cultures that practise it are convinced that the operation somehow makes the woman cleaner, more desirable. Unmutilated female genitals disgust them. A responsible mother in much of Africa and parts of the Middle East will ensure that her daughters undergo the same torture as countless generations before them.

Similarly, there is no passage in the Koran that says cousins must marry. (Anthropologists generally believe, as has already been noted, that the custom arises in some cultures that provide dowries, in order to keep money from flowing out of the family.) Nonetheless, it is seen as a requirement in pockets of the Arab world. I've already mentioned an Egyptian case discussed by Richard Critchfield in his remarkable book *Villages*. A sixteen-year-old girl named Batah refused to marry her cousin Ali, who was away serving as a soldier. Ali's family were no one's idea of desirable in-laws—his father was a well-known alcoholic—but Batah's refusal was actually rooted in her love for a member of an outcast clan.

All hell broke loose. Critchfield was present at a dinner when Ali's father broke in and attempted to carry Batah off. Among the many curses he flung at her was this threat: "By God, if you do not come I shall slit your throat and cut you into small pieces. Not even maggots shall find your body. We do not allow women to say yes or no."[3]

This is a mistaken belief. Islamic tradition prefers that a woman consent to her marriage, except when she is betrothed before puberty.[4] But because village custom was so deeply entrenched, Batah's refusal was seen as an intolerable insult to Ali's family. The outcome was brutal. Batah tried to marry the man she loved. Just before the wedding, her cousin Ali deflowered her—using his finger, another time-honoured local custom.[5] (In this truly barbaric ritual, the groom-to-be *publicly* breaks the bride's hymen with his middle finger, to prove her virginity.) He had thus humiliated and ruined the woman who had destroyed his honour.

Among the villagers, Critchfield notes, "sympathy tended to be with the soldier, not Batah. In their eyes breaking with village tradition was the greater guilt."[6] Again, an unnecessary custom of unknown origin overrides personal desire and shapes the duties and even the structure of the family.

Throughout history, all over the globe, family patterns exhibit these strange, esoteric twists. Why did the Baganda decide to give up their children to relatives? Why do some cultures send their daughters off with dowries, while others demand a bride-price to release them? How on earth did it become taboo for men and women to eat together in some Pacific societies? We can come up with ingenious theories, but it's unlikely we will ever rediscover the origins of these customs.

Above all, why did so many groups start to treat their women as property, and why have so many generations of women put up with it? We may not know why, but we do know *how* this happened. Gerda Lerner, in *The Creation of Patriarchy*, notes correctly that the exchange of women must necessarily have been preceded "by the indoctrination of women, from earliest childhood on, to an acceptance of their obligation to their kind to consent to such enforced marriages."[7] You can see this in practice even today in many parts of the world. The journalist Jan Goodwin noted that girls in some Islamic countries are taught from a very early age to be good wives and mothers—that is, "docile, obedient, and self-sacrificing."[8] They learn that their brothers come first in all things. Goodwin watched a seventeen-year-old girl rise as her nine-year-old brother entered the room, giving him her chair and reseating herself at his feet. Worse, she knew a mother who submissively stayed home after her *seven-year-old* son forbade her to attend a class in child-care.[9]

While we can never know how these irrational codes developed, some civilizations have left records that allow us to explore the evolution of their family systems. The map they provide, however, is not always entirely clear. We can't always separate folkways from the rules a society encodes. The Bible provides some obvious examples. Its rules on incest can be interpreted in two ways. On one hand, it's possible that the laws simply bolster accepted practice, reminding the ancient Hebrews that they weren't the kind of people who slept with their aunts or grandmothers.[10] On the other hand, the laws could be saying, "You people have *got* to stop sleeping with your grandmothers." A certain amount of speculation inevitably creeps into any discussion of the laws on marriage and family life.

What the laws *can* tell us, however, is what religions and governments saw as desirable—the practices they were trying to eliminate, and the values they wanted to reinforce. This is directly relevant to our lives now if we look at the world's dominant cultures—the civilizations that have shaped our own ideas of the family, and our own rules for governing it. In this chapter, and the ones that follow it, I will be concentrating largely on the history of the West.

Let's turn first to the question of self-interest and family laws. Most religions and governments like to present themselves as friends of the family. The major faiths are always keen to point out their efforts to strengthen family life, and the improvements they introduced to the lawless, heathen ways they replaced. And, while there have been some notable exceptions, most governments claim to have the interests of the family at heart.

But this is only partly true. Church and State are friendly to the family, in the words immortalized by Evelyn Waugh's *Scoop,* only "up to a point." They have good reason to distrust family allegiances, and to try to weaken them. For family ties represent a loyalty that competes with them, often working against their interests. Governments and clergy have often felt the need to sculpt the family a little or a lot—out of idealism, out of practical necessity and often out of an alliance of the two.

A classic example is the Roman Catholic Church's earlier insistence on six degrees of separation. That evocative phrase refers to the Church's exceptionally sweeping definition of incest from the sixth century on—you could not marry anyone related to you up to six degrees. A third cousin was still too close.[11]

Now, the Church drew on a truly beautiful idea to justify this stringency. It finds an able defender in Dr. Suzanne Scorsone, director of the office of family life for the Archdiocese of Toronto. The rule, she has said, kept people from becoming inbred and to some extent followed the prevailing folk customs of the local population. But its true purpose was the attempt to bring peace to warring peoples. Forcing families to look far afield for mates was designed to create ever-widening alliances. It opened the possibility of uniting all of Christendom into one great family under God.

That is lovely, and it is partly true. But even Dr. Scorsone acknowledges that the six-degree rule was also designed in part to block tight alliances within powerful families. On precisely that basis, it proved impossible to enforce. Royal families are notoriously unwilling to marry outside their own magic circle. As we'll see in the next chapter, Rome eventually had to retreat a considerable distance from its original vision; today, Catholics can sometimes even get dispensations to marry first cousins.

There are a few cultures that have gone much further in attempting to regulate family life; a handful have tried to suppress it altogether. The most thorough experiment of this kind belongs not to our own century, but to ancient Sparta. The Spartans were a uniquely militaristic society in ancient Greece. Because Sparta had colonized its neighbours, it was the only Greek state that had to maintain a standing army. The Spartans thus had good reason to distrust the taming effects of domestic life.

So they made it impossible for men to have one. Males over the age of seven lived separately from women.[12] They ate in a communal mess, dining off a black broth so vile that a visitor observed after tasting it that he now understood why Spartans did not fear death.[13] Sex was a trickier problem, since warrior cultures always need lots of children. But the Spartans found a way to keep men from any debilitating excess in that area as well. Their great (if mythical) law-giver, Lycurgus, made it a disgrace for a man to be seen visiting his wife.[14] Conjugal visits had to be furtive and brief.

Obviously, these extreme measures weakened the family tie. We should note, however, that it allowed Spartan women a rather more comfortable life than that available to any of their neighbours. Because Lycurgus believed that their most important function was bearing children, he emphasized their health.

So girls were raised to be athletic and sturdy, just like boys. They ate better than other Greek women, who were kept on short rations. Sparta's neighbours reasoned that malnutrition would help keep females where they belonged—sitting quietly at their spindles or looms. Spartan wives and virgins did not spend their time spinning, weaving or sewing. Lycurgus felt that making garments was work fit only for slaves. Left to their own devices, Spartan women carved out a life so pleasant that Aristotle condemned them roundly in his *Politics*.[15]

At least Sparta's rulers were open about their hostility to the family. The same dubious virtue attaches to the early Bolsheviks, who hoped to sweep away the "bourgeois family" along with the State. A more interesting example, because the antipathy was covert, also belongs to our century. The Third Reich was one of the worst friends the family ever had.

On the surface, the Nazis promoted a conservative, very middle-class vision of the family, which they called, tellingly, "the germ-cell of the nation."[16] This was literally true, in the sense that they wanted Germans to proliferate like germs. By the 1930s, the German birth rate had halved from its turn-of-the-century level. Thanks to the huge losses of the First World War, about a quarter of young adult women would be unable to marry. Desperate to boost its population, the Reich urged "restoring the family to its rightful place."[17]

It used a variety of methods to achieve this. It curbed equality for women, outlawed abortion, contraception, homosexuality and blatant prostitution, and dangled money and other incentives to marriage and fertility.[18] It developed its own cult of motherhood, placing greater emphasis on quantity than quality. On the birthday of Hitler's mother, August 12, fertile mothers received the Honour Cross of the German Mother. You needed at least four children to qualify for the bronze medal; gold was reserved for parents of eight or more.[19]

The *Lebensborn* (Well of Life) movement worked to speed up the process through less benign means. It provided what amounted to ss studs for racially suitable single women, working at the same time—necessarily—to remove the stigma attached to unwed motherhood. Once the war started, German officials snatched Aryan (or near-Aryan) children from invaded territories and gave them to upper-echelon German families.[20] Racially pure men were also encouraged to abandon their childless wives and remarry potentially fertile women.[21]

The Reich also tried to create the impression that it was nudging women out of the work force—a popular step among unemployed men. In a light-hearted passage she must have regretted once war broke out, Nancy Mitford puts these words in the mouth of a socialite chatting to a British fascist: "I don't know a thing about politics, but I'm sure Hitler must be a wonderful man. Hasn't he forbidden German women to work in offices and told them they never need worry about anything again, except arranging the flowers? How they must love him."[22]

That is precisely the image Hitler hoped to create, but it was never an accurate one. Nazi legislation removed women from the professions, but the government could not afford to remove cheaper female labour from humbler jobs. Once the country began mobilizing for war, female workers became essential. The number of women in the labour force increased by nearly 50 per cent between 1937 and 1939. By 1942, almost twice as many women worked outside the home as had before Hitler.[23] By the end of the war, they constituted three-fifths of the labour force.[24] Ideology was at war with practical concerns, and ideology lost.

Moreover, the family itself was inimical to the Nazi vision of an ideal society. Between political activity for adult males, the Nazi women's organization (*NS-Frauenschaften*), the Hitler Youth and the *Bund Deutschen Mädchen* for girls, there really wasn't much time left for home life. A popular German joke of the 1930s dealt with a family that was so busy with such activities that they met only once a year—at the Party rally in Nuremberg.

The ultimate effects of these conflicted and exploitive policies severely damaged the German family. The divorce rate soared even before the war. By the time it ended, an estimated 23 per cent of all young Germans had a venereal disease.[25]

The Spartans, the Bolsheviks and the Nazis are exceptions in the course of human history. Most cultures recognize that they need the family, and work instead to regulate and control it. They often damage it accidentally while pursuing other agendas, of course—no one deliberately set out to reduce the Ik to antisocial destitution. Moreover, many changes in human conduct and values develop without the agency of any conscious external force. Laws tend to follow human conduct, as well as lead it. They often merely encode values that are already current.

It's also important to remember that we don't necessarily get an accurate vision of past family life from the ruins, art, laws and records that come down to us. Human beings have a natural tendency to praise their own ways and denigrate those of others; we cannot trust a Roman historian's description of Gallic folkways or a *conquistador*'s account of Incan ones. Nor can we trust the moralists who devote their works to deploring contemporary degeneracy. From the moment humans invented writing, they seem to have spent a good deal of time lamenting the decline of their societies. Every generation appears afflicted with nostalgia for the good old days.

In addition, we tend to hear little about harmonious family life, because there's never much to say about it. (Tolstoy makes that point in the first sentence of *Anna Karenina*: "All happy families are alike; every unhappy family is unhappy in its own way."[26] Similarly, the novelist Brian Moore once told me that he writes about failure rather than success because failure is so much more interesting.) Laws get passed and diatribes written during times of change and stress. There's no need for intervention or even comment when everyone in a society (or at least anyone with any power) agrees on issues like hierarchy, inheritance, marriage and child-rearing. We tend to learn most about periods of transition and stress.

That is one obvious feature of a major influence on our own customs today: the Bible of the ancient Hebrews. Many of its stern laws have a direct bearing on the family: no more child sacrifice, no more cross-dressing, no more incestuous marriages. We know that many of these laws addressed actual practices of the time. Archaeologists have found buried piles of bones just outside Jerusalem, for instance, that confirm the existence of a child-sacrifice cult.

The new laws enforce an ethical standard, but at the same time they impose cultural homogeneity on the Hebrews, and effectively separate them from their neighbours.

Like every other religion I know, Judaism argues that it vastly improved the quality of family life, and the lot of women and children. You can certainly make a case for that. Norma Joseph, a professor in the Department of Religion at Montreal's Concordia University, talks about the magnificence of the Bible's vision of marriage. God himself, she points out, acted as the first matchmaker, creating Eve for Adam. The creation myth also stresses the inseparability of men from women, for Eve is bone of Adam's bone and flesh of his flesh. Like Pandora, of course, Eve is also responsible for man's fall. But marriage is a central value in Judaism, a religious obligation.

But what kind of marriage? What type of family life were the laws of Israel attempting to create? On the evidence of the laws themselves, the Hebrews (or their God, if you prefer) were anxious to enforce sexual purity and bolster patriarchal power. The fifth of the ten commandments orders Jews to honour their parents; the seventh specifically forbids adultery. The tenth touches on the same theme, ranking the sin of desiring your neighbour's wife with coveting his ox or his ass.

There is little of the revulsion against sex *per se* that you find in the early (and often later) Christian churches. As Norma Joseph remarks succinctly: "Judaism does not tolerate celibacy." In Genesis, Jews were told that it is "not good for man to be alone"[27]—marriage is part of the service owed to God.

But there is a horror of anything irregular: the adulterous wife, the harlot, any sexual act that cannot produce legitimate offspring.

That insistence on the straight and narrow has shaped Western attitudes right up to the present. Our laws on prostitution and homosexuality reflect values far more Hebrew than Greek or Roman.

The Old Testament also repeatedly emphasizes the blessings of fertility. Female barrenness is legitimate grounds for divorce. Children are valued; infanticide is out. The Bible refers to child sacrifice as an "abomination."[28] Finally, there are strict laws prohibiting incest, or any kind of confusion of roles in the family.

Both the laws and some of the narratives strongly suggest that the ancient Israelis were surrounded by and emerging from some fairly gruesome behaviour. That might explain the Bible's strong puritanical vein, its horror of unlicenced sexuality. Take, for instance, the story of Lot's difficulties as a host in Sodom. We learn in Genesis that the Sodomites are all too keen to mingle with Lot's overnight male guests—they want him to hand over the visitors for a gang rape. Lot—a good host but a poor father—offers his neighbours his two virgin daughters as a substitute.[29] There is a similar and equally hideous story about the town of Gibeah, involving the death of a concubine after a night of sexual abuse.[30]

The Bible attempts to stamp all that out. It objects not just to sexual violence, but to any form of unchastity. When a man sends his daughter out in marriage, she must be a virgin. If she doesn't bleed on her wedding night, Deuteronomy orders the elders to take her to the door of her father's house to be stoned to death. The community must rid itself of a woman who has played "the whore in her father's house: so shalt you put evil away from among you."[31]

Given what we know now about human anatomy, we can assume that some women died because they had no hymen, either from birth or through a non-sexual misadventure. Given what we know about human nature, we have to speculate that others may well have been seduced or raped by their own blood relatives. To be scrupulously fair, there are also provisions in the Bible for forcing a seducer to

marry his victim, which means that the ancient Hebrews must sometimes have tolerated the loss of virginity before marriage.

Apologists for Judaism (and Islam and Christianity) often argue
that those religious teachings on marriage and family that we find
unattractive are reflections of the social realities of their original
periods. The religion represents an advance on the past. Presumably
then, stoning was already the accepted punishment for illicit sex.

The Bible does mitigate this harshness slightly. If a betrothed
woman is raped in a field, it gives her the benefit of the doubt and
assumes she cried for help: "But unto the damsel thou shalt do nothing; there is in the damsel no sin worthy of death." The passage
explicitly compares the violated woman to a murder victim; this is
one case where tradition does not blame the victim.[32]

For adultery, the Bible and the Koran demand that four reputable
witnesses attest to the crime. In parts of the Muslim world today,
that requirement isn't always enforced. In the case of the Palestinian girl killed by her cousins, there can have been no witnesses to
her unchastity, because she was still a virgin.[33]

Many of the rules that can cause problems today probably also
had roots that predate the religion. Menstruation must already have
been seen as defiling—many cultures segregate women during their
periods[34]—and the idea of women as a form of property must
already have been firmly entrenched.

In other ways, however, the Hebrew laws are clearly an attempt
to change the existing rules. Feminist scholars see in many of them
an effort to root out both goddess-worship and the remnants of a
matrilineal society.[35] The ancient Hebrews do seem to have been a
matrilineal people at some point, because a child's Jewish status
derives from its mother, not the father. While matrilineal descent
does not imply matriarchy, a tradition of female descent doesn't fit
well with the enormous power and prestige of the Hebrew patriarch. I have heard it argued that reckoning religious affiiliation from

the mother is a medieval development, a concession to the prevalence of rape. Norma Joseph assures us that's not true: matrilineal descent is the original pattern. The switch must have occurred fairly early, because the division into tribes is not a late development and tribal affiliation comes from the father.

There is another rather startling piece of evidence in support of this opinion. It involves two of King David's children, Amnon and Tamar, the offspring of different mothers. Amnon's lust for Tamar was so strong it made him ill. When she visited him in his sickness, he forced himself on her. She fought him, not because such a liaison would be incestuous, but because it would be illicit. She begs him to ask their father's permission to marry: "... speak unto the king, for he will not withhold me from thee."[36] There is no reason to believe that she's simply trying to talk her way out of a sticky situation. It seems likely that Tamar's beliefs are a vestige of an earlier, purely matrilineal society. Where the question of paternity is irrelevant, there's no reason to bar relations between paternal half-siblings.

The triumph of a fully patrilineal system can be gauged by another biblical injunction: the levirate. It dictates that a man's widow must marry his brother, or at least secure his refusal before marrying anyone else.[37] (Since the Hebrews permitted polygyny, the fact that he might already be married was of no consequence.) The refusal was not a pleasant ritual. In the necessary ceremony, *chalitza*, the spurned widow had to unfasten her brother-in-law's shoe and spit in his face, in public.

You can interpret the levirate in different ways, according to your own biases. The most cynical explanation sees it as a way of keeping property in the family: both the woman herself, and her whole dowry. It is as if the marriage made the woman's reproductive capacity the property of all his kin. There is a less materialistic possibility: the levirate ensured that a widow would be able to carry on her husband's name and line, for her first child by her subsequent marriage was regarded as his. Norma Joseph notes that this would seem extremely important to a culture so intensely concerned with spiritual, as well as material, inheritance.

Finally, the arrangement does make provision for the widow, who would otherwise have to return to her own family, quite possibly as a lifelong burden. This is no small consideration. The lot of the widow and orphan cannot have been enviable, for the Bible repeatedly has to urge charity and integrity in dealing with them. They must often have been without resources. Otherwise, Elijah wouldn't have had to help out a widow with a miraculous self-replenishing jar of oil, and Ruth wouldn't have been out gleaning Boaz's fields.

The Bible's recurring concerns with patriarchy and purity—especially, but not exclusively female purity—created an orderly but not notably just culture. This is one of the central concerns of any institution governing a large group of people: keeping the chaos of sexual attraction under control. For the Mangaians, as we've seen, that meant allowing sexual licence during adolescence, in the hope that people would get it out of their systems and settle down to the serious business of life after marriage. The Hebrews found other solutions to the problem of male lust, at least: whores were out, but polygamy and concubines were just fine.

Marriage was both a pragmatic and a spiritual concern. At this point in Jewish history, no rabbi presided over the wedding service, and the engagement contract was the crux of the alliance. At the same time, marriage was—and is—a religious responsibility, and religious laws governed its conduct. Children were expected to obey and honour their parents; fathers could ask to have them killed if they failed in this duty. But, interestingly, at no point does the Old Testament say that women must obey their husbands.[38] Perhaps this reflects some level of egalitarianism within the marriage; perhaps it simply means there was no need to say it.

In sharp contrast to Catholic doctrine, the Old Testament permits divorce, but clearly disapproves of it except under particular circumstances. Nonetheless, during this period a man could put his wife away at will. By about A.D. 1000, Rebbenu Gershom, a German sage, ruled that a woman must accept her divorce for it to be valid: she must take her *get*, her bill of divorcement, willingly into her hands. This represents an enormous change; the earlier practice does not so much allow a couple to divorce, as allow a man to repudiate his wife. Gershom also prohibited polygyny within his own community. Both edicts eventually spread to all European Jewry.[39]

As I've already noted, the laws were also very keen on promoting fertility; they seem designed to achieve the largest possible number of children. If one does not work from the assumption that the Scriptures are the unaided work of God, it's hard not to be impressed by the acumen or simple good luck of their authors. According to the dictates of the law, women are unclean during their periods and for seven days afterwards[40]—removing them from action at precisely their least fertile time. Moreover, it is a sin for a man to abstain from sex with his wife for long; couples are supposed to have intercourse on the Sabbath except at times of illness or uncleanness. In polygynous households, Norma Joseph says, the man owes equal sexual attention to all his wives, along with equal accommodations and support. (Patriarchy does not come without responsibilities.) The laws ensure that the fertile will bear as many children as possible.

When Church or State chooses to interfere in family life, the desire to boost the population is often a prime motive. Until industry and technology sharply reduced the need for human labour, it was an obvious advantage to rule a state with many subjects. Nor is there anything unusual in the Hebrew mixture of spiritual and pragmatic elements. Professor Gunnar Heinsohn has pointed out that many scholars now agree the European drive against witchcraft was rooted partly in a desire to stamp out abortion and contraception—the provinces of herbalists and midwives.

We have to remember, moreover, that the apparently spiritual concerns of religious leaders in earlier cultures had pragmatic elements that the modern mind may have trouble grasping. The ancient Hebrews, like the other peoples around them, had a very concrete sense of their God. The prophets warn again and again that God will punish his people if they don't shape up. Nor will chastisement be delayed until the next life—this God is very free with floods and plagues and boils and destruction of cities. Obeying the laws of purity and hierarchy within the family became a safety measure. Moreover, it makes sense for priests and the Scriptures to determine the laws on family life. Since sexual misbehaviour is so offensive to this very dangerous God, even the most power-hungry king will want to leave the issues surrounding it to His word and His representatives.

The Hebrews tended to despise other cultures as intrinsically immoral. It's hard to make our own judgments on this, because we know so little about what was going on in most of the world during the periods the Bible describes. Even if we turn to the relatively late reigns of Saul and David in about the twelfth and eleventh centuries B.C., we have records for only a few other cultures. In India, the Aryan invasion would be about four hundred years old. The caste system was beginning to develop, but the warrior class— the *Kshatriyas*—were still on top. (The priestly Brahmins replaced them over time.) The Vedas, the Hindu scriptures, were beginning to appear. Marriage could be by abduction, purchase or consent; consent was regarded as rather *déclassé*.[41] Polygyny was allowed, but women were not sequestered. Widows were still permitted to remarry, although some groups practised *suttee*, the live cremation of widows. Female status was about to decline sharply.

For China, we have no true history for this period, only myths. The myths say that an early race of unclothed cannibals had already been tamed into a true civilization, including the institution of marriage. We have no clue about family life—or any other aspect of life—in Japan.

Similarly, we know very little about the nature of marriage or child-rearing in the western hemisphere. The patterns that survived until the first European arrivals suggest that some tribes, notably the Iroquois, held to matrilineal descent and matrilocal marriage. They were indifferent to virginity, and let young women lead lives of happy promiscuity in their own longhouses. In those societies, women played an important part in government and religion.[42] Unless something sharply changed social patterns, we can also assume at least some indigenous groups, including the Innu, had an easygoing approach to marriage, which could be broken at will, and a gentle, indulgent attitude to child-rearing.[43]

As you can see, we have only the patchiest notion of family patterns in most of the world at this time. But the Old Testament does touch on four nations who left behind substantial information. The Jews, by their own account, emerged from Sumeria, fled famine to Egypt, were exiled to Babylonia, and eventually ran into trouble with the Assyrians. That put them into contact (often unpleasantly) with the four great cultures of the central Asian world—Persian ascendancy comes a bit later.

Only a few features of family life in these societies have much relation to our world, and I want to dwell on those. The first concerns the most familiar of these cultures, Egypt. It's of interest because its family values were in some ways more congenial to the modern mind than those of ancient Israel, especially in Egypt's earlier periods. Thus, Egyptian women were equal to men under the law. Some achieved professional status, working as scribes, treasurers and priestesses—a striking difference from Israel.[44] Marriages were generally monogamous, at least below the level of royalty.[45] The Egyptians valued fidelity, in some cases for men as well as women. Relations within their families seem to have been gentle and affable; they passed down to us pictures of family treats—banquets, picnics and fishing trips.[46]

Egyptian moralists urged kindness to wives, and gratitude and love for the mother: "Three long years she carried thee upon her shoulder, and gave thee her breast to thy mouth. She nurtured thee, and took no offense from thy uncleanliness."[47]

Not every aspect of Egyptian practice was equally sympathetic. Upper-class women enjoyed high status partly because rank counted for more than gender. Although slavery was relatively rare,[48] royal retainers were frequently buried with their masters.[49] (Egyptian kings liked to depart this earth fully equipped for the journey to the beyond. They were buried with large quantities of food and a variety of attendants—priests, servants, dwarfs and even their favourite dogs.) There are no signs of violence or struggle in their tombs. Presumably the chosen retainers were poisoned and went more or less willingly—somewhat like the suicidal cults of Jonestown or Heaven's Gate.

Life further down the social scale had its own drawbacks. Peasant women, to an even greater extent than peasant men, probably didn't have terribly enjoyable lives. In addition to their own work, they were liable for the same forced labour as men. The name of a female scribe shows up on the lists of deserters from the dreaded *corvée*.[50]

At most social levels, women's own work took more time than we tend to realize. It's important to remember that in all of these societies, the business of staying fed and clothed required endless drudgery. Without refrigeration, food had to be preserved—and fast, for all of these ancient cultures sprang up in hot climates. Grain had to be ground, beer brewed, wine fermented. Moreover, the modern world has almost forgotten the ceaseless toil of spinning, weaving and sewing that was woman's lot. In all of these cultures, women made everyone's clothes, often from rather intractable materials. If you were rich enough, your slaves could do the work, or you could buy superior garments from gifted artisans. But for most of the female population, the spindle was a constant companion.[51]

So it makes perfect sense that the Bible's portrait of the woman of virtue—she whose "price is far above rubies"—concentrates on her value as a workhorse: "She looketh well to the ways of her household, and eateth not the bread of idleness."[52] Female labour was necessary; wives were a most useful commodity. When Egyptian records list housewives as "mistress of the house," the title went beyond empty flattery.

The status of children was also relatively high, especially in comparison to later practices in nearby cultures. Like the Hebrews, the Egyptians valued children and condemned infanticide. One observer claimed that parents guilty of it were sentenced to holding the dead child in their arms for three days and three nights.[53] Egyptian family values would look strikingly close to our own, were it not for the practice of incest.

It's true that incest is a rather large exception, and one that had considerable influence. The words "brother" and "sister" in Egyptian love poetry are the standard expressions for "beloved" or "lover."[54] As the centuries went on, the practice apparently trickled down from royalty to all social classes, and remained popular for at least two centuries after Christ.[55] This society endorsed not only brother–sister marriage, but also the union of daughters and fathers. As noted in an earlier chapter, that tolerance was a direct result of matrilineal inheritance: male relatives married siblings or offspring to preserve their share of the family's property, or to remain in positions of power. It is a classic example of the human willingness to sacrifice biological self-interest in favour of power or property.

Unlike many of the societies that would succeed it, Egypt allowed its women considerable freedom. The sexes mingled socially before and after marriage.[56] But over the centuries, women's position declined sharply, in part because of Greek influence. Under and after Alexander the Great (who captured Egypt in 323 B.C.), Egyptian women suddenly found themselves minors under the law, requiring a guardian to defend their commercial and legal interests.[57]

That gradual sinking of female standing seems to have infected all of the successive civilizations of the Near and Middle East. This is the other important feature of family life in the non-Judaic Near East. Between about 3200 B.C. and 600 B.C., you can trace a broad pattern: from Sumeria to Babylonia to Assyria, women's rights decline and their value decreases.

Thus, in Sumeria, well into the third millennium B.C., a wife kept control of her dowry and had equal rights with her husband in raising their children. She could own a business or slaves in her own right.[58] Under some circumstances, she could even seek a divorce.[59]

At the same time, she was not a free agent in the manner of a contemporary Western woman. If she was not an aristocrat, her husband could lease her and her children into slavery to pay his debts. The law did not concern itself with his extramarital affairs; adultery for her was a capital offence.[60] If she did not bear children, her husband had the right to take a second wife.[61]

But unlike his Hebrew contemporary, he did *not* have the right to repudiate her. The barren wife remained in her husband's household. In at least one of Sumeria's city-states, the law protected women against the injustice of their husbands. In Eshnunna, a man could be evicted and stripped of his belongings for divorcing a wife with children.[62]

The status of the Sumerian wife declined sharply as the civilization around her developed and became more complex. But why? A favourite feminist explanation is the ousting of goddesses by a patriarchal priesthood. Certainly goddesses figure in the theologies of Egypt and Sumeria. For the Sumerians, the original creator was a female god, Nammu.[63] Her prestige declined in time, but there were several others. The most potent was the virgin earth-goddess, the sexual Innini (Ishtar in the Semitic world).[64] Some areas served another female deity, Ninkarsag, the mother-goddess. As in Egypt, priestesses served the gods as well as priests; temples also housed sacred prostitutes or concubines as a matter of course.[65] For the people of the Nile, Isis, the Great Mother, was a popular focus of worship, particularly in her role as mother of the sun god, Horus.[66]

But the worship of female deities doesn't inevitably elevate the status of women. Hinduism has a full panoply of goddesses, without any noticeable exaltation of women's standing as a result. No major religion is more explicit about the natural inferiority of the female sex. The Code of Manu, Hinduism's oldest written guide to conduct,[67] proclaims: "The source of dishonour is woman; the source of strife is woman; the source of earthly existence is woman; therefore avoid woman."[68] In another passage, Manu writes:

> Though he be uncouth and prone to pleasure
> though he have no good points at all,
> the virtuous wife should ever
> worship her lord as a god.[69]

It is possible, of course, that India, too, experienced this descent of woman, from goddess to chattel. But I think it is evidence that goddesses alone are not enough to give women a less subservient role in the family. The ancient Greeks worshipped a number of goddesses, and—as we're about to see—they didn't have much use for women.

Theology alone isn't enough to explain the change in the relations of the sexes we see from Sumeria to Babylonia to Assyria. Nor does Helen Fisher's plough argument take us very far. The Sumerians were a relatively egalitarian society, yet they started using the plough early. They'd even already figured out how to attach a tubular seed-drill to it.[70]

On the other hand, the early Sumerians were not terribly advanced in other ways. Metal work was a rarity; homes were relatively primitive assemblies of reeds and sun-baked clay.[71] Commercial life was brisk, but unsophisticated. The Sumerians hadn't yet invented money, although they routinely used gold and silver as standards of value in barter. Political unification didn't come until about 2800 B.C., when the culture's city-states merged into an empire.

There's a general assumption that women fare worst in military nations, but the Sumerians were a warlike breed. They fought frankly for profit; they slaughtered their captives on the battlefield, or sold them into captivity, or sacrificed them to their gods. It does seem possible, however, that the escalation of Sumerian belligerency changed the status of women and possibly children.[72]

The greatest single factor, however, seems to be an increasing attention to and consolidation of property. The selling of children and wives by debtors, for instance, is closely associated with a steep rise in government taxation.[73] As the economy became both more sophisticated and more stratified, the tendency to treat family members as commodities became more pronounced. It's hard not to feel that Engels was on to something when he blamed the rise of private property for the degradation of women.

The process accelerated as power passed from the Sumerians to Babylonia, from about 2100 B.C. Some things did not change. Babylonia was not, for instance, in any way puritanical about sexuality. Not for nothing does the Bible refer to the "whore of Babylon." Both sacred and secular prostitution flourished.[74] Herodotus claimed that all Babylonian women were required once in their lives to have sex with a stranger in the Temple of Venus.[75] Like the Egyptians and the Sumerians, the Babylonians permitted considerable social mixing of the sexes before marriage. Indeed, they went further, allowing a kind of temporary "trial marriage."

Women could still inherit property; there is evidence that girls were educated, as well as boys.[76] But in other ways Babylonian law and custom show a growing attempt to control the behaviour of women after marriage, and to reinforce the status of wives and children as property. Upper-class women were increasingly confined to the house, in an early version of *purdah*. Married women could no longer own businesses; independent economic activity was seen as humiliating to the husband.[77] A man could divorce his wife and send her out penniless for a variety of flaws, including extravagance. He almost literally owned his children. As in Sumeria, he was allowed to lease them out as slaves if he was in debt.[78] A lower-class man could do the same thing to his wife for a period of up to three years.

In other ways, as well, the sense of wives and children as property had become stronger. The Code of Hammurabi makes it clear that the Babylonians saw the family almost as a single organism, with wives and children as extensions of the patriarch. Thus, if a building collapsed and killed its owner's son, the Code dictated that the builder's son should be put to death. If a man struck a girl and killed her, his own daughter had to die in recompense.[79]

A sense of patriarchal kinship also clearly emerges. In a form of the levirate, if the prospective husband of a betrothed woman died before the wedding, she had to marry one of his brothers or relatives.[80] Hammurabi established a man's children—his own blood— as his rightful heirs, not his wife.[81] Male prerogatives generally increased. Unlike his Sumerian predecessor, the Babylonian husband of a barren wife did have the right to expel her from his house, although she got to take her dowry with her.[82] Men were allowed secondary wives, but female adultery was a capital offence. A woman accused by anyone other than her husband was compelled to throw herself in the river.[83] The Sumerian woman could request a divorce and get it. In Babylonia, the Code of Hammurabi dictated that a wife could be drowned for trying to initiate proceedings.

As in the Bible, this harshness was mitigated somewhat in other passages. Divorce was permitted to a neglected wife who had lived a blameless life.[84] The law was even more indulgent (in a way unthinkable for the Hebrews) to a woman whose husband abandoned her for any length of time without providing financial support. She was allowed to cohabit with another man until her husband's return, without any legal penalty.[85] (Again like the Bible, the Code of Hammurabi seems to issue contradictory instructions about marriage and family life. That may be because the code isn't a code at all—it's a series of *ad hoc* legal decisions, designed to address specific situations.)

There are many other indications that material concerns were changing the nature and motives of the family. Many Babylonians, for instance, evaded the need to bequeath property to daughters by dedicating one or more as priestesses.[86] Nonetheless, women and children fared considerably better in Babylonia than in its successor, Assyria. (The Assyrians became a conquering power in the first millennium B.C.) The historian Georges Contenau noted: "Assyrian law made no mention of a number of legal rights which the mother of a family possessed in the much earlier epoch of Hammurabi."[87]

The Assyrians displayed a great concern with female fertility and fidelity. Abortion was a capital offence; the guilty woman was to be impaled on a stake even if she were already dead.[88] In Sumeria, the veil was a status symbol for upper-class wives; in Assyria, it was a legal requirement, the *chador* of its time. It was illegal to veil a slave or a prostitute, disguising these non-respectable women as decent, protected ones.[89]

Women could be punished severely for striking their husbands. A woman could not own property. If her husband divorced her, he kept all her possessions, plus, of course, the children. Perhaps the status of women is best summed up by Assyrian law on rape. In a bizarre version of "an eye for an eye," Assyrian justice could punish a man who violated a virgin by the rape of his own wife.[90] The penalty for raping a married woman was death, presumably because of the wrong done to the victim's husband. If he caught the couple *in flagrante delicto,* the husband could carry out the sentence himself.[91]

Studying changes in family life from Sumeria to Assyria is a depressing exercise—particularly since Babylonian law is so severe, and Assyrian law positively sadistic. We rather tend to assume that cultures become more socially liberal as they develop, but the ancient

Near East disproves the theory. At the same time, the simple proliferation of written laws is instructive. Even if they were enforc-
ing customary practice, they suggest a growing intervention by
rulers in private life.

After Assyria, it is heartening to turn to the next great round of
civilizations, Greece and Rome. (The rise of Greece coincides with
the final decline of the Assyrian empire; Rome triumphs about three
centuries later.) This is not because either of them offer pictures of
ideally happy family life. But they at least reverse the pattern of their
predecessors. They show the quality of family life, at least for
women and children, improving rather than degenerating.

We inherited little directly from Greece; its legacy comes to us
filtered through Rome. That seems to me a good thing. The nature
of Greek family life, to my mind, could cheer no one but a misogynist. The climate allowed men to spend most of their free time out
of doors, but women were kept in the house—indeed, in the
women's quarters of the house. Like the Assyrians, the Greeks
believed in keeping women safe indoors, where they could lead
blameless lives of industry (that spindle again) and procreation. The
women's section of the home was secured with bolts and bars.[92]
Greece banned women from most of the activities it valued—
notably athletics and politics—and segregated the respectable ones
from male social life. The Greek matron never dined in the presence of her husband's friends.

Greek creation myths stressed the destructiveness and chaotic
irrationality of women—and the consequent need for men to control them. It is telling that the best of the goddesses had no mother;
Athena sprang from her father Zeus's forehead. The myths reflect
a paranoia about women, no doubt of subconscious origin, that
invaded that culture's supposedly rational science and philosophy.
Greek beliefs about women were often tinged with a kind of dread.
Aristotle warned that a menstruating woman could turn a clear mirror a bloody red.[93] Plato believed that the uterus could travel around

the body, choking off life.[94] (These errors proved tenacious, influencing Roman and then European thinking well into the modern period. In the second century A.D., Aretaeus of Cappodocia wrote that "on the whole, the womb is like an animal within an animal," because of this ability to roam through the rest of the system.[95]) The Greek males' fear of women also shows up in their art. The decorative sculptures of many temples, including the Parthenon, depicted the battle of the Athenians against the Amazons.

Rome had its own brands of misogyny, but it placed far greater emphasis on domestic life than the Greeks did. The position of women was unquestionably better, because they were not segregated from the male world to the same extent. Moreover, while individual Roman sexual tastes were extremely catholic, especially in the later centuries, the culture had an underlying streak of puritanism. No matter how the élite behaved, Rome did not approve of a man who spread himself too thin. When Romans whispered that Julius Caesar was a husband to every woman and a wife to every man, they were not expressing admiration. The Romans preferred monogamy and self-control in both sexes. This presents a sharp contrast to Greek culture, which featured a notorious enthusiasm for pederasty.[96] The cultivated Athenian male could take pride in preferring his own sex.

Even by the first century A.D.—when Roman influence had considerably weakened this homosexual bias—contempt for heterosexual love was still a potent force in Greece. In his defence of romance between the sexes, *Dialogue on Love,* Plutarch puts these words in the mouth of a sophisticated Greek: "I certainly do not give the name 'love' to the feeling one has for women and girls any more than we would say that flies are in love with milk, bees with honey, or breeders with the calves and fowl which they fatten in the dark . . ."[97] This may be fiction, but it is clearly fiction based on reality—possibly on eavesdropping.

This is explicit in Plato's famous *Symposium*. This beautiful tract on love suggests that individual human beings were originally only halves of a single entity. Thus, we seek love to complete our fragmented selves. It's a resonant symbol, whose power has survived to the present. But Plato felt that the highest form of love was between two men. (To be fair, he also believed that the highest form of love transcended sex. "Platonic" love, which we have degraded to mean only unconsummated relationships, actually embraces a deep devotion to the moral goodness of the beloved, too profound to find sexual satisfaction.) For the culture's élite, the ideal relationship was between a mature man and a young boy—the mentor relationship carried to an extreme.

This created a moral atmosphere difficult for the modern observer to understand. A partiality for their own sex did not mean that men did not marry. Marriage was a political responsibility, and the Greeks took politics very seriously. But, at least among the élite, their emotions were often otherwise engaged. Not everyone preferred his own sex, of course. The statesman Pericles was openly fond of his mistress, Aspasia. The comedy *Lysistrata* would make no sense if most Greeks had no sexual interest in their wives. If all men were happier with slaves, prostitutes and young men, there would be nothing funny about a city's wives threatening to keep their husbands out of their beds.

Nonetheless, Greek society was distinctly tolerant of a man's passion for an adolescent male, and utterly intolerant of female self-assertion or sexuality. The orator Lysias (c. 458 – c. 380 B.C.) argued a case for a client whose home had been violated. The intruder was not a would-be thief. He was the client's romantic rival—both men were in love with the same boy. The rival had broken in to look for the boy. The client expressed prudish outrage that this drunken boor had penetrated the women's room: "Within were my sister and my nieces, whose lives have been so well ordered that they are ashamed to be seen even by their kinsmen." But the rival's suspicions were correct. The boy was sleeping in the house. The client was impervious to the irony of combining his exaggerated sensitivity about his women's honour with his pursuit of adolescent prey.

A Roman court would have seen the irony; their women held a different place in their lives. Greek marriage, understandably given the males' sexual tastes, was a purely practical business. Fathers arranged for girls' marriages at puberty—around the age of fifteen— ideally to men of about thirty.[98] The female role was running the *oikos*, the household that was the essential economic unit of the Hellenic world. At marriage, women were transferred from their own families to the husband's *oikos*: they were essentially a medium of exchange.

This did not mean they were without value. Like the Bible's woman of virtue, they needed prudence and industry to supervise the *oikos*. They were essential for producing sons to carry on the family, a significant role in a culture with ancestral religious rites. Moreover, their marriages were monogamous, and could not be dissolved lightly. Those marriages were not mere contracts between the males of two families. Weddings were very much a religious concern; the Greek bride could feel that the gods themselves sanctioned her nuptials.

But before and after marriage, her position was not enviable. The Greek attitude towards women seems at times positively vindictive. The poet Hipponax wrote, "The two days in a woman's life a man can best enjoy are when he marries her and when he carries her dead to her grave."[99] In Sophocles' tragedy *Tereus*, Procne laments her marriage (admittedly to a barbarian): "... I've given some thought to this life we women lead and what nothings we are. I think we're happiest as young children in our father's homes, where we lead the lives of human beings..."[100] Euripides' Medea is equally unenthusiastic about her lot: "Surely, of all creatures that have life and will, we women / Are the most wretched. When for an extravagant sum, / We have bought a husband, we must then accept him as / Possessor of our body."[101]

The function of women in Greek culture was summarized for all time in the fourth century B.C. by the orator Demosthenes: "Hetaerae [courtesans] we keep for the sake of pleasure; concubines [i.e., female slaves] for the daily care of our persons, wives to bear us legitimate children and to be the trusted guardians of our households."[102] In a depressing summary, the statesman Pericles pronounced, "The best reputation a woman can have is not to be spoken of at all."[103]

The devaluing and systematic deprivation of women had predictable results. (Remember that non-Spartan Greeks believed it was best not to feed girls much.) Female life expectancy was about ten years less than male. There is evidence that far more men than women survived into adulthood. Since men were more likely to die in battle, and their wars were almost unending, that means that the Greeks must have exposed substantial numbers of baby girls to die at birth. At least one estimate places the figure at 10 per cent of female births.[104] It might have been even higher. The Greeks had a saying: "Even a poor man will bring up a son, but even a rich man will expose a daughter."[105]

To be fair, there are a few indications of a balancing regard for women and marriage. Homer wrote in the *Odyssey:* "There is nothing finer than when a man and his wife live together in true union." Even Aristotle, whose low opinion of women influenced male thought for so many centuries to come, apparently felt his own marriage was happy. In his will, he was careful to provide (however paternalistically) for his wife's future: "I want the guardians and Nicanor[106] to remember what my relations were with Herphyllis and her fidelity to myself. If she wishes to take a husband, they should not give her to a man unworthy of me."[107] But in general, domestic affection must have been influenced and inhibited by the general disdain for marital love.

Rome held a less monolithic vision of both women and family life. It is extraordinary, given the early Roman image of the ideal family, that Roman families should have eventually become less authoritarian and controlling than Greek ones—but they did.

I have already noted the Romans' own version of the history of their families, a myth that many scholars now believe to be based on fact. The story is the familiar rape of the Sabine women. (The Romans had vanquished the Sabines completely by the third century B.C.) The significant point here is the form of marriage for which the story provided justification. The historian Livy tells us that on the morning after the rape (in both senses of the word), Romulus gathered together the women and their captors.[108] The couples were married on the spot. Romulus also made a long and pompous speech trying to reconcile the women to their new lot in life, namely the Roman form of marriage, which materially reduced their rights and put them under the power of the men who had just abducted and violated them. From the beginning, Rome was always complacently convinced that it knew best.

The kind of marriage that Romulus approved was called *confarreatio*—literally, the "sharing of spelt." The name comes from the religious ceremony of marriage. The couple offered a cake of spelt to the gods. Until the Empire, Roman marriage was very much a religious affair. Some of the rites that accompanied it would seem familiar today. The bride wore a wreath and veil—although the veil was not white, but flame-coloured, a reflection of the wife's role as keeper of the hearth. At the betrothal ceremony, the groom gave her a ring, which she wore on the same finger we do, in the belief that a nerve attaches the fourth finger of the left hand directly to the heart.[109] The wedding vows also emphasized the merging and affection of the couple. The bride pronounced *Ubi tu Gaius, ego Gaia.* (Where you are Gaius, I am Gaia.) It implied the same commitment as the biblical Book of Ruth: "Whither thou goest, I will go."

It also implied, of course, that the good wife willingly abdicated her own identity. In the words of J.P.V.D. Balsdon, "By such a marriage a wife was in the absolute power of her husband, and divorce was all but impossible. That is to say, she could not in any circumstances rid herself of her husband. He, on the other hand, in certain circumstances might rid himself of her. If she was unfaithful or if she took to drinking—drunkenness, it was argued, was the commonest cause of unchastity—she was punished summarily; her husband and her own relations were her pitiless judges."[110] (Balsdon is being charitable on the subject of drink. The early records suggest that women could be put to death for drinking any wine at all.) The relationship of the early Roman matron to her husband was essentially that of a daughter to a father.[111]

There were two other forms of marriage possible to a Roman.[112] Plebeian families often practised *coemptio*, marriage by purchase. This was not really a version of the bride-price system popular in so many other parts of the world, because the sale was purely symbolic. The ceremony involved placing a single coin in a ceremonial pair of scales. It was a less elaborate way of transferring a girl or woman from one family to another.

In a third form, about which we know very little, couples were "married" by *usus:* mutual consent and evidence of extended cohabitation. This was not an exact equivalent of our common-law relationships: There was a ceremony performed before witnesses. If the wife then remained in her husband's house for a full year, she automatically came under his authority. She could escape from falling under his control, however, by the simple expedient of spending three nights a year somewhere else.

As in Greece, none of these marriages (with the possible exception of *usus* arrangements) were love matches. In 60 B.C., Julius Caesar formed a political alliance with Pompey and Crassus. As a result, Caesar abruptly informed Servilius Caepio, fiancé of his daughter Julia, that the wedding was off. He married Julia to Pompey. When she died in 45 B.C., Pompey signalled his new independence by declining to marry some other female of Caesar's line. Instead, he married Cornelia, daughter of another political ally.[113]

This political dimension of marriage had pitfalls, of course. When Octavian (the future Emperor Augustus) fell out with his brother-in-law Mark Antony, he urged his sister to divorce his former ally. She refused, and loyally raised Antony's children by his first wife and by Cleopatra after his death.[114]

A woman had, at least until the start of the Empire, no legal personality. Like her Greek sister, she was always under someone's guardianship. (Roman girls did not originally even boast personal names. If a man named Cornelius had a daughter, she was called Cornelia. If she had sisters, they became Cornelia Two, Three, and so on.) She married very young, possibly before puberty.[115] But she was also *materfamilias domina,* a title that held more real power and dignity than the Greeks allowed their housewives. To a much greater extent than the Greeks, Romans valued not just child-bearing, but active motherhood. Greek women practised swaddling, and the prosperous employed wet nurses. Slaves played a major role in child-care; women who ran the equivalent of small factories in their home were probably not in a position to spend quality time with their young. Meanwhile, at least in the early centuries, Roman women generally nursed their own children, although slaves took care of some of the other chores of child-raising.[116]

In both Greece and Rome—indeed, in all the major ancient civilizations with the possible exception of Egypt—attitudes towards children were highly authoritarian. Nonetheless, there is plenty of evidence that men and women cared for their offspring in ways that we would recognize as familiar. From the fourth century B.C. on, Greek vases frequently featured pictures of young children (usually boys) happily at play.[117] Archaeologists have discovered a treasure trove of toys in their excavations.[118] There are passages in the great Greek dramas that show deep affection for children. Euripides has Hercules say, "The best mortals, and those who are not, love children." (In a stunning example of dramatic irony, he promptly goes mad and kills his own kids.)

In *The Myths of Motherhood*, Shari Thurer points out that the Athenians and other Greeks had good reason to cherish their children, at least the male ones. Athenian law required adult offspring to feed and house their parents; they constituted an insurance policy.[119] But the Roman mother may have made a better parent than her Greek counterpart, because her life was happier. Shari Thurer notes an arresting idea about Greece that originated with Philip Slater, in *The Glory of Hera*.[120] He suggested that Greek misogyny was the product of a cycle. Women, frustrated by their dull and restricted lives, took out their hostility on the only available males: their sons. With their husbands so often away on military campaigns, the women made their male offspring the target of all their conflicted feelings about men: possessiveness, anger, envy and vicarious pride. Boys, in return, learned to fear and resent women. In Thurer's phrase, "Misogyny bred misogyny."[121] It is perhaps no wonder that Socrates' wife Xantippe was such a shrew. If the theory is correct, then Roman men would have enjoyed rather less troubled relationships with their mothers.

Nonetheless, until at least the end of the Punic Wars in the second century B.C., Rome could safely be described as a highly patriarchal society. As in Greece, the head of a family derived power from a number of roles: judge, family priest, holder of all family property. In Rome's early years, he could sell his children into slavery, disinherit them and even put them to death—although custom required him to call a family council before exercising that last option.[122] He was free to marry them off as he wished, as long as they were physically mature and not too closely related (on the male side) to the prospective spouse.[123] (The Romans were strict about avoiding incest—until the emperors began tampering with the law. In the early period, the Emperor Claudius would never have been allowed to marry his niece Agrippina, the daughter of his brother Germanicus.)

Fertility was a woman's prime duty. One historian noted that the first lawsuit over a dowry came in 231 B.C., when one Spurius Carvilius divorced his wife because she was barren. The writer added approvingly that "this Carvilius dearly loved the wife whom he divorced, and held her in strong affection because of her character"—but he had yet higher regard for his oath to marry for the purpose of begetting children.[124] Another Roman reportedly divorced his wife because she appeared out of doors with her face uncovered.

Like every other ancient culture examined in this chapter, the Romans placed the highest possible value on female chastity. Adultery—a crime only in women—was a capital offence. Unless the wife had fallen under the *manus* of her husband, however, he did not act as her executioner. That was the privilege of her own family, which she had disgraced.[125]

If we can trust the historians, women sometimes found ways of escaping from this control. The nightmare that haunted Romans was not the overtly violent virago of the Greek unconscious. She was a more subtle killer, a poisoner.[126] She appeared frequently in the annals of Rome, making her debut in 331 B.C. A suspicious number of prominent citizens had died, and a female slave led the authorities to a place where a group of twenty women was found brewing a strange concoction. They insisted it was "a health-giving tonic." They were forced to drink it, and promptly died. In a subsequent investigation and trial, 170 women were condemned to death. This particular story may be a fabrication. We learn of it from the historian Livy, who added piously that the story did not figure in all the history books, so he hoped it might be untrue. But there were a number of other cases. In 180 B.C., a consul died, poisoned by his aptly named wife, Hostilia. She had hoped her son would fill the vacancy left by her husband's demise.[127]

Roman women also sometimes managed to assert their will less murderously. In 195 B.C., Rome's tribunes proposed repealing the Oppian Law, dating back to the Punic Wars twenty years earlier.

The law, an emergency measure, had barred women from owning more than half an ounce of gold, wearing clothes of different colours and riding in horse-drawn vehicles within cities or towns. Rome's female population mounted a vast public demonstration in support of repeal.

Their brazenness lacerated the delicate sensibilities of the consul Marcus Porcius Cato. He told his fellow citizens that "it made me blush to push my way through a positive regiment of women a few minutes ago in order to get here...."[128] Recovering from his embarrassment, he urged Rome to hold fast to austerity: "Woman is a violent and uncontrolled animal, and it is no good giving her the reins and expecting her not to kick over the traces." In an argument that has survived to this day, he warned of a potential domino effect: "Suppose you allow them to acquire or to extort one right after another, and in the end to achieve complete equality with men, do you think that you will find them bearable? Nonsense. Once they have achieved equality, they will be your masters."[129]

The tribune Lucius Valerius launched a counterattack, rather less eloquently than I, for one, could wish. The next day the women blocked the streets in even greater numbers. The law was repealed.

This feistiness would have been unthinkable for a Greek woman outside the fantasy world of a comedy. It makes some sense if you look at the evolution of the Roman family. By the third century B.C., the older *confarreatio* marriage was giving way to a freer form. Women no longer necessarily married *in manu* ("in the hand") of their husbands. To protect patrician property, a wife might retain her identity as a member of her birth family. She thus remained under the power of her own father until she turned twenty-five, at which time she was subject only to the nominal supervision of her guardian. She kept possession of her own property (which automatically became her husband's in *confarreatio* marriage) and was able to obtain a divorce with relatively little fuss if she (or her family) so desired.[130] The writer Gaius, in the second century A.D., observed that there seemed no reason to keep adult women under male guardianship; their reputation for levity and credulity, he felt, were "rather apparent than real."[131]

The change was originally meant to keep property from flowing out of the bride's birth family; as Romans became richer, they were less eager to lose control of a dowry forever. But in practice, it gave women a chance to become wealthy in their own right.[132]

The Punic Wars forced women into more active and public roles, by draining men from the city. Under normal circumstances, as in much of the ancient world, men outnumbered women. Censuses from the second to the fourth centuries A.D. showed the ratio of men to women in Rome itself as 131 to 100—higher in the rest of Italy and in Roman Africa. One reason for this discrepancy is obvious: families routinely exposed female children. The mortality rate in childbirth was also high, possibly as much as 5 to 10 per cent.[133] But the Wars may have altered the sex ratio.[134]

From this period on, it's easy to trace serious changes in family life. In theory, women in the upper stratum of Rome were still not much better off than their Greek neighbours. But in practice, paternal power had started to fade. Affection began to replace authority. The bond between many wives and husbands seems to have been real. Roman law originally ordered men on military or administrative tours of duty to leave their wives behind. But the rule had relaxed, possibly as early as the second century B.C.[135] Too many rumours started about the grass widows, damaging morale. And once women accompanied the governing men, they started to play a greater part in their husbands' careers.

The changes did not please everyone. We have seen Cato's fulminations on the growth of female liberty. As he lamented in his anti-repeal speech, "... we rule all men—and who rules us? Our wives."[136] The historian Jérôme Carcopino, writing in 1941 (in Italy, under fascist rule), tellingly titled his sub-chapter on this development "Feminism and Demoralization."

Carcopino particularly deplored the new indulgence of the Roman father. He traces the onset of the general rot to a change in the meaning of emancipation. In the early Roman family, to emancipate a child meant to cast him out—it was a punishment. But at the beginning of the empire, Julius Caesar gave sons the right to administer any property they acquired in the course of their military careers.[137] That made it possible for an emancipated son to control his own property without losing his inheritance. Emancipation became a reward.[138]

The result, in Carcopino's severe view, was disastrous. "Having given up the habit of controlling their children, they let the children govern them, and took pleasure in bleeding themselves white to gratify the expensive whims of their offspring.... The stern face of the traditional *paterfamilias* had faded out; instead we see on every hand the flabby face of the son of the house, the eternal spoiled child of society ..."[139]

Roman and later moralists also noted that the loss of authority led to a far less stable family life. During the Empire, divorce—once a rarity—became common. The satirist Juvenal wrote that some women divorced their husbands before their wedding garlands had faded. Seneca, using the rhetorical device of hyperbole, claimed that others measured time not by the administrations of Rome's consuls, but by the number of their husbands.

The emperor Augustus, that great advocate of family morality, had three wives (in succession, of course), two of them divorced from earlier husbands. Carcopino refers to "an epidemic of divorces —at least among the aristocracy whose matrimonial adventures are documented ..."[140] Cicero, in a famous scandal, divorced his wife Terentia after thirty years of marriage in order to wed the young heiress Publilia. (Cicero's secretary defended him by arguing that at least the orator's motive was greed, not sexual passion.) Terentia survived this blow; she married two more times, and lived to see her hundredth birthday.

In spite of his own marital history, Augustus was dedicated to the ideal of marriage—and to the future citizens it produced. He attempted to mould the Roman family in three sets of legislation, in 18 and 17 B.C., and again in A.D. 9. Essentially, he tried to compel upper-class Romans to marry by restricting the right of the celibate to inherit property. Inheritances were forbidden to bachelors between the ages of twenty and sixty, and unmarried women (a category that embraced the widow and the divorced) between eighteen and fifty.

Widows were supposed to marry within a year, a divorcée within six months. Augustus also transferred the responsibility for policing infidelity from the family to the state.[141] Families and neighbours were now compelled to inform on adulterers.

Augustus clearly felt, apparently with good reason, that Romans had become slack about the purity of their own families. Pliny the Younger was shocked by a case in which a centurion had seduced the wife of a superior officer. The most scandalous feature was the cuckolded husband's unwillingness to condemn his wife.

There was a crucial reason for Rome's extensive legislation on the family. Governments tend to intervene in family life when they become worried about demographics or morality. Rome fit the bill on both counts. The emperors might have been less concerned about changing sexual morality if the birth rate hadn't dipped so low. But Romans were becoming reluctant to marry and breed. In this, they were following a late development in Hellenistic Greece. As the religious and political motives for marriage evaporated, men became more concerned with personal satisfaction. In Greece, as we've seen, satisfaction did not necessarily demand a wife, or even a woman.[142]

In the first century A.D., the emperor Nero, admittedly not your typical Roman, reportedly "married" a man named Sporus in a traditional public ceremony. On that occasion he took the part of groom, but he supposedly played the bride at a later wedding, even imitating the screams and lamentations of a virgin being deflowered.[143] A little later in the century, Juvenal penned a dour passage about an invitation to the wedding of two men as if this were an everyday occurrence. (Boswell takes this passage to mean that it was, but I suspect that Juvenal was going for shock value.[144])

By the start of the Christian era, there was a substantial pool of bachelors and spinsters, much to Augustus's disgust. The great aristocratic families were dying out. By about A.D. 100, only half of the senatorial families listed in the census of 65 remained on the rolls.[145] Augustus's efforts to change the pattern had failed.

But why? It's an unpleasant conclusion, but they failed in part because Romans came to love property more than children and marriage. Imperial conquest brought wealth, and wealth seemed to stimulate greed. In the words of one sociologist, "Both men and women married for financial gain or they married not at all."[146] They were just as unenthusiastic about reproduction. The respectable Roman matron was under pressure to produce three children, and she rarely wanted to exceed her quota. Child-bearing after the age of twenty-five was considered rather *louche,* a sign that the unhappy mother had failed to conquer her physical passions.[147]

Abortion may have been widely practised (there is some disagreement about this), and it remained legal (except in connection with adultery) until Christianity took hold. The exposure of infants continued. Augustus tried to curb this rejection of children by raising taxes on inheritances for childless couples—by a whopping 50 per cent. Sophisticated Romans evaded that rule by "adopting" adults, who presumably got a cut of the take.

Some couples did manage to produce large families. Marcus Aurelius had thirteen children, all by the same wife. Germanicus, brother of the emperor Claudius, managed to produce nine children before dying young—quite possibly poisoned.[148] Considering how badly they turned out (the deranged emperor Caligula was his fourth), one might wish he had stopped at the prescribed three.

None of this meant, of course, that most Romans were leading lives of chaste self-restraint. The married woman often was: abortion was risky and contraception unreliable. The Romans were familiar with some relatively effective techniques—some physicians recommended blocking the entrance to the uterus with honey, wool or ointment. But they also relied heavily on amulets and magic. One authority advocated wearing the liver of a cat in a tube on the left foot.[149]

Sexual self-control within marriage was both common and admired.[150] The husband who continued to impregnate his wife was condemned as "uxorious,"[151] by no means a compliment. The well-bred Roman gentleman was expected to seek consolation elsewhere. Even Marcus Aurelius found comfort with a concubine after the death of his wife.[152] Women, on the other hand, ran grave risks if they strayed. Unlike men, they were vulnerable to charges of adultery or criminal fornication.[153]

There were women who rebelled spectacularly against this double standard. Some clearly valued sex over money: a few upper-class women registered themselves as prostitutes to elude the penalties for illicit intercourse, even though that rendered them ineligible to receive the legacies that other Romans prized so much.[154] Augustus had to exile a daughter and granddaughter for their notorious affairs; the second wife of the emperor Claudius, Messalina, has become a by-word for nymphomania.

This is not surprising in the context of our normal image of imperial Rome, derived largely from malicious histories of the ruling families, and the exaggerations of satirists. The emperors who followed Augustus can justly be described as degenerates; several of them must have been stark, raving mad. But that image of constant sexual excess leaves out several important elements of Roman life.

The first is social class. The great bulk of the population simply did not have the same opportunities for sexual adventures as their betters. Slaves (with the exception of prostitutes) were not supposed to have intercourse without permission; the prudent master controlled the number of children in his home. (The censor Cato, the same man who opposed indulging women's wishes, *charged* his male slaves money for the privilege of sleeping with his female drudges.[155]) Patricians took slaves as concubines, but concubines were essentially inferior wives. They were supposed to remain faithful to their masters, and to behave with circumspection.[156]

Slaves were not allowed any of the three official forms of Roman marriage, but they could enter an informal marital arrangement, known as *contubernium*.[157] Many did so, and their tombs show such common-law relations lasting a lifetime. There is evidence that both slaves and freed men valued chastity in the women given to them.[158]

Even among the upper classes, sexual licence could never be the guilt-free, natural pleasure possible in less puritanical cultures. The ancient Romans were not Trobriand Islanders or Mangaians. Their traditional image of the good life was austere. In spite of Augustus's legislation, they retained a sneaking admiration for the wife who stayed faithful after her husband's death—the *univira*, the one-man woman.[159] They loved stories of women who killed themselves *with* their husbands. One of the stars was Arria, whose husband, A. Caecina Paetus, was advised to commit suicide (a favourite imperial recommendation) during the reign of Claudius. She plunged a dagger into her own breast, withdrew it and expired with the immortal words, "It does not hurt, Paetus."[160]

In the back of the Roman mind lurked the image of Cornelia, the mother of the Gracchi, who scorned trinkets because, she said, her children were her jewels. Moreover, very much unlike his Greek predecessors, the Roman male was supposed to rise above physical self-indulgence; Cato, for instance, believed that Romans should have sex *only* for purposes of procreation. Not everyone lived this way, obviously, but the standard did not disappear.

The perfect analogy here is food. We see the Romans as uncontrolled gluttons and epicures. Thanks largely to a few celebrated pieces of satire, we imagine them feasting each night on dormice rolled in honey and roasted peacock. It is true that the wealthy and considerate host provided a *vomitorium* for his over-fed guests, and that it was considered a compliment to the chef to use it.[161]

But this revolting excess is only part of the picture. Many Roman residents did not have enough to eat; you can't distract a populace with bread and circuses if they all have enough bread. Rome maintained relief rolls precisely because so many people went hungry.

Moreover, even among the well-to-do, the Romans were light eaters until dinner, a more leisurely meal than we can easily imagine.[162] (Some banquets went on for eight or ten hours, embracing music and other entertainment as well as gorging.) Most importantly, not all Romans admired the frenzied gluttony of the fictional Trimalchio or the all-too-real Nero. Pliny the Younger preferred an "elegant and frugal repast";[163] Juvenal invited a friend to a simple but admirable meal consisting of a kid, some wild asparagus, eggs, grapes, pears and apples.[164]

The vision of Trimalchio's greed overwhelms the image of Juvenal's good taste; a Messalina overshadows the legions of chaste, industrious Roman matrons. This clearly became as true for them as for us. Many Romans were sickened by the corruption, emptiness and avarice of the society around them. They didn't have to put up with it for many more centuries, however; their world was about to disappear, overrun by the kind of barbarians that its ancestors conquered. History chose to reverse Rome's evolution from discipline and self-sacrifice to individualistic hedonism.

This might well worry us, for the later Romans often seem disturbingly like us. Our society is much closer to the conspicuous consumption and exaggerated self-expression of the later Empire than to the solidarity and austerity of the warrior cultures that destroyed it.

Like us, the Romans were distinguished by their often unstable marriages, pervasive greed, indulged children (at least among the rich), a search for self-fulfilment at the expense of public duty, a cult of celebrity and a general breakdown of the old order and values. From a contemporary perspective, it seems alarming that Rome lost its grip as its patriarchal family became freer—lost, moreover, to tribes who cherished power over affection and duty over individual desire. Centuries would pass before men again started to relinquish their power within the family.

But there were substantial differences between that Roman world and our own. It is difficult to identify completely with people who watched mortal combat and fed Christians to the lions as forms of entertainment. From its sternly disciplined origins, Rome became a highly evolved and refined civilization that nonetheless nurtured callous, even frivolous brutality. That careless cruelty inevitably infected at least some of its family life.

The Augustan dynasty's fondness for poisoning and executing its own members is a prime example. There was clearly something wrong with the descendants of Livia. Tiberius was paranoid and Caligula a monster. Claudius, despite some intelligent measures, seems to have fallen under the domination of two successive horrific wives, the second his niece Agrippina. She is believed to have poisoned him in A.D. 54, to slide her son Nero onto the throne. (Explanations for the family's peculiarities have ranged from Tourette's Syndrome to lead poisoning.)

Understandably, they only managed to hold on to power for a few decades, but they set a tone that did much to corrupt and later destroy Rome. Their family relations were outrageous. The emperor Nero not only had his wife killed, but arranged the death of his own mother, the admittedly appalling Agrippina. She reportedly commanded her assassins to stab her in the womb that had housed so unnatural a son.[165]

The terrible truth, of course, is that brutality and cruelty to others do not necessarily exclude family affection. The atrocious Caligula was reportedly dotingly fond of his spoiled brat of a daughter, Drusilla.[166] (It did her no good. When her father was overthrown, the rebellious soldiers killed her by dashing out her brains.) But brutal surroundings do tend to make for a brutal family.

Given this, it's hard to see Rome as a terrific model of family life. Yet what followed it was in some ways worse, for centuries to come. As the Roman Empire declined and fell, it gradually yielded its power to cultures whose patriarchal family patterns were almost as rigid and hierarchical as those of the original Romans.

However, Rome's final centuries also introduced an entirely new set of values, attitudes which deeply affect our own ideal of family life. Although much of its message remained submerged for centuries, nothing has done more to shape the ways that we think of marriage and children today. For as Rome degenerated, some of its citizens and subjects found an escape from the miseries and confusions of their lives. The great empire collided with a fringe religious cult in one of its less important colonies: Christianity was about to transform the face of the family in the West.

The Christian Family: Church & State, Part II

IN A SOCIETY AS HARSH and autocratic as Rome's, the search for release and comfort inevitably brought many people to religion. They generally did not turn to the state faith, whose gods (some of them former emperors) had ceased to inspire deep devotion. Rome was filled with other sects, seen by the orthodox as cults. Juvenal was scathing about the Eastern creeds infecting Rome, with their bizarre penitential rites and exploitive priests.[1] He did not differentiate between Isis, Jehovah or Jesus—all were foreign frauds.

But Christianity proved to be something very different. It was born in the unequal clash of two cultures: the victorious Romans and the defeated Jews. It was an ideal faith for underdogs, promising salvation in the next life as compensation for the suffering in this one. Yet we know that it also attracted a number of upper-class Romans, particularly women.[2] The reason is obvious. In a world drained of any larger meaning by empty consumerism, hedonism and a fully justified insecurity, Christianity turned life into a moral drama. For the slave drudging away in hunger and misery, for the rich man's wife dreading the next imperial temper tantrum,[3] the new religion offered potent consolations.

At its beginning, it was unquestionably what we would call a cult—a small, fringe faith tending to attract the powerless and to demand absolute dedication from them. Its aims and tenets were profoundly antithetical to the two surrounding societies. In its monotheism and radical politics, it was an affront to Rome. With its attack on the priesthood and scriptural authority, it issued a direct challenge to Judaism.

The new religion's effect on family life was paradoxical. On one hand, Christ said a number of things that ought to have transformed the nature of the family. As we've seen, he rescued the woman taken in adultery, implying that human beings were too sinful to judge one another. Saving her from death, he told the guilty woman only to go forth and sin no more.[4] Unlike either the Romans or the Jews, he did not seem to find women spiritually inferior to men. He included them in his teaching, and spent a good deal of time with them.[5] Women played key roles in his death and resurrection.[6] After his death, many worked to spread the faith. That gave them plenty of opportunities for martyrdom, first under the Romans and later under Rome's destroyers.

Similarly, Christ did not regard children merely as flawed embryonic adults, needing constant restraint. He seemed at times to exalt them above the mature: "Except ye be converted, and become as little children, ye shall not enter into the kingdom of heaven."[7] "Suffer the little children to come unto me, and forbid them not; for of such is the kingdom of God."[8]

There are other teachings that deal directly with the family. From the beginning, the spiritual kinship of the faithful took precedence over the ties of blood—"For whosoever shall do the will of God, the same is my brother, and my sister, and mother."[9] The believer was allowed to stay with a non-Christian spouse, but he was not commanded to waste much energy on preserving the marriage: "... if the unbelieving depart, let him depart. A brother or a sister is not under bondage in such cases..."[10] Christ even restrained a disciple from attending his father's funeral: "Let the dead bury their dead."[11] Yet ironically, because it attacked and eventually weakened the bonds of kinship, Christianity would come to strengthen the nuclear family as a social unit.[12]

At the same time, in setting an example of chastity, Christ lowered the status of marriage. His celibacy was an affront to the central tenets of both Romans and Hebrews. The religions of both demanded marriage, the only source of legitimate children. Christianity's early years coincided with increasing official pressure to force marriage on unwilling Romans. Judaism did not retreat from pressuring the reluctant to marry until the sixteenth century.[13] But the Christian was not merely permitted to remain single—he was vigorously encouraged to do so.

Christ's example had a profound effect on his religion from the start. Many early believers remained virgins; married couples sometimes agreed to forgo sexual relations.[14] At the same time, Christ's ideal of marriage was more stringent than those of the surrounding faiths. He condemned divorce, permissible to both Romans and Jews.[15]

His vision of the family is a radical one, based on ties of love and shared religious striving, rather than honour, prestige and prosperity. For both the Romans and the Hebrews (and every other major culture of the period), the family was very much a matter of property—of dowries, bride-prices, inheritance and accumulation. These have no place in a truly Christian vision; Christ told the faithful that they could not serve both God and Mammon.[16]

In all of this, Christianity turned the values of the surrounding societies upside down. At a time when hierarchy was paramount, it initially made no distinction between free man and slave, Roman and Jew, man and woman, even adult and child.[17] Christ's disciples preached that God is "no respecter of persons."[18] The apostle Paul, no lover of women, told the Galatian Christians that "[t]here is neither Jew nor Greek, there is neither bond nor free, there is neither male nor female: for ye are all one in Christ Jesus."[19]

This is all heady stuff, and the standards it set have had an immeasurable effect on our own civilization. But it had surprisingly little effect on the eventual shape of Christian family life. The early Church made little effort to apply Christ's teachings to relations between husband and wife, or parent and child. The reason is no mystery: the first Christians had little interest in the family. They had been told to set their affections above, "not on things on the earth."[20] St. Paul made the obvious connection: "... [H]e that is married careth for the things that are of the world, how he may please his wife ... The unmarried woman careth for the things of the Lord, that she may be holy both in body and in spirit ..."[21] Dualists to the core, the faithful were to place no value on the things of the flesh; they were to concentrate on the spirit. Marriage and procreation were inarguably physical—and therefore of no real value.

Moreover, the new sect was an apocalyptic one. Believers expected the Messiah to return at any moment; they did not anticipate that they would still be waiting two thousand years later. Given that, the faithful were under no compulsion to breed. After all, this world was going to end almost immediately. St. Paul acknowledged that it was better to marry than to burn with lust,[22] but it was a grudging concession. He made no bones about his preference for the celibate life.

The early church did not generally attempt to regulate family life, leaving such worldly concerns to secular authorities.[23] (The faithful, after all, were to "render therefore unto Caesar the things which are Caesar's."[24]) Instead, it encouraged abstinence from the family's pleasures and pains. This disdain for the family came to pervade Christian thought. In the fifth century A.D., St. Jerome wrote sourly of "the disadvantages of marriage, such as pregnancy, a crying baby, the tortures of jealousy, the cares of household management, and the cutting short by death of all its fancied blessings."[25] No previous religion had placed chastity so high among the virtues. Virginity, one early Father of the Church pronounced, was "supernaturally great, wonderful, and glorious... [the] best and noblest manner of life."[26]

Since human nature is weak, the Church found itself dealing with people who stubbornly married and had children. In some areas, therefore, its leader had to establish guidelines. The new religion remained firmly Jewish in its attitude to life, absolutely banning abortion and the exposure of babies. It retained Christ's condemnation of divorce, banning the remarriage of living partners and thus rendering marriage indissoluble.[27] St. Paul also took a keen interest in suppressing the emancipation of women, characteristic of upper-class Rome. In his first letter to the Corinthians, he commands that women keep silent in church; if they have any questions, they can ask their husbands later.[28] (He does not offer any advice to the puzzled virgin.) After all, woman was created for man, not vice versa.[29]

The role Paul outlines for women would meet with approval from the most traditional Jew or Roman: "... to be sober, to love their husbands, to love their children, to be discreet, chaste, keepers at home, good, obedient to their own husbands..."[30] From the beginning, the early Church failed to hold fast to Christ's egalitarian view of the sexes. The Church Fathers wrote with a misogyny that surpasses the nastiest satires of the Romans. In the third century A.D., Tertullian wrote in *On the Apparel of Women:* "You are the devil's gateway: You are the unsealer of that forbidden tree... You are she who persuaded him whom the devil was not valiant enough to attack."[31] The cult of Mary did surprisingly little to temper this harshness. Drawing on both Roman and Hebrew traditions, Christianity came to see women, in the words of a fifth-century theologian, as "a painted ill."[32]

Although the new dispensation freed believers from many of the rules of Judaism (including male circumcision), the Church was faithful to the Old Testament's sense of menstruation and women in general as polluting. St. Jerome wrote that nothing was as unclean as a woman during her periods; she contaminated all that she touched.[33] To a rather greater extent than Judaism, the new faith emphasized man's fall *through women,* tainting all mankind with original sin.[34]

You might have expected Christ's explicit words on children to have influenced Church thought, but they do not seem to have interested the early leaders much. The writings about them which survive focus on the need to raise offspring as good Christians. One source reminds parents of the need for stern discipline: "be not afraid to reprove them and to teach them wisdom with severity . . . bring them under with cutting stripes."[35]

A letter from St. Jerome in A.D. 403 is one of our most detailed guides to early Christian thinking about child-rearing. His tone in discussing the child Paula is affectionate, and his advice to her mother is generally kindly and shrewd. He urges her, for instance, to stimulate Paula's industry at her lessons through praise rather than scolding. Unsurprisingly, he is against cosmetics, jewellery or revealing clothing; he is for industry, prayer and strict chaperonage. He counsels against stringent fasts for the young, on the sound reasoning that long abstinence is dangerous for the unformed body.

In a famous passage, he recommends that Paula be allowed to bathe and eat meat, and "take a little wine for her stomach's sake."[36] (Remember that safe, pure water is a relatively modern luxury in Europe.) He does, however, insist that the child rise from each meal still hungry, that she never witness any form of entertainment or game, and that her constant companion be "some aged virgin," careless of worldly interests and "inclined to melancholy."[37] Note that Jerome disapproves of baths for any "full-grown virgin," whose modesty should make it impossible for her to strip. The melancholy aging virgin cannot have been an entirely delightful companion.

In the fourth century A.D., the emperor Constantine made Christianity Rome's preferred religion. Like many other early Christians, he may have converted under the influence of a woman—his mother, St. Helena, who acted as a kind of human divining rod in Jerusalem. Pilgrims still visit the sites that she identified with key moments in Christ's career, on the basis of absolutely no evidence.

It would be fair to say that power corrupted the original ascetic nature of Christianity. The first Christians tried as far as possible to restrict food, water, sleep and cleanliness, not to mention sex. As one might expect, most of its followers failed to keep up that life of deprivation indefinitely. Christianity's vision, the historian Barbara Tuchman notes, "was never the art of the possible."[38] But asceticism remained a Christian ideal, one that most deeply affected lives within monasteries and convents.

For one lasting consequence of Christian thought was the development of all-female religious communities. These were almost a mirror image of some of the Eastern cults, whose temples to goddesses so often housed sacred prostitutes. Instead, the first Christian convents were dedicated to chastity and every other form of physical deprivation, to foster spiritual growth.[39] In the centuries to come, they would offer a haven to at least some women who rejected the demands of marriage and motherhood. In 1691, Juana Inéz de la Cruz would write to another nun that she had taken the veil, even though she did not find a religious life entirely congenial, because "given my completely negative feelings about marriage, it was the least disproportionate and most fitting thing I could do." This alternative to marriage for women was an innovation in Western history.

In time, however, it must have occurred to the Church Fathers that a religion composed exclusively of virgins has a limited run on this earth. (The Shakers, a nineteenth-century sect that did insist on celibacy, are no longer among us.) To ensure a continuing supply of virgins, some believers have to breed. The religion eventually decided that family life was *not* one of the things that were Caesar's, and spent a number of centuries working to gain control of it.

As Rome began to lose control of its imperial possessions, Christianity proved adept at adjusting to the world's new masters. In the south, Byzantium replaced the old order. In the north, power returned to the Celtic and Germanic tribes Rome had long held in check.

At first blush, the northern cultures would seem particularly unlikely candidates for conversion, since their chief concern was war. But Christianity had something for everyone. After all, Christ had said he had come into the world not to send peace, but a sword.[40] Here, too, it was often women who led the way, converting their husbands and children. In the sixth century, Clovis, the king of the Franks, originally blamed his wife's Christian faith for the death of one of their children. Then, presumably in desperation, he tried praying to her God before battle. Victory led him to convert.[41]

Now, warrior peoples—Spartan, Viking, Mameluke or Mongol— rarely make domestic life a priority. Their men are supposed to be off doing battle, not lolling around a hearth. Like the Greeks, the Hebrews and the Romans, the tribes of Europe wanted chaste, industrious and obedient wives, raising healthy, hardy, preferably male children. The good woman would need to be both competent and stoical, for the warrior has little time to spare for household concerns, never mind emotional needs. The home's role must be sharply limited. Male children are often wrenched from their mothers early, to be trained for battle.

Cultures of this type are particularly likely to see women as property: women, after all, are usually excluded from warfare, and warfare is their most valued activity.[42] The most important social bond is the brotherhood of warriors, which tends to limit the female role.[43] Like her sisters to the south, the Anglo-Saxon or Frank or Germanic woman was always under the guardianship of a male.[44] In the early centuries, she was at her father's disposal; later, possibly under the influence of the Church, she gained the right to veto a proposed marriage.[45] Among the Germanic tribes, the head of the household had powers almost equal to those of the early Roman *paterfamilias.* He had the power of life and death, the right to inflict corporal punishment and, when necessary, to sell his children.[46]

Like the early Romans, the new rulers were organized into extended families and clans. The nuclear family does not appear to have been an important focus for them. Among the Anglo-Saxons, for instance, the most important unit of relation seems to have been the *maegth,* the body of kinsmen we call a sib.[47] It served in part as a unit of vengeance. If a member of one sib killed another, the victim's sib was responsible for avenging the crime—on any member of the perpetrator's sib it managed to catch.

This idea of collective responsibility was tenacious. As late as the reign of King Ethelred, at the turn of the first millennium, a law decreed that murder must be avenged on the killers "or their nearest kindred, head for head."[48] Fortunately, an alternative solution allowed escape from the eternal feuds that have done so much to depopulate Sicily and the Balkans. It was possible for the guilty sib to pay blood money, in the famous system of *wergild.* The money was dispersed throughout the sib, but women—no surprise—did not share in the spoils until very late.[49]

In one way, however, the status of women was higher than it had been among the Greeks, Romans or Jews. Those cultures were patrilineal; descent came from the father's family alone. As in traditional China, where women might not even appear on the ancestral tables, the female line was submerged. Even today, Jewish liturgy refers to the God of Abraham, Isaac and Jacob. The names of the matriarchs Sarah, Rebecca, Leah and Rachel figure only in self-consciously feminist services.

But the Germanic tribes reckoned descent from both lines. When a kinsman committed a crime, his father's family was responsible for only two-thirds of the compensating payment. The mother's family also owed a third. As in some later Roman marriages, her family also remained responsible for her good conduct—although her husband, inevitably, had the right to beat her as long as he didn't actually cause death.[50] (This privilege lived on in law almost until our own period. There has been considerable academic controversy over the past few years about the supposed derivation of the phrase "rule of thumb," believed to refer to a man's right to beat his wife with a stick no thicker than his thumb. I had come to believe this was a myth, but historian Lawrence Stone assures me that such a rule actually existed.) Nonetheless, the continuing relationship between the families must have had some effect on the treatment of wives, and possibly the status of mothers.

Aside from this, we know relatively little about personal life in the dark centuries that followed the fall of Rome.[51] They left few samples of literature or domestic art to give us a sense of how their families lived. Our knowledge of them is restricted largely to a few bleak law codes, wills and scraps of poetry and history. Their families may have lived in mutual love and enjoyment, or the whole household may have walked on eggshells, terrified of the master's tyrannical temper. Their feelings about one another and their children will remain forever a mystery.

That changes dramatically, however, as Europe entered the second millennium. We know an enormous amount about life in the Middle Ages, even though historians often disagree on the meaning of that information. I can only hope to offer the barest outline of the most significant features of medieval family life, and the enormous changes in it over time.

The first thing a contemporary observer would notice, were he to be miraculously transported back in time, would probably be the smell. It may seem an irrelevant point that the antique traditions of hygiene were largely lost during the Middle Ages. But I think it's important because it goes some way to explaining the prevalence of the Christian disdain for the body. In a world where most people believed that bathing was immoral and unhealthy (see

St. Jerome above), lovers would face a constant reminder that the flesh is corrupt. It must be easier to despise physicality in a society where everyone has terrible breath and body odour—not to mention fleas and lice.

If we were to live in that world for any length of time, our nerves would also be severely strained by the almost total absence of privacy.[52] At the low end of the social scale, an entire family squeezed into a small, single-roomed hovel. Witold Rybczynski says that the poor in town lived in homes that were "little more than shelters for sleeping," so lacking in any privacy that "family life was compromised."[53] Where there were two rooms, the second might well house animals; it took money to build a barn.[54]

Even in the homes of prosperous peasants, everyone slept on the large bedstead, "piled high with straw pallets," in the words of one writer, "all seething with vermin."[55] Any overnight visitors were welcome to join the grandparents, parents and children on this communal bed—along, all too often, with the pigs and chickens. (Pig bites were responsible for 5 per cent of the deaths of infants. Chickens pecking at the hearth often started fires; cradle fires were the leading cause of death for babies.[56])

Up at the castle, formality and pomp counted more than comfort. There were public and private rooms, if we make "private" a relative term. As with the Romans, a *ménage* embraced many more inhabitants than the nuclear family. Noble homes teemed with attendants of all kinds. Meals in the great dining halls were public spectacles.[57]

Personal space was available only at the top of the social order; the lord's bedchamber was the least accessible part of the house.[58] Even there, other people slept close at hand.[59] A lord or lady was surrounded by dependents all day. From rising to retiring, servants assisted—and watched. This thoroughly public life unquestionably had profound effects on intimacy and relationships.

Moreover, social attitudes reinforced this openness. The Middle

Ages did not have much of a concept of private life, or even individual selfhood. Peasants were so thoroughly lacking in self-consciousness that they went about naked in the summer.[60] The community was involved in spheres that we see as purely personal. Friends and relations accompanied newlyweds to the bridal bed. It is fortunate the bed was curtained because the guests often engaged in boisterous pranks just outside it to distract the groom from the task at hand. This practice must have died very late, at least in the lower and middle classes. In 1857, the fictional Emma Bovary begs to be spared the normal vulgar jokes of the wedding night; one cousin had hoped to spit water into the bridal chamber through the keyhole.

The outside world was even more intrusive when it disapproved of a match or of the conduct of a marriage. When an older man married a young woman, when a widow remarried, when a woman started to rove, when a couple failed to conceive within a few years, they ran the risk of a *charivari*. In this mocking ceremony, the victims were forced to ride back to back in a raucous, ribald parade of their masked neighbours.[61] Beatrice Gottlieb writes that its distinctive contributions were "noise, ridicule, and obscenity,"[62] adding in an interview that it must have been "an awful experience" for its victims. It was inflicted on the adulterous, on the shrewish wife, on the inappropriate couple. It survived and mutated into the gentler shivaree of the American frontier, a kind of group serenade of a bridal couple. But the original intent was punitive.

Relations within the family were far more hierarchical than our own, and—at least among the upper classes—much more formal. The head of the household occupied the place of God the Father within his own home.[63] He had the right to punish any of its members physically, from his wife and children down.[64] Relations between the sexes and the generations were supposed to be ceremonial, at least in public.[65] To an extent we can scarcely imagine, this was a world obsessed with issues of protocol, precedence and proper behaviour. (This concern, unfortunately, did not preclude a great deal of brawling.[66])

At the top end, medieval society was still organized into extended families and clans, with elaborate kin relations and inheritance laws. But lineage was of little importance to peasants, and kinship ties had weakened dramatically. The indigent peasant turned to parents, siblings and children for assistance, not to more distant relations.[67]

Male and female spheres were sharply divided, largely because of the familiar terror of female unchastity. Since actual knights were closer in conduct to Lear's attendants than to the knights of the Round Table, this was probably a wise precaution. But daily labour was a more crucial issue. There was little common ground in the work pursued by the genders. Women could not join in the hunt or battle-training; men took no interest in the distaff or the kitchen. In the castle, males belonged in the hall, women in the bedchamber.[68] For peasants, the fields and forests were men's domain, while women belonged in the house. That was the theory, at any rate, and the usual practice among the well-to-do. The less fortunate wife might spend much of her time in the fields as well, and even in the forests, gathering herbs and anything else a human could eat.

This was not the best of worlds for children. As we've already seen, the Middle Ages seems strikingly indifferent to them in a number of ways. They were rarely represented in art or discussed in the age's myriad books of advice on conduct.[69] The community sometimes intervened to stop men from assaulting their wives, but there is no case on record of public intercession in a case of child abuse.[70] At home and at school, the disciplining of children would seem wildly excessive to us. But this was a harsh age. Flagellation was a routine discipline for adults in monasteries and castles. The penalties for actual crimes would strike us as barbarous. Maiming, a common punishment, could involve gouging out eyes, lopping off ears or ripping out the tongue. There were lay courts in parts of Europe that cauterized the genitalia of adulterous wives with white-hot tongs.[71]

Royalty and nobles could afford large families, even if they were less than ecstatic over the need to dower their daughters. (There was in any case always the option of forcing a girl into a convent, a cheaper alternative.) But for the poor, fertility was a mixed blessing. On one hand, children could prove immensely useful. They were put to work almost as soon as they could walk—foraging, running errands, fetching water, fishing and tending babies.[72] The poor also needed children to guarantee their maintenance in old age, especially in a world in which kinship ties were so attenuated. But there was a drawback: the poor couldn't feed very many mouths. Then again, they usually didn't have to: the mortality rate for children ran as high as one or two in three.[73] Poor women also could not afford wet nurses, which gave them considerable protection against closely spaced pregnancies. Finally, malnutrition and ill health undoubtedly hindered conception and often caused miscarriages.

Remember also that a surprisingly large chunk of the population never married, because it could not afford to.[74] Others stayed single in religious communities. We do not know how many people lived in convents and monasteries, nor if religious communities drew their members from all social classes, or just the cream. But we do know that a significant percentage of the population lived in accordance with the Church's preferences, and renounced the possibility of family life of any kind.

Most medieval people also married late. It's true that kings and lords liked to marry off their daughters very young. Betrothal at the age of seven was not unusual. The ruling class wanted its alliances cemented the instant the girls hit the dangerous threshold of puberty. (Medieval Jews shared the same preference, in part because the financial future was always precarious, and in part because marriage provided some minimal protection for young women against a hostile

Christendom.[75]) But for the general population, the average age of marriage was not early—about twenty-five.[76]

For the average man or woman, marriage had nothing to do with romance. Where families had any property worth preserving, matches were usually arranged by parents or guardians.[77] Masters and lords felt free to marry off their vassals as they wished.[78] Even if they weren't quite that high-handed, their approval was necessary for a wedding. Nor was their blessing free. The vassal had to pay the lord for the privilege of marrying by paying a special fine called the "merchet."[79] He could not escape payment by living in sin, either. There was *another* fine for bearing an illegitimate child, the "leywrite." Like Cato charging his slaves for the right to have sex, the medieval lord liked to cover all the bases. Finally, even in families who were not dependent on some great man, personal preference ran a poor second to economic considerations. A couple could not marry on nothing.

And a man with a craft or some land or any kind of business needed to marry; he could not manage without a wife's labour.[80] Beatrice Gottlieb notes that where we often have two-career couples, this culture generally required whole-household careers.[81] Men needed women to help in the fields, to keep an eye on business when they were away, to supervise servants and apprentices, to make clothes, to prepare food. Like the women of the ancient civilizations before her, the medieval housewife spent a lot of time salting, drying, smoking or fermenting food. The female peasant, chronically overworked, might journey to the fields spinning as she walked.

The economic necessity of marriage is obvious in the high rates of remarriage among the widowed. The surges in marriage rates after the great plagues are also evidence for it, although other factors were at work.[82] Historians assume that people felt an urge to reproduce in the face of so much death. Moreover, the sudden reduction in the population created large inheritances, often in the hands of young orphans. Piers Plowman deplored the greed-based matches so common "since the pestilence."[83] Whatever the motive, Church and State took a keen interest in getting Europeans paired off and breeding after any depopulating catastrophe. Polygamy was even briefly permitted in parts of Germany after the carnage of the Hundred Years' War.[84]

But marriage was not merely pragmatic. It was not even inevitably arranged. The high-born teenager had little hope of finding her own husband, since too much rode on finding the right alliance for her. But if she managed to survive her first husband, she had a fair chance of pleasing herself the next time round. (The Church proved unable to prevent the remarriage of widows.) Moreover, peasants and burghers did not necessarily trust to the judgment of their elders and betters. The love match was seen as a problem, but it was a *common* problem.

This was possible because of a combination of cultural peculiarities. First, there was a tradition of marriage as a process, rather than a single event. To an even greater extent than in Judea or Rome, betrothal was a crucial ceremony, at least as important as the wedding. Once the knotty question of property had been ironed out, the couple was essentially regarded as wed. For the Germanic tribes in particular, the key issue was the payment of a bride-price. An agreement to marry carried the two families almost all the way to the wedding.

Secondly, medieval Europeans had inherited some of Rome's elastic approach to marriage. While arrangements remained highly formal for the élite and propertied, the laws of many areas reflected the idea that shaped lower-class unions in Rome: consent makes marriage. In this largely non-literate society, an exchange of vows between the couple constituted wedlock.[85] It was possible to marry without benefit of clergy, witnesses or written record.

Consummation, of course, was necessary to seal the marriage— not just for its own sake, but because only after taking it did the groom make his final payment, the morning gift. Although the origins of the custom were eventually lost, it constituted payment for the bride's virginity, which could not be established until someone tested it.[86]

Given all this, sex between fiancés, no matter how deeply it offended the church, constituted a minor sin in the secular world. Beatrice Gottlieb notes the surprising attitude towards it in Shakespeare's *Measure for Measure,* a play steeped in Christian beliefs. In it, the Duke—impersonating a priest—endorses the sexual substitution of Angelo's fiancée, Mariana, for the woman he actually wants, Isabella. Apparently, since Angelo and Mariana were engaged (he has jilted her), intercourse does not constitute fornication.[87]

That meant that the pregnant bride was not an unusual figure in the lower classes. Gottlieb reasons that it was not so much that the pregnancy forced couples to marry, as that the prospect of marriage freed them to have sexual relations.[88]

This system was not without problems. A steady procession of pregnant spinsters besieged the church courts, claiming that their seducers had spoken the magic "words of marriage." (By the second millennium, the church had jurisdiction over marital issues.) There are records from the fourteenth and fifteenth centuries of high drama at village churches. Men not infrequently disrupted the reading of banns, claiming to be the prospective bride's real husband.[89] Sometimes they brought witnesses to substantiate their claims; sometimes the Church had to base its judgment on nothing but two conflicting stories.

The result of this possibility was often chaos. Suzanne Scorsone performs a vivid re-enactment of an aged crone appearing at a funeral, swearing that she exchanged vows with the deceased in a field thirty years before. Clerics grilled bewildered peasants about the tense of the words used, because in theory a mere promise to marry in the future didn't count. For the vows to be valid, the couple had to say that they married one another, not just that they would do so one day.

The Church also recognized, albeit with distaste, that the combination of vows and sexual congress had to be recognized as a marriage. Surprisingly few couples availed themselves of this winning combination. We will never know if they lacked opportunity, knowledge of the Church's position, or simply courage. But the illegitimacy rates were very low, especially given the late age of marriage. Since premarital sex was largely the prerogative of fiancés, presumably the inconveniently pregnant simply proceeded with the wedding. The single mother was most likely to be a victim of breach of promise.[90]

Secular authorities were no more enamoured of this *ad hoc* betrothal system than the Church. Clandestine marriages permitted people to escape the control of their families—a challenge to public order. Lawrence Stone told me that historians now believe such marriages were particularly popular among the poor, as a means of escaping from their parents. But, he noted, they also proved useful for rebels in the upper classes.[91]

Beatrice Gottlieb cites a famous example from the reign of Henry II of France, in the sixteenth century. The king had arranged to marry his illegitimate daughter, Diane de France (aged seven) to the son of the Duc de Montmorency. But the young man admitted that he had already exchanged vows of marriage with a young lady-in-waiting. A papal court decided in favour of the enamoured couple, but the prelate of the French Church found a way to circumvent the ruling.[92] In an interview, Gottlieb added that the young man eventually yielded to pressure and repudiated his vows, but the young woman steadfastly refused to recant.

This licensed loophole in the laws on marriage is an astonishingly subversive tradition, and one that tells us something important about the family. It strongly suggests a recognition of romantic love, even a kind of grudging endorsement of its rights. In defiance of families, rulers and Church, it permitted some people to marry for love, evading the whole elaborate structure of obedience and duty.

A corollary of this, of course, is that people had the opportunity to meet, to fall in love, to snatch enough private time to blurt out the vows that united them in the face of opposition. It isn't surprising that this was possible in courts, but peasants and servants were able to form such marriages, too. It was an option in part because so many young people did not live under the watchful eyes of their own families. Remember that the medieval world believed strongly that it was good for children to leave home, for both practical and moral reasons. Sent out as servants or apprentices or courtiers, the young enjoyed more freedom than we often realize. Both Beatrice Gottlieb and Natalie Zemon Davis emphasize that they could mingle at festivals and outings.[93]

That meant that they often chose their own marriage partners, even if they sought and obtained the consent of their families or masters. Yet, even given all this, it is difficult to see why Church and State allowed the practice of unsanctioned marriage to last as long as it did. Catholic priests were not required to keep marriage registries until the Council of Trent finally ended the possibility of confusion in the sixteenth century—as a response, interestingly, to the new stringency of Protestantism. Britain waited much longer.[94]

This seems particularly odd because clandestine marriage is antithetical to the pattern of medieval life; it requires secrecy, privacy and insubordination. While the rest of society married at the church door and celebrated with a public feast, the secret match could take place anywhere—a field, a bedroom, an alehouse, even a brothel.[95]

Lawrence Stone notes that the idea sounds romantic, but—at least in Britain—the reality was often sordid. The law eventually forced eloping couples to find a willing minister; Stone describes the clergy who performed such ceremonies as "pretty dissolute characters"—often drunks or imprisoned debtors. Yet the practice was not abolished in England until the mid-eighteenth century—and even then, a really determined couple could escape to the more permissive legal climate of Scotland.[96] The flight to Gretna Green was a real option for the runaway bride.

The love match was not the Middle Ages' only contact with romance. It was a society obsessed with adultery.[97] Tales of cuckoldry were a favourite form of entertainment. The plot Chaucer used in the *The Merchant's Tale* shows up in at least three languages.[98] In it, a young wife takes advantage of her husband's blindness to have sex with her lover in a pear tree. The gods or their agents (Pluto for Chaucer, St. Peter in other versions) take pity on the wronged husband and restore his sight. But the young wife is able to talk her way out of trouble.

This fascination shaped the way men treated their wives in the real world. While the medieval wife did not precisely live in purdah, she was closely watched and guarded.[99] It was thought wise to keep this dangerous creature busy plying her needle or on her knees in prayer.[100] Idleness spelled danger. Writers advised fathers that reading was an unnecessary skill for females, unless they intended to take the veil. One expert argued that female literacy could only lead to the reading of love letters.[101]

The temptation to stray must have risen sharply as men's manners improved. For from the twelfth century on, it was possible to dress up adulterous lust in fancy clothes. The new cult of courtly love glorified the image of women, and changed the code of chivalry and etiquette to include a reverence for women—at least well-born women. (The peasant female remained eligible for a less chivalrous relationship, such as rape.[102]) Courtly love dictated total dedication to—even worship of—a worthy woman.

The idea of courtly love turned adulterous passion almost into a religion.[103] Georges Duby regards it as a form of education, "a pattern of sentimental behaviour."[104] Literary works like the *Roman de la Rose* created a new standard of knightly conduct—conveniently, at exactly the time that low-born merchants were starting to represent serious competition to the ruling class. Courtly love offered the young knight a new way to prove his superiority to others, through his devotion and purity in love. He was to be distinguished by his courtesy, his self-restraint and his consuming capacity for adoration. The new man of the Middle Ages, somewhat like his 1990s successor, was supposed to exhibit some of the female virtues along with his prowess in combat.

In the mouths of the original troubadours, this love was supposed to stay platonic: the poet loved his mistress without expecting a return. Obviously, this is not how things usually worked in the real world. But this literary tradition had an effect in that world, by creating the idea of woman as man's moral superior, his road to salvation.

This became an instance of life imitating art. The lady of romance improved the lot of the lady of the manor. Between the twelfth and fifteenth centuries, courteous treatment of women became—for the first time—a hallmark of the gentleman. During the Hundred Years' War, John, Duke of Bourbon, made his knights swear to maintain the honour of all women "of good birth." He lived up to his own vow, escorting the Duchess of Brittany to the nearest castle held by her own people, rather than holding her prisoner. "No, we do not war on ladies," he explained chivalrously.[105]

The idea was not the radical departure we used to assume, but it was of tremendous importance. The troubadour sighing over his perfect and unattainable mistress created a different way of looking at women, not as inferiors, but as saints. The Roman or Hebrew lover could not *think* about his mistress or wife in quite this way, no matter how he felt. We have inherited this idea of woman as potential Madonna, along with its reverse image of woman as temptress and whore. Without the tradition of courtly love, Dickens could never have created his more mawkish idealized heroines, and the sentimental agonies of *Love Story* would be beyond imagination.

The code of chivalry and courtly love was only one face of medieval relations. It belonged to the high culture, and co-existed with a less attractive and elevated set of attitudes that crossed all class lines. Medieval society twinned a second obsession with adultery; it was fixated on the idea of the shrewish, dominant woman. The termagant was a favourite theme of literature and folk tales. Beatrice Gottlieb acknowledges that medieval men had "an almost pathological fear of shrews."[106]

It is difficult to judge if this fear was rooted in reality. In theory, women were totally under the domination of men. Even as late as the eighteenth century, English common law worked on the blithe assumption that "[t]he husband and wife are one, and the husband is that one."[107] Church and State agreed on the wife's inferior status, and the desirability of obedience and compliance. The lord of the manor was free to regard his lady as one more feudal possession, a field he could plough at will. Confessors warned wives never to withhold their bodies from their lawful spouses.[108]

The crime of killing a husband was classified as treason, an offence against the State.[109] A wife's legal rights were meagre throughout Europe; her husband could pretty well do as he pleased, unless he actually murdered her. In the thirteenth century, St. Thomas Aquinas argued that woman, being more frail "both in vigour of soul and strength of body," necessarily should be "subject to man, in whom reason predominates."[110]

But men couldn't overcome the fear that women weren't subject to reason. Female power was personified in a magnificent fictional figure from the fourteenth century, Chaucer's Wife of Bath. This heroine has battled her way to dominance over five successive husbands. The moral of her tale is that what women most want is "sovereynetee"—mastery over their husbands.[111]

The Wife of Bath turns medieval values upside down. She starts her prologue with an erudite and well-reasoned attack on virginity. She also argues that women deserve to rule precisely *because* they are less reasonable than men. She even drubs one of her husbands into submission while he tries to read the great misogynist tracts of the age—including the works of St. Jerome. She uses words and her fists as weapons, and she wins.

The Wife of Bath is much, much larger than life, but there were women who did manage to rule their husbands. Margery Kempe, a very different kind of creature, is one example. She was a daughter of the mayor of Lynn in the fifteenth century. Married at twenty, she endured a series of miserable pregnancies—fourteen of them in all. She started to have religious visions, and enlisted the help of Christ to escape from her husband's apparently limitless sexual appetite. In one quarrel over her vow of chastity, he asked her if she would rather see him dead than sleep with him again. She agreed that she would, and pointed out that they had already kept chaste for eight weeks. He answered that he had refrained only because he was afraid of her. In the end, she had her way. He left her alone on condition that they share a bed, eat together on Fridays, and that she pay all his debts. They separated for a while, but when he was old and senile she took him back and nursed him.[112]

Most marriages, however, were nothing like this. The nagging, insubordinate or violent wife ran the risk of a *charivari* or her husband's revenge. There is a horrible story by Geoffroy de la Tour Landry about a woman who criticized her husband in public. He "smote her with his fist down to the earth," kicked her face, broke her nose and disfigured her forever. Landry notes with satisfaction that for the rest of her life, she "might not for shame show her visage." He sees this as rightful punishment for "her evil and great language she was wont to say to her husband."[113]

This "evil and great language" would probably have been acceptable in a male mouth. Even in our own more egalitarian age, the anthropologist Deborah Tannen has shown that our perceptions of the two sexes are skewed.[114] Women are seen as interrupting conversations often, even though they do so less frequently than men. We assume subconsciously that males have the right to dominate.

But there was nothing subconscious about the medieval belief in women's lower status. It was personified in another favourite cautionary tale, the story of patient Griselda. She showed up in print at least four times in the fourteenth century, in Chaucer, Boccaccio, Petrarch and Le Ménagier. In each version, she is a woman of humble birth who has the bad luck to attract a nobleman. He marries her, then determines to try her patience. He subjects her to a series of trials and humiliations, robbing her of her children and telling her they're dead. Finally, he informs her that he intends to remarry, and makes her wait on the bride. Griselda, a human dishrag, bears all this submissively. The bride turns out to be her daughter, and they all live happily ever after— Griselda is not the type to hold a grudge.

To be fair, Le Ménagier felt that the story was cruel and unreasonable. He was a gentle soul, who penned a monumental manual of advice for his young wife.[115] (At the age of at least sixty, he married a girl of fifteen.) He counselled her on everything from choosing a good horse to planning a menu for twelve guests during Lent. A realistic man, he also anticipated that he would predecease her, and considered the question of her second husband with equanimity. (He urged her to choose a successor worthy of him.) Nonetheless, even he held a kind of mirror image of the Wife of Bath's ideal marriage. "No man can be better bewitched," he advised wives, "than by giving him what pleaseth him."[116]

The Church was a powerful ally for men seeking to control their women. Female subordination was one area where secular and religious authorities enjoyed total agreement. But there were other, more contentious issues about family life. The Middle Ages witnessed an ongoing struggle between religious and secular authorities over control of the family. The Church's concerns went well beyond its particularly sweeping definition of incest. It maintained its rather Hebraic horror of any form of sexual deviance, and, as we've seen, its interpretation of deviance was exceptionally broad. Its exaltation of chastity made a celibate, monastic life a possibility for at least some of the population, occasionally in the teeth of parental opposition.

It also created an obsession with controlling sex, even in marriage. The Church was anxious that even married couples refrain from sex for any purpose other than procreation. It prescribed periods of abstinence for them, and urged them not to enjoy intercourse for its own sake.[117] At the same time, its horror of illicit sex indirectly weakened the bonds between mother and infant, at least among the well-to-do. Medieval folk wisdom dictated that it was wrong for a nursing mother to have sex, and the Church feared the consequences of keeping a man from the bed of his lawful spouse. Priests therefore urged the upper-class mother to find a wet nurse.[118]

I strongly doubt that Christ would have been in favour of this ruling. He certainly would have disapproved of other elements of medieval doctrine. A strong interest in property lay under a number of religious laws. The medieval Church opposed co-habitation without marriage, the remarriage of widows, marriage between relatives, the levirate and even adoption. It is no coincidence that these practices—all common in Rome's later centuries—tended to keep property within families. The Church preferred that as much property as possible should flow elsewhere—to itself. Ignoring Christ's condemnation of serving Mammon, it was fixated on legacies.[119]

It also liked power, and dealt harshly with challenges to its hegemony. It waged, for instance, an increasingly vicious war against "witches"—not just heretics, as during the Inquisition, but women believed to have supernatural powers. Some of these must have been mad, others just unlucky. There's a widespread belief among historians now that many were midwives, skilled in the arts of contraception and abortion. Certainly hysteria about them rose regularly after each round of deadly plague, at those times when the need to repopulate Christendom was particularly high.[120] The craze peaked a bit later, between 1560 to 1670, during periods of devastating wars and religious division.

As we've already seen, the Church's prohibitions on incestuous marriage conveniently worked to undermine the strength and cohesiveness of kinship, that rival loyalty. The Church also succeeded in establishing jurisdiction over contested marriages and marital conflict from an early period. In northwestern Europe, a priest usually officiated at the wedding ceremony—not, until much later, inside the church, but at its door.[121] (Marriage in front of the altar was a southern custom.) The Church also played a role *before* the wedding, since the priest read banns for weeks before the ceremony. In theory, that ensured there was no impediment to the union.

Nonetheless, the Church didn't even get around to officially declaring marriage a sacrament until the Fourth Lateran Council in 1215. The regulations governing matrimony did not become consistent until even later, at the Council of Trent in 1561. The Church's long, reluctant tolerance of clandestine marriage was only one example of its difficulties in controlling the faithful. Divorce proved very difficult to eradicate, although the Church obviously triumphed in the end.[122] Divorce is still not an option for devout Catholics, and sometimes their governments. Ireland only began to permit it in 1997.

The Church's efforts were sometimes wholly unsuccessful. While it could eventually keep people from dissolving their marriages legally, it could never entirely control individual couples. The medieval equivalent of divorce was desertion. We have no accurate figures on absconders, but in England deserted wives accounted for about a third of the poor rolls.[123] Similarly, canon law treated adultery as an equal crime in both sexes, but it couldn't convince anyone else to do so. Concubinage remained standard among the ruling class, and secular authorities generally punished only unfaithful women.[124] Like other patriarchal societies, feudal Europe did not expect sexual fidelity from upper-class men.

Despite the Church's teachings, courtiers ridiculed the faithful husband. Servants and peasant women were automatically fair game.

Homosexuality, although strictly forbidden, obviously flourished, especially in the monasteries. Boswell believes that a couple of poems of medieval love strongly suggest lesbian attachments, although I think allowances must be made for the flowery literary conventions of the age.[125]

The laws on incest proved similarly difficult to enforce. Aristocrats demanded blood relatives, the only available partners of equal rank.[126] In 1215, the Lateran Council relaxed some of the rules, reducing the prohibited range to the fourth degree.[127] The Church finally developed a system that allowed Christians to buy dispensations from the rules on kinship.[128] This escape hatch became an important source of income.

Ironically, that compromise sabotaged another apparently iron-clad rule, the ban on divorce. Royal husbands often suddenly discovered that unsatisfactory wives fell within the prohibited bounds of kinship. In 1152, Louis VII of France was persuaded to divorce Eleanor of Aquitaine, on the grounds that they were distant cousins. That left her free to marry Henry Plantagenet, a future king of England.[129] A husband could rid himself of his wife on the grounds that she was too closely related; God frowned on their union. That was precisely the issue that led to the fall of the Catholic Church in England. Rome refused to let Henry VIII wriggle out of his marriage to Catherine of Aragon, his brother's widow. Even today, these medieval conundrums have not disappeared. The current mayor of New York, Rudy Giuliani, successfully sued for the dissolution of his first marriage on the grounds that he and his wife were second cousins.

There is a pattern of advance and retreat in the history of the Church's efforts to prevent the faintest tinge of incest, for its own spiritual and pragmatic reasons. In other areas of family life, it encountered less resistance. In a society where primogeniture was absolute, its monasteries and priesthood were convenient asylums for younger sons. A religious vocation—genuine or imposed—was also a convenient answer for families unwilling to part with large dowries for their daughters.

It took a long time for the Church to insinuate itself fully into marriage. The first liturgical rituals of marriage did not appear in northern Europe until around 1100.[130] It took centuries to convince the cultures of the north that a priest was a necessary presence at the ceremony. The influence of the Church's thinking can nonetheless be gauged in the very low illegitimacy figures for this period.

Then, just as the Church seemed to have won, the system started to unravel. Much of the responsibility for this can be laid at the Church's own door. The sixteenth century witnessed a Roman-style moral slackness, followed by that revival of early Christian commitment, the Reformation. Many medieval Europeans had failed to live Christian lives, of course, but some sources make the sixteenth century sound like one long orgy. And some of the major players in this long Saturnalia were monks, priests and popes.

It may seem odd to discuss Catholic clergy in the context of marriage, since family ties were precisely what priests, monks and nuns were supposed to renounce. (In fact, priests had been allowed to marry until the eleventh century.) The gap between doctrine and practice, however, grew exceptionally wide during the fifteenth century. The theoretically celibate were in fact raising families, taking lovers and generally scoffing at their vows.

The scandalous tales of the period come not just from the pens of Reformation critics, but from the clergy themselves. Abbot Johannes Trithemius of Sponheim condemned his own monks: "The whole day is spent in filthy talk; their whole time is given to play and gluttony . . . They scorn the vow of poverty, know not that of chastity, revile that of obedience . . ."[131]

This picture might seem exaggerated, until we consider, say, the Borgias and the Medici, who both produced popes. The papacy of the fifteenth century rivalled the worst excesses of Rome. To take an almost unbelievable example, Pope Alexander VI (1431–1503), a

Borgia, set the worst possible example for the faithful. His behaviour—including full-blown orgies—deeply distressed his predecessor, Pius II, himself the father of various children by different mistresses.[132] Alexander openly raised his assortment of illegitimate offspring, including the infamous Lucrezia Borgia.[133] William Manchester writes of him, "Breaking any commandment excited him, but he was partial to the seventh."[134] He was equally fond of naked attendants at his parties, and, of course, money. Savonarola himself preached against Alexander's corruption, and was executed for his pains.

This type of pope—and Alexander was not unique—is naturally very expensive. Priests had to sell a lot of indulgences to support the Vatican's weakness for ostentation. The flagrant abuse of power combined with other cultural changes that were not friendly to the unreasonable authoritarianism of the medieval world. Those changes included a revival of interest in both classical learning and the Bible, propelled by the fifteenth-century invention of the printing press.

In 1517, a choleric priest at the University of Wittenberg grew tired of the Church's abuses, especially the sale of indulgences. He nailed his ninety-five articles against a church door, and launched the Reformation. Martin Luther initially set out to reform the Church, not the family. But the religious movement he eventually established, Protestantism, would again alter the shape of marriage, and relations between parent and child.

From Patriarchy to Romance

THE ORIGINAL PROTESTANT reformers were a dour and repressed set of men, but they ultimately placed the Western family on its current emotional basis. This was not their intention; they would undoubtedly have been disgusted by the developments that shaped family life in the centuries that followed. These changes are extraordinarily dramatic. Although a mere 450 years separate Martin Luther's first revolt from the glory years of our own sexual revolution, between him and us lies a whirlwind of changes—social, economic and technological. In the context of the whole of human history, moreover, these sharp alterations occurred at comparatively breakneck speed. They were to mould family life in the West into forms that had nothing to do with the world's other dominant cultures.

For until the Reformation, family patterns in Europe would have been largely recognizable to the other major civilizations. India, the Middle East, China and Japan were similarly patriarchal, authoritarian and hierarchical. Kinship was both deep and extended, especially at the upper end of the social scale. The essential similarities of all these cultures were to some extent masked by their more glaring differences, features such as the Islamic and Chinese toleration of polygamy, for instance, or the Hindu practice of *suttee*, the immolation of widows.[1] But they all rested on the same basic principles.

Like Europeans, fathers in all these societies assumed the right to marry off their children as they wished. All stressed the need for discipline with children, whose great debt to their fathers (and ancestors in the Far East) could never fully be repaid. Fundamentally, families in the major cultures of the world were organized like pyramids, with power and property concentrated at the top. Obedience, deference and industry were prime virtues in all of them.

Of course, just as Europe faced the insubordination of clandestine lovers, the other cultures harboured their own rebels. Human beings have a great capacity to subvert rules that become seriously inconvenient. Islam, for instance, places great value on filial piety. Yet in the seventeenth century, the Mogul prince Aurangzeb made himself emperor by overthrowing his own father, Shah Jahan. Aurangzeb then kept his parent a prisoner until the Shah's death— ignoring the Islamic principles he otherwise passionately embraced.

In the same way, it is impossible for any culture, no matter how rigid, to completely repress unlawful sexual passion. One example is the eponymous heroine of Jonathan Spence's *The Death of Woman Wang*.[2] Her revolt was cut short, but she managed briefly to evade the whole weight of Confucian doctrine on restraint and obedience. We know little of her life. She was married to a poor hired labourer named Jen. She lived with him and his seventy-year-old father until the old man moved, unable to get along with her. History remembers her only because, in 1671, she ran away with another man.[3]

Her lover soon abandoned her.[4] Her husband eventually took her back. In January 1672, he strangled her as she slept, intending to claim that a hated neighbour was both her lover and her murderer.[5] The plot failed, and Jen was executed for murder.

A European court might have forgiven him, but he was criminally culpable under the laws of China. His mistake was not murdering his wife, but waiting too long to do so. The Chinese legal code dictated that revenge had to be hot in a *crime passionnel,* exacted almost instantly.

Even in Japan, perhaps the world's most rigidly conformist society, we have accounts from the seventeenth century of a *demi-monde* that ran counter to all the culture's professed values. The Japanese merchant class developed a "floating world" of prostitutes, courtesans, gamblers and musicians that swayed sons from the paths of industry and duty. Satirical moralists, very much in the style of Rome, wrung every lascivious detail from their scolding tales of prodigal sons frittering away their time and money on worthless women and empty pleasures. Housewives, they nagged, had developed the fashions and manners of prostitutes.[6] Fathers slaved for sons who dissipated all they'd earned, leaving grandchildren to starve.[7] The floating world was bad news for families, but a great boon to literature.

Like Europe, all of these cultures were obsessively anxious about the chastity of their women. They also shared the Western worry about the dominant wife. In *The Thousand and One Nights,* one story concerns a cobbler named Ma'aruf, whose wife, Fatimah, is a genuine virago. When he fails to bring back to her precisely the pastry she wants (one made with honey rather than sugar), she knocks out one of his teeth and tries to pull out his beard.[8]

But these deviations from the norm were precisely that. The norm itself was not about to change dramatically; the shape of the family in these cultures was to remain consistent for centuries to come. In the West, the sixteenth century marks the beginning of truly radical changes that were to transform the nature of marriage and parenthood. We have come to live in a world where poor Woman Wang might have lived happily ever after.

In some ways, it is obvious why they started in the West. European women, restricted as they often were, nonetheless enjoyed considerably more freedom than their sisters to the East. By 1427, for example, 15.6 per cent of households in Florence were headed by women who had evaded male guardianship.[9] (These women, often widows, may not have seen their single status as a privilege, of course. Many of them must have been very poor.) From the twelfth century on, some women (often widows) were members of craft guilds in their own right, working as shoemakers, tanners, haberdashers, even smiths.[10]

Within the home, however, the husband still embodied both civil and religious authority as the domestic representative of both king and Christ. I do not think it would be unjust to say that the emphasis in all spheres of life was on behaviour: not how you felt or thought, but what you did. The Reformation went a long way to changing that, raising new issues in the conduct of family life.

When we left Martin Luther at the church door, he was a celibate priest (he still saw himself as a monk), with no intention of taking on the Church over the issue of clerical celibacy or any other aspect of sexual or family life. There can be no less likely figure to bolster the strength of the nuclear family. His childhood was wretched.[11] His father, a miner, believed that what children really needed was punishment—beatings severe enough to knock them out. Martin, the oldest of seven, bore the brunt of his sadism. His mother shared this zest for discipline.

Although Luther's mother was devout, it's not possible to blame the Church for his misery. His father's beliefs were pre-Christian, a jumble of terrors about goblins, demons and witches. For Luther, taking vows was an act of rebellion.

His initial desire was to reform the Church—in particular, to end the frenzied sale of indulgences initiated by Pope Leo X, another

Borgia. In 1476, an earlier pope had declared that money given to the Church on earth could rescue sinners from purgatory.[12] In the early sixteenth century, Leo X, broke and desperate, launched a major marketing campaign for indulgences. Luther attacked this bargain-basement approach to salvation, and a revolution started.

The Church fought back, summoning Luther to Rome. He declined. With support from Prince Frederick the Wise and other German rulers, he continued battling on his own turf. Opposition from Rome fed his anger; he turned against the papacy and the Church.

This matters to the history of the family because his fury eventually spilled onto other Catholic doctrines. In 1522, in his pamphlet *On Christian Marriage,* he savaged the Church's glorification of virginity and its ban on the marriage of clergy.[13] For the first time in Christian history, a theologian had declared marriage a *higher* good than chastity. Three years later, Luther took a wife himself. His spouse, Katherine von Bora, must have matched his fiery nature, for she had escaped from a convent in 1523.[14]

As you might expect from his upbringing, Luther remained ambivalent about sex even in the context of marriage. His own worked out well. He must have controlled his concerns about sexual sin, since the couple had six children. His best-known quotation on marriage is wholly positive: "There is no more lovely, friendly and charming relationship, communion or company than a good marriage."[15] (This seems to me a great improvement on the classical viewpoint expressed by Menander in the third century B.C.: "Marriage, if one will face the truth, is an evil, but a necessary evil.")

But Luther's vision remained close to the Church's in a number of areas. He had no desire, for instance, to alter the tradition of male supremacy. Although he blasted Catholic clergy for their misogyny, he also noted blandly that women's wide hips proved they were built to stay at home, raising children.[16]

Luther was also no fan of the love match, although he did not believe in forcing offspring into unwelcome marriages.[17] In 1524, he produced a pamphlet with the comprehensive title *Parents Should Neither Compel Nor Hinder the Marriage of Their Children, and Children Should Not Become Engaged without the Consent of Their Parents.*[18] Protestant authorities, however, interested themselves only in his second proposition. The new civil courts they established punished clandestine marriage, and the Catholic Church gradually followed suit.[19] The new stringency spread to the American colonies, where marriage required parental consent, notice of intent to marry, a ceremony performed by a recognized authority and official registration.[20] The loophole had finally closed.[21]

The Protestant ideal of family life changed the focus of the relationship between husband, wife and children in other ways. It was perhaps even more authoritarian than the Catholic vision, but it also placed more emphasis on feelings. Certainly, in the English family we can see a growing tendency to treat wives as friends and partners.[22] The Reformers also made a modest effort to end the most miserable marriages. Where the Church allowed only annulment (under very specific conditions) or legal separation, Luther and his followers endorsed the possibility of divorce.[23] Luther felt it should be permissible in cases of impotence, adultery and religious disbelief.[24] This position was the natural consequence of the high value Protestants placed on marriage. They saw no reason for a guiltless partner to live in celibate loneliness. Divorce rates for the early Reformers were nonetheless very low.

This new movement influenced family relations in less tangible ways. Like the early Church, the Reformers stressed the kinship of all believers. Their very names—the Moravian Brethren, the Children of Light, the Family of Love—suggest their hunger for strong family ties.[25]

At the same time, they added a new dimension to the essentially authoritarian spirit of the feudal age. For Luther, rebel that he was, every man was his own priest. Protestantism stressed the individual conscience, rather than obedience to authority. (Note, however, that it remained a very bad idea to oppose such Protestant stalwarts as Calvin, Zwingli, Knox or Luther himself.) Women, as well as men, were encouraged to read the Bible.[26] Lutherans, Calvinists and English Congregationalists all accepted the idea of a woman's individual tie to God. The German Baptists even asserted that women were the spiritual equals of men.[27] Ironically, this Protestant mutation came to enhance the status of Catholic women. The Church took a new interest in their piety, needing all the help it could get.[28] As in the days of the early Christian Church, women played a leading role in supporting and spreading the new faith.

Children must have benefited as well from this new endorsement of family life as the highest good. Conscientious Protestant parents inevitably had to pay considerable attention to their children, for whose spiritual health they were responsible. This new concern spread to the Counter Reformation. In the sixteenth century, for the first time, confessors' manuals advised Catholic priests to pay attention to parents' responsibilities to young children. Until that time, their sole concern had been the children's duties towards their parents.[29]

Nonetheless, the new churches did not enlarge the liberty of women or children. Proscribing convents and virginity, for instance, they could see no "natural" role for women outside of marriage. That did not mean that all women were able to marry, or even to live under male protection. But authorities became more concerned about the masterless female. (They were generally more anxious about any unattached person. The sixteenth century also witnessed a flurry of legislation about vagrants.[30]) The new Protestant rulers could not force all women to marry, but they could and did ensure that the unattached female was unable to earn more than a subsistence. In Protestant communities like Geneva, they also frequently appointed legal guardians for widows.[31]

In both Protestant and Catholic states, a new preoccupation with order made life inside and outside the family a more sober affair. Laws strove to introduce what was called the Triumph of Lent: restrictions on expensive clothing and public entertainments, combined with bans on gambling and prostitution.[32] Protestant clerics and administrators dealt more harshly with sexual sin than had the Church. In France and later England, new laws forced the authorities to pay close attention to any stillborn infant delivered by an unmarried woman. If she had attempted to hide her pregnancy, she ran the risk of execution—it was assumed she had intended to kill her child and dispose of the evidence.

The law did mercifully prevent the prosecution from torturing the accused in such cases, at least if it had failed to find a corpse.[33] Nonetheless, the number of executions for infanticide soared.[34]

Some Protestant communities went further. In 1566, Calvinist Geneva passed edicts dictating equal punishments for men and women for fornication: prison, on bread and water, for the single sinner; banishment, if one partner was married; death, if both were. In practice, however, only women were executed, and men managed to avoid banishment for exercising their traditional right to seduce or rape their servants.[35] The law was repealed in 1610.

In spite of this attempted external control, however, Protestant families were self-governing in ways that Catholic ones were not. The Catholic worshipped privately or at church. The Protestant family was supposed to gather daily for prayers under the direction of the father.[36] Where the celibate Catholic priest kept busy advising married couples on the conduct of their sexual lives, Protestants were largely left to their own consciences. Calvin and other leaders also held a more hopeful view of the male capacity for self-control than did the Church. While the Catholic wife was counselled against frustrating her husband's passions and leading him into sin, Calvin urged couples to restrict the size of their families. He envisioned, of course, that they would accomplish this by practising the only sanctioned method of birth control: abstinence.[37]

To the people living in the sixteenth century, the Protestant revolt would have been the sole conspicuous challenge to the kind of family life they knew. But other equally sweeping changes had started to gather momentum. They include the beginnings of capitalism and increased urbanization. In the centuries to come, other values would intrude on family life: a new concern for domestic privacy, an acceptance of the love match, a sudden surge in population from the mid-eighteenth century, even a sharp alteration in the idea of motherhood. They developed at different paces in different areas, and cannot be treated chronologically. I want to trace them separately, moving from the sphere of emotion to the realm of hard economic fact.

Let me start with the love match. As we've seen, it always existed, but underground, condemned by Church and State. It gained respectability first in England. This seems to make sense. The Church of England, after all, grew out of a king's thwarted desire for a divorce. Of Henry VIII's six marriages, four seem to have been rooted in love—or at least lust. His initial craving to remarry was dictated by his need for an heir, but his choice of mates seems less pragmatic. After his divorce from Catherine of Aragon, his only purely politic marriage was to Anne of Cleves. Disliking her looks, he had the marriage declared void after only six months.[38]

Henry seems to have consulted only his own preferences in selecting his other wives. His judgment was erratic. Jane Seymour, though rather insipid, might have done well as Queen had she lived. Catherine Parr, Henry's final wife, was his soundest choice, although her behaviour after his death seems foolhardy. (She married the charming and ambitious Thomas Seymour; the couple shared their home with the young Princess Elizabeth. After Catherine's death, Seymour was executed for treason, accused of plotting to marry Elizabeth and seize the crown himself. Witnesses at his trial testified that his behaviour with Elizabeth during Catherine's life was flirtatious to the point of indiscretion, including romping visits to her bedroom. Elizabeth was lucky to escape with her head.) Anne Boleyn and Catherine Howard were probably not the adulterous trollops portrayed by their enemies, but neither were they ideal material for queens of England.

Henry, of course, was a king; his subjects did not enjoy the same freedoms. Many, as I've already noted, were married off at the whim of their parents or masters. The aristocratic maiden, in particular, had no hope of choosing her first husband. Like Lady Jane Grey, she could be forced into a most unwelcome marriage. A century earlier, for instance, a daughter of the Paston household in Norfolk attempted to resist her parents' choice of a husband for her. She eventually gave in because for three months she was "beaten once in a week or twice, sometimes twice in one day, and her head broken in two or three places."[39]

(Remarkably, just a few years later, another Paston, Margery, secretly pledged herself to the family's steward and refused to back down under similar treatment. Her parents never spoke to her again—although they continued to employ her husband.[40] It should also be noted that at least one of the Pastons' arranged marriages turned out very well. The letters of John Paston and his wife Margaret are models of tender affection.[41])

But the mercenary arranged marriage fell out of favour exceptionally early in England. By the mid-eighteenth century, the Baron de Montesquieu noted disapprovingly that across the Channel daughters frequently married "according to their own fancy without consulting their parents."[42] (He admitted the absence of British convents as a mitigating factor. He reasoned that since French girls had the option of taking the veil rather than accepting their parents' choice, they had no excuse for selecting their own husbands.)

We cannot isolate the moment when the love match became respectable in Britain. Lawrence Stone, in my *Ideas* series, starts his discussion of the history of marriage in England by noting dryly that until the end of the seventeenth century at the earliest, it was a legal procedure designed to ensure the legitimization and education of children; the control of sexual behaviour; and the orderly transfer of property. (As we've seen, it could be more emotional than that, but Stone's summary reflects the thinking of pre-modern society in general.) He continued: "This was what it was all about. It was not about love, it was not about sex: it was about that."

Moreover, European society rather distrusted love in marriage. In the sixteenth century, Montaigne wrote severely that "[a] good marriage, if such there be, rejects the company and condition of love. It tries to reproduce those of friendship."[43] A century later, an Englishwoman named Dorothy Osborne wrote that out of a thousand couples who married for love, "hardly one can be brought for an example that it may be done and not repented of afterwards."[44] This statement, conventional for its time, is made extraordinary by Osborne's own history. She had insisted on marrying for love, and apparently did not regret her choice. Her denigrating attitude towards the love match continued to prevail in the Latin countries into the nineteenth century, sometimes even later.

Stone locates the first stage of the change in the eighteenth century. The focus of marriage moved slightly, from what was called "interest"—money—to the need for an emotional bond. That bond, however, was not a burning romantic connection. It was what people called "settled affection"—attachment, rather than passion. You were also supposed to regulate your feelings sufficiently to bestow your affections appropriately. There should be no question of any kind of misalliance.

Somehow, by the end of the eighteenth century, the emphasis shifted. It is as if Shakespeare's comedies were slowly incorporated into real life. For, as we've seen repeatedly, people knew about love, and enjoyed entertainments based on the ideal of the romantic marriage. In *Much Ado About Nothing*, Beatrice and Benedict come to feel a great deal more than "settled affection" for one another. But the Elizabethans who watched those plays probably enjoyed them in the same spirit as a Bombay movie audience now: as an escape from reality. The businessman or peasant watching a love match develop through endless song and dance has no intention of letting his children marry in the same flighty way.

We know that this must have changed radically in England by 1813, the year that Jane Austen's *Pride and Prejudice* was finally published. (In 1797, a publisher had rejected an earlier version of the novel.) The immoral taint that once clung to the love match was moving to the marriage based purely on "interest." We know because Elizabeth Bennet is horrified by a marriage that would have seemed laudable to earlier generations. Charlotte Lucas, the plain daughter of an impecunious minor aristocrat, accepts the proposal of a very silly but well-to-do clergyman, Mr. Collins. In doing this, she delights her parents, ensures her future and clears the way for her younger sisters to enter the marriage market. Elizabeth ought to have commended her common sense.

Instead, the heroine is appalled by Charlotte's mercenary insensitivity. She feels their friendship is over. There is nothing really novel about Elizabeth's own love for Darcy—it's a standard prince-and-beggar-maid theme bathed in the moral light of the courtly love tradition. An imperfect man becomes better in his attempt to gain the love of a good woman. But the condemnation of Charlotte's eminently sensible arrangement is new.

It's possible to argue, of course, that *Pride and Prejudice* is fiction, having no connection to real life. Many historians do not refer to literature for that reason. But Austen's books are realistic; she clearly does not intend to shock her readers with an unfamiliar vision. Somewhere along the line, a different approach to marriage has crept in. There's a subterranean sense that it's degrading, even disgusting, for a woman to share the bed of a man she doesn't much like.

Austen's treatment of marriage is suggestive in other ways. Although her own writing coincides with the start of the Romantic movement, she is clearly no fan of mad passion. In *Sense and Sensibility,* she roundly condemns Marianne Dashwood's high-flown sentiments and lack of restraint. Her heroines walk a tightrope between their desire for love and their need for a decent maintenance.

All of them succeed in the end—in every case, without parental guidance. In most of the novels, parents learn of an attachment only when a couple announces their engagement. (Of all of these parents, Mr. Woodhouse in *Emma* is the least suspicious: "[I]t seemed as if he could not think so ill of any two persons' understanding as to suppose they meant to marry till it were proved against them."[45]) Without sentimentality, Austen even suggests that parental control is a fantasy: "Who can be in doubt of what followed? When any two young people take it into their heads to marry, they are pretty sure by perseverance to carry their point, be they ever so poor, or ever so imprudent, or ever so little likely to be necessary to each other's ultimate comfort."[46]

One heroine alone accepts the advice of a quasi-parental figure, and she is a cautionary example. In *Persuasion,* Anne Elliot originally agrees to renounce Captain Wentworth under pressure from her friend Lady Russell, and lives to regret her compliance. That interference is unusual, although in *Pride and Prejudice* Mrs. Bennet attempts ineffectually to force Elizabeth to marry the noxious Mr. Collins, and in *Sense and Sensibility* Mrs. Dashwood gently manoeuvres her daughter Marianne into accepting Colonel Brandon. In most of Austen's work, older people show considerable restraint about even questioning their charges. Elizabeth's aunt and uncle, the Gardiners, do not dream of interrogating her about Mr. Darcy's obvious interest in her. Mrs. Dashwood, characteristically going overboard, declines even to ask her daughter if she is engaged.

In a couple of centuries, Britain somehow moved from breaking a daughter's head to respecting her reserve. The concept of the private conscience had extended to marriage, once a highly public and pragmatic affair. The result is not what Luther intended, but individual values have obviously triumphed over collective ones within the family.

But then, the family itself was becoming a smaller and more private place. From the sixteenth century on, we begin to see a far greater sense in people of themselves as individuals, and as members of a *nuclear* family. In the early fifteenth century, a status-obsessed Florentine patrician named Leon Battista Alberti wrote *Della famiglia*, an inquiry into the quality that "exalts and ennobles families." His definition of the family was broad. It included "Children, wife, other relatives, retainers, and servants."[47]

Two centuries later, a wealthy Italian might still see his family in the same way, but a Dutch merchant's list would be much smaller. When it comes to domestic privacy, the social leader was not Britain, but the Netherlands. In the tightly restricted space of Dutch cities, a household might well consist of only a couple and their children. Even the prosperous had few or no servants, since Dutch authorities discouraged hiring them by imposing special taxes for hiring domestic help.[48]

Moreover, their homes contained rooms that were never open to outsiders. In the old days, Edward Shorter notes, "The family's shell was pierced full of holes, permitting people from outside to flow freely through the household, observing and monitoring."[49] Among the Dutch bourgeoisie, that openness was gone. They were the first group to develop a thoroughly private domestic life.[50]

These values were not, however, uniquely Dutch. The French upper classes began to relegate their servants to the backstairs by the sixteenth century. Servants in English country homes joined them about a century later, expelled from the public hall to perform their work out of sight.[51] Unlike Leon Battista Alberti, their masters no longer saw them as part of the family. By the Victorian period, the wealthy country family preferred to banish the help to a separate servants' wing.[52] If one needed their services, one sounded the bell that rang in their quarters.

During these centuries, the family shrank in terms of time, as well as size. Alberti believed that lineage was one of the ennobling factors in a good family: an aristocrat is apt to cherish a keen sense of pedigree. But, as the middle classes began to displace hereditary landowners in social importance, that concern with ancestry declined. Edward Shorter and other historians mourn the loss of the chain of generations, of family continuity.[53] But it was an inevitable casualty of the new emphasis on individualism, the same source that nourished romantic marriage and personal fulfilment in the family. Shorter himself notes that, in this new ideal of family life, "Spouses and children came to be prized for what they were, rather than for what they represented or could do."[54] It is difficult to see this as a deprivation.

Note that the attitude towards children was changing, along with marriage. Philippe Ariès observes that the dead child first begins to appear on parents' tombs in the sixteenth century.[55] By the seventeenth century, the living child had become commonplace in portraits.[56] In other words, at least among people wealthy enough to commission portraits, the vision of the family was moving closer to a cosy, nuclear unit—husband, wife and kids at happy leisure together.

A new sense of childhood as a separate state was also emerging, in part because more children were in schools, rather than apprenticed out to learn adult work. The charms of small children became fashionable. During this period, Mme de Sévigné went into raptures over her little daughter's pretty ways, acknowledging frankly: "I simply adore her."[57]

This doting fondness was not a personal idiosyncrasy. The diarist John Evelyn wrote of the death of his son, aged five, in 1657: "Here ends the joy of my life, and for which I go ever mourning to the grave."[58] The Dutch mother had already started to raise her own children, without the assistance of a nurse.[59] About a century before it happened anywhere else, the Dutch family centred itself on its children.

You can see some residual tensions about the place of children in the family towards the end of that next century in England— once again, in the works of Jane Austen. Except for Charles Blake, in her fragment *The Watsons,* children do not play a leading role in her fiction. But the heroines of many of her novels are doting aunts, and one of them—Emma in *The Watsons*—is good-natured enough to invite the ten-year-old Charles to stand up with her at a dance. Nonetheless, Austen's attitudes towards children seem distinctly astringent. Children run riot through *Persuasion* and *Sense and Sensibility,* to the distress of the heroines of those novels. Lady Middleton, a blindly indulgent mother in *Sense and Sensibility,* is an object of ridicule. At least two of Austen's heroes, Mr. Knightley and Captain Wentworth, have a brisk, no-nonsense approach; *Emma*'s Mr. Woodhouse feels Knightley is too rough with his visiting grandsons.

When it comes to children, Jane Austen's *Persuasion,* her last novel, reflects one extraordinary social change that few readers today would even notice. The shock lies in the marriage of Admiral and Mrs. Croft. Jane Austen presents them as a singularly happy couple: Mrs. Croft, through the combination of her husband's fortune and her own force of character, occupies an honoured position among the novel's other women, and her husband's naval cronies. She is, in other words, treated as an admirable and enviable wife— yet she has no children.

In ancient Greece, in pre-revolutionary China, in most of Africa, Asia and Latin America today, a novelist could not portray a childless woman in this way. Mrs. Croft is only possible as a character in a world where a wife's main function has ceased to be childbearer. She is valued because she makes her husband happy, and that is something new. A family's central concern has shifted from the transmission of genes and property to emotional fulfilment.

This new emphasis on emotion unquestionably went some way towards changing the public manners of husband and wife to one another. But this is another area where we have to be careful about seeing the past as monolithic. There is plenty of evidence that formality and reserve were not consistent in earlier generations. In the Restoration comedy *The Way of the World* (1700), Millamant agrees to marry the hero Mirabell—on certain conditions. These include her refusal to be called names—"as wife, spouse, my dear, joy, jewel, love, sweetheart, and the rest of that nauseous cant..." She continues, "... don't let us be familiar or fond, nor kiss before folks..."[60]

Now, *The Way of the World* is not reality, but theatre—and a comedy, at that. But Millamant's speech would not be funny if no one ever behaved in the way she deplores. Long before the triumph of the love match, in other words, some upper-class English couples *were* publicly "familiar or fond."

On the other hand, the attitude to this marital affection is obviously disapproving. The cream of society preferred cool restraint. At least a century later, such manners still prevailed in the upper classes. But by 1840, Queen Victoria—however formal in public—was gushing to her diary about the perfection of her dearest Albert: "Already the 2nd day since our marriage; his love and gentleness is beyond everything, and to kiss that dear soft cheek, to press my lips to his, is heavenly bliss."[61] The next day did nothing to cool her ardour: "My dearest Albert put on my stockings for me. I went in and saw him shave; a great delight for me."

This sentimentality—for one can give it no other name—extended to children, as well. As we've seen, the pre-modern European chatelaine or merchant's wife tended to farm out her infants to wet nurses, placing the interests of her husband and his property above her own maternal feelings. The peasant had no choice about rationing the time spent on child-care. If her family were to survive, she needed to be out in the fields, working. But from the nineteenth century on, motherhood became the primary concern of the good woman. Every other concern was to be sacrificed to the well-being of the child.[62]

This obsessive concern did not extend to the children of the poor. In the nineteenth century, while thousands of readers wept over the deaths of Dickens's little Nell, real children worked punishing hours in factories and mines. (Compulsory education for the young is an innovation of our own century.[63]) A Royal Commission reported in 1842 that some mines employed children as young as four, working shifts of up to fourteen hours.[64] Their job was to open and close the passage doors for each coal carriage, to keep draughts of air from starting fires. The child was thus alone for the whole shift, in mines infested with "rats, mice, beetles, and other vermin . . ." The rats were so bold that they sometimes snatched lighted candles from miners and ran off with them. We know that detail because the candle flame sometimes ignited gas explosions.[65]

Thousands of other children earned their bread by selling themselves. The Victorian era, for all its prudery, was a pedophile's paradise.[66] Some child prostitutes worked in brothels, of which London had an estimated 5,000 at mid-century. Thousands of others walked the streets; the little match girls of fairy-tale fame were selling more than matches. And London was not even the major centre for child prostitution. That distinction went to Brussels, where a corrupt police force assisted the trade.[67] (This is disturbingly relevant today, as a major scandal on the sexual abuse of Belgian children continues to unfold.)

Bizarrely, this sexual and economic exploitation of children thrived in a society that was increasingly interested in their well-being. In the middle classes, the ideas of the philosophers Jean-Jacques Rousseau and John Locke had percolated down, creating a sense of children as fragile beings, needing constant affectionate care.[68]

Some schools were being reformed—not a moment too soon— to be less chaotic, autocratic and violent. You can find some of the more advanced theories in the novels of Louisa May Alcott, which often specifically concern ideas about child-rearing. Alcott herself was raised in an extremely progressive home for her time—her parasite of a father was a radical thinker—but she wasn't writing in a vacuum. She did not come up with her rather enlightened prescriptions about a healthy diet and exercise (and the evils of corporal punishment) all by herself.

A Marxist would have no difficulty in explaining this contrast in the treatment of children from different social classes, seeing bourgeois hypocrisy as inherent to capitalism. Certainly a brutal exploitation of the poor continued through all these essentially emotional developments—the love match, the new appreciation of domestic privacy, even the exaltation of passion by the Romantic movement. For these alterations in the family's emotional basis rest in part on vast economic change. The newly nuclear family was possible because Western society had found a new system for producing goods.

This is not the place, nor am I the author, to deal in any detail with the rise of capitalism. I want to deal with it very broadly, and only as it directly affects family life. Its earliest stages, for instance, need little attention here. They slightly predated the rise of Protestantism, and passed virtually unnoticed. Production very slowly began to shift from small, local units to long-distance trade and larger manufacturing centres.[69]

The eventual effects of these changes on the family are incalculable. Instead of working as a single unit, men, women and children began to drift into separate spheres. Families gradually ceased to be the essential economic unit, as capitalism and later industrialization made it more feasible for young people to survive without the help of their parents. The adventurous fifteenth-century peasant had few options for leaving home. One could become a servant elsewhere. All too frequently, men had the opportunity for a truly frightful life as soldiers. By the nineteenth century, however, there were other possibilities: work in offices and factories.

This new division of labour was not necessarily good news for wives and children. The medieval woman's status may not have been particularly high, but it was difficult to accuse her of being a parasite. Since there was no division between the home and work, she was *seen* to pull her own weight. But under capitalism, work becomes defined as labour for which you are paid.[70] Women could be viewed increasingly as dependents, both financial and social.

Capitalism and industrialization altered the economic basis of the family out of recognition. For the first time in Western history, most women could put away the distaff, the loom and the needle. Of course, they were able to do so only because other men and women did the same work, under far greater pressure, in factories or, as piece-workers, in their own homes. (The piece-work system has always been defended because it lets women stay home while earning money. Unfortunately, it usually pays so little as to cancel out that advantage.)

At the same time, technology removed much of the drudgery of household labour. This was a clear advantage, but it did hide a drawback: it made the housewife's role more amorphous. Nor did it necessarily create vast new stores of leisure. From the late-nineteenth century on, experts of all stripes found new tasks for women. As attention focused increasingly on childhood as a separate and delicate state, motherhood became a more taxing responsibility. Standards of cleanliness and tidiness rose to a positively Dutch level throughout the West, buttressed by the discovery of germs and their connection to disease. In a book on advice to women over the past 150 years, Barbara Ehrenreich and Deirdre English title one chapter "Microbes and the Manufacture of Housework."[71]

These changes also introduced a consumer mentality: people (at least people with money) could buy what they needed or wanted. By the early decades of this century, advertisers had already become skilled in transforming want into need: the new emphasis on the germ-free home owed as much to manufacturers as to doctors. The Victorians emphasized the ideal of the home as haven from a

bruising world. Our century dispersed among all classes the aristocratic model of the home as showcase. It took about one and a half
centuries to make domesticity both a science and an art—the vision
so ably exploited by Martha Stewart and her K-Mart line of sheets.

The family also became far more mobile. To a much greater
extent than their ancestors, people in the West could change jobs,
because those jobs were no longer attached to land and their families. All of these considerations inevitably made the family a far
more fragile structure. This corollary of our economic system was
not obvious in the nineteenth century, because the middle class, concerned with respectability, did not push consumerism and individualism to their logical conclusions in family life. The successful man
did not look for a younger and more attractive wife (although he
could always keep a mistress); young people were not free to move
in together without marriage. But the seeds of our own unstable
family units had already started to germinate.

It is important not to exaggerate the rate or drama of all of these
changes. The majority of Europeans and North Americans lived
outside cities, supporting themselves through agriculture, until this
century. Until at least 1800, most goods were produced in a household—not necessarily one's own home, but not in a factory.[72] The
world would not have seemed dramatically different to most European peasants from the sixteenth to the nineteenth centuries. Even
life expectancy (and consequently the population) did not begin to
shoot up until around 1750.[73]

We can see omens of change much earlier, however. England
passed its Poor Laws in 1597 to ensure the support of the indigent. Responsibility for this fell first on relatives: parents, children,
grandparents and grandchildren. The parish took over only if none
of these existed or could afford another dependent. Family responsibility was of course traditional; the interesting feature is that the
law had to spell it out. The law implicitly recognized that the bonds
of kinship were weakening.[74] In the succeeding centuries, that

trend accelerated: with industrialization, millions would eventually leave their rural homes to find work in the city. Mobility is no friend of kinship.

It is fashionable in intellectual circles to see these changes as disastrous, and to mourn the old communal life of the Middle Ages. Certainly life in the West slowly became more competitive, more fragmented and potentially much more lonely.[75] But, as we've seen, the good old days were not all that good for everyone. The child sweating away in an ill-lit, hot and noisy factory is a poignant image. But there is nothing enviable about the lot of his ancestors, slaving endlessly to produce prosperity for their masters and a subsistence for themselves.

What are the most striking features that separate our family life from Luther's age, only a few centuries ago? The most important changes include the dramatic rise in divorce and single-parent homes. We have also developed both the ability to limit the number of our children and new attitudes towards the ones we have. Sexual behaviour has changed almost beyond recognition. Women at all social levels work outside the home. Most members of our society subscribe at least to the ideal of egalitarianism between the sexes, with inevitable effects on the ways we manage our domestic lives. Our courts recognize domestic violence as a crime. Our idea of what constitutes a family has changed to the point that some jurisdictions are attempting to let gay partners enter a form of marriage.

Let's start with the growing fragility of marriage. It begins with a religious change: remember that Protestant reformers had reintroduced divorce as a possibility in the West, but only under highly restricted conditions. France was the first country to take the next steps. In the heady days of the Revolution, the Constitution of 1791 made marriage a purely secular arrangement.[76] A year later, France adopted a remarkably liberal divorce law, permitting seven grounds. They included insanity, conviction for certain crimes, notorious immorality, abandonment and brutality. More important, any couple could divorce by mutual consent with a delay of no more than four months. The Napoleonic Civil Code trimmed back that liberality considerably, and again curtailed the rights of women, which had flourished so briefly. Typically, a man could divorce an adulterous wife, but a woman could rid herself of an unfaithful husband only if he actually brought his mistress into the home.[77]

The history of divorce in the rest of the West shows a more steady progression. In colonial New England, for instance, the grounds for it were fairly liberal for men, embracing adultery, desertion and cruelty by the wife.[78] Women required additional grievances. Adultery had to be accompanied by desertion or failure to provide financial support. Laws in the South were more restrictive for both sexes. Over time, the various colonies and later states liberalized their legislation on divorce piece by piece. Changing laws did not instantly lead to a flurry of dissolutions. In 1860, there were fewer than 8,000 divorces in the entire country. By 1900 there were 55,000; in 1962, more than 400,000.[79]

You can find a similar but generally less dramatic pattern in the non-Catholic European countries. By 1950, about 230 of every thousand American marriages were ending in divorce. The figure for France was 106.9; for Sweden, 147.7; for England and Wales, 86.1. (For purposes of comparison, note that the figures were higher in a number of Muslim countries, where divorce was both accepted and legally simple. The Iranian figure was 211, and Egypt's 273. Algeria kept no records for 1950, but its 1940 rate was 292.)[80]

If the British rate looks exceptionally low, that's because it took Britain much longer to ease the process of divorce. By the 1830s, reformers were already arguing vigorously that the existing system not only made divorce impossible for all but the wealthiest, but was conspicuously unjust to women. Women could not even testify in the proceedings against them, making it all too simple for an unscrupulous man to rid himself of an unwanted wife by falsely claiming she had been unfaithful. Moreover, British law gave husbands monetary compensation from the "seducer" for the loss of their wives' fidelity and services—which struck many legislators as degrading for all parties involved.

In 1857, the House of Lords finally approved the country's first Divorce Act. That Act continued the tradition of awarding damages, but in a less scandalous way, recompensing the couple's now motherless children as well as their father.[81] Not until 1923 did Britain make divorce possible for the wife of an adulterous husband. In 1937, the law again intervened, this time to prevent divorces based on collusion—with a willing husband allowing his wife to sue on the basis of a bogus sexual escapade. No-fault divorce did not become an option until 1969.

The British example is familiar to me because I am a Canadian, and we liberalized our divorce laws at about the same time. I can remember as a child devouring a story about a woman who made her living providing evidence of adultery for couples who wanted to end their marriages. She spent several nights each week sharing a motel bed with a stranger, lying beside him clothed chastely in her slip, waiting for the obligatory photographer.

It's no longer necessary to indulge in a farce of this type to obtain a divorce. Today, as I've mentioned before, the U.S. divorce rate hovers at almost one in two marriages. (The divorce rate recently has declined slightly in most of the industrialized nations, but not nearly as much as the marriage rates.) There is no scandal attached to dissolving a marriage; it has become so commonplace that Canada, France and Japan have breezy magazines devoted to the subject. The Japanese one is called *Liz*, in homage to Hollywood's most married (and remarried) star.

Some Catholic countries resisted this trend towards easy divorce rather longer. (The number of annulments granted by the Church, on the other hand, is surprisingly high. In 1993, it permitted 60,000 annulments in the United States alone.) Ireland did not legalize divorce until 1997, and only then after prolonged and acrimonious debate. But this was inevitably a losing battle from the French Revolution on. As noted above, the Revolution introduced secular marriage, formalized before a municipal official and stressing the importance of mutual consent and the approval of *civil* authorities.[82] That legacy was lasting. By the beginning of this century, 50 per cent of couples in some French regions were choosing civil, rather than religious weddings. The Western family had gradually floated out of the religious control that the Catholic Church worked so hard to impose.

The incidence of divorce in all the Western countries is high enough to discomfit the historian Lawrence Stone, who wants to see the laws toughened up again for couples who are raising children. Nonetheless, Stone acknowledges that the rate did not rise with legislative change; other factors were at work.

What were they? War was a big one: the number of divorces bounded up during and after both world wars. In the United States, about 321,000 couples divorced in 1942, 485,000 in 1945, and 610,000 in 1946.[83] Nor is that phenomenon limited to our century. It was evident as early as the American Civil War.

You don't have to look far to find reasons for this. Many marriages contracted in wartime are based on the flimsiest previous acquaintance. Adultery is endemic during the chaos and mobility of a major conflict. Moreover, war gives couples a chance to live apart, and many women may have found they liked life better that way. In addition, life without a husband became a stronger possibility for women after the Second World War in particular, because they had entered the work force and knew they could support themselves.

That has of course remained true; it is fashionable in conservative circles to link the rising divorce rate to feminism. But women's demands are not the only force weakening our marriages. In *The Hearts of Men*,[84] Barbara Ehrenreich makes a convincing case for a change in male thinking that predates the great wave of feminist activism of the 1960s. Essentially, under the influence of such gurus as Hugh Hefner, North American men in the 1950s began to apply a consumer philosophy to their private lives. In a world where sex had become easily available, some of them lost their desire to share their time and money with a wife and children. Even if they were willing to face the disciplines of domesticity, vast numbers of them began to do so on a serial basis. Over the intervening decades, it has become socially acceptable to treat marriage as a transaction much like buying a car. You marry a woman, and trade her in a few years later for a new model. We could call it the Donald Trump school of family life.

But there is nothing to be gained by trying to blame one sex or the other for the epidemic of marital breakdowns. The root cause lies elsewhere, in the nature of the bonds that hold our families together. They are almost entirely emotional. Unlike medieval peasants, most of us do not need two adults plus some children to earn one living. (It's no accident that so many variety stores are owned by recent immigrants; it's the one contemporary career that still requires the labour of an entire family.) No religious or secular court punishes extramarital sex or desertion. There is no longer even a social price—no scandal attaches to divorce.

Countless experts have noted that our model for marriage is therapeutic: we are supposed to grow together, to work on our relationship. That ideal does work for a lot of people, but it's inevitably less powerful than economic need or stringent legislation. In some ways, this is a good thing: wretchedly unhappy couples no longer have to stay together. Yet the ease of divorce in our society has probably added little to the sum of human happiness. In the immortal words of Professor Gunnar Heinsohn, "Essentially, we have traded one form of misery for another." That misery ripples out beyond the couple; a Statistics Canada survey in 1993 found that 66 per cent of divorcing couples had children.[85] As discussed in Chapter 5, children suffer disproportionately under our system; there is a growing body of evidence that divorce causes them serious, sometimes irreparable damage.

Marriage in our society is also fragile in another sense: it's easy to avoid. In Canada, only 65 per cent of the population outside Quebec is expected to marry before the age of fifty. In Quebec, that figure is only *40* per cent.[86] (By contrast, in Japan, 85 per cent of men and 90 per cent of women are married by the age of 34.[87]) Between 1939 and 1972, 90 per cent of Quebeckers had married by that age. In 1994, there were only 5.5 marriages per 1,000 Canadians—fewer than in 1932, at the worst point of the Depression. In releasing the new data, an official at Statistics Canada announced, "We're witnessing the disappearance of marriage as an institution."

Of course, large numbers of those unmarried Canadians are not living alone, since common-law relationships have become both respectable and common. These are, however, even more delicate than marriages. If a common-law couple fails to marry, they will almost certainly separate. Only 15 per cent of such relationships last for ten years.[88]

These elastic arrangements are possible in part because women can earn their own livings. In 1994, the woman earned more than the man in almost a quarter of two-parent Canadian homes.[89] Conversely, the man was the sole wage-earner in just under one quarter of homes. (Women were the sole providers in 7.5 per cent of two-parent families.) Under these conditions, the prospect of divorce apparently becomes less disastrous for wives and offspring.

But those statistics are only part of the picture. More than half of single-parent families in Canada are poor. In 1993, the median income for two-parent families was $47,000. For single-parent households, it was $20,200.[90] Women, unsurprisingly, headed 87 per cent of those single-parent homes. U.S. research suggests that after a divorce, women's standard of living falls an average of about 30 per cent, while men's *rises* by 10 per cent.[91] Our flexible family arrangements carry a cost.

They also mean that the blended family is at least as common as it was in earlier centuries, when death, rather than divorce, severed families. In the early 1990s, almost a quarter of Canadian weddings celebrated remarriages.[92] (The rates for men and women re-entering marital bliss differed by a single percentage point, contradicting a widespread belief that men are more likely to marry a second time. The widowed, significantly or not, were more likely to tie the knot again than the divorced.) In 1993, 10 per cent of couples getting married or entering a common-law relationship brought with them children from previous relationships.[93]

Ten per cent does not sound like a huge proportion, but it must be remembered that Western fertility rates are exceptionally low.[94] The proliferation of birth control, sterilization and abortion in our world is just as striking as the changes in marriage patterns.

Now, most Europeans were familiar all along with at least two methods of preventing conception: abstinence and *coitus interruptus*. The second option is of course a sin for Catholics, but many pre-modern couples may not have known that—it might have been too intimate a matter to discuss with a priest. In our century, however, other contraceptive techniques gained popularity with extraordinary speed.

This is all the more startling because Westerners made so little use even of the available possibilities in earlier centuries. Thus, although condoms have been around for more than four hundred years (Casanova sometimes wore one made of sheep's gut), they were generally used as a prophylactic against disease, not pregnancy, until the last century.[95] A German developed the first diaphragm in 1838, and the first clinic to fit it opened in Holland in 1882, yet its use spread rather slowly.[96]

But from the start of this century, a variety of birth-control techniques rapidly gained wide social acceptance. In 1900, only 18 per cent of British working-class families had used contraceptives; by 1935–39, that figure had grown to 68 per cent.[97]

Civil authorities had conflicted attitudes towards this new ability to limit family size. Conservative forces worried about the effects of birth control on family life and public morality. From the nineteenth century on, they fretted about the dangers of licentiousness in homes where women were not mothers above all else. But they were also often tempted by the possibility of reducing the number of dependent poor—by the eugenic possibilities of contraception. One of the disciples of the birth-control campaigner Margaret Sanger was Dr. Lydia de Vilbiss, who opened a Florida family-planning clinic in the 1930s specifically targeting the poor. Dr. de Vilbiss rather hoped the state would eventually make contraception compulsory for couples on welfare, with forced "eugenic sterilization" as a follow-up measure for the recalcitrant.[98]

Popular demand and pragmatic concerns eventually defeated the desire to legislate morality. The United States Supreme Court, for instance, removed birth-control devices from the jurisdiction of federal anti-obscenity laws in 1936.[99] The American Medical Association waited a year longer before permitting doctors to dispense contraceptives.[100] Legislators and doctors were similarly reluctant to endorse birth control in all of the West, but most had started to come around by the 1930s. Germany, for obvious reasons, abstained from this trend during its Nazi years; the U.S.S.R. adopted it earlier.

Any attempt to keep up the birth rate in the democratic nations was essentially doomed by two technological advances of the 1950s: the birth-control pill and the intra-uterine device (IUD). While they are not without risks for the health of the women who use them, they have an almost irresistible advantage. They offer the option of preventing pregnancy without sacrificing sexual spontaneity or pleasure.[101]

By 1990, the pill was the choice of 48 per cent of French women of child-bearing age who did not want to conceive. Twenty-six per cent used an IUD.[102] West Germans and Belgians similarly favour the pill; Scandinavians were more apt to use IUDs. In the Netherlands, United Kingdom and particularly Canada and the United

States, surgical sterilization remains popular. In the mid-1980s, nearly half of married women in Quebec either had tubal ligations or husbands with vasectomies.[103]

Yet Quebec is nominally a Catholic province, and its governments are traditionally keen to promote fertility among French-speakers. In 1995, the current premier of Quebec, Lucien Bouchard, publicly mourned the fact that Quebeckers are "one of the white races that has the least children."[104] As you might expect, the statement got him into considerable trouble with both feminist and anti-racism groups.

Premier Bouchard has his own nationalist motives for deploring a low birth rate. Most Western governments have good reason to welcome it. Children born under their jurisdictions must be educated at their expense. Many countries also provide medical care and even income supplements. It is much cheaper to import adult labour from the Third World than to raise it at home. It is no accident that Western countries offer few genuine incentives to boost the fertility of their populations.

Our understanding of the factors that influence the birth rate is limited—if it were better, authorities in India and some of the African nations might be able to control their populations more effectively. Yet we can identify two crucial determinants. First, the birth rate almost always declines as the standard of living rises. (The holdouts are religiously orthodox communities, including Saudi Arabians and ultra-orthodox Jews, whose clergy forbid contraception.) Second, where women gain substantial rights and status, the number of births also tends to decline: most women do not seem to want large families.

It's important to recognize that contraceptives are not the only factor in the falling birth rate. Abortion has become so common in a number of societies as to constitute a method of birth control. In 1993, 1.3 million abortions were performed in the United States[105]— the equivalent of a medium-sized city. In Russia, as we've already seen, terminations currently outnumber births two to one.[106] In Canada, about 16.5 per cent of women had had one or more abortions by 1993—up from 4.1 per cent in 1975.[107] As noted in Chapter 4, the Canadian rate now stands at 26.9 abortions for every 100 live births.[108]

We know that these figures represent a huge increase over earlier periods, but we cannot be sure *how* huge: the Western nations did not begin to legalize abortion until well after the Second World War, and people are reluctant to report illegal activities. Attitudes towards this issue today are complex and in some ways unexpected. The *Lovelaw* television series, on family life around the world, recorded a group of Italian women discussing their *multiple* abortions. All were Catholics, and the Catholic Church absolutely condemns abortion. One woman even talked about becoming anxious before her most recent termination, to the point of fearing she might die. As a result, she went to confession the day before the procedure, and asked for absolution in advance. She was offended when the priest laughed uproariously, pointing out (not unreasonably) that he was in no position to offer her forgiveness for her plan to violate one of the Church's central teachings. When the interviewer asked her why she had not listened to her confessor and cancelled the operation, she replied angrily that abortion was a woman's concern, no business of a priest's.

This has obviously been a common female attitude in earlier societies, where women often dealt with controlling the size of their families behind the backs of men. It is the principle that led to landmark decisions like the United States Supreme Court's *Roe vs. Wade* ruling in 1973—the idea that contraception and abortion are a female prerogative. (Canada has no such clear-cut ruling. It functions by ignoring its own abortion legislation.) Today, that attitude has come under pressure from groups, often composed of conservative Christians, who see abortion as a form of murder. It is also perfectly possible to oppose abortion from a purely secular perspective, by seeing it as a question of children's rights. The focus of the intellectual debate over abortion lies in the question of when life begins: at conception, at some specific point in the development of the fetus, or only at birth.

There are, however, less rational values at play in the abortion issue. Communities that oppose abortion are apt to stress the helpless, victimized fetus, but they also are often repelled by the idea of sex without consequences. In Shreveport, Louisiana, a stronghold of the anti-abortion movement, the militant Christian groups picketing clinics are also against women's liberation, preaching a form of family life that draws as much from the fascist movements of this century as from the Bible. Their beliefs are neither realistic nor attractive, but such groups are right about one thing: support for abortion in our society is generally linked to a strong sense of the rights of women.

The two are not necessarily linked: as we've seen repeatedly, some earlier cultures permitted contraception, abortion *and* infanticide as long as a male got to make the decision. But for us, support for abortion rights generally goes hand in hand with the belief that women should have the right to *choose* pregnancy or termination, without reference to the father's desires.

That assumption has come under increasing attack over the past few years. Men have started to sue to prevent their pregnant partners from aborting. Picketers routinely surround abortion clinics, harassing the women who enter them. Doctors who perform the procedure have been killed. A growing number of hospitals have retreated from offering abortions, unwilling to face the hassle and the risks.

I suspect that the Western nations are on the point of making abortion more difficult, appalled by the sheer number of pregnancies being terminated. The question of late-term abortions is currently a contentious political issue in the United States; this could be the thin edge of the wedge.

New legal restrictions on abortion would unquestionably reduce its popularity significantly. It is unlikely, however, that women will abandon it altogether. It flourished, in back alleys, through all the centuries when it was banned. In 1974, Hungary and Romania imposed restrictions on both abortion and birth control. They enjoyed, if that is the right word, a temporary rise in the birth rate, followed by rapid drops.[109] The family often remains resistant to legislative control.

If modern governments have failed to shape the family as they wish, however, it's not from lack of trying. Canadian prime minister Pierre Trudeau said memorably that the state has no place in the bedrooms of the nation—but all Western governments intrude into its nurseries. It is illegal to abuse a child physically anywhere in the West; in Sweden, the definition of abuse extends as far as a spanking or a single slap. Children must attend school, unless their parents can afford the time necessary to educate them—under state-dictated guidelines—at home.

The so-called welfare state has thus assumed some of the responsibilities that once lay under control of the family alone. Conservative thinkers, particularly in the United States, often argue that governments intrude too much into domestic life today, weakening the family and sapping initiative. I think that's nonsense: the state stepped in largely because it had to. I can see no social or individual advantage in restoring a family's freedom to starve, for instance, a strong possibility in its more independent days. The decline of the supportive extended family preceded the rise of welfare measures, not vice versa.

And, as we've seen far too often in earlier chapters, not all parents are good or wise. Anyone studying the current state of the Western family has to support more rigorous and swift intervention in violent families, and far more support for alternatives. I believe that biological parents still enjoy too many rights over their children's lives—a belief bolstered by a ruling at the end of 1997, when a Maryland judge returned a toddler to a mother who had killed his older sister.[110]

That ruling is not an isolated case. Canadian courts have dispatched pre-teens raised in middle-class suburbs to their biological families on native reserves, in violation of the most basic common sense. American ones have yanked children out of foster homes where they've spent happy years, returning them to parents they remembered only with horror.

These decisions point to the great paradox of contemporary family life. No society has ever claimed to be more child-centred, yet we allow hundreds of thousands of children to endure sickening violence and neglect. The media heap abuse on social workers who fail to remove kids from dangerous homes, but there's almost nowhere to put a child at risk. The number of homes willing to accept foster children is shrinking, because the financial incentives are so low. Our laws and our social policies favour biological parents only in part out of genuine belief. Keeping children with their own families, no matter how terrible those are, is much cheaper than creating adequate alternatives.

And, just like the Victorians, we let some children suffer while exalting the value of others to the skies. In Chapter 4, I discussed the pressures on contemporary parents, inundated with ceaseless contradictory advice from any number of experts. We know far more about children than any previous society, and that makes it much harder to raise them. It's easy for the modern mother, in particular, to despair of getting things right. In the 1950s, she worried about dominating and overprotecting her children, especially her sons. Today, she's apt to feel guilty about neglecting them, since she almost certainly works outside the home. (I will not enter into the debate on whether mothers of young children should work, because it seems to me purely academic. Until middle-class families can survive on one income, we might as well discuss the number of angels that can dance on the head of a pin.) For much of history, parents' main worry was keeping their children alive. Today, at least in our world, that's less of a problem, but it's also no longer good enough. In the therapeutic family model, children also have to be communicative, successful and well-adjusted—goals which can never be totally met.

It's perhaps no wonder that our attitudes to children are so contradictory. Our birth rates are low, we start bearing children exceptionally late, and an unprecedented number of couples choose not to have any. Yet we are also the first culture in history to make it possible for a sixty-three-year-old grandmother to enjoy her very own new baby. An infertile Western couple (or single woman) may pay tens of thousands of dollars for fertility treatments or adoption. In my immediate social circle, there are families who've tried both routes. Where medical help has failed, they've found (and paid for) children in Romania, Hungary, Russia, Guatemala and Vietnam.

Nor is it their fault that they have not chosen unfortunate children from their own countries. Our system makes that extremely difficult. Precisely because abortion is so readily available, a woman who chooses to continue her pregnancy will almost certainly want to raise her own child. Our courts will back her right to retain custody even if she proves disastrous as a mother. The candidates for adoption in the contemporary West tend to be so damaged as to daunt a prospective family—even if that family meets the rigid criteria set by our social agencies. They also tend not to be white, one reason for the thriving trade in babies from the former Communist nations.

Whatever their criteria, these couples want children for their own sake. In this society, you don't have to be a parent to qualify as an adult. Offspring no longer even ensure support or companionship in old age. To a far greater extent than other cultures, we segregate people by age. The affluent and relatively healthy senior citizen (the "golden ager," in one contemporary euphemism) can enjoy the leisure of a retirement village; the less fortunate may find themselves cared for by strangers in old-age homes. People from other cultures often cite this as evidence of Western barbarism—we discard the aged like old shoes. It will be interesting, to put it gently, to see what happens to this particular development as the masses of baby boomers grow old. With few children to provide help, and the sheer pressure of their numbers, they are going to constitute a social crisis in the coming decades.

In a world where so many women work, however, it's difficult to imagine returning to the days when three or more generations shared a home. As I argued in Chapter 6, it's unlikely that the West will be able to revive a truly united extended family. If you see that as a tragedy, try to remember that in extended families, *every* meal would be like Christmas or Thanksgiving, without even the sedative buffer of excessive amounts of food.

Where does this leave us? Overall, if we live in families at all, we're stuck with nuclear ones, very loosely tied to other relatives, held together by the flimsy bonds of emotional attachment. For, as the family's responsibilities and role have shrunk, we have loaded more and more emotion on to it. It is no wonder that so many people are reluctant to marry: we've made marriage frighteningly important. Barbara Ehrenreich, for one, feels that we expect too much from it: no other culture in history has demanded that husbands and wives be financial associates, co-parents, passionate lovers, best friends, constant companions *and* even exercise partners.[111] In cultures with lower divorce rates, marriage is often less demanding. Lawrence Stone notes that in Japan, couples spend only an average of 18½ minutes a day talking to one another.[112]

Yet that emotional base is really all we've got. We don't demand that people reproduce; we don't even insist that they start their families as couples. We don't force people to stay with their spouses. We don't expect adults to remain strongly linked to their parents. If people do produce children, they are held responsible for raising them to adulthood, and that's about it.

Given that, it's difficult to see how Western governments can sustain their objections to gay marriage. If we no longer recognize parenthood as the essential aim of the family, and if we permit people to pair up and part at will, there seems to be no rational reason to prevent two adults of the same sex from calling themselves a family. Hawaii has already attempted to permit such marriages (an effort quashed by Washington), and some governments and businesses have started to allow gay partners access to pensions and benefit plans.

In fact, I find it heartening that some homosexual and lesbian couples feel this longing for a committed, socially sanctioned family life. It's a testament to the strength of the ideal of the family, to the human desire for a stable, loving domestic life. In 1994, I interviewed a lesbian couple who had just celebrated a kind of wedding in an exceptionally liberal United Church.[113] (Traditionalists, they both wore white bridal gowns.) Of the dozens of couples with whom I've discussed marriage, they were the most moving and the most eloquent. Their union brought them no tax benefits, little social approval and a great deal of trouble with their families. Precisely because of that, they had devoted a tremendous amount of thought to the meaning of their decision. It seemed to me a very brave thing to do.

I do not know if gay marriage will become a legal possibility in our world; I have no predictions about the family at all.[114] Nor can I offer any prescriptions for new laws or policies.[115] I can see that our current systems are deeply flawed. Our families are far too unstable. Too many children are growing up in the worst possible homes. But I don't believe that we are uniquely unhappy, or that our unhappiness is a direct result of the way we organize family life. I don't believe that our homes are, to use a loathsome modern term, any more dysfunctional than many families in the past. The great difference is that we live in a world where people expect to be happy.

What I hope to have created is a sense of context—a recognition that family life is imperfect and difficult everywhere, all the time. I do not believe that there is some golden age to which we can return. We cannot now go back to the forests to live communally as hunter-gatherers. The restoration of supposedly "traditional" values is a hopeless dream: there is no one tradition, and economics, technology and irreversible social change in any case bar the way.

What I would like to see is a more realistic vision of the family in both individuals and governments. I wish children in our world were raised with more models of couples making their way through each stage of life, instead of our enormous concentration on courtship and romance. I wish that families dealing with disabled children—and adults—received more social support, in recognition that they no longer have crowds of relations to draw on for help. I wish that Westerners would renounce their delusion that they can be happy all the time, and learn to deal with the less-than-perfect families they have.

Above all, I wish that social critics would stop calling for a return to "family values" as a cure-all for our various ills. No father, no matter how caring, can lift his family out of poverty if he cannot make a living. No mother, no matter how desperately she desires it, can do a great job of parenting on the streets. We keep forgetting the lesson of the Ik: when life becomes unbearably hard, the family dissolves.

For all this, I often see hopeful signs about the future of the family, especially when I look at my students. Their attitudes seem to me far healthier than the ones I imbibed in university—less promiscuous, more thoughtful, less selfish. (They also generally get along much better with their parents.)

The terrible truth I see, in all the research devoted to this book, is that good people create good families, and vice versa. This is not a soothing conclusion, because we don't know how to create virtue. But from classical Rome to Confucian China to Los Angeles today, the structure of the family seems to matter less than the ways that we choose to behave within it. That is particularly true for people in the West now, because they *can* choose so much. In a world where the family has changed so much and so fast, we need to learn how to live with restraint and kindness and intelligence within the choices we make.

P R E F A C E

1 Jane Austen, *Northanger Abbey, Lady Susan, The Watsons and Sanditon* (Oxford: Oxford University Press, 1990), 84.

C H A P T E R   O N E

1 Beatrice Gottlieb, *The Family in the Western World from the Black Death to the Industrial Age* (New York: Oxford University Press, 1994), 12–18.
2 In much of the world, a young girl like Red Riding Hood would never under any circumstances be allowed to walk anywhere alone.
3 Helen Fisher, *Anatomy of Love: The Natural History of Monogamy, Adultery and Divorce* (New York: Fawcett Columbine, 1992), 64, and interview with author.
4 Adrian Forsyth, *A Natural History of Sex: The ecology and evolution of mating behaviour* (Shelburne, VT: Chapters Publishing, 1993), 66.
5 Jane Goodall, *In the Shadow of Man*, rev. ed. (London: Weidenfeld and Nicolson, 1988), 188–91.
6 Tony D. Williams, *The Penguins* (Oxford: Oxford University Press, 1995), 158.
7 *Ibid.*, 157.
8 Alex Shoumatoff, *The Mountain of Names: A History of the Human Family* (New York: Simon and Schuster, 1985), 19.
9 Fisher, *Anatomy of Love*, 64; interview with author.
10 Forsyth, *Natural History of Sex*, 32.
11 *Ibid.*, 30–31.
12 Matt Ridley, *The Red Queen: Sex and the Evolution of Human Nature* (New York: Penguin, 1995), 216–17.
13 *New York Times* Special Features, 7 May 1993, and Associated Press, 7 May 1993. Both stories deal with a report by the Battelle Human Affairs Research Centers in Seattle, which found that only 2.3 per cent of men

aged twenty to thirty-nine reported any homosexual activity in the past decade, while a mere 1.1 per cent said that their relations were exclusively homosexual.

14 Forsyth, *Natural History of Sex*, 71–75, 79–80.

15 Desmond Morris, *The Naked Ape* (Toronto: Bantam, 1969), 83.

16 Ridley, *Red Queen*, 216.

17 Goodall, *Shadow of Man*, 182–83.

18 It's also difficult for a human to understand exactly what constitutes a really attractive chimpanzee. The Marilyn Monroe or Sharon Stone of Goodall's troop was Flo, an aged and distinctly battered veteran of life in the wild.

19 Fisher, *Anatomy of Love*, 149; interview with author.

20 Morris, *Naked Ape*, 18.

21 Elaine Morgan, *The Descent of the Child: Human Evolution from a New Perspective* (New York: Oxford University Press, 1995), 59–61.

22 *Ibid.*, 104.

23 Fisher, *Anatomy of Love*, 149; interview with author.

24 Robert Ardrey, *African Genesis* (London: Collins, 1961); Robert Ardrey, *The Territorial Imperative* (New York: Atheneum, 1966); Robert Ardrey, *The Social Contract* (New York: Atheneum, 1970); Lionel Tiger and Robin Fox, *The Imperial Animal* (New York: Holt, Rinehart and Winston, 1971); Desmond Morris, *The Naked Ape* (Toronto: Bantam, 1969); Desmond Morris, *The Human Zoo* (New York: McGraw-Hill, 1970).

25 Morris, *Naked Ape*, 62.

26 Morgan drew heavily for her theory from the writings of Sir Alastair Hardy. See A.C. Hardy, "Was man more aquatic in the past?" *New Scientist* 7 (1960), 642–45.

27 Morris, *Naked Ape*, 58.

28 *Ibid.*

29 Elaine Morgan, *The Descent of Woman* (New York: Bantam, 1973), 87.

30 Fisher, *Anatomy of Love*, 150; Morgan, *Descent of Woman*, 179.

31 Morgan, *Descent of Woman*, 181.

32 André Burgière, Christiane Klapisch-Zuber, Martine Segalen and Françoise Zonabend, trans. Sarah Hanbury Tenison, Rosemary Morris and Andrew Wilson, *A History of the Family, Volume II: The Impact of Modernity* (Cambridge, MA: The Belknap Press of Harvard University Press, 1996), 427. The Canadian rate is closer to 40 per cent; France's and Britain's are running at about one in three.

33 Fisher, *Anatomy of Love*, 109–12; interview with author. See also Diane

Ackerman, *A Natural History of Love* (New York: Random House, 1994), 167.

34 Fisher, *Anatomy of Love*, 112.

35 *Ibid.*, 115–16.

36 *Ibid.*; Fisher, interview with author.

37 Fisher, interview with author.

38 *Ibid.*, 56–57. See also Dorothy Tennov, *Love and Limerence* (New York: Stein and Day, 1979); John Money, *Love and Love Sickness: The Science of Sex, Gender Difference, and Pair-Bonding* (Baltimore: Johns Hopkins University Press, 1980); Bonnie Kreps interview with author for CBC Radio's *Ideas* series "Instant Intimacy."

39 Ernest Jones, *The Life of Sigmund Freud* (Harmondsworth: Penguin, 1981), 177.

40 Fisher, *Anatomy of Love*, 52–56; Ackerman, *Natural History of Love*, 165–66.

41 Ridley, *Red Queen*, 217.

42 Fisher, *Anatomy of Love*, 34–36; Forsyth, *Natural History of Sex*, 44–45, 52–53.

43 Forsyth, *Natural History of Sex*, 37.

44 Deborah Tannen, *You Just Don't Understand* (New York: Ballantine, 1990).

45 Gerda Lerner, *The Creation of Patriarchy* (New York: Oxford University Press, 1986), 17.

46 Alex Shoumatoff, *Mountain of Names*, 34–35.

47 W.R. Jankowiak and E.F. Fischer, "A cross-cultural perspective on romantic love," *Ethnology* 31 (no. 2): 149–55.

48 William Jankowiak, interview with author.

CHAPTER TWO

1 Will Durant, *The Story of Civilization: Our Oriental Heritage* (New York: Simon and Schuster, 1963), 39.

2 Gerda Lerner, *The Creation of Patriarchy* (New York: Oxford University Press, 1986), 46.

3 Nora Waln, *The House of Exile* (Boston: Little, Brown, 1992), 69.

4 A young Chinese woman who asked to be identified as Ooming—"no one"—in interview with author.

5 For the sake of brevity, I will generally use the present tense when citing anthropological studies of different cultures. But the reader should

note that the massive influence of Western culture on most places (and fundamentalist Islam on a few others) has often caused enormous social change in this century.

6 Helen Fisher, *Anatomy of Love: The Natural History of Monogamy, Adultery and Divorce* (New York: Fawcett Columbine, 1992), 66–67.

7 In a conversation with the anthropologist Janice Boddy, I suggested that the Sudanese women she had studied obviously counted for little in their culture, since one of the women had said to her, "We are cattle." Dr. Boddy retorted: "But you have to remember how important cattle are to these people!"

8 Fisher, *Anatomy of Love*, 66–67.

9 William Jankowiak, ed., *Romantic Passion: A Universal Experience?* (New York: University of Columbia Press, 1995).

10 Fisher, *Anatomy of Love*, 350.

11 In a survey of 1,510 teenagers by the Henry J. Kaiser Family Foundation, only 29 per cent reported they had had sex. (Associated Press, 28 June 1996). Another extremely authoritative study of American sexual mores by the National Opinion Research Center at the University of Chicago found that the median number of partners over a lifetime for men was six, and for women, two (*The New York Times*, 7 October 1994).

12 See note 5.

13 The Mangaians, like almost every other group we know about, do experience the kind of crush we call love; it just has no place in their social system.

14 Donald Symons, *The Evolution of Human Sexuality* (Oxford: Oxford University Press, 1979), 110–12.

15 Murasaki Shikibu, *The Tale of Genji*, trans. Edward G. Seidensticker (New York: Alfred A. Knopf, 1978), 82.

16 Jane Goodall, *In the Shadow of Man*, rev. ed. (London: Weidenfeld and Nicolson, 1988), 182–83. Note that some of the males Goodall observed did display sexual interest in their sisters.

17 Adrian Forsyth, *A Natural History of Sex: The ecology and evolution of mating behaviour* (Shelburne, VT: Chapters Publishing, 1993), 137.

18 *Ibid.*, 138.

19 Judith Lewis Herman and Lisa Hirschman, *Father-Daughter Incest* (Cambridge, MA: Harvard University Press, 1971), 12.

20 *Genesis* 19: 30–36.

21 Forsyth, *Natural History of Sex*, 140.

22 Associated Press, reprinted in *The Globe and Mail*, 17 July 1997.

23 Claude Lévi-Strauss, "The Social Use of Kinship Terms Among Brazilian Indians," in Paul Bohannan and John Middleton, eds., *Marriage, Family and Residence* (Garden City, NY: The Natural History Press, 1968), 176–79; also Sarah Hobson, *Family Web: A Story of India* (London: John Murray, 1978).

24 Forsyth, *Natural History of Sex*, 140.

25 Richard Critchfield, *Villages* (New York: Doubleday, 1983), 156.

26 Gerda Lerner, *The Creation of Patriarchy* (New York: Oxford University Press, 1986), 47.

27 Laura Bohannan, "Dahomean Marriage: A Revaluation," in Bohannan, *Marriage, Family and Residence*, 88–89.

28 E.R. Leach, "Polyandry, Inheritance and the Definition of Marriage," in Bohannan, *Marriage, Family and Residence*, 75–77; E. Kathleen Gough, "The Nayars and the Definition of Marriage," in Bohannan, *Marriage, Family and Residence*, 52–65.

29 Ruth Benedict, *Patterns of Culture* (Boston: Houghton Mifflin, 1989), 76, 100–101.

30 Colin M. Turnbull, *The Forest People* (New York: Simon and Schuster, 1961), 132.

31 Nick Haslam, "Favored status of Indian women attacked," *The Toronto Star*, 29 April 1996.

32 Benedict, *Patterns of Culture*, 130–72.

33 Lucy Mair, *Marriage* (Harmondsworth: Penguin, 1971), 67–68.

34 Waln, *House of Exile*, 69.

35 The possibilities for self-expression within tradition are virtually infinite, and not always benign. In a Hindu marriage, the bride does not only bring a dowry into her new family, she is also entitled to gifts from her new in-laws. In 1982, I attended the Brahmin marriage of two young lawyers in Kuala Lumpur. It was an arranged match, but both bride and groom were clearly very happy. At the correct point in the lengthy ceremony, the groom placed a lovely silver ring—the gift of his female relations—on his bride's toe. It required a struggle; the ring was a size too small. The bride limped her way in agony through the rest of the festivities.

36 Reuters News Service, ex Zenica, Bosnia, 29 June 1996.

37 David Maybury-Lewis, *Millennium: Tribal Wisdom and the Modern World* (New York: Viking, 1992), 101–2.

38 *Ibid.*, 102.

39 *Ibid.*

CHAPTER THREE

1 Alice Thomas Ellis, *The Sin Eater* (Harmondsworth: Penguin, 1986), 122.

2 The authors of *Healing Your Aloneness: Finding Love and Wholeness Through Your Inner Child* (San Francisco: HarperCollins, 1991).

3 Doug Bennet and Tim Tiner, *Up North: A Guide to Ontario's Wilderness from Blackflies to the Northern Lights* (Markham, ON: Reed, 1993), 44.

4 Helen Fisher, *Anatomy of Love: The Natural History of Monogamy, Adultery and Divorce* (New York: Fawcett Columbine, 1992), 66; Alex Shoumatoff, *The Mountain of Names: A History of the Human Family* (New York: Simon and Schuster, 1985), 26. Only 4 per cent of recorded societies permit polyandry.

5 Fisher, *Anatomy of Love,* 66.

6 Will Durant, *The Story of Civilization, Vol. 1: Our Oriental Heritage* (New York: Simon and Schuster, 1963), 37.

7 *Ibid,* 37.

8 *Ibid.,* 40.

9 Fisher, *Anatomy of Love,* 69.

10 Durant, *Story of Civilization,* 40.

11 The Second World War killed fifteen million Russian men, depriving millions of women of existing or potential husbands. Shoumatoff, *Mountain of Names,* 29.

12 "Adultery: A New Furor Over an Old Sin," *Newsweek,* 30 September 1996, 54–59.

13 Timothy Taylor, *The Prehistory of Sex: Four Million Years of Human Sexual Culture* (New York: Bantam, 1996), 77.

14 William Manchester, *A World Lit Only by Fire: The Medieval Mind and the Renaissance, Portrait of an Age* (Boston: Little, Brown, 1992), 69.

15 Thomas Gregor, *Mehinaku: The Drama of Daily Life in a Brazilian Indian Village* (Chicago: University of Chicago Press, 1977), 132.

16 *Ibid,* 132.

17 *Ibid.,* 136.

18 *Ibid.,* 137–38.

19 *Ibid.,* 138.

20 *Ibid.,* 141.

21 *Ibid.,* 142–45.

22 Bennet and Tiner, *Up North,* 21.

23 *Ibid.,* 16–17.

24 *Mother Nature,* BBC Worldwide, Wildvision Production, seen on Canadian Discovery Channel, *Sunday Showcase,* 11 May 1997.

25 Helen Fisher, in interview with author for "The Idea of Marriage," *Ideas,* CBC Radio, 22 and 29 November 1994.

26 Fisher, *Anatomy of Love,* 160.

27 Robert Wright, "Our Cheating Hearts," *Time,* 15 August 1994, 32.

28 Helen Fisher, interview with author.

29 Bonnie Kreps, *Authentic Passion: Loving Without Losing Yourself* (Toronto: McClelland & Stewart, 1991).

30 *Ibid.*

31 Barbara Graham, "The Future of Love," *Utne Reader,* November–December, 1996, 49.

32 W.R. Jankowiak and E.F. Fischer, "A cross-cultural perspective on romantic love," *Ethnology* 31 (no. 2): 149–55.

33 Jonathan Spence, *The Death of Woman Wang* (New York: Penguin, 1978).

34 Nora Waln, *The House of Exile* (Boston: Little, Brown, 1992), 32–34.

35 *Ibid.,* 293.

36 *The Toronto Star,* 4 September 1993.

37 Helen A. Regis, "The madness of excess: Love among the Fulbe of North Cameroun," in William Jankowiak, ed., *Romantic Passion: A Universal Experience?* (New York: University of Columbia Press, 1995), 141–51.

38 David M. Buss, *The Evolution of Desire: Strategies of Human Mating* (New York: Basic Books, 1994), 126–29.

39 Henry Hess, "How the Mating Game Evolved," *The Globe and Mail,* 6 July 1994.

40 Shana Alexander, *Very Much a Lady: The untold story of Jean Harris and Dr. Herman Tarnower* (Boston: Little, Brown, 1983), 192–282.

41 Nancy Friday, *Jealousy* (New York: Perigord Press, William Morrow, 1985), 407–10.

42 Simone de Beauvoir, trans. Patrick O'Brian, *The Woman Destroyed* (New York: G. Putnam's Sons 1969), 123–254.

43 *New York,* 7 August 1995, 18.

44 Su Tong, *Raise the Red Lantern: Three Novellas* (New York: Penguin, 1996).

45 James Boswell, *Life of Johnson,* ed. R.W. Chapman (Oxford: Oxford University Press, 1980), 1035.

46 Natalie Zemon Davis, *The Return of Martin Guerre* (Cambridge, MA: Harvard University Press, 1983).

47 Julia O'Faolain and Lauro Martines, eds., *Not In God's Image: Women in*

History from the Greeks to the Victorians (New York: Harper Torchbook, 1973), 142.

48 J.P.V.D. Balsdon, *Roman Women: Their History and Habits* (New York: Barnes and Noble, 1983), 27.

49 *Ibid*, 27.

50 "The Maya," *The Globe and Mail*, 28 June 1996.

51 Jan Goodwin, *Price of Honor* (New York: Penguin, 1995), 246.

52 Martin Regg Cohn, "Upholding men's honor takes deadly toll," *The Toronto Star*, 16 September 1996.

53 *Ibid*.

54 Balsdon, *Roman Women*, 28.

55 James Houston, *Confessions of an Igloo Dweller* (Boston: Houghton Mifflin Company, 1996), 19–20.

56 Waverley Root, *The Food of France* (New York: Alfred A. Knopf, 1978), 424.

57 Lisa Herman, in "The Idea of Marriage," *Ideas*, 22 and 29 November 1994.

58 Theodore Zeldin, *An Intimate History of Humanity* (London: Minerva, 1995), 110.

59 *The Works of Geoffrey Chaucer*, ed. F.N. Robinson (Boston: Houghton Mifflin, 1961), 480–518.

60 Christopher Lasch, *Women and the Common Life* (New York: W.W. Norton, 1996), 33.

CHAPTER FOUR

1 A psychiatrist I know assures me that these cases are examples of denial. By the third term, aside from any other symptoms, the baby is kicking.

2 Elaine Morgan, *The Descent of Woman* (New York: Bantam, 1973), 230.

3 Genesis 30:1.

4 Genesis 30:3.

5 1 Samuel:1–14.

6 Morgan, *Descent of Woman*, 230–31.

7 *Ibid.*, 154.

8 *Report on Business Magazine*, August 1991.

9 "Good mom gene? Trigger prompts mice to care for young," Associated Press, 27 July 1996.

10 V.S. Naipaul, *A House for Mr. Biswas* (London: Andre Deutsch, 1961), 18. We know now that such exercises are essential to the child's physical

development. Many cultures seem to understand this instinctively, because these rituals are common all over the world.

11 "Canadian research shows loving rats have stress-free babies," Reuters, ex London, 27 November 1996.

12 *The Lancet*, 10 August 1996. The study examined the eating habits and lives of twenty-nine abnormally short children, aged from three to thirteen. The nature of their home lives can be guessed in part from the fact that some of the children found food to binge on by foraging in garbage cans. The doctors identified the problem as a new syndrome, "hyperphagic short stature."

13 Canadian Press, 2 June 1995.

14 Canadian Press, ex Miramichi, NB, 7 June 1995.

15 The Turners appealed unsuccessfully in October 1996. Their lawyer acknowledged that they were terrible parents, but argued that their failure to love their child was not a crime. See *The Globe and Mail*, 11 October 1996.

16 *The Toronto Star*, 2 April 1996, quoting Vera Rabie Azoory, author of *They Love You, They Love Me Not* (Toronto: HarperCollins, 1996).

17 *The Globe and Mail*, 20 June 1996.

18 Jerome Kagan, *The Nature of the Child* (New York: Basic Books, 1984), 264.

19 Desmond Morris, *The Naked Ape* (Toronto: Bantam, 1969), 105–6.

20 Canadian Press, ex Princeton, BC, 21 August 1996.

21 Nancy Mitford, *Don't Tell Alfred* (New York: Popular Library, 1976), 99.

22 *Ibid.*, 16–17.

23 Celestine Bohlen, "Italy's comfortable mamma's boys opting to remain at home longer," *The Globe and Mail*, 4 March 1996, reprinted from the New York Times Service.

24 "Fewer marriages, more divorces in Catholic Italy," Reuters, ex Rome, 27 September 1995.

25 Nicholas Kristof, "Japanese women have almost stopped having babies," *The Globe and Mail*, 11 October 1996. In recent years, Sweden has managed to raise its fertility rate to 1.9, from a low of 1.7 in 1980. In the United States, the rate has risen to about 2.0 from less than 1.8 in 1975. Germany, Spain and Hong Kong are running at 1.2, and Italy stands at 1.3.

26 Canadian Press, ex Ottawa and Montreal, 15 and 16 October 1995.

27 Jérôme Carcopino, *Daily Life in Ancient Rome*, trans. E.O. Lorimer (Harmondsworth: Penguin, 1975), 104.

28 Kristof, "Japanese women have almost stopped having babies," New York Times Service, ex Kyokushi, Japan, The Globe and Mail, 11 October 1996.

29 Ibid.

30 "Contraception through the ages," Reuters, ex Sydney, Australia, 27 November 1995. Also Sarah B. Pomeroy, Goddesses, Whores, Wives, and Slaves: Women in Classical Antiquity (New York: Schocken, 1975), 166–67.

31 Reuters, ex Sydney, Australia, 27 November 1995.

32 Canadian Press, ex Washington, 28 April 1996.

33 The Globe and Mail, 17 August 1996.

34 "Canadian abortion rates steadily rise: study," Canadian Press, ex Toronto, 5 February 1997.

35 Reuters, ex Moscow, 4 September 1995.

36 Associated Press, ex Washington, 9 January 1995.

37 Paul Veyne, ed., A History of Private Life, Vol. 1: From Pagan Rome to Byzantium, trans. Arthur Goldhammer (Cambridge, MA: The Belknap Press of Harvard University Press, 1992), 164.

38 "Impoverished Indian women caught in abortion trap," The Globe and Mail, 27 November 1996.

39 Ibid.

40 "Moms who give up kids fight the norm," Canadian Press, ex North Bay, ON, 30 August 1995.

41 D. James Romero, "Fear and Ignorance Seed a Bitter Harvest," Los Angeles Times, 9 February 1997.

42 "Dead baby found in garbage was alive when born," Canadian Press, ex Camrose, AB, 29 January 1997.

43 "Bright young things could face execution for infanticide," Associated Press, 18 November 1996, and 17 December 1996.

44 Shari L. Thurer, The Myths of Motherhood: How Culture Reinvents the Good Mother (New York: Penguin, 1995), 96 and 132.

45 "Romania Acting to Keep Families Together," The New York Times, 14 December 1996. The government increased the state allowance to mothers fivefold in an attempt to reduce the number of children being abandoned. In 1995, there were 104,000 children in state-run institutions.

46 "Mother indicted in daughter's abuse death," Associated Press, 28 November 1995; David Van Biema, "Abandoned to Her Fate," Time, 11 December 1995, 38–42.

47 Maclean's, 19 May 1997, 33; The Toronto Sun, 10 May 1997, 5 June 1997, 15 June 1997, 2 July 1997, 9 July 1997, 8 August 1997.

48 "Mother sentenced for killing child who saw her having sex," Associated Press, ex Dayton, OH, 15 February 1996.

49 "Disabled twins found emaciated, mother charged," Associated Press, ex Ceres, CA, 17 September 1996.

50 Thurer, *Myths of Motherhood*, 132.

51 Psychiatrist William Johnston of Toronto, interview with author.

52 Thurer, *Myths of Motherhood*, 6.

53 "Woman sold teenage son to settle drug debt: police," Associated Press, ex Detroit, 19 November 1996.

54 Thurer, *Myths of Motherhood*, 238–39.

55 *Ibid.*, 238.

56 Valerie Solanas, *The Scum Manifesto* (San Francisco: A.K. Press, 1996).

57 Shulamith Firestone, *The Dialectic of Sex* (London: Women's Press, 1979), 75.

58 *Ibid.*

59 Germaine Greer, *The Female Eunuch* (London: Granada, 1971), 235.

60 Philippe Ariès, *Centuries of Childhood: A Social History of Family Life*, trans. Robert Baldick (London: Jonathan Cape, 1962), 39.

61 Edward Shorter, *The Making of the Modern Family* (New York: Basic Books, 1975), 174–81.

62 *Ibid.*, 171.

63 *Ibid.*, 170.

64 Ariès, *Centuries of Childhood*, 39.

65 Ferdinand Mount, *The Subversive Family: An Alternative History of Love and Marriage* (London: Jonathan Cape, 1982), 106.

66 Ariès, *Centuries of Childhood*, 130.

67 Shorter, *Making of the Modern Family*, 170.

68 Thurer, *Myths of Motherhood*, 236–38.

69 Mary McCarthy, *The Group* (New York: Harcourt Brace, 1989), 292, 300–302, 311–12, 437–39.

70 Maxine Hong Kingston, *The Woman Warrior* (New York: Vintage, 1976) 125.

71 Emmanuel Le Roy Ladurie, *Montaillou: Catholics and Cathars in a French Village* (London: Scolar, 1978), 210.

72 Jane Goodall, *In the Shadow of Man*, rev. ed. (London: Weidenfeld and Nicolson, 1988), 80–81.

73 *Ibid.*, 82.

74 Sarah Hobson, *Family Web: A Story of India* (London: John Murray, 1978), 149.

75 Redmond O'Hanlon, *In Trouble Again* (London: Hamish Hamilton, 1988), 240.

76 Sholom Aleichem, *The Old Country*, trans. Julius and Frances Butwin (New York: Crown, 1946), 194.

77 Ian Buruma, *A Japanese Mirror: Heroes and Villains of Japanese Culture* (London: Jonathan Cape, 1984), 20.

78 *Ibid.*

79 Tobias Wolff, *The Night in Question* (New York: Knopf, 1996), 202.

80 Thurer, *Myths of Motherhood*, xi.

81 *Ibid.*, xiii.

82 Bruno Bettelheim, *A Good Enough Parent: A Book on Child-Rearing* (New York: Vintage, 1988).

CHAPTER FIVE

1 Edmund Gosse, *Father and Son* (London: William Heinemann, 1908), 37.

2 John Winokur, comp. and ed., *Father* (New York: Dutton, 1993), 179.

3 *Ibid.*, 86.

4 *Amazing But True* (Toronto: Owl Books, Greey de Pencier, 1990), 75.

5 Several nature documentaries on television. The author adores watching fish.

6 Adrian Forsyth, *A Natural History of Sex: The ecology and evolution of mating behavior* (Shelburne, VT: Chapters Publishing, 1993), 66.

7 BBC Worldwide, Wildvision Production, "Mother Nature," seen on Canadian Discovery Channel, *Sunday Showcase*, 11 May 1997.

8 Jane Goodall, *In the Shadow of Man*, rev. ed. (London: Weidenfeld and Nicolson, 1988), 230.

9 Ursula Owen, *Fathers, Reflections by Daughters* (New York: Pantheon, 1985), 56.

10 *Ibid.*, 57.

11 Ruth Benedict, *The Chrysanthemum and the Sword: Patterns of Japanese Culture* (New York: Meridian, New American Library, 1974), 52.

12 Jan Goodwin, *Price of Honor: Muslim Women Lift the Veil of Silence on the Islamic World* (New York: Penguin, 1995), 6.

13 Bronislaw Malinowski, *The Sexual Life of Savages* (London: Halcyon House, 1929), 20.

14 Georges Contenau, *Everyday Life in Babylon and Assyria* (London: Edward Arnold, 1954), 17.

15 "Refugee selling seven-year-old son to pay bills," Associated Press, ex Sidon, Lebanon, 12 October 1996.

16 Owen, *Fathers*, 114.

17 Lawrence Stone, *Broken Lives: Separation and Divorce in England, 1660–1857* (Oxford: Oxford University Press, 1994), 14.

18 Goodwin, *Price of Honor*, 71, 150.

19 This situation became familiar through the book *Not Without My Daughter* (New York: St. Martin's Press, 1987) by Betty Mahmoody, an American woman who eventually did manage to wrest her daughter from her Iranian husband. Her story was made into a movie starring Sally Field. But in Toronto, where I live, I read about several similar cases each year. On 17 August 1996, *The Globe and Mail* ran such a story under the headline, "Mother reunited with son: Father in custody after arrest in airport on abduction charge." The father, Masoud Kolahchahi-Sabet, had abducted his six-year-old son, Peyman, after his divorce. He held the boy for three years in Tehran. The child's mother, Homiera Massah-Rabbani, only got the boy back because the father attempted to return to Canada on an expired passport, giving her a basis for bargaining with her former in-laws.

20 "U.S. doctor gets $7.835 million in Alberta adoption case," Associated Press, ex Huntington, wv, 4 December 1995.

21 Canadian Press, ex Montreal, 25 September 1995.

22 "Murder-suicides sparked by men trying to get back at wives: psychiatrist," Canadian Press, ex Hamilton, ON, 4 November 1995.

23 *Ibid.*

24 "Man accused of throwing children from window in domestic violence case," Associated Press, 28 January 1997.

25 Canadian Press, ex Toronto, 7 March 1995.

26 Edith Hamilton, *Mythology* (New York: Signet, 1969), 65–68.

27 B.S. Hewlett, "Husband-wife reciprocity and the father-infant relationship among Aka pygmies," in *Father-Child Relations: Cultural and Biosocial Contexts*, ed. B.S Hewlett (New York: Aldine De Gruyter, 1992), 153–76.

28 Interview by Finbar O'Reilly.

29 Genesis 42:38, and also 44:29.

30 2 Samuel 18:33.

31 Joyce Tyldesley, *Daughters of Isis: Women of Ancient Egypt* (Harmondsworth: Penguin, 1995), 66–67.

32 Quoted in Owen, *Fathers*, 116.

33 Patrice Engel and Cynthia Breaux, *Is There a Father Instinct? Fathers' Responsibility for Their Children* (Washington, D.C.: The International Centre for Research on Women, and New York: The Population Council, New York, February 1994), 16.

34 V. Pandya, "Gukwelonone: The game of hiding fathers and seeking sons among the Ongee of Little Andaman," in Hewlett, *Father-Child Relations,* 263–80.

35 Sarah Hobson, *Family Web: A Story of India* (London: John Murray, 1978), 101.

36 Tyldesley, *Daughters of Isis,* 66

37 David M. Buss, *The Evolution of Desire: Strategies of Human Mating* (New York: Basic Books, 1994).

38 Henry Hess, "How the Mating Game Evolved," *The Globe and Mail,* 6 July 1994.

39 F. Furstenberg, "Good dads – bad dads: Two faces of fatherhood," in *The Changing American Family and Public Policy,* ed. A. Cherlin (Lanham, MD: Urban Institute Press, 1988), 216.

40 *The Toronto Star,* 19 June 1996.

41 R.L. Munroe and R.H. Munroe, "Fathers in children's environments: A four culture study," in Hewlett, *Father-Child Relations,* 213–30. In the other two cultures the Munroes studied, the Logoli in Kenya and the Newar in Nepal, fathers were absent from only 4 and 15 per cent of families.

42 Engel and Breaux, *Is There a Father Instinct?,* 26–27.

43 Nicholas Kristof, "Japanese women have almost stopped having babies: If trends last, population could be half," *New York Times* Service, ex Kyokushi, Japan, *The Globe and Mail,* 11 October 1996.

44 Will Durant, *The Story of Civilization: Our Oriental Heritage* (New York: Simon and Schuster, 1963), 32.

45 Lucy Mair, *Marriage* (Harmondsworth: Penguin, 1971), 148.

46 Paul Bohannan and John Middleton, eds., *Marriage, Family and Residence* (Garden City, NY: The Natural History Press, 1968), 321–32.

47 J. Brown, P. Anderson and B. Chevanne, *Report on the Contribution of Caribbean Men to the Family* (Kingston, Jamaica: Caribbean Child Development Centre, 1993).

48 William Davenport, "The Family System of Jamaica," reprinted from *Social and Economic Studies,* Vol. 10, 1961, 420–54, in Bohannan and Middleton, *Marriage, Family and Residence,* 251.

49 *Ibid.,* 282.

50 Engel and Breaux, *Is There a Father Instinct?*, 27.

51 *Ibid.*, 15.

52 Anne Boston, "Growing Up Fatherless," in Owen, *Fathers*, 31.

53 Alex Shoumatoff, *The Mountain of Names: A History of the Human Family* (New York: Simon and Schuster, 1985), 17–18.

54 Helen Fisher, *Anatomy of Love: The Natural History of Monogamy, Adultery and Divorce* (New York: Fawcett Columbine, 1992), 155.

55 *Ibid.*, 154–55.

56 BBC Worldwide, Wildvision Production, "Mother Nature," on Canadian Discovery Channel, *Sunday Showcase*, 11 May 1997.

57 Helen Fisher, in interview with author.

58 *New Scientist*, 16 December 1995, 9.

59 Desmond Morris, *The Naked Ape* (Toronto: Bantam, 1969), 34.

60 *Ibid.*, 36.

61 *Ibid.*

62 *Ibid.*

63 Helen Fisher, in interview with author; Gerda Lerner, *The Creation of Patriarchy* (New York: Oxford University Press, 1986), 29–30.

64 Colin M. Turnbull, *The Forest People* (New York: Simon and Schuster, 1961), 126–28.

65 Elizabeth Marshall Thomas, *The Harmless People* (New York: Vintage, 1959), 49.

66 Engel and Breaux, *Is There a Father Instinct?*, 33.

67 K. Endicott, "Fathering in an egalitarian society," in Hewlett, *Father-Child Relations*, 281–96.

68 Helen Fisher, in interview with author.

69 Stanford anthropologist Renato Rosaldo, in interview with author.

70 Durant, *Civilization*, 40.

71 Helen Fisher, in interview with author.

72 J. Bronowski, *The Ascent of Man* (London: Macdonald Futura, 1981), 38.

73 Jennifer Veale, Scripps Howard News Service, ex London, 24–25 July 1995.

74 *Ibid.*

75 Engel and Breaux, *Is There a Father Instinct?*, 30.

76 Jasper Becker, *Hungry Ghosts: Mao's Secret Famine* (New York: The Free Press, 1996), 20–21, 136–38, 160, 211–13.

77 Elliott Skinner, "Intergenerational Conflict Among the Mossi: Father and Son," in Bohannan and Middleton, *Marriage, Family and Residence*, 237–45.

78 N. Folbre, "Rotten kids, bad daddies, and public policy," paper prepared for presentation at the International Food Policy Research Institute, World Bank Conference on Intrahousehold Resource Allocation: Policy Issues and Research Methods, Washington, D.C., 12–15 February 1992.

79 Engel and Breaux, *Is There a Father Instinct?*, 43.

80 F.G. Bolton, "Today's father and social services delivery system: A false promise," in M.E. Lamb, ed., *The Father's Role: Cross-Cultural Perspectives* (Hillsdale, NJ: Lawrence Erlbaum Associates, 1987), 429–41.

81 *The Globe and Mail*, 14 June 1997.

82 "Instant Intimacy," *Ideas*, CBC Radio, 10 and 17 December 1991.

83 Quoted in David Blankenhorn, *Fatherless America: Confronting Our Most Urgent Social Problem* (New York: HarperPerennial, 1996), 56.

84 Gunnar Heinsohn, in interview with author. For instance, sociological studies of the Nazi Party before the Second World War found that a disproportionate number of high-ranking officials were from fatherless homes. Similar studies in contemporary Scandinavia have found the same disturbing pattern.

85 K.A. Clarke-Stewart, "And daddy makes three: The father's impact on the mother and young child," in *Child Development* 49, 1978, 466–78, and K.A. Clarke-Stewart, "The fathers' contribution to children's cognitive and social development in early childhood," in F.A. Pedersen, ed., *The Father-Infant Relationship, Observational Studies in the Family Setting* (New York: Praeger Publishers, 1980), 111–46.

86 Dorothy Lipovenko, "Children of single mothers face troubles: Statscan study finds more behavioural problems, school failures caused by greater stress," *The Globe and Mail*, 19 October 1996.

87 Y.Y. Al-Mazrou, K.M. Aziz and M. Khalil, "Association of parents' education and fathers' occupation with prevalence of diarrhoea among children less than five years of age in Saudi Arabia," *Journal of Diarrhoeal Disease Research*, 9, 1991, quoted in Engel and Breaux, *Is There a Father Instinct?*, 24.

88 Engel and Breaux, *Is There a Father Instinct?*, 17.

89 *Ibid.*

CHAPTER SIX

1 *The Globe and Mail*, 2 July 1996.

2 Alex Shoumatoff, *The Mountain of Names: A History of the Human Family* (New York: Simon and Schuster, 1985), 60.

3 Gerald R. Leslie, *The Family in Social Context* (New York: Oxford University Press, 1967), 36.

4 George Murdock, "World Ethnographic Sample," *American Anthropologist*, No. 59 (August 1957): 664–87.

5 George Murdock, *Social Structure* (New York: The Macmillan Company, 1949), Chapter 1.

6 *Ibid.*, 2.

7 Meyer F. Nimkoff and Russell Middleton, "Types of Family and Types of Economy," *American Journal of Sociology*, No. 66 (Nov. 1960), 215–25, quoted in Leslie, *The Family in Social Context*, 37.

8 Beatrice Gottlieb, interview with author; and Beatrice Gottlieb, *The Family in the Western World from the Black Death to the Industrial Age* (New York: Oxford University Press, 1994), 5–6.

9 *Ibid.*, 59–62.

10 *Ibid.*, 50.

11 *Ibid.*

12 *Ibid.*, 72.

13 Quoted in Gottlieb, *Family in the Western World*, 252.

14 Stuart A. Queen and Robert W. Habenstein, eds., *The Family in Various Cultures*, 3rd ed. (Philadelphia: J.B. Lippincott, 1961), 46–47.

15 David Maybury-Lewis, *Millennium: Tribal Wisdom and the Modern World* (New York: Viking, 1992), 109.

16 Keith F. Otterbein, "Marquesan Polyandry," in Paul Bohannan and John Middleton, eds., *Marriage, Family and Residence* (Garden City, NY: The Natural History Press, 1968), 287–96.

17 Queen and Habenstein, *Family in Various Cultures*, 91–92.

18 *Ibid.*, 144.

19 Leslie, *Family in Social Context*, 166–67.

20 Shoumatoff, *Mountain of Names*, 53.

21 *Ibid.*, 55.

22 Leslie, *Family in Social Context*, 205.

23 *Ibid.*, 205–6.

24 Queen and Habenstein, *Family in Various Cultures*, 69.

25 Murdock, *Social Structure*, 268.

26 Maybury-Lewis, *Millennium*, 123.

27 James Houston, *Confessions of an Igloo Dweller* (Boston: Houghton Mifflin, 1996), 199.

28 Queen and Habenstein, *Family in Various Cultures*, 77.

29 *Ibid.*, 82.

30 The Nazi vision of the family is a complex issue. See Chapter 7 for a more complete discussion of its conflicts and paradoxes.

31 Shoumatoff, *Mountain of Names*, 167.

32 *Ibid.*

33 Joseph Mitchell, *Up in the Old Hotel and Other Stories* (New York: Vintage, 1992), 156–57.

34 John Reader, *Man on Earth: A Celebration of Mankind* (New York: Harper & Row Perennial Library, 1988), 56.

35 Leslie, *The Family in Social Context*, 35–36.

36 Louis Finkelstein, ed., *The Jews: Their History* (New York: Schocken, 1970), 275.

37 Nora Waln, *The House of Exile* (Boston: Little, Brown, 1992), 36.

38 *Ibid.*, 35.

39 "Woman gets 10 years for daughter-in-law strangulation," Canadian Press, ex Vancouver, 10 April 1996.

40 Sarah Hobson, *Family Web: A Story of India* (London: John Murray, 1978).

41 *Ibid.*, 32–33.

42 *Ibid.*, 39.

43 *Ibid.*, 53.

44 Erika Friedl, *Women of Deh Koh: Lives in an Iranian Village* (New York: Penguin, 1991).

45 Witold Rybczynski, *Home: A Short History of an Idea* (New York: Viking, 1986), 39, 86–87.

46 Paul Veyne, ed., *A History of Private Life, Vol. 1: From Pagan Rome to Byzantium*, trans. Arthur Goldhammer (Cambridge, MA: The Belknap Press of Harvard University Press, 1987), 71.

47 Gerda Lerner, *The Creation of Patriarchy* (New York: Oxford University Press, 1986), 24.

48 Veyne and Goldhammer, *History of Private Life*, 462.

49 Pauline Schmitt Pantel, ed., *A History of Women: From Ancient Goddesses to Christian Saints* (Cambridge, MA: The Belknap Press of Harvard University Press, 1992), 311.

50 H.D.F. Kitto, *The Greeks* (Harmondsworth: Penguin, 1973), 90.

51 *Ibid.*, 142.

52 Jérôme Carcopino, *Daily Life in Ancient Rome*, trans. E.O. Lorimer (Harmondsworth: Penguin, 1975), 69.

53 Veyne and Goldhammer, *History of Private Life*, 51.

54 *Ibid.*, 52.

55 Carcopino, *Daily Life*, 71.

56 *Ibid.*, 70.

57 Veyne and Goldhammer, *History of Private Life*, 65.

58 This seems not to have been a uniquely Roman tic. Salic Law forbade castration, yet in the eighth century A.D., Charlemagne was also obliged to double the fine for it. It was permissible only as a punishment for slaves caught stealing. Veyne and Goldhammer, *History of Private Life*, 457.

59 *Ibid.*

60 Veyne and Goldhammer, *History of Private Life*, 68.

61 *Ibid.*, 79.

62 Schmitt Pantel, *History of Women*, 320.

63 *Ibid.*, 311.

64 Veyne and Goldhammer, *History of Private Life*, 79.

65 Schmitt Pantel, *History of Women*, 320–21.

66 Veyne and Goldhammer, *History of Private Life*, 73.

67 *Ibid.*, 88–109.

68 *Ibid.*, 88.

69 Clark Blaise and Bharati Mukherjee, *Days and Nights in Calcutta* (Garden City, NY: Doubleday, 1977), 152.

70 William Davenport, "The Family System of Jamaica," in Bohannan and Middleton, *Marriage, Family and Residence*, 251.

71 R.D. Laing and A. Esterson. *Sanity, Madness and the Family* (Harmondsworth: Penguin, 1970).

72 *Ibid.*, 176–201.

73 John Welwood, *Love and Awakening: Discovering the Sacred Path of Intimate Relationship* (New York: HarperCollins, 1996).

74 1 Samuel 1:8.

75 Marvin Lowenthal, trans., *The Memoirs of Glückel of Hameln* (New York: Schocken, 1977).

76 *Ibid.*, 34.

77 *Ibid.*, 1.

78 *Ibid.*, 150.

79 Shoumatoff, *Mountain of Names*, 137.

80 Queen and Habenstein, *Family in Various Cultures*, 27.

81 Elaine Carey, *The Toronto Star*, 5 May 1996.

82 Waln, *House of Exile*, 133. See also Jonathan Spence, *The Death of Woman Wang* (New York: Penguin, 1978), 126.

83 "Court returns passports of doctor's family held in dowry case," Associated Press, ex Bangalore, 18 January 1996.

84 Rita Daly, "Women cast off in homeland: husbands took their passports and ID papers, wives charge," *The Toronto Star*, 14 May 1995.

85 Colin M. Turnbull, *The Mountain People* (New York: Simon and Schuster, 1987).

86 *Ibid.*, 112.

CHAPTER SEVEN

1 Geraldine Brooks, *Nine Parts of Desire: The Hidden World of Islamic Women* (New York: Doubleday, 1996), 33–36.

2 *Ibid.*, 37.

3 Richard Critchfield, *Villages* (New York: Doubleday, 1983), 156.

4 Julia O'Faolain and Lauro Martines, eds., *Not in God's Image: Women in History from the Greeks to the Victorians* (New York: Harper Torchbooks, 1973), 109.

5 The Egyptian doctor and writer Nawal El Saadawi has a savagely disturbing short story about this form of defloration in her collection *She Has No Place in Paradise* (London: Minerva, 1991), 9–14. The protagonist, filled with rage against his mother and all women, deliberately holds back and fails to break the bride's hymen. (It's obviously much easier for a man to control the depth of penetration if he's using his finger rather than his penis.) The vicious anti-hero displays the obligatory handkerchief, unmarked by blood, knowing it will mean the girl's death.

6 *Ibid.*, 157.

7 Gerda Lerner, *The Creation of Patriarchy* (New York: Oxford University Press. 1986), 47.

8 Jan Goodwin, *Price of Honor: Muslim Women Lift the Veil of Silence on the Islamic World* (New York: Penguin, 1995), 45.

9 *Ibid.*

10 In a patriarchal and polygamous society, of course, a grandfather's wife might well be the same age as or younger than a grandson.

11 Beatrice Gottlieb, *The Family in the Western World from the Black Death to the Industrial Age* (New York: Oxford University Press, 1994), 56.

12 Sarah B. Pomeroy, *Goddesses, Whores, Wives, and Slaves: Women in Classical Antiquity* (New York: Schocken, 1975), 37–38.

13 H.D.F. Kitto, *The Greeks* (Harmondsworth: Penguin, 1973), 93.

14 O'Faolain and Martines, *Not in God's Image*, 6.

15 *Ibid.*, 6–8.

16 Richard Grunberger, *A Social History of the Third Reich* (Harmondsworth: Penguin, 1977), 298.

17 *Ibid.*, 300–3.

18 *Ibid.*, 304.

19 *Ibid.*, 305.

20 *Ibid.*, 314–18.

21 *Ibid.*, 302.

22 Nancy Mitford, *Wigs on the Green* (Toronto: Popular Library Edition, 1976), 61.

23 *Ibid.*, 308.

24 *Ibid.*, 328.

25 *Ibid.*, 318.

26 Leo Tolstoy, *Anna Karenina* (New York: Bantam, 1960), 1.

27 Genesis 2:18.

28 Shari L. Thurer, *The Myths of Motherhood: How Culture Reinvents the Good Mother* (New York: Penguin, 1995), 52.

29 Genesis 19:8.

30 Judges 19:22–29.

31 Deuteronomy 22:1.

32 Deuteronomy 22:26.

33 See Chapter 3.

34 Thurer, *Myths of Motherhood*, 35. The biblical passages on menstruation can be found in Leviticus 15:19–24 and 18:19. A man cannot have intercourse with his wife during her period. Even touching her is defiling. She is not "clean" again until she has visited the ritual bath, the *mikvah*.

35 See, for instance, Lerner, *Patriarchy*, 167–79.

36 2 Samuel 13:12–13.

37 Gerald R. Leslie, *The Family in Social Context* (New York: Oxford University Press, 1967), 30, 161.

38 Renate Bridenthal, Claudia Koonz and Susan Stuard, *Becoming Visible: Women in European History*, 2nd ed. (Boston: Houghton Mifflin, 1987), 73.

39 Paul Johnson, *A History of the Jews* (London: Weidenfeld and Nicolson, 1987), 200; Elie Kedourie, ed., *The Jewish Word: Revelation, Prophecy and History* (London: Thames and Hudson, 1979), 175.

40 Leviticus 15:19–28.

41 Will Durant, *The Story of Civilization: Our Oriental Heritage* (New York: Simon and Schuster, 1963), 401.

42 Ronald Wright, *Stolen Continents: The "New World" Through Indian Eyes* (Toronto: Penguin, 1993), 118–19.

43 Bridenthal et al., *Becoming Visible*, 23.

44 *Ibid.*, 49.

45 Joyce Tyldesley, *Daughters of Isis: Women of Ancient Egypt* (Harmonds-worth: Penguin, 1995), 49–50.

46 *Ibid.*, 143–44.

47 Durant, *Story of Civilization*, 165.

48 Tyldesley, *Daughters of Isis*, 135.

49 *Ibid.*, 181–83.

50 *Ibid.*, 136–37.

51 See Elizabeth Wayland Barber, *Women's Work: The First 20,000 Years: Women, Cloth, and Society in Early Times* (New York: W.W. Norton, 1994).

52 Proverbs 31:27.

53 Tyldesley, *Daughters of Isis*, 166.

54 Leonard Cottrell, *Life Under the Pharoahs* (London: Evan Brothers, 1955), 51.

55 Durant, *Story of Civilization*, 164.

56 Cottrell, *Life Under the Pharoahs*, 50.

57 Bridenthal et al., *Becoming Visible*, 57.

58 Durant, *Story of Civilization*, 130.

59 William Rowbotham, in interview with author.

60 Durant, *Story of Civilization*, 130.

61 Bridenthal et al., *Becoming Visible*, 61.

62 *Ibid.*, 65.

63 *Ibid.*, 63.

64 Durant, *Story of Civilization*, 127.

65 *Ibid.*, 130; Bridenthal et al., *Becoming Visible*, 65.

66 Durant, *Story of Civilization*, 201.

67 The Code of Manu was once believed to date back to about 1200 B.C. Today, scholars place it no later than the start of the Christian era.

68 Quoted in Durant, *Story of Civilization*, 493.

69 Clark Blaise and Bharati Mukherjee, *Days and Nights in Calcutta* (Garden City, NY: Doubleday, 1977), 236.

70 Leonard C. Woolley, *The Sumerians* (Oxford: Oxford University Press, 1928), 112–14.

71 Durant, *Story of Civilization*, 124–25.

72 Bridenthal et al., *Becoming Visible*, 62.

73 *Ibid.*, 62–63.

74 Durant, *Story of Civilization*, 244–46.

75 *Ibid.*, 245. Note that Herodotus is not always to be trusted.
76 *Ibid.*, 247.
77 Bridenthal et al., *Becoming Visible*, 68.
78 Georges Contenau, *Everyday Life in Babylon and Assyria* (London: Edward Arnold, 1954), 18.
79 Bridenthal et al., *Becoming Visible*, 69; Durant, *Story of Civilization*, 231.
80 Contenau, *Everyday Life*, 18.
81 Durant, *Story of Civilization*, 231.
82 *Ibid.*, 153.
83 Bridenthal et al., *Becoming Visible*, 68; and William Rowbotham, in interview with author.
84 Bridenthal et al., *Becoming Visible*, 68.
85 Durant, *Story of Civilization*, 247.
86 Bridenthal et al., *Becoming Visible*, 62.
87 Contenau, *Everyday Life*, 18.
88 Durant, *Story of Civilization*, 275.
89 Bridenthal et al., *Becoming Visible*, 70.
90 *Ibid.*, 70.
91 Durant, *Story of Civilization*, 275.
92 Kitto, *The Greeks*, 219, 230. Kitto argues, rather weakly in my opinion, that the bars protected the virtue of the home's slaves, and the possessions of the women's quarters, which were, after all, partly a clothing factory.
93 Bonnie Anderson and Judith Zinsser, *A History of Their Own: Women in Europe from Prehistory to the Present*, Vol. 1 (New York: Harper and Row, 1988), 28.
94 *Ibid.*, 29.
95 *Ibid.*
96 Pauline Schmitt Pantel, ed., *History of Women: Fron Ancient Goddesses to Christian Saints* (Cambridge, MA: The Belknap Press of Harvard University Press, 1992), 319.
97 Quoted in O'Faolain and Martines, *Not in God's Image*, 30.
98 Pomeroy, *Goddesses*, 64.
99 Mary Lefkowitz and Maureen Fant, *Women's Life in Greece and Rome* (Baltimore: Johns Hopkins University Press, 1982), 18.
100 Quoted in Bridenthal et al., *Becoming Visible*, 90.
101 Euripides, *Medea*, trans. Philip Vellacott (Harmondsworth: Penguin Classics, 1971), 24.
102 Kitto, *The Greeks*, 221.

103 *Ibid.*

104 Anderson and Zinsser, *History of Their Own*, Vol. 1, 30; Thurer, *Myth of Motherhood*, 70.

105 O'Faolain and Martines, *Not in God's Image*, 19.

106 His adopted son.

107 O'Faolain and Martines, *Not in God's Image*, 11.

108 Livy, *History of Rome*, Vol. 1, trans. Rev. Canon Roberts (London: J.M. Dent & Sons, 1912), 12–13.

109 Jérôme Carcopino, *Daily Life in Ancient Rome*, trans. E.O. Lorimer (Harmondsworth: Penguin, 1975), 94.

110 J.P.V.D. Balsdon, *Roman Women: Their History and Habits* (New York: Barnes and Noble, 1983), 24.

111 O'Faolain and Martines, *Not in God's Image*, 34.

112 Carcopino, *Daily Life*, 93–97; Pomeroy, *Goddesses*, 152.

113 Balsdon, *Roman Women*, 47; Pomeroy, *Goddesses*, 156.

114 Pomeroy, *Goddesses*, 156.

115 Schmitt Pantel, *History of Women*, 303–4.

116 Stuart A. Queen and Robert W. Habenstein, eds., *The Family in Various Cultures*, 3rd ed. (Philadelphia: J.B. Lippincott, 1961), 167.

117 Thurer, *Myths of Motherhood*, 68.

118 *Ibid.*, 69.

119 *Ibid.*

120 Philip Slater, *The Glory of Hera* (Boston: Beacon Press, 1968).

121 Thurer, *Myths of Motherhood*, 76.

122 *Ibid.*, 170.

123 *Ibid.*

124 Aulus Gellius, *The Attic Nights*, quoted in O'Faolain and Martines, *Not in God's Image*, 35.

125 Pomeroy, *Goddesses*, 159.

126 Quoted in Balsdon, *Roman Women*, 30–31.

127 *Ibid.*

128 Livy, *History of Rome*, Vol. 11, trans. Rev. Canon Roberts (London: J.M. Dent & Sons, 1912), 129–30.

129 Quoted in Balsdon, *Roman Women*, 34–35; O'Faolain and Martines, *Not in God's Image*, 38–39.

130 Balsdon, *Roman Women*, 45; Susan Treggiari, Professor in the School of Humanities and Sciences, Stanford University, in interview with author; Susan Treggiari, *Roman Marriage: Iusti Coniuges from the Time of Cicero to the Time of Ulpian* (Oxford: Clarendon Press, 1991).

131 Quoted in O'Faolain and Martines, *Not in God's Image*, 44.

132 Gerald R. Leslie, *The Family in Social Context* (New York: Oxford University Press, 1967), 174.

133 Schmitt Pantel, *History of Women*, 298.

134 Remember that Professor Gunnar Heinsohn suggested to me that the original Roman pattern may have been to keep all healthy males, but only one girl. She could be exchanged for a bride for the family's eldest son. The younger boys would thus have a strong impetus to get out into the world and wage war so that they could capture wives for themselves.

135 Balsdon, *Roman Women*, 59.

136 Plutarch, *The Lives of the Noble Grecians and Romans: The Dryden Translation* (Chicago: Encyclopedia Britannica, 1952), 287.

137 Leslie, *Family in Social Context*, 174.

138 Carcopino, *Daily Life*, 91.

139 *Ibid.*, 92.

140 *Ibid.*, 111.

141 Schmitt Pantel, *History of Women* 313–14, among many others.

142 Pomeroy, *Goddesses*, 132.

143 Suetonius, *Nero 29*, quoted in John Boswell, *Same-Sex Unions in Premodern Europe* (New York: Villard, 1994), 80–81.

144 Boswell, *Same-Sex Unions*, 80.

145 *Ibid.*, 317.

146 Leslie, *Family in Social Context*, 175.

147 Schmitt Pantel, *History of Women*, 321.

148 *Ibid.*, 322.

149 Pomeroy, *Goddesses*, 167.

150 Schmitt Pantel, *History of Women*, 320.

151 *Ibid.*, 322

152 Carcopino, *Daily Life*, 116.

153 Pomeroy, *Goddesses*, 160.

154 *Ibid.*; Professor Gunnar Heinsohn, in interview with author.

155 Pomeroy, *Goddesses*, 192.

156 Schmitt Pantel, *History of Women*, 320; Carcopino, *Daily Life*, 116.

157 Pomeroy, *Goddesses*, 193.

158 Schmitt Pantel, *History of Women*, 324.

159 Pomeroy, *Goddesses*, 161.

160 Carcopino, *Daily Life*, 99–100; Pomeroy, *Goddesses*, 161.

161 M.F.K. Fisher, *Here Let Us Feast: A Book of Banquets* (San Francisco: North Point Press, 1986), 61–62.

162 Carcopino, *Daily Life*, 287.

163 *Ibid.*, 288.

164 *Ibid.*, 298.

165 Anderson and Zinsser, *History of Their Own*, 43.

166 See Robert Graves, *I Claudius* (Harmondsworth: Penguin, 1953), 362.

CHAPTER EIGHT

1 Jérôme Carcopino, *Daily Life in Ancient Rome*, trans. E.O. Lorimer (Harmondsworth: Penguin, 1975), 147–49.

2 André Burgière, Christiane Klapisch-Zuber, Martine Segalen, and Françoise Zonabend, *A History of the Family. Volume I: Distant Worlds, Ancient Worlds,* trans. Sarah Hanbury Tenison, Rosemary Morris and Andrew Wilson (Cambridge, MA: The Belknap Press of Harvard University Press, 1996), 306.

3 Carcopino, *Daily Life*, 101. He notes that the emperors who followed Claudius and Nero no longer forced women to kill themselves with their condemned husbands, but adds that "the cruelty of daily life still left all too many opportunities" for women to display the ancient Roman resolution in the face of suicide.

4 John 8:7–11.

5 Bonnie Anderson and Judith Zinsser, *A History of Their Own: Women in Europe from Prehistory to the Present*, Vol. 1 (New York: Harper and Row, 1988), 67–68.

6 Pauline Schmitt Pantel, ed., *A History of Women: From Ancient Goddesses to Christian Saints* (Cambridge, MA: The Belknap Press of Harvard University Press, 1992), 410.

7 Matthew 18:3.

8 Mark 10:14.

9 Mark 3:35.

10 1 Corinthians 7:15.

11 Matthew 8:22.

12 Alex Shoumatoff, *The Mountain of Names: A History of the Human Family* (New York: Simon and Schuster, 1985), 117.

13 Mendell Lewittes, *Jewish Marriage: Rabbinic Law, Legend, and Custom.* (Northvale, NJ: Jason Aronson Inc., 1994), 12. The injunction against this kind of pressure can be found in the *Shulchan Aruch*. It is by no means universally accepted even today.

14 Schmitt Pantel, *History of Women*, 411.

15 Matthew 19:6; Matthew 5:32.

16 Matthew 6:24; Matthew 19:21.

17 Anderson and Zinsser, *History of Their Own*, 67.

18 Acts 10:34; Romans 2:11.

19 Galatians 3:28.

20 Colossians 3:2.

21 I Corinthians 7:33–34.

22 I Corinthians 7:9.

23 John Boswell, *Same-Sex Unions in Premodern Europe* (New York: Villard, 1994), 165.

24 Matthew 22:21.

25 Quoted in Stuart A. Queen and Robert W. Habenstein, eds., *The Family in Various Cultures*, 3rd ed. (Philadelphia: J.B. Lippincott, 1961), 185.

26 *Ibid.*, 184.

27 Gerald R. Leslie, *The Family in Social Context* (New York: Oxford University Press, 1967), 213.

28 I Corinthians 14:34.

29 I Corinthians 11:8–9.

30 Titus 2:4–5.

31 Tertullian, quoted in Queen and Habenstein, *Family in Various Cultures*, 186.

32 John Chrysostom, quoted in *ibid.*, 186.

33 Anderson and Zinsser, *History of Their Own*, 81.

34 Barbara Tuchman, *A Distant Mirror: The Calamitous 14th Century* (New York: Ballantine, 1978), 211.

35 Queen and Habenstein, *Family in Various Cultures*, 191.

36 Quoted in Queen and Habenstein, *Family in Various Cultures*, 192.

37 *Ibid.*

38 Tuchman, *Distant Mirror*, 212.

39 *Ibid.*, 73–74.

40 Matthew 10:34.

41 Anderson and Zinsser, *History of Their Own*, 72–73.

42 *Ibid.*, 32–33.

43 Burgière et al., *History of the Family, Volume I*, 337. In the Middle Ages, this emphasis on male bonding united with the Graeco-Roman practice of formally swearing brotherhood with another male, who might or might not be a lover. The Church developed a ceremony for consecrating friendship, the subject of John Boswell's *Same-Sex Unions in Premodern Europe*. Boswell believes many of these were a form of homosexual marriage.

While this was probably true in a few cases, I suspect that most were simply vows of friendship in a world that took that relationship much more seriously than we do.

44 Queen and Habenstein, *Family in Various Cultures*, 209.

45 *Ibid.*

46 Burgière et al., *History of the Family, Volume I*, 339.

47 Queen and Habenstein, *Family in Various Cultures*, 205.

48 *Ibid.*, 206, quoting from B. Thorpe, *Ancient Laws and Institutes of England*, Vol. 1 (London: Commissioners on the Public Records for the Kingdom, 1840), 249.

49 *Ibid.*, 209.

50 *Ibid.*, 205.

51 Burgière et al., *History of the Family, Volume I*, 318–19.

52 Witold Rybczynski, *Home: A Short History of an Idea* (New York: Viking, 1986), 24; Tuchman, *Distant Mirror*, 210.

53 Rybczynski, *Home*, 24.

54 Beatrice Gottlieb, *The Family in the Western World from the Black Death to the Industrial Age* (New York: Oxford University Press, 1994), 28.

55 William Manchester, *A World Lit Only by Fire: The Medieval Mind and the Renaissance, Portrait of an Age* (Boston: Little, Brown, 1992), 53.

56 Barbara Hanawalt, *The Ties That Bound: Peasant Families in Medieval England* (New York: Oxford University Press, 1986), 175–77.

57 Georges Duby, ed., *A History of Private Life, Vol. 2: Revelations of the Medieval World*, trans. Arthur Goldhammer (Cambridge, MA: The Belknap Press of Harvard University Press, 1987), 75.

58 *Ibid.*, 60.

59 *Ibid.*, 63.

60 Manchester, *World Lit*, 22.

61 Burgière et al., *History of the Family, Volume I*, 450.

62 Gottlieb, *Family in the Western World*, 81.

63 Duby, *History of Private Life, Vol. 2*, 68.

64 Gottlieb, *Family in the Western World*, 92.

65 *Ibid.*

66 Duby, *History of Private Life, Vol. 2*, 76.

67 Hanawalt, *Ties That Bound*, 83.

68 Duby, *History of Private Life, Vol. 2*, 77.

69 Tuchman, *Distant Mirror*, 50.

70 Hanawalt, *Ties That Bound*, 183.

71 Manchester, *World Lit*, 59.

72 Hanawalt, *Ties That Bound*, 158–61.

73 Tuchman, *Distant Mirror*, 50.

74 Gottlieb, *Family in the Western World*, 50–51.

75 Natalie Zemon Davis, in interview with author.

76 Gottlieb, *Family in the Western World*, 61.

77 Burgière et al., *History of the the Family*, *Volume I*, 446.

78 Duby, *History of Private Life*, *Vol. 2*, 71.

79 Julia O'Faolain and Lauro Martines, eds., *Not In God's Image: Women in History from the Greeks to the Victorians* (New York: Harper Torchbook, 1973), 161.

80 Gottlieb, *Family in the Western World*, 93.

81 Beatrice Gottlieb, in interview with author.

82 Tuchman, *Distant Mirror*, 117.

83 *Ibid.*

84 Gunnar Heinsohn, in interview with author.

85 Gottlieb, *Family in the Western World*, 72–73.

86 Boswell, *Same-Sex Unions*, 169–70.

87 Gottlieb, *Family in the Western World*, 77.

88 *Ibid.*

89 *Ibid.*, 84.

90 *Ibid.*, 64.

91 See also Lawrence Stone, *The Family, Sex and Marriage in England, 1500–1977* (London: Oxford University Press, 1977).

92 Gottlieb, *Family in the Western World*, 84–85; Burgière et al., *History of the Family: Volume II: The Impact of Modernity*, trans. Sarah Hanbury Tenison, Rosemary Morris, and Andrew Wilson (Cambridge, MA: The Belknap Press of Harvard University Press, 1996), 124.

93 Gottlieb, *Family in the Western World*, 62–64; Natalie Zemon Davis, in interview with author.

94 Burgière et al., *History of the Family*, *Volume II*, 109–10.

95 Lawrence Stone, in interview with author.

96 Lawrence Stone, in interview with author; Leslie, *Family in Social Context*, 193.

97 Duby, *History of Private Life*, *Vol. 2*, 82; Tuchman, *Distant Mirror*, 210–1.

98 Anderson and Zinsser, *History of Their Own*, 435.

99 Duby, *History of Private Life*, *Vol. 2*, 77.

100 *Ibid.*, 79.

101 O'Faolain and Martines, *Not in God's Image*, 167.

102 Renate Bridenthal, Claudia Koonz and Susan Stuard, *Becoming Visible:*

Women in European History, 2nd ed. (Boston: Houghton Mifflin, 1987), 179.

103 Anderson and Zinsser, *History of Their Own*, 313–16, 332–33.

104 Georges Duby, *Love and Marriage in the Middle Ages*, trans. Jane Dunnett (Chicago: University of Chicago Press, 1994), 75–79.

105 *Ibid.*, 315.

106 Gottlieb, *Family in the Western World*, 95.

107 William Blackstone, quoted in Gottlieb, *Family in the Western World*, 91.

108 Duby, *Love and Marriage*, 27.

109 Hanawalt, *Ties That Bound*, 214.

110 Quoted in Tuchman, *Distant Mirror*, 214.

111 *The Works of Geoffrey Chaucer*, ed. F.N. Robinson, 2nd ed. (Boston: Houghton Mifflin, 1961), 86.

112 Hanawalt, *Ties That Bound*, 212–13.

113 Quoted in Tuchman, *Distant Mirror*, 214.

114 Deborah Tannen, *You Just Don't Understand* (New York: Ballantine, 1990), 210–15.

115 Eileen Power, *Medieval People* (Garden City, NY: Doubleday, 1924), 99–124.

116 Tuchman, *Distant Mirror*, 215.

117 Burgière et al., *History of the Family, Volume I*, 332–33.

118 Gottlieb, *Family in the Western World*, 148.

119 *Ibid.*, 332.

120 Professor Gunnar Heinsohn, in interview with author.

121 Gottlieb, *Family in the Western World*, 69.

122 Boswell, *Same-Sex Unions*, 172.

123 Lawrence Stone, in interview with author.

124 Gottlieb, *Family in the Western World*, 100.

125 Boswell, *Same-Sex Unions*, 259.

126 Duby, *History of Private Life, Vol. 2*, 119–20.

127 *Ibid.*, 135.

128 *Ibid.*, 133–36; Shoumatoff, *Mountain of Names*, 116–17.

129 Shoumatoff, *Mountain of Names*, 117.

130 Duby, *History of Private Life, Vol. 2*, 124.

131 Quoted in Manchester, *World Lit*, 128–29.

132 *Ibid.*, 75. Clerical misbehaviour was naturally not restricted to this period. The famous university lecturer Abelard, who seduced his private student Héloïse and suffered greatly for it, lived from the eleventh to the twelfth century.

133 Lucrezia suffers from an unjustly noxious reputation. She probably, for instance, did not have incestuous relations with her father and brothers. Nonetheless, not only did Alexander openly acknowledge his children, he used Lucrezia to further his political aims through marriage, and annulled the unions when their use had passed. She was on her third marriage by the age of eighteen, but lost that husband when her brother had him killed. She mourned his death most sincerely but lived to marry again.

134 Manchester, *World Lit*, 77.

CHAPTER NINE

1 Will Durant, *The Story of Civilization, Vol. 1: Our Oriental Heritage* (New York: Simon and Schuster, 1963), 495.

2 Jonathan Spence, *The Death of Woman Wang* (New York: Penguin, 1978).

3 *Ibid.*, 117.

4 *Ibid.*, 123.

5 *Ibid.*, 131–32.

6 Howard Hibbett, *The Floating World in Japanese Fiction* (Rutland, VT: Charles E. Tuttle, 1975), 101.

7 *Ibid*, 114.

8 M.F.K. Fisher, *Here Let Us Feast: A Book of Banquets* (San Francisco: North Point Press, 1986), 45–47.

9 Bonnie Anderson and Judith Zinsser, *A History of Their Own: Women in Europe from Prehistory to the Present*, Vol. 1 (New York: Harper and Row, 1988), 357.

10 *Ibid.*, 369.

11 William Manchester, *A World Lit Only by Fire: The Medieval Mind and the Renaissance, Portrait of an Age* (Boston: Little, Brown, 1992), 136–37.

12 *Ibid.*, 133.

13 Renate Bridenthal, Claudia Koonz and Susan Stuard, *Becoming Visible: Women in European History*, 2nd ed. (Boston: Houghton Mifflin, 1987), 205.

14 *Ibid.*

15 John Bartlett, *Familiar Quotations*, 15th ed., ed. Emily Morrison (Boston: Little, Brown, 1980), 156.

16 Julia O'Faolain and Lauro Martines, eds., *Not In God's Image: Women in History from the Greeks to the Victorians* (New York: Harper Torchbook, 1973), 196–97.

17 Beatrice Gottlieb, *The Family in the Western World from the Black Death to the Industrial Age* (New York: Oxford University Press, 1994), 55.

18 Bridenthal et al., *Becoming Visible*, 207.

19 *Ibid.*

20 Gerald R. Leslie, *The Family in Social Context* (New York: Oxford University Press, 1967), 202.

21 Yet the Colonies retained one northern European practice greatly at odds with Puritanism. "Bundling" allowed a courting couple to pass their evenings together in bed—sometimes separated by a board, and in theory fully clothed—as long as they did not actually have intercourse. The custom must have been a holdover from the days when a betrothed couple was regarded as virtually married. It had some obvious practical advantages for the northern nations that allowed it. In the freezing winters of Scandinavia or New England, it at least kept lovers warm. Nonetheless, it seems an anomaly in the context of Protestant Puritanism. Authorities are divided on the question of self-restraint; we do not know how many couples yielded to temptation. Gottlieb, *Family in the Western World*, 42; Leslie, *Family in Social Context*, 200–201.

22 Stuart A. Queen and Robert W. Habenstein, eds., *The Family in Various Cultures*, 3rd ed. (Philadelphia: J.B. Lippincott, 1961), 249.

23 *Ibid.*, 78; Bridenthal et al., *Becoming Visible*, 205.

24 O'Faolain and Martines, *Not in God's Image*, 195.

25 Gottlieb, *Family in the Western World*, 251.

26 Bridenthal et al., *Becoming Visible*, 207.

27 Anderson and Zinsser, *History of Their Own*, 228.

28 *Ibid.*, 229.

29 Gottlieb, *Family in the Western World*, 251.

30 Bridenthal et al., *Becoming Visible*, 228. This concern was based in part on a surge in the numbers of the homeless and unemployed, thanks to a new concentration in the ownership of land. The enclosure movement in Britain and the rise of ground rents in France vastly swelled the ranks of dispossessed peasants. André Burgière, Christiane Klapisch-Zuber, Martine Segalen and Françoise Zonabend, *A History of the Family. Volume II: The Impact of Modernity*, trans. Sarah Hanbury Tenison, Rosemary Morris and Andrew Wilson (Cambridge, MA: The Belknap Press of Harvard University Press, 1996), 24.

31 Bridenthal et al., *Becoming Visible*, 216.

32 *Ibid.*, 227.

33 O'Faolain and Martines, *Not in God's Image*, 226.

34 Bridenthal et al., *Becoming Visible*, 216.

35 *Ibid.*, 206.

36 Burgière et al., *History of the Family, Volume II*, 107.

37 *Ibid.*, 101.

38 This is far from the only royal entanglement to suggest that the marriage of Prince Charles and the late Lady Diana was not an aberration in English history. The idea that British royalty stoically and privately endured unhappy matches is a fabrication.

39 From *The Paston Letters*, ed. John Warrington (London: Everyman, 1924); reprinted 1975, quoted in O'Faolain and Martines, *Not in God's Image*, 172.

40 *Ibid.*, 172–74.

41 Quoted in Bel Mooney, ed., *From This Day Forward* (Harmondsworth: Penguin, 1991), 239–43.

42 *Ibid.*, 30.

43 *Ibid.*, 15.

44 Quoted in Gottlieb, *Family in the Western World*, 55.

45 Jane Austen, *Emma* (Boston: The Riverside Press Cambridge, Houghton Mifflin Company, 1957), 148.

46 Jane Austen, *Persuasion* (Oxford: Oxford University Press, 1990), 233

47 Quoted in Gottlieb, *Family in the Western World*, 252.

48 Witold Rybczynski, *Home: A Short History of an Idea* (New York: Viking, 1986), 59.

49 Edward Shorter, *The Making of the Modern Family* (New York: Basic Books, 1975), 8.

50 *Ibid.*, 59.

51 Mark Girouard, *Life in the English Country House* (Harmondsworth: Penguin, 1980), 138.

52 *Ibid.*, 276.

53 Shorter, *Making of the Modern Family*, 5.

54 *Ibid.*, 6.

55 Philippe Ariès, *Centuries of Childhood: A Social History of Family Life*, trans. Robert Baldick (London: Jonathan Cape, 1962), 40.

56 *Ibid.*, 46–47.

57 *Ibid.*, 49.

58 Quoted in Ferdinand Mount, *The Subversive Family: An Alternative History of Love and Marriage* (London: Jonathan Cape, 1982), 115.

59 Rybczynski, *Home*, 59.

60 William Congreve, *The Comedies of William Congreve*, ed. Eric S. Rump (Harmondsworth: Penguin, 1985), 379.

61 Quoted in Helga Rubenstein, ed., *The Oxford Book of Marriage* (Oxford: Oxford University Press, 1992), 97–98.

62 Shorter, *Making of the Modern Family*, 5.

63 Sheila M. Rothman, *Woman's Proper Place: A History of Changing Ideas and Practices, 1870 to the Present* (New York: Basic Books, 1978), 166.

64 Ronald Pearsall, *The Worm in the Bud: The World of Victorian Sexuality* (Harmondsworth: Penguin, 1971), 361.

65 *Ibid.*

66 Thurer, *Myths of Motherhood*, 220–21.

67 Pearsall, *Worm in the Bud*, 368.

68 Thurer, *Myths of Motherhood*, 219.

69 Anderson and Zinsser, *History of Their Own*, 408.

70 Bridenthal et al., *Becoming Visible*, 224.

71 Barbara Ehrenreich and Deirdre English, *For Her Own Good: 150 Years of the Experts' Advice to Women* (Garden City, NY: Doubleday, 1979), 141–82.

72 Gottlieb, *Family in the Western World*, 269.

73 *Ibid.*, 121.

74 Queen and Habenstein, *The Family in Various Cultures*, 250.

75 Shorter, *Making of the Modern Family*, 3.

76 Michelle Perrot, ed., *A History of Private Life, Vol. IV: From the Fires of Revolution to the Great War* (Cambridge, MA: The Belknap Press of Harvard University Press, 1990), 30–33.

77 *Ibid.*, 33.

78 Leslie, *Family in Social Context*, 204.

79 *Ibid.*, 586–87.

80 *Ibid.*

81 Lawrence Stone, *The Road to Divorce, England 1536–1987* (Oxford: Oxford University Press, 1987), 288–95.

82 Perrot, ed., *A History of Private Life, Vol. IV*, 29–30.

83 David Blankenhorn, *Fatherless America: Confronting Our Most Urgent Social Problem* (New York: HarperPerennial, 1996), 60.

84 Barbara Ehrenreich, *The Hearts of Men: American Dreams and the Flight from Commitment* (New York: Doubleday, 1983).

85 "Changing Family," Canadian Press, ex Ottawa, 11 April 1996.

86 *The Toronto Star*, 17 June 1996.

87 Burgière et al., *History of the Family, Volume II*, 263.

88 *Ibid.*

89 Dorothy Lipovenko, "More women primary breadwinners," *The Globe and Mail*, 15 August 1996.

90 Canadian Press, 12 September 1995.

91 Susan Faludi, "Statistically challeged: media coverage of incorrect statistics is often influenced by politics," *The Nation*, 15 April 1996.

92 Canadian Press, ex Ottawa, 10 February 1994.

93 "Changing Family," Canadian Press, ex Ottawa, 11 April 1996.

94 Burgière et al., *History of the Family, Volume II*, 404.

95 Germaine Greer, *Sex and Destiny: The Politics of Human Fertility* (London: Picador, 1985), 130.

96 *Ibid.*, 132.

97 Françoise Thébaud, ed., *A History of Women: Toward a Cultural Identity in the Twentieth Century* (Cambridge, MA: The Belknap Press of Harvard University Press, 1994), 111.

98 Rothman, *Woman's Proper Place*, 204.

99 *Ibid.*, 79.

100 *Ibid.*

101 Today, of course, the condom has regained popularity among casual sexual partners because of its original purpose—as a defence against infection.

102 Rothman, *Woman's Proper Place*, 441.

103 *Ibid.*

104 *The Globe and Mail*, 16 October 1995.

105 Canadian Press, ex Washington, 4 April 1996.

106 Reuters, ex Moscow, 4 September 1995.

107 Alanna Mitchell, "Abortion rate rises steadily," *The Globe and Mail*, 5 February 1997, quoting a study published 4 February 1997 in the U.S. journal *Family Planning Perspectives*.

108 *The Globe and Mail*, 17 August 1996.

109 Burgière et al., *History of the Family, Volume II*, 413.

110 *Boston Globe*, 3 January 1998.

111 "The History of Marriage," Part 2, *Ideas*, CBC Radio, 29 November 1994.

112 *Ibid.*

113 *Ibid.*

114 The one possible exception lies in our policies on indigent single mothers. I see a growing vindictiveness about them that may well translate into legislation, particularly in the United States.

115 Again, I can offer a single exception. I think the United States should stop penalizing the married by forcing them to pay higher taxes, a system that strikes me as insane.

Ackerman, Diane. *A Natural History of Love*. New York: Random House, 1994.

Aleichem, Sholom. *The Old Country*. Trans. Julius and Frances Butwin. New York: Crown Publishers, 1946.

Alexander, Shana. *Very Much a Lady: The untold story of Jean Harris and Dr. Herman Tarnower*. Boston: Little, Brown, 1983.

Anderson, Bonnie, and Judith Zinsser. *A History of Their Own: Women in Europe from Prehistory to the Present*, Vols. 1 and 2. New York: Harper and Row, 1988.

Ariès, Philippe. *Centuries of Childhood: A Social History of Family Life*. Trans. Robert Baldick. London: Jonathan Cape, 1962.

————, and Georges Duby, gen. eds. *A History of Private Life, Vol. 1: From Pagan Rome to Byzantium*. Ed. Paul Veyne and trans. Arthur Goldhammer. Cambridge, MA: The Belknap Press of Harvard University Press, 1992.

————, gen. eds. *A History of Private Life, Vol. 2: Revelations of the Medieval World*. Ed. Georges Duby and trans. Arthur Goldhammer. Cambridge, MA: The Belknap Press of Harvard University Press, 1988.

————, gen. eds. *A History of Private Life, Vol. 3: Passions of the Renaissance*. Ed. Roger Chartier and trans. Arthur Goldhammer. Cambridge, MA: The Belknap Press of Harvard University Press, 1989.

————, gen. eds. *A History of Private Life, Vol. 4: From the Fires of Revolution to the Great War*. Ed. Michelle Perrot and trans. Arthur Goldhammer. Cambridge, MA: The Belknap Press of Harvard University Press, 1990.

Austen, Jane. *Emma*. Boston: Houghton Mifflin Company, 1957.

————. *Northanger Abbey, Lady Susan, The Watsons and Sanditon*. Oxford: Oxford University Press, 1990.

————. *Persuasion*. Ed. John Davie. Oxford: Oxford University Press, 1990.

Balsdon, J.P.V.D. *Roman Women: Their History and Habits*. New York: Barnes & Noble Books, 1962.

Barber, Elizabeth Wayland. *Women's Work: The First 20,000 Years: Women, Cloth, and Society in Early Times*. New York: W.W. Norton, 1994.

Barnes, Virginia Lee, and Janice Boddy. *Aman: The Story of a Somali Girl, by Aman*. Toronto: Knopf Canada, 1994.

Becker, Jasper. *Hungry Ghosts: Mao's Secret Famine*. New York: The Free Press, 1996.

Benedict, Ruth. *Patterns of Culture*. Boston: Houghton Mifflin, 1989.

Bennet, Doug, and Tim Tiner, *Up North: A Guide to Ontario's Wilderness from Blackflies to the Northern Lights*. Markham, ON: Reed Books, 1993.

Bernikow, Louise. *Among Women*. New York: Harmony, 1980.

Bettelheim, Bruno. *A Good Enough Parent: A Book on Child-Rearing*. New York: Vintage Books, Random House, 1988.

Blaise, Clark, and Bharati Mukherjee. *Days and Nights in Calcutta*. Garden City, New York: Doubleday, 1977.

Blankenhorn, David. *Fatherless America: Confronting Our Most Urgent Social Problem*. New York: HarperPerennial, 1996.

Boddy, Janice. *Wombs and Alien Spirits: Women, Men and the Zar Cult in Northern Sudan*. Madison, WI: University of Wisconsin Press, 1994.

Bohannan, Paul, and John Middleton, eds. *Marriage, Family and Residence*. Garden City, NY: American Museum Sourcebooks in Anthropology, The Natural History Press, 1968.

Boswell, John. *The Kindness of Strangers: The Abandonment of Children in Western Europe from Late Antiquity to the Renaissance*. New York: Pantheon, 1988.

————. *Same-Sex Unions in Premodern Europe*. New York: Villard Books, 1994.

Bridenthal, Renate, Claudia Koonz and Susan Stuard. *Becoming Visible: Women in European History*. Boston: Houghton Mifflin, 1977, 2nd edition, 1987.

Briffault, Robert. *The Mothers*. New York: Atheneum, 1977.

Bronowski, J. *The Ascent of Man*. London: Macdonald Futura, 1981.

Brooks, Geraldine. *Nine Parts of Desire: The Hidden World of Islamic Women*. New York: Doubleday, 1996.

Burgière, André, Christiane Klapisch-Zuber, Martine Segalen and Françoise Zonabend. *A History of the Family, Volume I: Distant Worlds, Ancient Worlds*. Trans. Sarah Hanbury Tenison, Rosemary Morris and Andrew Wilson. Cambridge, MA: The Belknap Press of Harvard University Press, 1996.

————. *A History of the Family, Volume II: The Impact of Modernity*. Trans.

Sarah Hanbury Tenison, Rosemary Morris and Andrew Wilson. Cambridge, MA: The Belknap Press of Harvard University Press, 1996.

Buruma, Ian. *A Japanese Mirror: Heroes and Villains of Japanese Culture.* London: Jonathan Cape, 1984.

Buss, David M. *The Evolution of Desire: Strategies of Human Mating.* New York: Basic Books, 1994.

Carcopino, Jérôme. *Daily Life in Ancient Rome.* Trans. E.O. Lorimer. Harmondsworth: Penguin, 1975.

Contenau, Georges. *Everyday Life in Babylon and Assyria.* Translated from the French by K.R. and A.R. Maxwell-Hyslop. London: Edward Arnold, 1954.

Critchfield, Richard. *Villages.* New York: Anchor Books, Doubleday, 1983.

Cushing, Frank Hamilton. *Zuni: Selected Writings.* Lincoln, NE: University of Nebraska Press, 1979.

Dalley, Stephanie. *Mari and Karana.* London: Longman, 1984.

Davis, Natalie Zemon. *The Return of Martin Guerre.* Cambridge, MA: Harvard University Press, 1983.

De Beauvoir, Simone. *The Woman Destroyed.* Trans. Patrick O'Brian. New York: Putnam, 1969.

De Mause, Lloyd, ed. *The History of Childhood.* New York: Psychohistory Press, 1974.

Duby, Georges. *Love and Marriage in the Middle Ages.* Trans. Jane Dunnett. Chicago: University of Chicago Press, 1994.

Duby, Georges. See also under Ariès, Philippe, and Georges Duby, *A History of Private Life, Vol. 2.*

————, and Michelle Perrot, gen. eds. *A History of Women, Vol. 1: From Ancient Goddesses to Christian Saints.* Ed. Pauline Schmitt Pantel. Cambridge, MA: The Belknap Press of Harvard University Press, 1992.

————, gen. eds. *A History of Women, Vol. 2: Silences of the Middle Ages.* Ed. Christiane Klapisch-Zuber. Cambridge, MA: The Belknap Press of Harvard University Press, 1992.

————, gen. eds. *A History of Women, Vol. 3: Renaissance and Enlightenment Paradoxes.* Ed. Natalie Zemon Davis and Arlette Farge. Cambridge, MA: The Belknap Press of Harvard University Press, 1993.

————, gen. eds. *A History of Women, Vol. 4: Emerging Feminism From Revolution to World War.* Ed. Geneviève Fraisse and Michelle Perrot. Cambridge, MA: The Belknap Press of Harvard University Press, 1993.

————, gen. eds. *A History of Women, Vol. 5: Toward a Cultural Identity in the Twentieth Century.* Ed. Françoise Thébaud. Cambridge, MA: The Belknap Press of Harvard University Press, 1994.

Durant, Will. *The Story of Civilization, Vol. 1: Our Oriental Heritage*. New York: Simon and Schuster, 1963.

Ehrenreich, Barbara. *The Hearts of Men: American Dreams and the Flight from Commitment*. New York: Doubleday, 1983.

———. *The Worst Years of Our Lives*. New York: Pantheon, 1990.

———, and Deirdre English. *For Her Own Good: 150 Years of the Experts' Advice to Women*. Garden City, NY: Anchor Books, 1979.

Embree, John F. *Suye Mura: A Japanese Village*. Chicago: University of Chicago Press, Phoenix Books, 1964. (First published 1939.)

Engel, Patrice, and Cynthia Breaux. *Is There a Father Instinct? Fathers' Responsibility for Their Children*. Washington, D.C.: The International Centre for Research on Women, and New York: The Population Council, New York, February 1994.

Engels, Friedrich. *Origin of the Family, Private Property and the State*. Ed. Eleanor Leacock. New York: Pathfinder Press, 1972.

Farah, Madelein. *Marriage and Sexuality in Islam: A Translation of al-Ghazālī's Book on the Etiquette of Marriage from the Ihyā'*. Salt Lake City, UT: University of Utah Press, 1984.

Firestone, Shulamith. *The Dialectic of Sex*. London: Women's Press, 1979.

Fisher, Helen. *Anatomy of Love: The Natural History of Monogamy, Adultery and Divorce*. New York: Fawcett Columbine, 1992.

———. *The Sex Contract: The Evolution of Human Behavior*. New York: William Morrow and Company, 1982.

Forsyth, Adrian. *A Natural History of Sex: The ecology and evolution of mating behavior*. Shelburne, VT: Chapters Publishing, 1993.

Friday, Nancy. *Jealousy*. New York: Perigord Press Books, William Morrow & Co., 1985.

Friedan, Betty. *The Feminine Mystique*. New York: Dell Publishing Co., 1974.

Friedl, Erika. *Women of Deh Koh: Lives in an Iranian Village*. New York: Penguin, 1991.

Girouard, Mark. *Life in the English Country House*. Harmondsworth: Penguin, 1980.

Glückel of Hameln. *The Memoirs of Glückel of Hameln*. Trans. Marvin Lowenthal. New York: Schocken Books, 1977.

Goldberg, Herb. *What Men Really Want*. Toronto: Signet, 1991.

Goodall, Jane. *The Chimpanzees of Gombe: Patterns of Behavior*. Cambridge, MA: The Belknap Press of Harvard University Press, 1986.

———. *In the Shadow of Man*, rev. ed. London: Weidenfeld and Nicolson, 1988.

Goodwin, Jan. *Price of Honor: Muslim Women Lift the Veil of Silence on the Islamic World*. New York: Penguin Books 1995.

Gottlieb, Beatrice. *The Family in the Western World from the Black Death to the Industrial Age*. New York: Oxford University Press, 1994.

Graves, Robert. *I Claudius*. London: Penguin, 1953.

Greer, Germaine. *Sex and Destiny: The Politics of Human Fertility*. London: Picador, 1985.

————. *The Female Eunuch*. London: Granada, 1971.

Gregor, Thomas. *Anxious Pleasures: The Sexual Lives of an Amazonian People*. Chicago: University of Chicago Press, 1984.

Grunberger, Richard. *A Social History of the Third Reich*. Harmondsworth: Penguin, 1977.

Hamilton, Edith. *Mythology*. New York: New American Library, 1965.

Hanawalt, Barbara. *The Ties That Bound: Peasant Families in Medieval England*. New York: Oxford University Press, 1986.

Herman, Judith Lewis, and Lisa Hirschman. *Father-Daughter Incest*. Cambridge, MA: Harvard University Press, 1971.

Hewlett, B.S., ed. *Father-Child Relations: Cultural and Biosocial Contexts*. New York: Aldine De Gruyter, 1992.

Hibbert, Christopher. *The English: A Social History, 1066–1945*. London: Paladin Books, 1988.

Hobson, Sarah. *Family Web: A Story of India*. London: John Murray, 1978.

Horton, Patricia. *Mother Without a Mask*. London: Kyle Cathie, 1993.

Houston, James. *Confessions of an Igloo Dweller*. Boston: Houghton Mifflin Company, 1996.

Jankowiak, W.R., and E.F. Fischer. "A cross-cultural perspective on romantic love." *Ethnology* 31 (no. 2): 149–55.

Jankowiak, William, ed. *Romantic Passion: A Universal Experience?* New York: University of Columbia Press, 1995.

Kagan, Jerome. *The Nature of the Child*. New York: Basic Books, 1984.

Kingston, Maxine Hong. *The Woman Warrior: Memoirs of a Girlhood Among Ghosts*. New York: Vintage, 1977.

Kinsey, A.C., W.B. Pomeroy and C.E. Martin. *Sexual Behavior in the Human Male*. Philadelphia: Saunders, 1948.

————. *Sexual Behavior in the Human Female*. Philadelphia: Saunders, 1953.

Kitto, H.D.F. *The Greeks*. Harmondsworth: Penguin, 1973.

Kreps, Bonnie. *Authentic Passion: Loving Without Losing Yourself*. Toronto: McClelland & Stewart, 1991.

Laing, R.D., and A. Esterson. *Sanity, Madness and the Family*. Harmonds-worth: Penguin, 1970.

Lamb, M.E., ed. *The Father's Role: Cross-Cultural Perspectives*. Hillsdale, NJ: Lawrence Erlbaum Associates, Publishers, 1987.

Lasch, Christopher. *The Culture of Narcissism: American Life in an Age of Diminishing Expectations*. New York: Warner Books, 1979.

————. *Women and the Common Life*. Ed. by Elisabeth Lasch-Quinn. New York: W.W. Norton & Company, 1996.

Lerner, Gerda. *The Creation of Patriarchy*. New York: Oxford University Press. 1986.

Le Roy Ladurie, Emmanuel. *Montaillou: Catholics and Cathars in a French Village*. Trans. Barbara Bray. London: Scolar, 1978.

Leslie, Gerald R. *The Family in Social Context*. New York: Oxford Univer-sity Press, 1967.

Lévi-Strauss, Claude. *The Elementary Structures of Kinship*. Boston: Beacon Press, 1969.

Lewittes, Mendell. *Jewish Marriage: Rabbinic Law, Legend, and Custom*. North-vale, NJ: Jason Aronson, 1994.

Mair, Lucy. *Marriage*. Harmondsworth: Penguin, 1971.

Malinowski, Bronislaw. *The Sexual Life of Savages*. London: Halcyon House, 1929.

Manchester, William. *A World Lit Only by Fire: The Medieval Mind and the Renaissance, Portrait of an Age*. Boston: Little, Brown, 1992.

Masters, W.H., and V.E. Johnson. *Human Sexual Response*. Boston: Little, Brown, 1966.

Masters, William H., Virginia E. Johnson and Robert C. Kolodny. *Masters and Johnson on Sex and Human Loving*. Boston: Little, Brown, 1986.

Maybury-Lewis, David. *Millennium: Tribal Wisdom and the Modern World*. New York: Viking, 1992.

McCarthy, Mary. *The Group*. New York: Harcourt Brace & Company, 1989.

Money, John. *Love and Love Sickness: The Science of Sex, Gender Difference, and Pair-Bonding*. Baltimore: Johns Hopkins University Press, 1980.

Mooney, Bel, ed. *From This Day Forward*. London: John Murray, 1989.

Morgan, Elaine. *The Descent of the Child: Human Evolution from a New Perspective*. New York: Oxford University Press, 1995.

————. *The Descent of Woman*. New York: Bantam, 1973.

Morris, Desmond. *The Naked Ape*. Toronto: Bantam, 1969.

Mount, Ferdinand. *The Subversive Family: An Alternative History of Love and Marriage*. London: Jonathan Cape, 1982.

Murdock, George. *Social Structure*. New York: The Macmillan Company, 1949.

————. "World Ethnographic Sample," *American Anthropologist*, No. 59, August 1957.

Naipaul, V.S. *A House for Mr. Biswas*. London: Andre Deutsch, 1961.

O'Faolain, Julia, and Lauro Martines, eds. *Not in God's Image: Women in History from the Greeks to the Victorians*. New York: Harper Torchbooks, 1973.

Olasky, Marvin. *Abortion Rites: A Social History of Abortion in America*. Wheaton, IL: Crossway Books, 1992.

Owen, Ursula. *Fathers, Reflections by Daughters*. New York: Pantheon Books, 1935.

Pearsall, Ronald. *The Worm in the Bud: The World of Victorian Sexuality*. Harmondsworth: Penguin, 1971.

Perrot, Michelle. See under Ariès, Philippe, and Georges Duby, *A History of Private Life, Vol. 4*.

Pollitt, Katha. *Reasonable Creatures: Essays on Women and Feminism*. New York: Knopf, 1994.

Pomeroy, Sarah. B. *Goddesses, Whores, Wives, and Slaves: Women in Classical Antiquity*. New York: Schocken Books, 1975.

Power, Eileen. *Medieval People*. Garden City, NY: Doubleday Anchor Books, n.d. (originally published in 1924).

Queen, Stuart A., and Robert W. Habenstein, eds. *The Family in Various Cultures*. 3rd edition. Philadelphia: J.B. Lippincott Company, 1961.

Rabie-Azoory, Vera. *They Love You, They Love Me Not: The Truth About the Family Favorite and Sibling Rivalry*. Toronto: HarperCollins Publishers, 1995.

Reader, John. *Man on Earth: A Celebration of Mankind*. New York: Perennial Library, Harper & Row, 1990.

Report of the Committee on Sexual Offences Against Children and Youths. *Sexual Offences Against Children*. Vol. 1. Ottawa: Minister of Supply and Services Canada, 1984.

Ridley, Matt. *The Red Queen: Sex and the Evolution of Human Nature*. New York: Penguin, 1995.

Rosaldo, Michelle, and Louise Lamphere. *Women, Culture and Society*. Stanford: Stanford University Press, 1974.

Rothman, Sheila M. *Woman's Proper Place: A History of Changing Ideas and Practices, 1870 to the Present*. New York: Basic Books, 1978.

Rubinstein, Helga, ed. *The Oxford Book of Marriage*. Oxford: Oxford University Press, 1992.

Rybczynski, Witold. *Home: A Short History of an Idea*. New York: Viking, 1986.

Scarfe, Maggie. *Intimate Partners: Patterns in Love and Marriage.* New York: Ballantine Books, 1987.

Schmitt Pantel, Pauline. See under Duby, Georges. *A History of Women, Vol. 1.*

Shorter, Edward. *The Making of the Modern Family.* New York: Basic Books, 1975.

Shoumatoff, Alex. The *Mountains of Names: A History of the Human Family.* New York: Simon and Schuster, 1985.

Spence, Jonathan D. *The Death of Woman Wang.* New York: Penguin, 1979.

Stone, Lawrence. *Broken Lives: Separation and Divorce in England, 1660–1857.* Oxford: Oxford University Press, 1994.

———. *The Family, Sex and Marriage in England, 1500–1977.* Oxford: Oxford University Press, 1977.

———. *The Road to Divorce, England 1536–1987.* Oxford: Oxford University Press, 1987.

———. *Uncertain Unions: Marriage in England, 1660–1753.* Oxford: Oxford University Press, 1994.

Symons, Donald. *The Evolution of Human Sexuality.* Oxford: Oxford University Press, 1979.

Tannen, Deborah. *You Just Don't Understand.* New York: Ballantine Books, 1990.

Tennov, Dorothy. *Love and Limerence: The Experience of Being in Love.* New York: Stein and Day, 1979.

Thurer, Shari L. *The Myths of Motherhood: How Culture Reinvents the Good Mother.* New York: Penguin, 1995.

Tiger, Lionel, and Robin Fox. *The Imperial Animal.* New York: Holt, Rinehart and Winston, 1971.

Treggiari, Susan. *Roman Marriage: Iusti Coniuges from the Time of Cicero to the Time of Ulpian.* Oxord: Clarendon Press, 1991.

Tuchman, Barbara. *A Distant Mirror: The Calamitous 14th Century.* New York: Ballantine Books, 1978.

Turnbull, Colin M. *The Forest People.* New York: Simon and Schuster, 1961.

———. *The Mountain People.* New York: Simon and Schuster, 1987.

Tyldesley, Joyce. *Daughters of Isis: Women of Ancient Egypt.* Harmondsworth: Penguin, 1995.

Veyne, Paul. See under Ariès, Philippe, And Georges Duby, *A History of Private Life, Vol. 1.*

Waln, Nora. *The House of Exile.* Boston: Little, Brown, 1992.

Zeldin, Theodore. *An Intimate History of Humanity.* London: Minerva, 1995.

abandonment, 94, 97, 193

abduction, 14, 48–52, 201

abortion, 7, 92, 93, 120, 149, 192, 200, 209, 225, 235, 255, 288, 291, 292, 293, 295

abuse, 36, 39, 64, 84, 85, 96–97, 113, 118, 120–22, 165, 196, 240, 243, 270, 278, 293, 294

Adam and Eve, 8, 9, 195

adoption, 6, 43, 84–86, 93, 113, 120, 125, 156, 255, 289, 295

adultery, 5, 6, 14, 20, 53, 56–59, 61, 67–69, 71, 72, 73, 127, 195, 197, 205, 208, 223–25, 232, 242, 244, 250, 252, 256, 266, 270, 283, 284, 285

Africa, 4, 25, 31, 56, 74, 81, 85, 89, 105, 109, 117, 125, 128, 130–31, 139, 150, 167, 180–81, 183, 187, 221, 276

African hornbills, 115

Agrippina, 35, 218, 228

Aka, 123, 139, 143

Akan tribe, 149

Alberti, Leon Battista, 152, 274

Alcott, Louisa May, 278

Aleichem, Sholom, 108

Allodi, Federico, 62, 180, 182

Ambati, Balamurali, 179

American Samoa, 128

Anatomy of Love, The (see also Fisher, Helen), 19

animals, 4, 7, 8, 13, 17, 21, 27, 33, 37, 59, 60, 80, 82, 102, 135, 137, 139, 141, 164, 241

annulment, 266

antelopes, 13

apes, 9, 14, 16–18, 137–38

Aquinas, Thomas, 252

Ardrey, Robert, 14

Aretaeus of Cappodocia, 211

Ariès, Philippe, 99–102, 275

aristocrats, 27, 32, 70, 106, 151, 224, 270, 281

Aristotle, 190, 210, 214

Ascent of Man, The (see also Bronowski, Jacob), 141

Ashanti, 152

Asia, 4, 31, 43, 47, 48, 74, 95, 109, 150, 176, 184, 276

Asmat tribe, 176

Assyria, 117, 118, 141, 205–6, 209, 210

Augustus, 167, 217, 222–26

Aurangzeb, 262

Aurelius, Marcus, 224–25

Austen, Jane, 156, 269, 270, 272, 276

Australia, 28, 131, 187

babies, 4, 7, 12, 13, 17, 80–83,
    89–91, 94, 95, 99–100, 102–3,
    108, 113, 121, 124, 125, 133, 136,
    137, 146, 235, 241, 244, 295
baboons, 11, 20, 60, 81, 133–35;
    hamadryas, 133–134
Babylonia, 117, 118, 141, 202, 205–9
Baganda tribe, 155, 156, 188
Bakhtiari, 141
Balsdon, J.P.V.D., 215–16
Barrett Browning, Elizabeth, 125,
    143
Batek tribe, 139
Bedouin, 37, 73, 141
Belize, 128
Benedict, Ruth, 117
Bennet, Elizabeth, 272
Bengal, 171
Benin. See Dahomey
Bettleheim, Bruno, 112
Bible, The, 35, 57, 70, 81, 117, 123,
    125, 153, 174, 189, 194–99, 201,
    203, 207–8, 213, 215, 259, 267,
    292
birth control. See contraception
Black Caribs, 128
Blaise, Clark, 171
blue jays, 6
Bly, Robert, 143
Bohannan, Laura, 40
Bolsheviks, 98, 100, 184, 192, 194
Boswell, James, 71
Bouchard, Lucien, 90, 290
Brazil. See Meninaku tribe, 58
breasts, 15, 16, 54, 58, 79, 80, 104
Breaux, Cynthia, 142
Bremen, University of, 48, 61
Britain, 69, 93, 182, 249, 270, 273,
    274, 283, 284, 288, 289

Bronowski, Jacob, 141
Burkina Faso, 143
Burma, 131, 157
Burton, Richard, 154
Buruma, Ian, 109
Bushmen, 139
Buss, David, 67, 68, 127
butterflies, 15
buttocks, 15–16
Byron, Lord, 53, 74

Caesar, Julius, 211, 216, 222
Caligula, 224, 228
Calvinism, 267, 268
Canada, 92, 95, 108, 128, 146, 159,
    177, 178, 179, 180, 181, 284,
    286–89, 291, 293, 294
Carcopino, Jérôme, 90, 165, 221–22
Catholicism, 265, 266–68, 284, 285,
    288, 290, 291
Cato, Marcus Porcius, 165, 220, 221,
    226, 245
cats, 80, 87, 106, 116
cavemen, 9
celibacy, 7, 10, 39, 195, 223, 233,
    234, 237, 258, 264, 266, 268
Centuries of Childhood (see also
    Ariès, Philippe), 100, 101
charivari, 242, 253
Chaucer, Geoffrey, 76, 250, 252, 254
Chicago, University of, 57, 60
chickadees, 6, 59
child abuse, 120, 121, 243
childbirth, 17, 55, 187, 221
childless, 6, 63, 70, 88, 91, 95, 99,
    130, 193, 224, 276
child-rearing, 102–4, 111, 139, 236,
    277
children, 3, 4, 6, 8, 13, 18–19, 22, 23,

27–28, 30, 33, 34, 37, 39, 40–43,
45–46, 49, 52, 55, 57, 60, 70–71,
79–113, 158, 165, 167–70,
174–175, 177–81, 183–84, 188,
191, 192, 195, 198, 200, 204–5,
207–9, 210, 213–14, 217–19,
221–22, 224, 226–27, 229,
232–33, 235–36, 238, 239–44, 249,
254, 259, 262, 264–67, 271, 272,
274–82, 284–86, 288, 290, 292–98
chimpanzees, 5, 6, 9–12, 21, 26, 39,
59, 87, 106, 116, 135, 137, 176
China, 11, 28, 29, 36, 48, 63–65, 69,
70, 91, 96, 118, 119, 143, 146,
152–54, 156, 161, 166, 175, 178,
179, 201, 239, 261, 263, 276, 298
Chopich, Erica, 53
Christ, 72, 204, 232, 233, 234, 235,
236, 237, 238, 253, 255, 264
Christianity, 197, 224, 229, 231, 233,
235, 237, 238, 258
Cicero, 152, 222
Claudius, 166, 218, 224–26, 228
Clovis, 238
Conaty, Anne, 120
Concordia University, 69, 195
Confucianism, 36, 105, 117, 262, 298
Congo, 44, 123
Constantine, 237
Contenau, Georges, 209
contraception, 7, 89, 90–92, 106,
149, 192, 200, 225, 255, 268,
288–93
Costa Rica, 15
Creation of Patriarchy, The (*see also*
Lerner, Gerda), 189
Crew, Nola, 179–80
Critchfield, Richard, 37, 187–88
Cronus, 122

Dahomey, 39, 154
Daily Life in Ancient Rome (*see also*
Carcopino, Jérôme), 91, 165
Darwinism, 6, 9
Davis, Natalie Zemon, 71, 159, 249
de Beauvoir, Simone, 68
de Vilbiss, Lydia, 289
Death of Woman Wang, The, 65, 262
Deh Koh (*see also* Iran), 163,
170–72
Della famiglia, 152, 274
Descent of Women, The (*see also*
Morgan, Elaine), 80
divorce, 14, 18–20, 120, 130, 178–80,
193, 196, 200, 205, 208, 215, 217,
220, 222, 233, 235, 256, 257, 266,
269, 282, 283, 284, 285, 286, 287,
296
Dobu. *See* Trobriand Islands
Douglas, Mary, 119
dowry, 37, 47, 48, 161, 179, 187,
188, 198, 205, 208, 219, 221, 233,
258
Drusilla, 228
Duby, Georges, 250
Durant, Will, 27, 54–56, 131, 140

Egypt, 38, 92, 123, 124, 126, 141,
202, 204, 205, 207, 217, 283
Ehrenreich, Barbara, 280, 285, 296
Elliot, Anne, 273
Ellis, Alice Thomas, 53
Emma, 273, 276
Engel, Patrice, 142
English, Deirdre, 280
Esterson, A., & R.D. Laing, 173
estrus, 10–13, 15, 18, 60, 137
Europe, 3, 48, 55, 57, 74, 88, 90, 94,
109, 111, 128, 141, 144, 150, 151,

159, 236, 238, 240, 244, 252, 256,
258, 261–64, 271, 277, 281, 283,
288
Evelyn, John, 275
evolution, 9, 14, 15, 16, 18, 22, 31,
54, 124, 141, 157, 189, 220, 227
Evolution of Desire, The (see also
Buss, David), 127
Eyre, Jane, 64

family: extended, 3, 150–54, 157–63,
169–73, 175–77, 179, 181, 182,
184, 239, 243, 293, 296; imperial,
35, 151; nuclear, 3, 36, 98, 113,
117, 138, 145, 147, 150–52, 157,
160, 176, 184, 233, 239, 241, 264,
274, 275, 279
Family Web (see also Hobson,
Sarah), 107, 126, 170
fatherhood, 43, 120, 122, 127, 128,
132, 133, 137, 143, 144
female circumcision, 186–87
feminism, 9, 44, 68, 76, 99, 100, 141,
205, 197, 239, 285, 290
fertility (see also infertility), 10, 81,
91, 126, 149, 171, 186, 192, 196,
200, 209, 218, 244, 288, 290, 295
Firestone, Shulamith, 99
Fischer, Edward, 63
fish, 5, 6, 58, 79, 87, 115, 116, 133,
176
Fisher, Helen, 13, 19, 20, 28, 30, 63,
134–35, 138–40, 206
Forest People, The (see also Turnbull, Colin M.), 139
Foundling Hospitals, 95, 97
Fox, Robin, 14, 157
France, 268, 282, 283, 284, 285
French Polynesia, 153

Freud, Sigmund, 20, 33, 34, 37, 89,
145
Fulbe tribe, 66

Gaius, 220
Geerewol celebration, 51
genetics, 6, 7, 19, 33, 35–38, 42, 54,
59, 60, 71, 83, 88, 105, 112–13,
125, 127, 130, 134, 142, 143
George V, 115
Germanicus, 224
Germany, 48, 192, 193, 200, 246,
265, 267, 288, 289
Gershom, Rebbenu, 200
Ghana, 149, 152
Glory of Hera, The, 218
Glückel of Hameln, 174, 175
godfather, 158
Goldberg, Herb, 144
Gombe, 87, 106
Good Enough Parent, A, 112
Goodall, Jane, 11, 106, 116
Goodwin, Jan, 118, 133, 189
gorillas, 11, 60, 82
Gosse, Edmund, 115
Gottlieb, Beatrice, 151, 242, 245,
247, 248, 249, 252
Gouge, William, 117
Gowdas of Karnataka, 162
grandchildren, 106, 162, 181, 263,
281
Greece, 36, 92, 95, 117, 154, 164,
166, 168, 191, 196, 204, 210–23,
226, 234, 276
Greenberg, Michael E., 82
Greer, Germaine, 99
Gregor, Thomas, 58
Grossberg, Amy, 94

Hammurabi, Code of, 208
Hannah (*see also* Bible, The), 70,
    81, 174
harems, 5, 9, 59
Harmless People, The, 139
Harris, Jean, 68
Harvard University, 75
Hashimoto, Ryutaro, 91
Haub, Carl, 92
Hebrews, 72, 153, 189, 194, 195, 197,
    198, 199, 201, 204, 208, 233, 238
Heinsohn, Gunnar, 48–49, 61, 75,
    200, 286
Henry II of France, 248
Henry IV of France, 74
Henry VIII, 269, 270, 257
Hester Street, 111
Hinduism, 11, 47, 48, 117, 150, 154,
    162, 201, 262
Hitler, Adolf, 192–93
Hobson, Sarah, 107, 126, 162, 170
hominids, 8, 12, 15
homosexuality, 7, 192, 196, 211–12,
    257, 297
Hopi Indians, 152, 153
Horus, 206
House of Exile, The (*see also* Waln,
    Nora), 65, 161
household size, 3, 151, 177, 282
housing, 34, 177, 178
Hungary, 293, 295
hunter-gatherers, 14–15, 21–23,
    122–23, 139–40, 151, 298

Igarot tribe, 29–30, 140
Ik tribe, 183, 194, 298
incest, 33–38, 195, 198, 204, 256–57
India (*see also* Khasi tribe, Nayar),
    4, 26, 40, 44, 47, 126, 150, 157,

161, 162, 179, 201, 206, 261, 290;
    Malabar Coast, 40, 41
Indian Council of Medical
    Research, 93
Indonesia, 176
Inéz de la Cruz, Juana, 237
infanticide, 7, 35, 94, 96, 97, 116,
    143, 149, 196, 204, 214, 268, 292
infidelity. *See* adultery
Innu, 202
Inuit, 55, 74, 107, 131, 154, 155
Iran, 36, 57, 67, 163, 283
Iraq, 73
Iroquois, 202
Isis, 206, 231
Islam, 8, 49, 72, 74, 120, 187–89,
    197, 262
Israel, 34, 98, 195, 202
Istroni, Giovanni, 89

jacana, 5, 115, 117, 134
jackals, 6
Jamaica, 42, 132, 172
Jankowiak, William, 63, 64, 66
Janus Report of Sexual Behavior, 57
Japan, 32, 36, 48, 58, 64, 70, 91,
    109, 110, 117, 119, 130, 142, 154,
    157, 201, 261, 263, 287, 296;
    Heian, 32, 58, 70
jealousy, 4, 9, 32, 52, 58, 67–69, 71,
    74, 75, 127, 167, 175, 235
Jerome, St., 234, 236, 241, 253
Jews. *See* Judaism
Johnson, Samuel, 71
Joseph, Norma, 69, 195, 198–200
Judaism, 26, 69, 70, 111, 149,
    153–54, 164, 177, 195, 197, 202,
    231–33, 236, 239, 244, 290
Juvenal, 165, 222, 224, 227, 231

Kabir, Homaira and Humayan, 65
Kagan, Jerome, 86
Kelly, M.T., 67
Kessel, John, 120
Khan, Abdur, 162
Khan, Naazish, 162
Khan, Rashida, 162
Khasi tribe, 44–45
kibbutz, 34, 98, 184
Kingston, Maxine Hong, 104–5
Koran, The, 72, 117, 120, 186–87, 197
Korea, North, 143
Korea, South, 36
Kreps, Bonnie, 61, 76
Krishnamoorthy, P.V., 157
!Kung tribe, 139

Laing, R.D., and A. Esterson, 173
Lamb, Lady Caroline, 74
lambs, 7
langurs, 60
Lasch, Christopher, 76
Lebanon, 119
Lele, 117, 119
Lerner, Gerda, 141, 189
Lévi-Strauss, Claude, 33, 37, 39
lions, 60, 228
Locke, John, 278
loons, 53, 54
Louis VII, 257
love: attachment, 19, 20, 21, 30, 53, 62, 64, 83, 152, 271, 273; courtly, 250, 251, 272; platonic, 212, 251; romantic, 24, 27, 29–30, 63, 64, 65, 66, 75, 107, 248; sexual, 20
Luther, Martin, 259, 261, 264–67, 273, 282
Lycurgus, 191–92

magic, 46, 54, 60, 61, 93, 191, 225, 247
Mahabharata, 4
Malaysia, 139, 157
Malinowski, Bronislaw, 23, 118
Manchester, William, 259
Mangaians, 31, 199, 226
Manu, Code of, 206
marriage (see also polyandry, polygamy), 11, 14, 25–32, 34, 36–37, 39–45, 47–50, 54–55, 59–64, 66, 69–70, 76, 90, 104, 107, 118, 121, 125–26, 129, 140, 149, 151, 155, 157, 161–63, 179–80, 186–89, 192–99, 201–2, 204, 207, 209, 213–17, 220, 222–24, 226, 229, 233–35, 237, 239, 242, 244–49, 254–59, 263, 265, 266, 267, 269–77, 281, 282, 284–88, 296, 297; arranged, 14, 28, 31, 63, 65, 163, 178, 270; gay, 297; Jamaican model, 42, 172; romantic, 64, 265, 269, 270, 271, 272, 275, 277, 279
marriage by purchase, 216
Marshall, Elizabeth, 139
Maslow, Abraham, 75
matchmaker, 49, 195
matriarchy, 44, 134, 172, 197–98
matrilineal, 44, 72, 135, 197, 198, 202, 204
Maya, 69, 72
Maybury-Lewis, David, 50–52
McCarthy, Mary, 103
Mehinaku tribe, 58
Menander, 265
menstruation, 11, 26, 28, 41, 55, 79, 194, 197, 200–202, 210, 236, 255
Michener, James, 32

Middle Ages, 24, 72, 104, 164, 240, 243, 251, 254, 282

Michigan, University of, 67, 127

Millennium: Tribal Wisdom and the Modern World (*see also* Maybury-Lewis, David), 50

minks, 7

mishpochah, 153

misogyny, 98, 211, 218, 235, 265

Mitchell, Joseph, 158

Mitchell, Margaret, 163

Mitford, Nancy, 88, 193

Mohammed, 55, 73

monogamy, 5, 6, 54, 56, 69, 139, 150, 202, 211, 213

Morgan, Elaine, 14, 16, 17, 23, 80, 90

Morris, Desmond, 8, 14, 15, 54, 86, 137

Mossi tribe, 143

motherhood, 79, 82, 88, 98, 110, 113, 135, 143, 192, 217, 237, 269, 277, 280

mother-in-law, 28, 46, 74, 163, 171

Mount, Ferdinand, 101

Mountain People, The (*see also* Turnbull, Colin M.), 183

Moyers, Bill, 143

Murasaki, Lady, 34, 134

murder, 67, 73, 94, 97, 120–21, 161, 162, 197, 219, 239, 263, 291, 294

Murdock, George, 150, 152, 155

Myths of Motherhood, The (*see also* Thurer, Shari), 97, 111, 218

Naipaul, V.S., 83, 173

Naked Ape, The (*see also* Morris, Desmond), 14, 18, 86

Nammu (*see also* Sumeria), 205

National Opinion Research Center, University of Chicago, 57

Nature of the Child, The (*see also* Kagan, Jerome), 86

Nayar, 40–47, 74, 131

Nazis, 55, 156, 192, 193, 194, 289

Neanderthal, 14

Nepal, 4

Nero, 34, 166, 223, 227, 228

Netherlands, 274, 275, 280, 288, 289

New Mexico (*see also* Zuñi), 43

Niger (*see also* Wodaabe), 50, 119

Nigeria, 40, 48

Nikanov, Johnny, 158

North America, 3, 57, 88, 92, 94, 104, 107, 128, 130, 132, 141, 144, 157, 159, 180, 182, 281, 285

Old Bags Club, 69

Old Testament, 154, 196, 199, 202, 236

On the Apparel of Women (*see also* Tertullian), 235

On Christian Marriage, 265

Ooming, 64

orgasms, 31

Osborne, Dorothy, 271

Paharis, 47

pair bond, 18, 54

Pakistan, 118

Palestinians, 73, 143, 197

papacy, 8, 258, 259, 264, 265

Parolin, Caroline, 88

patriarchy, 44, 49, 123, 125, 129, 140, 143, 145, 153, 158, 166, 167, 170, 195, 197, 199, 205, 208, 218, 228, 229, 256, 261

Paston family, 270

Paul, Margaret, 53
peacocks, 116
penguins, 5, 6, 115, 134
Persuasion, 273, 276
Peterson, Brian, 94
Philippines, 29, 165, 169
pigs, 80, 131, 241
Plato, 210, 212
Pliny the Younger, 223, 227
polyandry, 4, 5, 43, 74, 153, 177
polygamy, 55, 56, 70, 150, 199, 246,
    262
polygyny, 54, 55, 69, 128, 143, 198,
    200
poverty, 112, 143, 258, 298
pregnancy, 10, 12, 23, 35, 79, 92, 93,
    99, 234, 247, 268, 288, 289, 292,
    295
Pride and Prejudice, 272
privacy, 30, 158, 163, 175, 177, 183,
    241, 249, 269, 274, 279
promiscuity, 5, 10, 11, 31, 202
prostitution, 11, 63, 118, 192, 196,
    205, 207, 209, 212, 225, 237, 263,
    268, 278
Protestantism, 249, 259, 261, 266,
    267, 268, 269, 279, 282
puffins, 59
pygmies. *See* Aka

Raise the Red Lantern, 70
rape, 6, 11, 51–52, 131, 196–98, 209,
    250, 268
rats, 80, 83, 90, 98, 106, 278
Red Riding Hood, 3, 4
Reformation, 261, 264, 266, 267
Regis, Helen, 66
religion, 69, 173, 186, 195, 197, 200,
    202, 206, 231, 232–37, 244,

247–50, 250–59, 264, 265, 266,
    267, 268, 269, 284, 285, 291, 297
reproduction, 7, 8, 17, 99, 136, 166,
    224
Return of Martin Guerre, The, 71
Rifai, Nabil, 119
Ritchie, Terressa Jolyn, 96
Roe vs. Wade, 291
Roman Catholic (*see also* Catholi-
    cism), 9, 190
Romania, 95, 293, 295
Rome, 9, 27, 34, 38, 48, 49, 50, 57,
    72, 74, 91, 93, 95, 96, 117, 141,
    152–68, 190, 191, 194, 196,
    210–40, 246, 250–51, 255, 257,
    258, 263, 265, 298
Rosaldo, Renato, 29
Rousseau, Jean-Jacques, 278
royalty, 36, 58, 151, 202, 204, 244,
    257
Russia, 290, 295
Rybczynski, Witold, 241

Sabine women, 48, 49, 215
Samoans, 128
Saudi Arabia, 9, 29, 146, 149, 290
Scorsone, Suzanne, 61, 190, 247
Sense and Sensibility, 273, 276
Sex and Destiny, 99
sex, premarital, 31, 155, 248
Shakers, 237
Shakespeare, William, 53, 61, 62,
    66, 71, 247, 271
Shalom Bayis, 70
Shorter, Edward, 157, 274, 275
Shoumatoff, Alex, 23, 133, 149
sib, 152, 154, 239
Sierra Leone, 56, 66, 89, 103, 107,
    125, 182

Singapore, 90

Slater, Philip, 218

slavery, 15, 27, 40, 42, 49, 69, 118, 140, 152, 153, 163–69, 181, 192, 203, 205, 208, 212, 214, 217, 218, 226, 245

Smith, Susan, 52, 97

snow geese, 6

South Africa, 105, 139, 167

Sparta, 191–92

Spence, Jonathan, 65, 262

Stone, Lawrence, 240, 248, 249, 270, 271, 285, 296

Story of Civilization, The (*see also* Durant, Will), 54, 140

Streisand, Barbra, 85, 115

Subversive Family, The (*see also* Mount, Ferdinand), 101

Sudden Infant Death Syndrome, 97

Sumeria, 69, 117, 118, 141, 202, 205–9

susu. *See* Trobriand Islands

Sweden, 283, 293

Tamils, 126, 157

Tannen, Deborah, 253

Tertullian, 235

Thousand and One Nights, The, 263

Thurer, Shari, 97, 111, 112, 218

Tibet, 4

Tiger, Lionel, 14, 157

Tiwi tribe, 28, 39

Trobriand Islands, 23, 45, 47, 118, 123, 133, 135, 143, 155, 156, 226

Troilus and Criseyde. See Chaucer, Geoffrey

Trudeau, Pierre, 293

Tulane University, 63

Turnbull, Colin M., 139, 183

Turner, John Ryan, 84

Turner, Tina, 31, 85

turtles, 79

Tyldesley, Joyce, 124

Uganda, 155

United States, 92, 103, 128, 144, 146, 179–82, 284, 285, 287, 289, 290, 291, 292, 293

Uruguay, 111

Vedas, The, 201

Veale, Jennifer, 142

Veyne, Paul, 166

Villages. See Critchfield, Richard

violence, 11, 14, 43, 107, 112, 121, 122, 170, 188, 196, 203, 240, 243–44, 278, 294

virginity, 38, 72, 73, 167, 188, 196, 197, 202, 205, 209, 223, 235, 236, 247, 252, 265, 267

von Bora, Katherine, 265

Waln, Nora, 28, 48, 65, 161

Watson, John, 103

Watsons, The, 276

Waugh, Evelyn, 190

Way of the World, The, 277

wedding, 25, 29, 38, 47, 48, 151, 171, 185, 188, 196, 199, 208, 213, 215, 216, 222, 223, 242, 245, 246, 248, 256, 297

Welwood, John, 174

Wife of Bath, 252–54

Wittenberg, University of, 259

Wodaabe, 50–52, 69, 94, 119, 140

wolves, 6, 81

Wolff, Tobias, 110

Woman Destroyed, The, 68

Woman Warrior, The, 104

Women and the Common Life, 76

World Ethnographic Sample (see also Murdock, George), 150

zebras, 80

Zeldin, Theodore, 75

Zimbabwe, 85

zoos, 8, 82, 107, 145

Zuñi, 43, 44, 48, 74, 152